Ideal & Practice
in Council-Manager Government

Edited by
H. George Frederickson

ICMA
Washington, D.C.

The views expressed in this book are those of the contributors and do not necessarily represent the views of ICMA.

Library of Congress Cataloging-in-Publication Data

Ideal and practice in council-manager government / edited by H. George Frederickson.
    p.   cm.
  ISBN 0-87326-057-0
  1. Municipal government by city manager—United States.
I. Frederickson, H. George.
JS344.C5I34 1989
352'.0084'0973—dc20
                                                    89-20015
                                                      CIP

Printed in the United States of America.

949392919089
54321

For Edwin O. Stene

Contents

Foreword

From time to time it is useful for those of us in the local government management profession to reflect on our heritage, our present condition, and our future. Periodically, we gather with our peers at seminars or conferences and exchange ideas among ourselves. One perspective that we consider is the one provided by academics who have examined our profession from the outside—through empirical research—and drawn conclusions about us and our work.

ICMA, PTI, and the University of Kansas joined together to cosponsor such a conference on local government management and the council-manager plan. The purpose of the conference was to provide an opportunity for dialogue between scholars and practitioners—to give researchers a chance to discuss their findings and managers a chance to relate these findings to their experience.

The timing was appropriate. ICMA was launching a celebration of its 75th anniversary, highlighting public service through professional management and the council-manager plan. A consortium of ICMA-recognized communities was simultaneously embarking on a FutureVisions program designed to focus attention on national trends and pressures that will affect managers and management in local communities in the years to come. As the research and development arm of ICMA and the National League of Cities, PTI has a mandate to be a change agent for city and county governments, so it was an important part of the discussion. As a technology development organization, PTI recognizes that technology must serve our communities under the policy direction of elected leaders and the management of appointed administrators. Only then can technology help accomplish the service delivery goals that are shaped in the context of the council-manager partnership.

As the following pages will show, the conference raised many questions about the changing roles and responsibilities of the professional manager vis-a-vis the governing body and the community, the state of the profession and the plan on the threshold of the 1990s, and prospects for the future. It also raised questions about the role of professional management in economic development, innovation, and technological change.

The dichotomy inherent in the title of this volume was clearly evident in the discussion among participants. Professional managers in the council-manager system have a strong sense of idealism and are motivated by a commitment to public service. At the same time they are realists, accepting the facts of the political environment as they work to serve both their councils and their communities. The research papers presented a framework for examining these two aspects of professional management, offering empirical data on managers' daily activities and interactions, leadership roles, skills, and values in the context of council-manager government. Much of the research presented here focuses specifically on cities. This is not to imply that the ideas or principles discussed here are limited to cities in their applications. Similarly, writers and participants often use the pronoun "he" as shorthand for "he or she." This is not meant to ignore the growing number of women in professional local management.

We are grateful to George Frederickson, Edwin O. Stene Professor of Public Administration, University of Kansas, who conceived the idea for the conference and for this volume; to Buford Watson, manager in the host city of Lawrence, Kansas, who arranged for the conference to be held in the local commission chambers; and to the many participants who contributed their time and ideas to make the conference a success.

William H. Hansell
Executive Director
International City
  Management Association

Costis Toregas
President
Public Technology, Inc.

Preface

The National Conference on the Study of City Management and the Council-Manager Plan was a singular event. It was the first time the leading scholars of city management collected together to assess both city managers and the plan.

It was fitting that the Edwin O. Stene Department of Public Administration of the University of Kansas, the nation's leading source of city managers, be a conference co-host. I am especially appreciative of the support of Professor John Nalbandian, past chairman of the department, and Professor Barbara Romzek, present chairwoman, for their support of the conference. The College of Liberal Arts and Sciences, the Graduate School and the Division of Continuing Education of the University of Kansas all provided significant support for the conference. It was, however, the Kansas University City Managers and Trainees (KUCIMATS), the Public Administration Department's alumni group, that provided important financing for the conference and for this publication. I am especially grateful for the continuing loyalty and support of the KUCIMATS.

It was equally fitting that the International City Management Association and Public Technology, Inc., the primary professional association and service organization in local government administration, be conference co-hosts. Without their financial support neither the conference nor this publication would have been possible. I am gratified by the strong support of this project by both William Hansell of ICMA and Costis Toregas of PTI.

It was, of course, the scholars who wrote the papers, the managers who responded to them, and their collective dialogue which made the conference a success.

Several persons contributed importantly to the editing and production of this volume, particularly Mary Frederickson, Kit Pittier, Thomas Michael Rundle, and Barbara Watkins.

Finally, the ICMA Director of Publications, Barbara Moore, participated in the project from beginning to end. She was a vital part of the conference and guided the publication of this volume. All associated with the conference and the book are in her debt.

H. George Frederickson
Lawrence, Kansas

Introduction

H. George Frederickson
University of Kansas

This is America's urban century. We are now a nation primarily of city dwellers. In the latter half of this century, we have been especially influenced by the two most salient features of city life--suburbanization and administration.

The first, suburbanization, characterizes where most city dwellers have chosen to live, not in the core but on the edge, being of the city but not in the city. The majority of Americans are a suburban, commuting, mall shopping people. Each American city—St. Louis, San Francisco, Cincinnati—is actually a sprawling, multijurisdictional complex of large and small general purpose governments with the inner city at the core and concentric rings of autonomous suburban cities with more inhabitants when taken together than the central city. Laid over, around and across these general purpose jurisdictions are county governments and special purpose governments with the same ability as the cities to tax, borrow, and spend: school districts, flood control districts, bridge authorities, weed abatement districts, economic development authorities, and so on. The 305 largest American metropolitan areas include an *average* of 23 suburban cities and 38 single purpose districts or authorities. The 50 largest American cities are much more complex, most of them doubling the above numbers.

Given this complexity, we cannot speak of the government of our cities and counties, for *government* implies a singular or unitary status. We can only describe and understand *governance*—the myriad of jurisdictions, processes, and relationships by which the city or county is in the broadest sense governed.

The second salient feature of the last half of America's urban century is administration, and administration is closely associated with suburbanization and intergovernmental complexity. While council-manager government for American cities began in the first half of the century, it has flourished since 1945, essentially at the same time as the growth of suburbanization and single purpose governments. While some large central cities have the council-manager form (Kansas City, Dallas, Ft. Worth, Phoenix, San Diego, Cincinnati), most do not. By contrast, most suburbs in the nation's largest 305 metropolitan areas have the council-manager form (about 55%). Smaller cities, towns and villages not in metropolitan areas are also predominately council-manager in form.

Single purpose districts and authorities are considerably more administrative in form (having nonpartisan, at-large elected boards, professional administrators, merit systems, etc.) than are traditional city or county governments. In fact, most single purpose governments were established to distance a particular public function (schooling, flood control, etc.) from politics.

As we moved from the central city to the suburbs we also moved from the political city to the administrative city. The council-manager form is now the dominant system of city government. Administration has come to be as important as suburbanization in contemporary local government.

At two points in the emergence of the suburbanized administrative city, scholars have engaged in extensive research, debate and discourse. In the later stages of the reform era political scientists and some sociologists studied how American cities were changing. They were also very active as advocates for change, generally away from traditional political forms toward administrative forms.

With the flourishing of the academic field of public administration in the 1950s and the generally accepted use of the master's degree in public administration as the appropriate academic preparation for city management, there came a second wave of research and debate over suburbanization and the administrative city. And then, from the mid-1960s to the early 1970s there was considerable growth in the study of urban affairs and the development of academic journals in that specialization. But in this scholarly work there was little interest in or research on the uniqueness of the council-manager form, the rapid growth of "management" in non-council-manager cities and in counties (the "chief administrative officer" being a familiar means of incorporating administrative expertise into traditionally more political forms of local government), or the dramatic changes that were under way in council-manager cities. Unlike earlier research done primarily by political scientists and sociologists, much of this research was being done by specialists in public administration or urban studies. Those specialists were often multidisciplinary in training, not usually working from the limited perspective of a single paradigm (the market model in economics, interest group pluralism in political science, etc.). As a result, contemporary research on the administrative city tended to be less fundamentally critical than the research in the 1950–60 period, which expressed alarm at suburbia and the loss of traditional politics.

Beginning in the early 1980s, there was once again a great interest in both urban affairs and administration on the part of researchers and scholars. The present emphasis appears to be on the maturing of council-manager government and on the mid-course corrections under way both in the government of particular cities and in the governance of metropolitan areas.

It is increasingly clear that we are at an especially dynamic point in local government in America. The financial withdrawal of the national government from urban concerns and the consequent devolution of responsibilities has had a dramatic effect on local governments. The increasing use of public-private partnerships, third party governments and other innovative means of service provision has redefined both the traditional work of the city or county and the role of both elected officials and appointed administrators. In all of this, both in the metropolitan areas and in the suburbs, the administrative form of government has proven to be remarkably adaptable and resilient.

This resurgence of scholarly interest in council-manager government sparked an interest in bringing together the leading students of contemporary local government. That possibility raised several questions. Could these scholars, through specially commissioned research papers, assess the knowledge base of city management and council-manager government? Was 1988-89 a good time to attempt a status report on what we know about city management and attempt to predict what the future holds?

I initially discussed the idea of such a conference with William Hansell, Executive Director of the International City Management Association (ICMA). As the concept of the conference evolved, we agreed that a meeting limited to researchers and professors would probably be overly scholarly. An alternative was to put the scholars together with some of the nation's seasoned city and county managers who would act as a reality check on the research findings and conclusions. Although we wondered if such a mix would result in more combustion than wisdom, we concluded that bringing scholars and practitioners together was a risk worth taking.

We also agreed that the timing for such a conference was good. If the conference were held in 1988 the proceedings could be published as part of ICMA's 75th anniversary celebration, scheduled to begin at the association's conference in Des Moines, Iowa, in September 1989.

Three organizations came together to sponsor the conference: the University of Kansas, the International City Management Association and Public Technology, Inc. The conference was held November 10-12, 1988, in Lawrence, Kansas. (Appropriately, Lawrence has the council-manager form of government, and the meetings were held in the commission chambers at city hall.) Many leading researchers in urban studies and city management were contacted and papers were commissioned. City managers were invited to act as respondents to the papers. The research papers were collected in advance of the meeting, duplicated and sent to all participants so they could read them before the conference. Respondents prepared their comments in advance and distributed them at the conference. To the considerable relief of virtually everyone, the papers were not formally presented or read. Each was discussed briefly by the author, and then the respondent started the general discussion. The conference dialogue, edited and condensed, constitutes a considerable portion of this volume.

Following the conference three important published research articles on council-manager government were added to this volume. These articles, written by conference participants, are reprinted here with the permission of *Public Administration Review* and the American Society for Public Administration. They are: "Role Emphases of City Managers and Other Municipal Executives" by Charldean Newell and David N. Ammons (May/June 1987); "Abandonments of the Council-Manager Plan: A New Institutionalist Perspective" by Greg J. Protasel (July/August 1988); and "Dichotomy and Duality: Reconceptualizing the Relationship between Policy and Administration in Council-Manager Cities" by James H. Svara (January/February 1985).

Finally, because of the importance of the subject, we commissioned a post-conference essay on city management and technological innovation: "Professionalism, Innovation, and Entrepreneurship: Evolution in a Changing Society" by Richard D. Bingham and Claire L. Felbinger.

This volume presents timely research reports on council-manager government and on city managers. It also presents the reactions of city and county managers, through their prepared responses and through the condensed dialogue. It is, of course, left to the participants and the reader to make their own evaluations of our works and to draw their own conclusions.

Participants

David N. Ammons, University of Georgia
Eric A. Anderson, City Manager, Eau Claire, Wisconsin
James M. Banovetz, Northern Illinois University
Donald A. Blubaugh, City Manager, Walnut Creek, California
Donald Borut, Deputy Director, International City Management Association
G. Curtis Branscome, City Manager, Decatur, Georgia
Larry J. Brown, County Administrator, Hillsborough County (Tampa), Florida
William N. Cassella, Jr., Dobbs Ferry, New York
E. H. Denton, County Administrator, Johnson County (Olathe), Kansas
H. George Frederickson, University of Kansas
James J. Glass, University of North Texas
Michael Gleason, City Manager, Eugene, Oregon
Martha L. Hale, Emporia State University
William H. Hansell, Jr., Executive Director, International City Management Association
David W. Hinton, University of Nebraska, Omaha
Karl Johnson, University of Missouri-Kansas City
Lawrence F. Keller, Cleveland State University
John E. Kerrigan, University of Houston, Downtown Campus
Norman King, City Manager, Palm Springs, California
Donald F. McIntyre, City Manager, Pasadena, California
Barbara Moore, International City Management Association
John Nalbandian, University of Kansas
Charldean Newell, University of North Texas
Chester A. Newland, University of Southern California
Terry L. Novak, City Manager, Spokane, Washington
David H. Olson, City Manager, Kansas City, Missouri
Donald E. Pipes, City Manager, Overland Park, Kansas
Gary F. Pokorny, City Manager, El Cerrito, California
Greg J. Protasel, Idaho State University
Karma Ruder, Deputy City Manager, Concord, California
Edward G. Schilling, San Francisco, California
Enrique G. Serna, City Manager, South Tucson, Arizona
Elaine B. Sharp, University of Kansas
James H. Svara, North Carolina State University
Howard D. Tipton, City Manager, Daytona Beach, Florida
Costis Toregas, President, Public Technology, Inc.
David F. Watkins, City Administrator, Lenexa, Kansas
Buford M. Watson, Jr., City Manager, Lawrence, Kansas

Students in the MPA program as well as faculty from the University of Kansas were conference observers.

The Context of
City Management

City Management in an
Era of Blurred Boundaries

Elaine B. Sharp
University of Kansas

Contemporary city managers are faced with the task of managing in an increasingly complex environment. Such a statement would surely elicit considerable agreement. It might also elicit considerable criticism, on the grounds that it is too vague and superficial. In what sense is the context for city management more complex? What do we mean by complexity, and in what specific areas are there identifiable aspects of increased complexity?

This essay argues that the context for city management has become more complex in a special way that can best be captured by the phrase "the blurring of boundaries." The phrase is borrowed from Ira Sharkansky, who used it to describe the difficulties of pinpointing exactly what the modern state includes, because of the tendency of governments to hide some of their activities in quasi-government organizations and other activities "on the margins of the state."[1] The implications of this particular trend at the local level will be explored. But blurring of boundaries means more than this. It means that spheres of action that once were distinct have become more interrelated. We see patterns of action that span once-separate spheres. Categories that once seemed to meaningfully distinguish important phenomena from each other have broken down. New forms have developed that muddy the distinctions that have been so important before. All these forms of blurring of boundaries create an increasingly complex environment for urban management.

This theme of increasing complexity in the sense of blurred boundaries will be explored in four key topical areas: (1) the changing character of local governing institutions, especially the emergence of hybrid arrangements to replace classic reform structures; (2) interaction between the public and private sectors at the local level; (3) intergovernmental relations, including changing patterns of conflict and cooperation in the federal system; and (4) changing economic roles in a post-industrial, "internationalized" economy. These topics have been selected for discussion because they encompass important trends in contemporary urban affairs. They also illustrate, in detail, how complexity is increasing because previously distinct roles are merging, previously autonomous spheres of action are becoming more interdependent, and previously meaningful categories are breaking down. In short, they reveal city management in a context of "blurred boundaries."

Reform Structures and Hybridization

Consider, for example, the meaning of reform in contemporary urban management. Traditionally, identifying reformed cities has been a clearcut task. A city government was reformed to the extent that it had adopted the governing structures that have been promoted by the reform movement. Specifically, reformism has meant the adoption of nonpartisan elections at the local level, the replacement of ward or district-based systems of representation with at-large representation, and the adoption of the council-manager form of government.

In contemporary urban administration, however, there has been a blurring of the boundaries between "reformed" and "nonreformed." Hybrid governing arrangements, combining some of the structures of reform with unreformed structures, have proliferated. It is no longer a simple, straightforward matter to determine which cities are "reformed" and which are not.

Consider, for example, the compilation of governing institutions, in the 1987 edition of ICMA's *Municipal Year Book*. For purposes of analysis, a random sample was drawn from the enormous listing of cities provided.[2] Two important aspects of "hybridization" can be observed in this sample. First, a number of cities that would otherwise be in the unreformed, mayor-council category have added city manager-like positions to their governing institutions. These professional chief administrators modify the basic mayor-council form--enough so that ICMA recognizes this hybrid--the mayor-council-manager arrangement--as a separate category. In the sample of 252 cities drawn for this analysis, 8.7% of all cities were of this hybrid type.[3] In some states, this hybrid form is even more prevalent. One-fifth of all cities in Missouri, for example, are mayor-council cities with professional chief administrative officers. Nearly one-third (32%) of the cities in Minnesota have this hybrid form.

Perhaps more important is the development of hybrid systems of representation. Analysis of this is somewhat hampered because there is incomplete information for a large number of communities in ICMA's listings.[4] However, the development of reform hybrids is apparent in Table 1, which shows the number of at-large council members reported by various types of cities. Less than half (48.4%) of mayor-council cities have strictly ward-based representation. About one-quarter of these cities have between one and three at-large council members, and another one-quarter have four or more at-large members. In short, the reform feature of at-large representation has been grafted onto many ostensibly unreformed mayor-council cities, at least to some degree. This grafting of at-large representation is even more apparent in the cities that are already hybrids in another respect--the mayor-council-manager cities.

Meanwhile, the majority of council-manager cities do *not* rely exclusively upon the reform model of at-large representation. In fact, Table 1 shows that a little over one-third of council-manager cities in the sample *have no at-large council members*. Roughly another one-fourth of the council-manager cities have either one, two, or three at-large council members. Since city councils typically have more than three members, this means that these cities have a combination of at-large and ward representation.

Challenges to at-large systems, on grounds that they prevent minority representation on city council, are an important part of the

Table 1
Extent of At-Large Representation,
by Form of Government, 1987

Number of At-Large Council Members	Form of City Government		
	Mayor-Council	Mayor-Council-Manager	Council-Manager
	48.4%	45.5%	34.6%
1-3	25.8	18.2	24.0
4 or More	25.8	36.4	41.4
Total Cities	124	22	104

Figures shown are percentages of cities of each type that have the number of members indicated

trend toward either abandoning at-large representation or supplementing at-large with ward representation. For example, in Springfield, Illinois, a federal judge ruled that the city's at-large election system (in the commission form of government) was discriminatory and illegal. Under the newly instituted governing arrangement, which includes a 10-member council elected from wards, two black residents were elected to the city council--the first black representation since the establishment of the at-large system in 1911.[5] Similar challenges have been mounted in other cities, while still others have moved to modify representation systems in an effort to head off such legal challenges. The concern here is with the complexity that these changes have introduced to the very conception of reform. Reformism can no longer be taken to mean that a city has the city manager form, at-large elections and nonpartisanship. Many communities with the city manager form of government now have either full ward representation or mixed ward and at-large systems. Does this make them less reformed? Perhaps it is useful to say that reform has become more complex, and that the principles of professionalism, nonpartisanship, and centralized, merit-based management must be worked out within a context that places greater emphasis on particularistic interests.

If the emergence of hybrid structures of government has blurred the boundaries between traditional reform and nonreform categories, perhaps it is also time to reexamine reformism as a concept and to consider what the essential core of that concept really is. Perhaps reform means more than the simple adoption of a set of institutional structures. Perhaps reform is a more subtle concept, having to do with community expectations about the role of government and the nature of the relationships between citizens, elected representatives, and administrators.

This awakens remembrance of Banfield and Wilson's controversial ethos theory.[6] Without adopting all the baggage associated with that approach, it may still be possible to think about reformism in a way that directs attention to the local political culture as well as formal institutions of government. For example, challenges to the city-manager plan, or to other reform institutions, are a recurrent feature of contemporary local government. Greg Protasel suggests that these challenges constitute "legitimation crises" brought on when the need for leadership exceeds the limits that classic council-manager systems can provide.[7] More broadly, this suggests that in some settings, prevailing public attitudes about what reform government can and should accomplish are at odds with institutional realities. A conceptualization of reform that focuses on these public expectations and understandings, i.e., the local political culture, might help us better understand and predict these episodes of challenge to reform institutions.

Public and Private Spheres of Action

The blurring of the boundaries between the public sphere and the private sphere has been, if anything, even more dramatic than the disintegration of clear categories of reform and nonreform. In a variety of ways, it is becoming difficult to distinguish what the public sector is doing from what the private sector is doing or indeed to distinguish public organizations from private organizations.[8]

The intersection of two distinct trends accounts for this dramatic blurring of boundaries. With respect to traditional urban service delivery, the public sector has been challenged to use the private sector more. For more than a decade now, there have been calls for increased "privatization" of traditional service delivery through arrangements such as contracting with private sector providers. City governments have responded to these calls, as we will see below.

At the same time that city governments have been asked to "privatize" traditional service delivery, they have also been pressed to take on a greater role with respect to economic development. Risk-taking ventures and investments that will shape the community's future economy are no longer viewed as matters for private sector entrepreneurs alone. Increasingly, city governments have created public-private partnerships for economic development, or quasi-public development organizations that operate in the "twilight zone" between the public and the private sphere.[9]

In short, the boundaries between public and private have been blurred from two directions--the increased privatization of what have traditionally been governmental service delivery functions and the increased "public-ization" of what have traditionally been private, entrepreneurial functions. The following section details these two trends.

As a number of authors have noted, privatization of a service or function does not necessarily mean that local government completely turns over its role in that area to the private sector. Rather, privatization includes a host of special arrangements in which nongovernmental organizations are responsible for the actual "production" of the service, while government plays the role of "provider" or "arranger"--a role that includes decision making about the scope and quality of service, monitoring, and the like.[10] These privatization arrangements include franchising, grants or subsidies to private and nonprofit organizations, voucher systems, and contracting for service.[11]

Contracting, one of the more widely used and controversial of these arrangements, amply illustrates the pervasiveness of privatization in local government. A survey of local governments shows that nearly 80% either now use or are planning to use private contractors in some aspect of service delivery.[12] One analyst has found that the volume of local government contracts with private sector organizations increased from $22 billion in 1972 to $66 billion in 1980.[13]

Many of the services contracted for are internal or staff services, like data processing or legal services. But contracting has also taken strong hold in other service areas. An ICMA survey of residential solid waste collection practices showed that only 34.1% of cities had municipally-produced service exclusively; a little over one-fifth (21.6%) contracted with private haulers, 11.8% left private haulers to contract directly with citizens, and 17% had a combination of methods.[14] Contracting is also prominent where other public works or transit services are involved and in the health and human service area.[15] Contracting is even found in law enforcement, which many view as a very traditional core function of local government.[16]

While local government has increasingly privatized its basic service delivery functions, it has simultaneously taken on greater involvement in economic development. This involvement ranges from promotional strategies to provision of financial inducements such as tax abatements and low cost loans to cooperative ventures with specific private sector firms or investor groups.[17] The blurring of boundaries between public and private is more evident in some of these forms of involvement than in others. Promotional strategies may yield little blurring, but financial inducement strategies do. Local government, in the latter case, effectively becomes a joint investor and entrepreneurial partner and shares the risks of investment with private capital.

Blurring of boundaries between what is public and what is private is even more dramatic in many cooperative ventures. This is especially the case when special, quasi-public, quasi-private corporations are created to conduct development activities. These entities have many of the features of public bodies, including powers of eminent domain and tax-exempt bond status; yet they are typically directed by boards dominated by local business executives and they are exempt from many of the rules, regulations, and accountability controls that govern government bureaus. They enjoy, as it were, the best of both the private and the public spheres.[18]

Each of the areas of increased public-private interpenetration has generated a variety of effectiveness and efficiency questions. For example, there is still controversy over the real level of cost savings that can be realized through service privatization[19] and debate rages over the effectiveness of financial incentives for businesses.[20]

Of greater interest here is the fact that blurring of boundaries between public and private simultaneously makes urban governance more complex and raises a host of thorny accountability questions. For example, when it contracts for services, local government is still responsible for the quality of those services, but it must live up to its responsibility in a realm that is beyond the usual governmental control mechanisms of budget review, personnel administration, and the like. Privatization, in other words, creates the need for more elaborate systems of monitoring, oversight, and contract compliance than many cities have traditionally had. There is evidence, fortunately, that cities are developing innovative methods to enhance contractor accountability.[21]

Similarly, the proliferation of quasi-public corporations and other hybrid public-private organizations raises important questions about potential policy bias, misuse of power, and the propriety of

7

organizational forms that circumvent accountability to the public.[22] In general, the interpenetration of public and private activity in economic development jangles alarms about the potential for the public interest to be subverted to the interests of business.[23]

Blurred Boundaries in the Intergovernmental System

In the area of intergovernmental relations, blurring of boundaries has to do with the interpenetration of activities and spheres of influence among local, state, and national levels of government. Stated another way, "...in the intergovernmental arena there is a trend toward more integration of federal, state, and local activities in the formulation and implementation of public policy."[24] But this is certainly a long term trend, and the resultant blurring of boundaries between levels of government is by no means a new phenomenon. It has been acknowledged at least since Morton Grodzins' introduction of the metaphor of "marble cake federalism."[25]

What is interesting about the contemporary status of intergovernmental relations is the staying power of blurred boundaries, despite important political developments. The election of a conservative Republican administration at the national level and the unfolding of its cutback agenda constitute one of the most important of these political developments. The demise of General Revenue Sharing and cuts in other federal programs are often assumed to be ushering in a period in which the federal government moves away from an interdependent role vis-a-vis state and local government.

There is some truth to this assessment, but the decline in the federal government's fiscal presence at the state and local levels does not come close to approximating a full retreat. Table 2, for example, shows that federal grants-in-aid, as a percent of total state-local government outlays, have declined noticeably since the high point of federal aid in 1978-1979. However, federal aid still constitutes nearly one-fifth of all state and local spending. When measured as a percentage of the federal government's total outlays, the decline in federal grants to state and local government seems even less dramatic.

For a number of reasons, declining federal aid does not necessarily translate into a marked lessening of federal-local interdependence. For one thing, despite visible cutbacks, substantial federal aid programs remain, along with the various mandates that they bring in the form of conditions-of-aid. As Lovell and Tobin[26] have noted, these federal mandates tend to have even more dramatic effects on local government than state mandates do. This is because federal mandates are less consistent with local priorities and values than are state mandates, and federal mandates are more likely to introduce wholly new activities to the jurisdiction. In short, the "strings" that are attached to federal-aid "carrots" are far from trivial. They provide a mechanism whereby national priorities and standards are injected into local affairs. Furthermore, "in mandate situations, where the local government is not responsible for what it does or for the way that it must do it, accountability becomes blurred and impossible to place."[27] In short, the blurring of boundaries between the federal government and local government remains, despite real cuts in grant-in-aid programs.

Another reason for continuing federal-local interdependence, or blurred boundaries, is the development of collaborative processes in the

Table 2
Federal Grants-in-Aid
Relative to Total Spending, 1965-1987

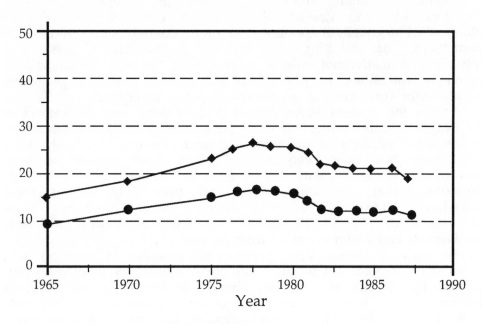

Federal Aid As:
◆ Percent of state-local expenditure
● Percent of federal expenditure

Source: U.S. Government Bureau of the Census. *Statistical Abstract of the United States* 1988. Washington, D.C.: U.S. Government Printing Office, adapted from Table 434, p. 260.

regulatory realm. Federal-local relations are not, after all, limited to subsidy via grant-in-aid programs. There are also substantial areas of regulatory policy in which local compliance, the appropriateness of federal standards in local areas, and similar issues can constitute the basis for heated conflict. At least in environmental policy there is a trend towards "regulatory negotiation," which invites local interests to join in bargaining and consensus building in the rule making process.[28] Such processes provide a vehicle for local government to have substantial input into federal regulatory policy making. In so doing, of course, the boundaries between what is federal and what is local are further blurred.

Interpenetration of federal and local affairs is also likely to continue because public officials at both levels have such deeply ingrained expectations about the mutuality of their roles. Years of intergovernmentalization of problems via federal aid programs leave their mark in the form of patterned responses to problems. This is evident in recent responses to the homeless problem, which evoked familiar calls from local officials for federal assistance. There are, as it were, prevailing assumptions about the nature of the federal-local connection--assumptions that approximate the model of federalism offered by Paul Peterson.[29] According to that model, local governments are constrained from pursuing redistributional social programs with local initiatives and resources; instead, local government is limited to serving as an implementing organization for federal programs.

Finally, seemingly dramatic changes in federal grant-in-aid programs, like the Reagan administration cutbacks, may distract attention from equally important and more durable intergovernmental phenomena. Gurr and King argue that the "national state's" presence in any city is a matter not only of grants-in-aid, but also "social transfer payments, the siting of public institutions and public employment, private-sector contracts and investment in public enterprises."[30]

Amidst the ferment about federal-local relations and the impact of the Reagan administration, the states have quietly reasserted themselves as important partners in the intergovernmental arena. Actually, state government has long been a key player with respect to local government finance systems -- setting limits, authorizing or failing to authorize various revenue sources, and prescribing various fiscal procedures.[31] However, the proliferation of direct federal-local fiscal connections in the 1960s and 1970s helped to short-circuit state involvement and divert attention from its role.

As Table 3 shows, state government's relative importance as a provider of grants-in-aid to cities has grown noticeably in recent years. In part this is due to the retrenchment of federal grants-in-aid, as discussed above. It is also the result of state responses to other fiscal pressures on cities, such as the populist tax revolt that spawned California's Proposition 13, Massachusetts' Proposition 2 1/2 and similar tax-limit measures in other areas.

As with the federal government, however, a flood of state mandates on local government has come along with the aid. In addition, a large number of state mandates have come in the form of direct orders rather than conditions of aid.[32] The combination of increasingly centralized state-local revenue systems, coupled with an increased state presence in local affairs via mandates, makes it increasingly difficult to draw sharp boundaries between the state and the local government realm.

Of course, much the same could be said about the boundaries between different units of local government. The explosion of special districts and authorities is a well-documented trend.[33] Meanwhile, there has been little change in the likelihood of consolidating the many municipal governments that exist in metropolitan areas. The result, in the eyes of some observers, is fragmentation, duplication of services,

Table 3
City Government Intergovernmental Revenues Per Capita,
by Source of Revenue, 1977-78 to 1985-86

Year	From State Government	From Federal Government
1977-78	$104.52	$73.86
1981-82	134.30	77.95
1982-83	139.76	75.56
1983-84	142.26	72.34
1984-85	157.34	70.15
1985-86	164.29	65.47

Source: Adapted from U.S. Bureau of the Census, *City Government Finances in 1985-1986*, Table 3, and same item from other years in this Government Finances series. Washington, DC: U.S. Government Printing Office.

lack of coordination, and chaos. Others, however, interpret the crazy quilt pattern of local government organization in metropolitan areas somewhat differently, emphasizing the benefits of multiple, autonomous local governments and the ways in which these various local governments collaborate with each other to achieve coordination and service efficiencies.[34] Recent evidence showing the extensiveness of intergovernmental service agreements and joint service arrangements between and among cities and counties supports this positive assessment.[35] A little over half (52%) of cities and counties surveyed by ICMA have contracted with another local government for some service and 55% provide some service jointly with another local government unit. Whether viewed positively or negatively, however, this is a portrait of complexity via blurred intergovernmental boundaries.

The Blurring of Economic Roles

The final area in which we will explore the theme of blurred boundaries involves the role of American urban economies in the contemporary international economic order. A brief look at economic trends suggests increasing interdependency between national and international economic developments and the economic fortunes of individual American cities. Partly as a result of these trends and partly as a result of choices made at the local level, many American cities are caught in a sometimes painful transition between industrial and post-industrial roles.

The decline of goods-manufacturing relative to service industries is an important and frequently observed feature of the U.S. post-industrial economy. In the period 1970-1985, for example, 26.7 million jobs were created, but nearly all of that employment growth is attributable to non-manufacturing industries.[36] Census Bureau figures show that manufacturing jobs declined from one-quarter of total jobs in 1970 to less than one-fifth of the total in 1984.[37]

Many of these industrial jobs have effectively been exported to other countries. Barry Bluestone and Bennett Harrison have documented this process of corporate disinvestment and reinvestment in foreign settings:

> Between 1950 and 1980, direct foreign investment by U.S. businesses increased *sixteen times*, from about $12 billion to $192 billion. Over the same period, gross private domestic investment grew less than half as rapidly, from $54 billion to about $400 billion...The total overseas output of American multinational corporations is now larger than the gross domestic product of every country in the world except the United States and the Soviet Union.[38]

But, while this "deindustrialization of America" is fairly well recognized, the full scope of the international economic order that is emerging, and the implications for American communities, are not fully recognized. Countries like South Korea, Brazil, and Taiwan are no longer manufacturing only products like clothing, shoes, and toys that require cheap labor but little capital investment or technological sophistication. Rather, many of these countries are replicating Japan's involvement in more "capital-intensive processing industries" while Japan and other countries have moved on to still more technologically sophisticated manufacturing processes.[39]

Within the United States, jobs involving the manufacture of sophisticated technological products are replacing some of the lost jobs in traditional manufacturing enterprises. For example, the manufacture of semiconductors, optical devices, X-ray apparatus, biological products and medicinals have increased dramatically in the period 1972-1987.[40] Many communities eagerly attempt to jump on the high-technology bandwagon as a way to prosperity in the face of an otherwise deindustrializing America.

As Manuel Castells observes, however, there are several reasons manufacturing jobs involving "high technologies" are even easier to move overseas than traditional manufacturing jobs. Many high technology products are very small and lightweight, which diminishes the significance of shipping costs and invites production wherever in the world labor costs are most favorable. The existence of new telecommunications technologies further enables high technology companies to locate their research and design and headquarters operations far from their assembly operations.[41]

On the manufacturing side, then, U.S. communities cannot really hide from increasing internationalization. They are competing for a place in a global economic order. The location of many manufacturing enterprises is a function of labor costs and investment opportunities not only in alternative U.S. sites, but in sites across the globe. Furthermore, manufacturing jobs in U.S. communities are not necessarily the result of investment decisions by U.S. firms. Direct foreign investments in the U.S. have increased seventeen-fold since 1970 to a level of over $25 billion in 1986.[42] In short, the contemporary industrial order is increasingly an international one, and the fortunes of many U.S. communities are bound up in it. The boundaries between local economic development issues and international economic issues are increasingly blurred.

Many communities have service-oriented rather than manufacturing-dominated economies. As noted above, this is a key feature of "post-industrial" society. But here too there is blurring of boundaries, in the form of a certain fuzziness about the contents and implications of a post-industrial service economy. At one level, a service economy suggests the dominance of traditional professional occupations in the health-care, education, and governmental sectors, coupled with the rise of newer technical occupations in both the communications field and other technical fields. This interpretation of the service economy is consistent with those many analyses which point to the dominance of knowledge-intensive activities and information-workers in post-industrial society.[43] High income and high education levels characterize the service workers in this emphasis.

However, many different sorts of jobs are part of a service-dominated economy. Traditional white-collar jobs in real estate and insurance are included. Very low-status, low-wage jobs such as restaurant worker, hotel worker, and retail clerk are also included. Census Bureau projections of the categories of greatest job growth between the years 1986 and 2000 show the diverse face of the post-industrial service economy. Along with general managers/top executives, computer programmers, and teachers are the following, even more dominant, categories for job growth: retail salespersons, waiters/waitresses, janitors/cleaners, general office clerks, food counter workers, and nursing aides/orderlies.[44]

Diversity within the service sector, coupled with new economic roles in an international industrial order, means that U.S. cities are sorting themselves into a variety of economic roles. One analyst,[45] for example, describes some cities as having "government-education" economies, dominated by jobs in those sectors by virtue of the fact that the city is a state capital, federal regional center, site of a major institution of higher education, or all three. Other cities are national or regional "nodal" centers, serving as corporate headquarters centers and having diverse service economies that include arts, recreation, and business support services. By contrast, some cities have economies that remain rooted in the industrial world. Some of these are "education-manufacturing" centers, where one or more local universities are helping to provide a transition to new technologies and industrial processes. Others are "production centers" which are dominated by routine assembly operations. There are also "Third World Entrepot" cities, which serve as immigration entry points and specialize in economic activities requiring low-wage labor, while others are retirement or resort centers.[46]

City officials cannot simply choose the economic role that they find most desirable for their city, even if they are willing to work in partnership with private sector entrepreneurs. The community's history, geography, and demography are too important. The extent to which local public officials can mold the economic fortune of the community in the face of powerful economic and demographic trends is a continuing question confronting both practitioners and scholars of economic development. The consequences of not trying are such that most local officials cannot afford to consider that option. Yet, because of the interpenetration of local and international economic forces and because of the complexity of the post-industrial service economy, the boundary between choice and inevitability is extremely blurred.

Conclusions

This essay has explored the theme of increased complexity through blurred boundaries from a variety of different perspectives. Whether we consider the relationships between and among units of government in the federal system, the relationships between the private sector and the public sector at the local level, the changing role of local economies in a post-industrial, international economic order, or the very meaning of urban reform itself, we find that distinctions are not clear cut, categories are shifting, and interdependent relationships are more common than autonomous spheres of activity. In short, we find that boundaries are blurred and that the complexity of urban governance is correspondingly increased. In many respects, this blurring of boundaries is helpful, beneficial, or necessary. In other respects, most notably having to do with accountability, this blurring of boundaries is problematic. Whether welcome or unwelcome, however, this blurring of boundaries appears to be a trend not likely to be reversed.

Notes

1. Ira Sharkansky, *Whither the State* (Chatham, NJ: Chatham House Publishers, 1979).

2. The sample was selected by first drawing a random sample of six states (Georgia, Idaho, Ohio, New Mexico, Oregon, and Delaware). All cities listed for each state were included in the sample.

3. In addition, 41.3% of the sample cities have the ICMA-recognized council-manager form and 49.2% are mayor-council cities. Less than one percent have the commission form of government, and no town-meeting communities are included in the sample.

4. In particular, while information on the number of at-large council members is typically available, many cities have missing data on the number of council members elected from wards. In those cases, the total council size cannot be conclusively determined either.

5. "Era Ends as Two Blacks Join Springfield Council," *New York Times*, Thursday, December 3, 1987, p. 9.

6. James Q. Wilson and Edward C. Banfield, "Public-Regardingness as a Value Premise in Voting Behavior," *American Political Science Review* (December, 1964): 876-887.

7. Greg J. Protasel, "Abandonments of the Council-Manager Plan: A New Institutionalist Perspective," *Public Administration Review* 48 (July/August, 1988): 807-812.

8. Mark Emmert and Michael Crow, "Public, Private and Hybrid Organizations: An Empirical Examination of the Role of Publicness," *Administration & Society* 20 (August, 1988): 216-244.

9. Harold Seidman, *Politics, Position, and Power* (New York: Oxford University Press, 1975).

10. E. S. Savas, *Privatizing the Public Sector: How to Shrink Government* (Chatham, NJ: Chatham House, 1982); Ted Kolderie, "The Two Different Concepts of Privatization," *Public Administration Review* 46 (July/August, 1986), p. 286.

11. Harry P. Hatry and Carl F. Valente, "Alternative Service Delivery Approaches Involving Increased Use of the Private Sector," *Municipal Year Book* (Washington, DC: International City Management Association, 1983), p. 204.

12. Elizabeth Voisin, "Surveyed Cities Would Privatize," *City & State*, October, 1987, p. 33.

13. Stephen Moore, "Contracting Out: A Painless Alternative to the Budget Cutter's Knife," in Steve Hanke, ed., *Prospects for Privatization* (New York: Academy of Political Science, 1987), p. 62.

14. Annie Millar, "Residential Solid Waste Collection," *Municipal Year Book* (Washington, DC: International City Management Association, 1983), p. 193.

15. Hatry and Valente, op. cit., p. 203.

16. Robert Poole, Jr., *Cutting Back City Hall* (New York: Universe Books, 1980), p. 40.

17. Harold Wolman and Larry Ledebur, "Concepts of Public-Private Cooperation," in Cheryl Farr, ed., *Shaping the Local Economy* (Washington, DC: ICMA, 1984), pp. 26-27.

18. Robert Stoke, "Baltimore: The Self-Evaluating City," in Clarence Stone and Heywood Sanders, eds., *The Politics of Urban Development* (Lawrence, KS: University Press of Kansas, 1987).

19. Poole, Jr., op cit., pp. 85-86; Savas, op cit.; Michael Fitzgerald, "The Promise and Performance of Privatization: The Knoxville Experience," *Policy Studies Review* 5 (February, 1987), p. 609; Moore, op. cit.

20. Peter S. Fisher, "Corporate Tax Incentives: The American Version of Industrial Policy," *Journal of Economic Issues* 19 (March, 1985): 1-19; Michael Wasylenko, "The Location of Firms: The Role of Taxes and Fiscal Incentives," in Roy Bahl, ed., *Urban Government Finance* (Beverly Hills: Sage, 1981); Paul Peretz, "The Marketplace for Industry: Where Angels Fear to Tread," *Policy Studies Review* 5 (February, 1986): 624-633.

21. Philip Fixler Jr. and Robert Poole, Jr., "Status of State and Local Privatization," in Steve Hanke, ed., *Prospects for Privatization* (New York: Academy of Political Science, 1987), p. 172.

22. Jameson Doig, "'If I See a Murderous Fellow Sharpening a Knife Cleverly...': The Wilsonian Dichotomy and the Public Authority Tradition," *Public Administration Review* 43 (July/August, 1983): 292-304.

23. Scott Cummings, "Private Enterprise and Public Policy: Business Hegemony in the Metropolis," in Scott Cummings, ed., *Business Elites and Urban Development* (Albany: State University of New York Press, 1988), pp. 3-21.

24. Robert D. Thomas, "Implementing Federal Programs at the Local Level," in Harlan Hahn and Charles Levine, eds., *Urban Politics: Past, Present and Future*, 2nd Edition (New York: Longman, 1980), pp. 264-279.

25. Deil S. Wright, *Understanding Intergovernmental Relations* (North Scituate, MA: Duxbury Press, 1987), p. 47.

26. Catherine Lovell and Charles Tobin, "Mandating—A Key Issue for Cities," *Municipal Year Book* (Washington, DC: ICMA, 1988), p. 75.

27. Ibid., p. 76.

28. Daniel J. Fiorino, "Regulatory Negotiation as a Policy Process," *Public Administration Review* 48 (July/August, 1988): 764-772.

29. Paul Peterson, *City Limits* (Chicago: University of Chicago Press, 1981).

30. Ted Robert Gurr and Desmond King, *The State and the City* (Chicago: University of Chicago Press, 1987), p. 82.

31. Susan MacManus, "State Government: The Overseer of Municipal Finance," in Alberta Sbragia, ed., *The Municipal Money Chase* (Boulder: Westview Press, 1983).

32. Lovell and Tobin, op. cit., p. 74.

33. Alberta Sbragia, "Politics, Local Government, and the Municipal Bond Market," in Alberta Sbragia, ed., *The Municipal Money Chase* (Boulder: Westview Press, 1983), p. 100; James T. Bennett and Thomas J. DiLorenzo, *Underground Government: The Off-Budget Public Sector* (Washington, DC: Cato Institute, 1983).

34. Vincent Ostrom, Robert Bish and Elinor Ostrom, *Local Government in the United States* (San Francisco: ICS Press, 1988).

35. Lori Henderson, "Intergovernmental Service Arrangements and the Transfer of Functions," *Municipal Year Book* (Washington, DC: ICMA, 1985), pp. 194-202.

36. David Barton, "Highlight of the 1987 U.S. Industrial Outlook," in U.S. Department of Commerce, *U.S. Industrial Outlook 1987* (Washington, DC: U.S. Government Printing Office, 1987), p. 6.

37. U.S. Department of Commerce, Bureau of the Census, *Statistical Abstract of the United States 1987* (Washington, DC: U.S. Government Printing Office, 1987), p. 389.

38. *The Deindustrialization of America* (New York: Basic Books, 1982), p. 42.

39. Robert B. Reich, *Tales of a New America* (New York: Vintage Books, 1987), p. 43.

40. Barton, op. cit., p. 7.

41. Manuel Castells, "High Technology, Economic Restructuring, and the Urban-Regional Process in the United States," in Manuel Castells, ed., *High Technology, Space, and Society* (Beverly Hills: Sage, 1985), p. 30.

42. U.S. Department of Commerce, Bureau of the Census, op. cit. p. 757.

43. John Naisbitt, "From an Industrial Society to an Information Society," in Cheryl Farr, ed., op cit.; Richard Knight and Gary Gappert, "Cities and the Challenge of the Global Economy," in Richard Bingham and John P. Blair, eds., *Urban Economic Development* (Beverly Hills: Sage, 1984).

44. U.S. Department of Commerce, Bureau of the Census, op. cit., p. 375.

45. Thomas Stanback, Jr., "The Changing Fortunes of Metropolitan Economies," in Manuel Castells, op. cit.

46. John Logan and Harvey Molotch, *Urban Fortunes* (Berkeley: University of California Press, 1987).

Response

Terry L. Novak
Spokane, Washington

I have been given the difficult task of commenting upon an article whose conclusions I largely accept. Nonetheless, I have one concern about the argument stated in the essay and will attempt to suggest further areas in which the concept of "the blurring of boundaries" can be applied to contemporary city government.

A Concern

The author suggests that boundaries have been blurred in the: (a) distinction between reformed and nonreformed city governments; (b) difference between public and private sector activities; (c) intergovernmental relations; (d) changing economic roles in an international economy. My concern is that in at least two of these areas, the perception of a blurring of boundaries is closely related to what we were taught in graduate school in the first place. My personal graduate program, more than twenty years ago, did not stress the pride in the municipal reform movement, which perhaps others stressed, and heavy emphasis was placed on intergovernmental relations. Thus, I do not find as extraordinarily striking the statement that "hybrid governing arrangements, combining some of the structures of reform with unreformed structures, have proliferated." Someone educated in a different tradition in public administration where the pride in the reform movement was stressed, would perhaps see the trends differently. Similarly, the trend toward more integration of federal, state, and local activities in the formulation and implementation of public policy depends on your expectations. My point is not that the author has over-stated the case or that she states it superficially; my point is that our concern for these blurred boundaries may be related to how we were taught public administration decades ago.

Going Further

With this caveat, I find the article quite persuasive. Since I'm a practitioner, and thus not bound by the rules of research and academic evidence, let me suggest some additional boundaries that have been blurred, giving rise to suggestions on the meaning of blurred boundaries in our daily affairs. I can readily perceive at least four areas in which additional boundaries have been blurred: (a) the distinction between the "ins" and the "outs"; (b) the distinction between campus and community; (c) the distinction between secular and sacred; (d) the shift in major areas of service within typical city budgets.

1. Research is readily available on the increase in "permeability" of modern local governments. City councils which used to be controlled by the golf team of the local Rotary Club are now peppered with minorities, women, and people from lower economic orders. A similar pattern can be discerned, I'm sure, in county commissions and school district boards. What was once viewed as a hierarchial structure has considerably flattened, and the debates

which used to rage in academic circles two decades ago about "who governs" are now, to me, irrelevant.

2. With the growth of the community college system and the changes in the demography of most urban universities, the distinction between what was once the cloistered campus and the outside community has also blurred. Professors and students have become active participants in the community governance process and the community is seeking more involvement in the campus. The opportunities for professors and students to contribute are broadened as are opportunities to reduce ivory-tower teaching and bring higher education into closer touch with reality. The use of community political and administrative leaders as adjunct faculty is just one example of this trend.

3. I am sure religious communities and their leadership have long participated in the governance of most communities. I cannot, however, remember the last time I heard the phrase "separation of church and state." With the debate on intensely moral issues such as abortion, AIDS, and sexual preference, religious groups and their leaders are actively involved in the governance of the community. Perhaps it has always been that way. But are we shedding our commitment to that phrase in the Constitution regarding separation of church and state?

4. Finally, I can cite at least five areas of public service in which the definitions we were taught to expect two decades ago have shifted. The fire service now, in most communities, spends more of its time and effort on medical emergencies and environmental controls than it does on putting water on flames. The fire service nationwide is in drastic need of renaming, but we have yet to come up with one that represents the diversity of its activities. Similarly, most police departments have moved away from authoritarianism and toward a social work ethic and a community education role. Park departments now are deeply involved with recreation programs which border on social services, represented by school-parks joint use agreements, and the community schools movement. Modern electronic library equipment has allowed the integration of regional libraries into elaborate systems bringing knowledge of the world directly to the doorstep of every citizen. Finally, in many metropolitan areas, what was one a central city system for water, sewer, refuse collection, and transit has given way to a regional system.

Meaning of Blurred Boundaries

What does this all means for the practice of local government management and the training for its future leaders? I would suggest that MPA programs place less emphasis on the history of the movement, more on intergovernmental relations, more on the international aspect of both our economies and our relation with cities elsewhere in the world, and provide closer interaction with business schools. If I have any personal complaint about my own MPA program, it is the fact that I have now had twenty-five years of on-the-job training in business law, real estate, the banking system, and contracts.

Secondly, internship programs should, I believe, be revised to internalize the true problems facing cities. Students need to *internalize* a perspective of the community beyond city hall, of the problems of those who don't carry briefcases, to conceptualize total community governance. This brings to mind the "urban plunge" that my son took when he was a college senior. He and a group of other students spent several days roaming the alleys with the homeless, eating at the gospel mission, and sleeping in church basements to internalize an understanding of the problems of the homeless. Perhaps any student aspiring to a city manager career should spend at least one week working as an orderly in the emergency room of a hospital. Or, a true heresy, perhaps all aspiring city managers should be forced to work as volunteers in a political campaign, to learn what council members put up with in order to get elected. I am sure hundreds of similar ideas could be developed to bring internship programs closer to the reality which the students face once they leave the university.

In summary, I find this article persuasive in its presentation and, undaunted by the need for academic research, I have suggested some further areas in which the boundaries have become blurred and the meaning this holds for the training of managers for the future.

Discussion

Hansell: Bill Cassella, you've been working for a long time on the new model-city charter; are you going to blur things further?

Cassella: Certainly. I think things are very blurred. I'm going to make a comment now that probably I should make later. I think that one word which is used in several papers should be stricken from all of them. That word is "unreformed." What does that word really mean? "Reformed" means different things at different times. I've been spending all my life reforming "reform." The preoccupation with saying one city is reformed and another city is unreformed is nonsense.

I am critical of the use of that term. It does injustice to the reformers of every generation. It suggests that some of them are not reforming and others are, because of some static notion of what reform is. It is not static, it is always changing. This restructuring and rearranging of government has been going on for a long time and will continue. When we say that we have introduced "unreformed elements" into a system, that's a non sequitur. Having been involved with a lot of the "reformers" most of my life, I feel we misread them in many cases and make them overly dogmatic. There are some dogmatic, classic structures. If you read about how people debated those structures, they did not unanimously support acceptance of absolutes.

Kerrigan: The academicians are now wearing a new suit of clothes. Instead of just doing research we also wear the clothing of economic development. Any university in the nation is now a third partner in community development along with the public and private sectors. That's an important thing we have overlooked.

Keep in mind that financial management was, is, and will be an important part of the training of managers. At one point it was more a traditional, in-house, in-service type of training. Now we're into the *real* economics; we're in the economic development game. In the future, MPA programs across the country are going to have more case studies and an international dimension. They've also added interpersonal relations and organizational theory, but finance, personnel, and planning still are very important.

The one issue that has not come up here is ethics. Ethics is the dominant issue that many managers have identified for inclusion in the curriculum of MPA programs. In the last ten years the curricula have changed, and it is now a dominant part in the MPA program.

Keller: One of the purposes of the council is to make sure that the public business is not just a shell game in which certain individuals have more access than others. What do you do with accountability? If you keep blurring boundaries, citizens hardly have a handle on city government. The more you continue to blur boundaries, the more difficult it is for people to understand what is going on in local government.

King: Just a follow-up comment on privatization. I think the point was well made in the paper that we're moving in that direction and also toward "public-ization" too. The trend toward privatization has been overemphasized in our city and others. The economics of the private sector change all the time. The thing that's often left out in graduate schools is the increasing importance of contract administration. Many city officials assume that once they contract out computer services, sewer account maintenance, or even custodial work, their worries are over. In fact, councils have to be talked into giving ten percent in-house support to be on top of those contracts. If there's anything managers have bombed out on in privatization, it's to convince councils of the need to have in-house staff who are on top of those contracts.

Toregas: This is equally true for procurement practices in dealing with privatization.

Branscome: I sense a blurred boundary between what Howard Tipton has called a political-action role and what Michael Gleason has called a broker role. Are they the same or different? Tipton says you have to aggressively identify the needs of the community. I can't figure out whether those are different words for the same thing or whether there's a real distinction there.

Gleason: Tipton can respond for himself, but I believe that they're the same thing. They are the forms of management that I was trying to describe: working with council members as individuals and working with the group dynamics of the council. Sometimes you are much more assertive and sometimes you are much more subdued.

Hansell: Maybe that's what is distinctive about a professional orientation to the brokering or political role. A manager does not engage in brokering for purposes of self-interest, although there is an element of self-interest you can never ignore. The purpose is not to develop an independent political base and advance a personal agenda, but rather to try to identify the relevant actors in the city--on the council, in the community, in the power structure, in neighborhoods. How can they communicate? With change after elections one of the issues is seeking ways to improve the interface between government and the public. How can the electoral mechanism better transmit public opinion to the council? It's never going to be perfect. One of the problems with district elections is that they do not seem to represent Hispanic voters as well as black voters because of differing degrees of residential segregation. Districts are not perfect. Proportional representation has never caught on. Community sentiments are reflected only in part to the council.

Frederickson: I'm interested in the observations of some of the senior managers regarding Elaine Sharp's argument. If the city has been significantly redefined in the last 15 to 20 years, and if that redefinition meant having less at the core and more at the margins, there is less government in the traditional sense and more governance with lots of participants. We deal with contractors, public-private partnerships, the federal government and the state in our business. Is there now less at the core of local government and more at the margins?

Branscome: We've gone from an establishment/business city commission that made policy which we administered, to a brokering role. We have three out of five elected officials who are women, with a very conservative element among those five, a couple in the middle, and another on the other side. Working with this commission is a completely different experience in terms of the issues and how they have been dealt with over the past fifteen years.

McIntyre: There's been a lot of cutback management in California since Proposition 13. We've taken on an average of 13 new programs every year since then. We have a much more activist council. If you ask whether we're doing more things than we used to do and fewer traditional things, I don't think there's been much reduction in traditional efforts but there's been a fragmentation of what we are required to do. Although the council agrees we're trying to do too much, they don't seem to have the capacity to control their own appetites to take on more things. The council's philosophy is populist in character. They see these as legitimate issues. Now we're into health and human services. I don't see any end. We just keep taking on more and more.

Novak: Washington is a state in which everything we do has to be approved by the legislature. There are outside pressures in addition to the legislature. You can trace similar patterns to other influences.

McIntyre: Part of the fragmentation is due to a new layer of bureaucracy in our system--advisory boards and commissions. We have so many now we can't keep track of them. They are playing a much more active role in the system. That also complicates and fragments decision making.

Hansell: I would argue that there is more work than in the past. New parties are getting involved in government, and citizens groups are being formed. Trends include regulation in land development. The changes taking place in open meeting laws, academic involvement in economic development, independent sector involvement in economic development, and the growing influence of nonprofit associations. In the background, local government is orchestrating these trends. Our enticement for major economic developments in Washington, D.C. was from local government and its incentives. Many would say that was an independent decision and isn't it wonderful that economic development happened and government didn't do it? Of course government was very much involved. We're using the private sector. There is a mythology that if you contract with the XYZ corporation to run the sewer plant, the city doesn't have a sewer plant any more. Somehow it just disappears. It is important to teach alternative ways of dealing with an underlying rhetoric that runs counter to what most government managers and local government elected officials really experience. We're doing more, not less.

Frederickson: It seems close to what Harlan Cleveland was describing as governance. It is not government in the orthodoxy, but it is governance in a broad sense with many participants, many more than in the past.

Banovetz: Much of this governance is shared with nonprofit groups. Our city council, which is distributing money to nonprofit human service organizations, is doing the same thing as United Way allocation committees did.

Watson: Government does work. People take for granted all the things that are being done. They want more, not less government. They want more programs. A few years ago Ed Stene would have never believed that a city manager had to know something about economic development. People expect you to create jobs. They expect you to help with getting retail facilities. While that's going on, this old city hall is working on sewers, water, and all the things that people have grown to expect and that they take for granted. People say, "We want to be represented, the neighborhoods want to be represented." They want to force you into new programs. It's not what we're doing, it's what we're not doing that they want us to get into. That's why representation is important. It lets the whole group decide what we're going to do and to raise taxes accordingly.

King: We're beginning to touch on why the public sector is increasing, whether or not we have privatization or contract administration. It's unfortunate that our economy does not capture the true cost to the consumer of doing so many things that turn out to be government problems--too much waste, smog, or water overuse, or the social implications of certain products. Until the federal government and state government--it's beyond a local issue--begin to capture, through various mechanisms, the true cost of consuming certain products, our local government load will continue to increase. We'll be out of money to deal with these issues. I think occasionally we have to step back and say that the fundamental problem is that the public sector is increasing because of faults in our economic system. That has to be changed somehow.

Banovetz: Government chokes on its own success. If we provide more services, we create demand for more services. Government exists to solve problems. One of the things the council-manager form of government has done is to prove itself adept at solving problems. When we first evolved as a form of government, the problems we faced were essentially modern kinds of matters: engineering, personnel systems, and purchasing; managers mastered these new tasks and technologies and delegated them as they took on new kinds of problems or added new agencies. In part, we're confronting new problems because we're mastering and solving the old ones. They don't go away. We just delegate them to lower levels and proceed then to turn the manager's attention to something more challenging.

Gleason: We're anointed because of our efficiency. We're making money; therefore, the devil take the hindmost. And guess who the devil is? We turn to the public side and say, "That's just a bunch of people who are sucking off the private side and they're just hanging around picking up the pieces." That's exactly what we're doing. And as a result of accepting that role, and that metaphor--which is an inaccurate metaphor, by the way--we have done a tremendous disservice to our country by not being able to articulate the costs involved in a rationalized relationship between private and public. I have not been able to find any literature that draws an appropriate metaphor for public service *vis-a-vis* Adam Smith. We fall into a false dichotomy between administration and policy.

Abandonments of the Council-Manager Plan
A New Institutionalist Perspective

Greg J. Protasel
Idaho State University

This article reconceptualizes the way abandonments of the council-manager form of local government have come to be portrayed. As in most contemporary theories of politics, abandonments have been depicted as reflections of social dimensions of politics, particularly those associated with large cities in a popular political development model. This research shows, however, that size is now a better indicator of nonabandonments of the council-manager plan. An institutionalist perspective is offered as a more accurate explanation of abandonments. The community leadership gap that sometimes exists in the traditional council-manager plan and which city managers may fill at considerable institutional peril is more often encountered in smaller cities than in large ones. Changes in the council-manager form of government, most particularly adoption of direct election of the mayor, have been made most conspicuously in larger cities, reducing pressures for abandonments.

The council-manager (CM) form of government has been on the scene for about 75 years. Since the first large city (Dayton, Ohio) adopted the council-manager form in 1914, it has become a well established feature of the local political landscape. Today, over 2,500 cities operate under the council-manager plan.[1]

Despite the spread of the council-manager form of government, the impetus behind the movement to reform local government seems to have lessened with time. During the 1960s, growth of the council-manager form began to slow down as many unreformed cities started hiring chief administrative officers (CAOs). In 1969, in recognition of this change, the International City Managers' Association changed its name to the International City Management Association.[2] Also, after over seven decades of reform, the unreformed mayor-council (MC) form of government still constitutes a majority of all U.S. cities.[3] Finally, every year a number of local referenda in reformed cities propose the abandonment of the council-manager plan. A survey of municipalities conducted in 1981 by the International City Management Association indicated that 3.5 percent of council-manager cities had abandoned the form of government during the previous 12 years.[4] While this rate of abandonments of the council-manager plan is roughly only one-third of that for cities abandoning the mayor-council plan, nagging questions remain. Why do elections proposing the abandonment of the council-manager plan continue to be a feature of politics in many reformed cities? To be sure, most of these elections result in retention of the plan, but why is the issue raised in the first place? And, most importantly, why do some communities choose to abandon reform?

This article reconceptualizes the way in which abandonments of the council-manager plan have come to be portrayed. The first section reviews the prevailing theoretical framework used to explain abandonments. As in most contemporary theories of politics, abandonments have been depicted as a function of the exogenous political environment and social context. Empirical flaws in this contextual theory of abandonments are presented in light of both the 1981 ICMA survey data and data from a 1986 ICMA survey, supplemented by information from a 1987 survey by the author of cities that had abandoned the council-manager plan in the previous ten years. This is followed by a reconceptualization of abandonments from a new institutionalist perspective. The institutional design of the council-manager form of government is shown to be important as a cause of abandonment of the plan.

Contemporary Contextual Theory

Traditional political institutions no longer capture the theoretical spotlight as they did in earlier theories of political scientists.[5] From the behavioral point of view, formally organized institutions are merely stages upon which political actors, who are driven by calculated self interest, perform. According to most contemporary theories of politics, institutions play no autonomous role but are portrayed merely as reflections of society.

The contemporary contextual perspective of institutions is well illustrated by the research which has been conducted to explain the growth and distribution of the council-manager plan in the United States.[6] The form of government for cities has been shown to vary by region, socioeconomic characteristics, and city size. The council-manager plan has been discovered to be predominant in the West, verified as the habitat of the upper middle class, and associated primarily with medium-size cities. This latter finding which highlights adoption variation by city size has also been used to explain abandonments of form of government. It is elaborated below as a model of political development.

Abandonments as Political Development

A model of political development has frequently been used to explain adoptions and abandonments of the council-manager plan.[7] According to the political development model, as small mayor-council towns grow into middle-size towns they begin to encounter critical resource management problems which require the professional skills of full-time managers. Thus, these cities abandon the mayor-council form of government and reform their governmental structures by adopting the council-manager plan. In time, according to the political development model, as these reformed, middle-size towns grow into large cities, the management of political conflict becomes paramount, causing a shift to political leadership. The council-manager form is abandoned in favor of the mayor-council form of government.

The evidence used to support this explanation of abandonment is a pattern found in a set of cross-municipal data. The distribution of municipalities by form of government varies according to city population size.[8] Mayor-council cities outnumber council-manager cities in the under 10,000 population range by over a 2:1 ratio, 2,702 to 1,315. In the middle population range of 10,000 to 249,999 the relationship reverses with council-manager cities slightly outnumbering mayor-council cities 1,239 to 1,074. Finally, in cities of 250,000 and over the relationship reverses again, with mayor-council cities outnumbering council-manager cities 35 to 20.

Another way to view the distribution of forms of local government is in terms of percentages. The council-manager form of government is found in 30% of all cities less than 10,000; in 48% of all cities of 10,000 to 249,999; and in 35% of all cities 250,000 and over. Or alternatively, the mayor-council form of government is found in 61% of all cities below 10,000; in 42% of all cities of 10,000 to 249,999; and in 61% of all cities 250,000 and over. The commission form and other structures account for the tiny percentage not in these totals.

The distribution of U.S. municipalities makes it strikingly clear that the mayor-council system is most common in small towns and large cities. In contrast, the council-manager form has its greatest acceptance in middle-size cities, and a majority of the population lives in these cities. The pattern of distribution of dominant forms of local government with respect to population from MC to CM to MC is interpreted by the political development model as the manifestation of a historical trend. However, as is pointed out below, the use of a model of political development to explain the cross-sectional distribution of dominant forms of city government is inappropriate in light of survey data regarding cities that have changed their forms of government. The political development model approximates reality so poorly that, instead of explaining why cities abandon the council-manager plan, it raises the question of why cities do not abandon the council-manager plan as predicted. This shift in the use of the political development model from an explanation of abandonment decisions to delineating nondecisions is explained below.

The Rise of Nonabandonments in Larger Cities

For the political development model to explain the cross-sectional distribution of dominant forms of government, two conditions would need to be met. First, the highest rates of change in form of city government should occur near the borders separating the middle-size cities from the small-size towns and large-size cities. Second, the rate of abandonments of the mayor-council form of government should be highest in the lower population range, while the rate of abandonments of the council-manager form of government should be highest in the upper population range. In other words, one would expect that abandonments of the mayor-council form of government would occur primarily near the transition point between small and middle-size cities and that abandonments of the council-manager form of government would mainly be found at the border between middle-size and large-size cities.

Surprisingly, data from the Form of Government surveys conducted in 1981 and 1986 by the International City Management Association support only the first condition necessary for acceptance of the political development model. The 1981 data indicate that the highest rates of change in city government between 1970 and 1981 occurred in cities with populations near the borders of the middle-size population range.[9] In cities of 5,000 to 9,999 population, 11.6% had changed their form of government during the period 1970 to 1981. Likewise, in cities of 250,000 to 499,999 population, 11.5% had changed their form of government during the same period. These data clearly show that these two population ranges were then in rapid transition as predicted by the political development model. However, it is a serious error to jump to the conclusion (as some have done) that changes within these population ranges completely conform to the predictions of the political development model.[10] Contrary to the political development model, the data indicate that the rate of abandonments of the mayor-council form of government is highest in the upper population range, while the rate of abandonments of the council-manager form of government is highest in the lower population range.

As one more closely examines the data for cities abandoning the council-manager plan across population groups, it turns out that cities of 5,000 to 9,999 have the highest rate of abandonments of the council-manager form of government.[11] This contradicts the developmental notion that the rate of abandonments of the council-manager form of government will be highest in the upper population ranges where political conflict supposedly increases requiring a shift to mayoral political leadership. In fact, both the 1981 and 1986 data indicate that abandonments of the council-manager form of government appear least likely in the large cities. No cities over 250,000 reported abandoning the council-manager plan in either survey.[12] However, in 1984 one city over 250,000 not in the surveys (Rochester, New York) dropped the council-manager plan. Still, this single case does not erase the doubts raised earlier about the political development model. When viewed from the 17-year perspective of the two most recent ICMA Form of Government surveys, it is clear that most abandonments are happening at the middle and lower population ranges.

Rather than explaining why cities abandon the council-manager form of government, the political development model appears most useful in raising the question of why more large cities are not abandoning the council-manager plan as predicted. As a theoretical baseline, the political development model in fact serves to account for decisions against abandonment or an absence of abandonment attempts.[13] Although this research set out to analyze abandonment decisions, it suggests conclusions about how changed mayor-manager relationships in council-manager cities may reduce pressures for abandonment.

The traditional view of mayors in council-manager cities as only titular heads of government has changed. In a study of 45 large council-manager cities, Boynton and Wright found that a collaborative or team relationship involving the manager and the mayor in policy-making activities was the most frequently found leadership pattern.[14] This finding was amplified in Wikstrom's study of mayors in 41 council-manager cities in Virginia where mayors were found to be exercising leadership as members of council-manager teams.[15]

Whether this rise of mayoral leadership in council-manager cities fundamentally alters the form of government is open to debate. Studies of some large council-manager cities have reported mayors emerging as chief executives who rival their city managers for power and who have essentially transformed the council-manager system into a version similar to the strong-mayor system with a chief administrative officer.[16]

However, Svara's study of the five largest cities in North Carolina suggests another variation in which effective nonexecutive mayoral leadership can occur without changing the basic character of the council-manager form of government.[17]

As research on the mayor's role in the council-manager form of government indicates, mayors have become guiding if not driving forces in city government. This may well mean that large council-manager cities have made practical adjustments which have eliminated pressures for abandonment. In short, large council-manager cities may not have abandoned their form of government as predicted by the political development model because they have adapted to the increasing political demands on city government. Perhaps new leadership activities undertaken by the mayors of large council-manager cities account for the fact that these cities appear least likely to abandon their form of government.

A New Institutionalist Perspective

Trying to explain why council-manager cities abandon their form of government in terms of the context of political development does not get very far. The fact that large council-manager cities appear least likely to abandon their form of government confounds the political development model. Therefore, a different theoretical approach is needed. What follows is an analysis of abandonments of the council-manager form of government from an institutionalist perspective.[18]

Institutionalism is not really new. While long neglected, the social sciences never dropped the concept of institutions. However, interest in political institutions has been revived recently, and it challenges much contemporary theoretical thinking because of the greater autonomous role claimed for political institutions.

With regard to the council-manager form of government, there has been a long history of interest in the design of this "good government" institution.[19] From the Progressive Period when Richard S. Childs, founder of the National Short Ballot Organization, vigorously promoted the council-manager form of government to the time when the behavioral movement began to gain momentum after World War II, the council-manager plan was praised for the way it supposedly separated politics from administration. Subsequent studies have demolished the dichotomy, but this does not prevent one from making the argument that the basic structure of local government does make a difference.[20]

Abandonments as Legitimation Crises

Along with the many other reforms of the Progressive Era, the council-manager plan is usually viewed as a reaction to corruption and inefficiency in government.[21] It was crafted with the underlying premise of the short ballot movement in mind--that "popular government" would lead to "good government." Richard S. Childs did not stress a public leadership role of the manager but rather the unification of authority in the city council and the short ballot as the hallmarks of the commission plan.[22] The feature of concentration of administrative authority in a city manager, subordinate to the council, was grafted onto the commission plan as an intellectual afterthought to improve the commission plan and thereby further the short ballot movement. Like so many inventions, the council-manager plan took on a life of its own and overran the short ballot movement in terms of its national significance.[23] Among public administrators, the concentration of administrative authority in a city manager became the primary feature of the council-manager plan. But vesting chief executive authority in the city manager was to have some unforeseen consequences.

The idea that the city manager would ever assume the role of community leader was generally unanticipated by the "good government" reformers.[24] The council-manager plan was designed to insulate the city manager from the political realm. The council-manager plan provided no institutional basis for political leadership by the manager. Legally, the city manager was supposed to be a neutral administrator, not a community leader. However, the role of community leader came to be thrust upon city managers by the circumstance of having to deal with amateur city councils which look to the professional city manager for expert advice.

As Banfield and Wilson remarked over two decades ago, "Probably the functional requirements of the plan, and not the 'good government' ideology behind it, account for the political aspects of the city manager's role."[25] The time is long past since city managers distinguished "policy" from "politics" in order to justify their participation in policy making. The literature on community power and politics depicts city managers not merely as participants in policy making but as community leaders as well.[26] Studies of city managers' policy orientations indicate that many managers view themselves as political types who should innovate and provide professional leadership on policy matters, in contrast to more traditional administrative types who see their policy role in neutral terms and who reject visible involvement in community affairs.[27]

The very design of the council-manager plan may require that the city manager exercise political leadership, but when the city manager does, it can be a risky political business. As Banfield and Wilson have pointed out:

> An experienced manager knows perfectly well that his council will use him for its political purposes if it can. For the sake of good relations with the council, he is usually willing to be accommodating and play its game--up to a point. As a rule, he stops short of getting into a position that would jeopardize his job or his professional standing. Sometimes, however, through a mistake of judgment or through wanting to accomplish something of importance, he goes beyond the point of safety, and takes responsibility for something that, according to the orthodoxy, should be in the council's sphere. This, when it succeeds--but only then--is called "providing leadership."[28]

But, what if the city manager is not successful in providing leadership? What if the city manager goes beyond the point of safety and takes responsibility for something that should be in the council's sphere--and fails? Might not the city manager, under these circumstances, provoke a legitimation crisis that threatens the council-manager form of government?

Legitimacy is at the very core of political leadership, and its most solid foundation is recognition by the people of the rightful authority

27

by which they are governed. In a democracy, that rightful authority is vested ultimately in the rule of law, but it relies on many standards, including professional expertise and, more particularly, the electoral process. Those who most visibly possess governmental authority exercise it legitimately because they are duly elected to exercise authority and because they do so within the law. But, as Lowi has pointed out, "legitimacy is bound to suffer if the real veers too far away from the formal."[29]

In the council-manager form of government, direct political legitimacy is in the elected members of the council. They have a political base which results from their election and the fact that they are accountable to the electorate for their actions. In contrast, the city manager depends on professional expertise, authoritative appointment, and legal provisions as bases for acts of community leadership, and, no matter how well intentioned, the manager runs risks that visible community leadership may be perceived as illegitimate. The city manager is hired by the council and is supposed to serve, subject to charter provisions, at its pleasure. In fact, the city manager is the one public chief executive in the United States who is legally subordinate to the legislature and who needs continuous legislative approval.

In the next section, changes in the council-manager plan are examined that provide for institutional mechanisms for the development of legitimate community leadership.

The Leadership Gap in the Council-Manager Plan

The original council-manager plan attempted to separate politics from administration, yet city managers have frequently been required to act as community leaders. But because city managers have severely limited legal bases for acting visibly as leaders, such actions may under some circumstances create legitimation problems for the council-manager form of government and trigger abandonments. One hypothesis which follows from this line of reasoning is that legitimation problems are most severe--and therefore abandonments most likely--in small- and medium-size cities where the agendas are crowded with critical resource management problems that city managers are expected to resolve. In other words, it is in situations where city managers are most visibly dominant that the potential for legitimation problems and abandonments is greatest.

Previous research findings are compatible with this hypothesis. Boynton's and Wright's study of mayor-manager relationships in large council-manager cities discovered dominant managers only in isolated instances in larger cities and revealed no evidence of bosslike managers in larger cities.[30] Also, as noted earlier, data from the 1981 and 1986 ICMA Form of Government surveys found small- and medium-size cities to be more likely than large cities to abandon the council-manager plan.

One type of institutional arrangement, the directly elected mayor, has a significant effect on the dominance of city managers. Where mayors are directly elected, they are a focal point for leadership in the public arena.[31] In larger cities and mayor-council cities where most mayors are directly elected, the public arena belongs foremost to the mayor. In smaller cities and council-manager cities where fewer mayors are directly elected, the focal point of leadership is absent or located elsewhere.

This is not to say that stronger leadership occurs in all council-manager cities with directly elected mayors than in those where the mayor is selected by the council. Rather, the point is that more visible leadership is apt to be located elsewhere in the formal institutional structure, in the hands of the city manager, if the mayor is not directly elected. This, in turn, may create legitimacy problems for the manager which, if not adroitly handled, may provoke an abandonment referendum.

One of the most important and pervasive changes in the institutional structure of the council-manager plan since its inception has been the adoption of a directly elected mayor. Today, approximately 65 percent of the council-manager cities in the United States have directly-elected mayors.[32] This modification of the council-manager plan was formally acknowledged in 1987 by the National Civic League's Model Charter Revision Project, although the revised edition of the Model City Charter does not indicate a preference for the way mayors are selected in council-manager cities.[33] Before the charter revision, preference had been given to council election of the mayor from among the council's members.

By comparing the percentage of directly-elected mayors in cities which have abandoned the council-manager plan with the national percentage, one gets an indication of the leadership gap in former council-manager cities. To supplement data from ICMA's 1981 and 1986 surveys, the author conducted a 1987 telephone survey of all the cities which had abandoned the council-manager plan during the ten-year period 1976-1986.[34] The results from this phone survey indicated that the mayor had been directly elected by the voters in only 26 percent of the cities which abandoned the council-manager plan.

It must be pointed out that this was a fact-finding type of survey concerned with testing a very specific hypothesis about the parameter for a single variable. Since the percentage of council-manager cities with a directly-elected mayor was known, it was possible to do something quite rare in the social sciences and test a hypothesis about a population proportion.

The null hypothesis was that cities which abandoned the council-manager form of government did not have a significantly lower percentage of directly-elected mayors than council-manager cities did nationally. Because this hypothesis was specific enough to predict a value for the population proportion, a single sample test proved practical. The aim of the survey was not to focus on the relationships between abandonments of the plan and other variables. The primary concern was to obtain a sample proportion from a single sample and compare it with the hypothesized population parameter.

As suspected, the cities which abandoned the council-manager form of government did not modify the council-manager plan to provide for mayoral leadership in the public arena to the extent that council-manager cities throughout the nation have. The research problem of evaluating the leadership gap in cities which abandoned the council-manager plan was investigated using a single-sample test involving proportions.

The percentage of directly elected mayors in the sample of former council-manager cities was compared to the known national percentage for all council-manager cities. A single-sample Z test statistic was computed using the formula for proportions. The statistical test indicated that such a relationship would occur less than one time in one thousand by chance. Thus, the null hypothesis was rejected at the .000 significance level.

While direct election of the mayor seems like a moderate alteration in the council-manager plan, it turns out to be a significant institutional feature.[35] Of course, such an "institutional fix" is no guarantee of leadership, but the implication is that, without an institutional focal point for political leadership, council-manager cities may face severe legitimation problems.[36]

Conclusion

The institutionalist perspective of abandonments described above does not challenge the health and robustness of the council-manager plan. After all, the rate of adoptions of the council-manager plan is roughly three times greater than the rate of abandonments and "The Plan" continues to enjoy the affection of professionals in local government.[37]

What has been shown is simply that the organization of government makes a difference. This institutionalist assertion is only new in the sense that it challenges some contemporary thinking that has depicted abandonments as the results of contextual, exogenous forces. Perhaps more importantly, focusing on the formal provisions of the council-manager plan emphasizes the importance of such endeavors as the Model Charter Revision Project which addresses "constitutional-choice" questions at the local level.

Notes

1. International City Management Association, *Municipal Year Book* (Washington: ICMA, 1987), p. xv.

2. Ibid., p. xiii.

3. Ibid., p. xv.

4. Heywood T. Sanders, "The Government of American Cities: Continuity and Change in Structure," *Municipal Year Book* (Washington: ICMA, 1982), p. 184.

5 . James G. March and Johan P. Olsen, "The New Institutionalism: Organizational Factors in Political Life," *American Political Science Review*, vol. 78 (September 1984), pp. 734-749.

6. Raymond Wolfinger and John Field, "Political Ethos and the Structure of City Government," American *Political Science Review*, vol. 60 (June 1966), pp. 306-326; Leo Schnore and Robert Alford, "Socioeconomic Characteristics of Suburbs," *Administrative Science Quarterly*, vol. 8 (June 1963), pp. 1-17; Wallace Sayre, "The General Manager Idea for Large Cities," *Public Administration Review*, vol. 14 (Autumn 1954), pp. 253-258; John Kessel," Governmental Structure and Political Environment," *American Political Science Review*, vol. 56 (September 1962), pp. 615-620.

7. Richard J. Stillman II, "Status of the Council-Manager Plan: Continuity in a Changing Society," *Public Management* (July 1985), p. 3.

8. International City Management Association, p. xv, Table 3.

9. Sanders, p. 184, Table 3/10.

10. Stillman II, p. 3; Sanders, p. 184.

11. Sanders, p. 184, Table 3/13.

12. The author obtained the 1986 Form of Government survey data from ICMA. The 1981 data was reported in Sanders, p. 184.

13. For an excellent study of nondecision making in cities, see Matthew A. Crenson, *The*

30

Un-Politics of Air Pollution (Baltimore: The Johns Hopkins University Press, 1971). For a classic discussion of nondecisions, see Peter Bachrach and Morton Baratz, "The Two Faces of Power," *American Political Science Review*, vol. 56 (December 1962), pp. 947-953.

14. Robert Paul Boynton and Deil S. Wright, "Mayor-Manager Relationships in Large Council-Manager Cities: A Reinterpretation," *Public Administration Review*, vol. 31 (January/February 1971), pp. 28-36.

15. Nelson Wikstrom, "The Mayor as a Policy Leader in the Council-Manager Form of Government: A View from the Field," *Public Administration Review*, vol. 39 (May/June 1979), pp. 270-276.

16. Jeffrey L. Pressman, "Preconditions of Mayoral Leadership," *American Political Science Review*, vol. 66 (June 1972), pp. 511-524; Glen Sparrow, "The Emerging Chief Executive: The San Diego Experience," *National Civic Review*, vol. 74 (December 1985), pp. 538-547.

17. James H. Svara, "The Mayor in Council-Manager Cities: Recognizing Leadership Potential," *National Civic Review*, vol. 75 (September/October 1986), pp. 271-281, 305; James H. Svara, "Mayoral Leadership in Council-Manager Cities: Pre-conditions versus Preconceptions," *Journal of Politics*, vol. 49 (February 1987), pp. 207-227.

18. March and Olsen, pp. 734-749.

19. William Bennett Munro, *The Government of American Cities* (New York: The Macmillan Company, 1920), pp. 386-400; Leonard D. White, *The City Manager* (Chicago: The University of Chicago Press, 1927); Harold A. Stone, Don K. Price, and Kathryn H. Stone, *City Manager Government in the United States* (Chicago: Public Administration Service, 1940).

20. For critical accounts of the dichotomy, see John East, *Council-Manager Government: The Political Thought of Its Founder, Richard S. Childs* (Chapel Hill: University of North Carolina Press, 1965); James H. Svara, "Dichotomy and Duality: Reconceptualizing the Relationship Between Policy and Administration in Council-Manager Cities," *Public Administration Review*, vol. 45 (January/February 1985), pp. 221-232.

21. Munro, pp. 358-385.

22. Stone et al, pp. 14-17.

23. Stone et al, pp. 9-10.

24. Ronald O. Loveridge, *City Managers in Legislative Politics* (New York: The Bobbs-Merrill Company, Inc., 1971), pp. 25-30.

25. Edward C. Banfield and James Q. Wilson, *City Politics* (New York: Vintage Books, 1963), p. 176.

26. Oliver Williams and Charles Adrian, *Four Cities* (Philadelphia: University of Pennsylvania Press, 1963); Aaron Wildavsky, *Leadership in a Small Town* (Totowa, NJ: Bedminister Press, 1964).

27. Loveridge, pp. 44-77.

28. Banfield and Wilson, p. 176.

29. Theodore J. Lowi, *The End of Liberalism* (New York: W. W. Norton & Company, 2d ed., 1979), p. 163.

30. Boynton and Wright, p. 33.

31. Thomas R. Dye, *Politics in States and Communities* (Englewood Cliffs, NJ: Prentice-Hall, Inc., 5th ed., 1985), p. 317.

32. International City Management Association, Form of Government survey, 1986.

33. Model Charter Revision Project, "Working Paper IV" (New York: National Civic League, Inc., 1987), p. 2.

34. In fall 1987, the International City Management Association was asked for a list of cities which had abandoned the council-manager plan. After some delay, ICMA sent a list of cities which had abandoned the council-manager plan from 1976-1986. It should be noted that 95 percent of these were small- and medium-size cities of less than 100,000 population. This is compatible with the institutional hypothesis discussed earlier that abandonments are most likely in the lower population ranges.

35. Although not concerned with abandonments, two studies with contrasting conclusions have

31

examined the impact of direct election of the mayor on the manager's authority. See Gladys M. Kammerer, "Role Diversity of City Managers," *Administrative Science Quarterly*, vol. 8 (March 1964), pp. 421-442; David A. Booth, "Are Elected Mayors a Threat to Managers?" *Administrative Science Quarterly*, vol. 12 (March 1986), pp. 572-589.

36. In a 1954 study, one of the causes of abandonment was traced to the dangers of not following the model charter. See Arthur W. Bromage, *Manager Plan Abandonments* (New York: The National Municipal League, 1954). In contrast, this study charges that the model charter itself, before the recent 1987 revision by the National Civic League, may have been a cause of abandonments.

37. Robert B. Denhardt, "Romancing the Plan," *Public Management*, vol. 67 (July 1985), p. 9.

City Managers and Federalism
Intergovernmental Relations
in the Administrative City

Lawrence F. Keller
Cleveland State University

Governing the contemporary American city involves complicated sets of relationships, both within and external to the city. In the convoluted setting of American metropolitan areas, city managers as chief executives must interact with leaders from other levels of government as well as with other local officials. Conceptually, the successful conduct of such relations depends upon the ability of the city manager to create and maintain appropriate intergovernmental networks of both individuals and organizations. In fact in the larger cities, city managers may deal with state and federal officials directly.

The networks must be able to generate public services *and* create legitimate systems of authority and power. Thus, the strategic conduct of intergovernmental affairs requires a network perspective. The network perspective helps to determine who should be at what table and at what time so that interactions with other governments will be guided by the effects on public services and systems of authority and power.

This paper examines how city managers have participated in intergovernmental relations in the past and the extent to which such participation is relevant to the creation and maintenance of appropriate networks. The first section examines the results of surveys of the roles managers play in contemporary intergovernmental relations. The final two sections examine the structure of networks in urban America and the extent to which the participation of city managers meets current and future problems in intergovernmental relations.

Methodology

This analysis of the intergovernmental roles of city managers utilizes data from four surveys. Two are national surveys using the same instrument. The first national survey, conducted by Bob Boynton and Deil Wright in 1965, included all city managers in cities over 100,000. The second, conducted by Larry Keller in 1976/1977, first surveyed all managers in cities over 100,000 and then all managers in cities between 50,000 and 100,000 in population.

Two are state surveys. In 1981 all managers in Colorado cities of less than 50,000 population were surveyed with a revised version of the questionnaire used in the two national surveys. The same revised instrument was used in a 1985 survey of all managers in Ohio. All four surveys had return rates over 60%.[1]

The surveys focused on the roles managers perceive for themselves and for other key actors and on how the latter affected the former. The effects were measured by comparing the preferred roles of managers in three policy areas to their assessments of the roles of others. Both the national and Colorado surveys were augmented with data on the characteristics of the cities.[2]

Thus the preferred roles of city managers were assessed and appraised in a two step process. First, the roles of city managers were compared to their views of the roles of others, especially mayors. Second, the effects of the characteristics of the city on their roles were tested.

The two national samples are directly comparable for cities over 100,000 in population. That is, a sub-sample of the second national sample (cities over 100,000) can be directly compared to the 1965 sample. However, the analysis here has concentrated on the full 1976 sample and because this sample includes cities between 50,000 and 100,000 it is not directly comparable to the first national sample.

Both state surveys are singular and thus are not comparable to each other or to the national samples. Methodologically, the empirical portion of the analysis utilizes four distinct samples from different time periods. The results are richly suggestive but not strictly comparable.

The Survey Questions

Two survey questions centered on the roles of major actors in intergovernmental relations. Managers assessed their general roles by ranking their preferred behavior in four phases of three policy areas[3]. Specifically, managers noted whether they played "predominant," "prominent but not dominant," "secondary," or "no role" in: proposing policy; developing support for policies among council; developing such support among the public; and leading and maintaining support for policies. This assessment was performed for the provision of "physical facilities," that is, public works, parks, etc., for "economic growth and industrial development" and "social problems."

Intergovernmentally, the managers noted who in their cities had the most contact with elected officials from other local, state and national units and who had the most contact with appointed officials from other units at all levels of government. In addition, several other questions sought information related to intergovernmental relations. In the revised versions of the survey instrument used in Colorado and Ohio, managers ranked intergovernmental relations with five other activities in terms of the time spent, the contribution to program success and how well they liked doing it.

Conducting the External Business of the Administrative City

Top officials in the administrative city spend much of their time interacting with officials from other governments. The development of the council-manager plan, however, generally ignored intergovernmental relations.[4] Thus, little tradition was formed around how the manager should interact with both elected and appointed officials from other levels. A first cut at analysis must look at who interacts with each type of elected and appointed intergovernmental official. Tables 1 through 6 summarize who plays the major external role with various actors from other governments in the four samples of council-manager cities.[5]

The mayor tends to be the point of contact with other local elected officials. In the national samples, the only other significant category

Table 1
Actor Contacting Local Elected Officials from Other Units

	1965 National Survey	1976 National Survey	Colorado Survey	Ohio Survey
City Manager	16%	16%	34%	33%
Mayor	53%	51%	34%	54%
Councilperson	4%	10%	15%	4%
Other City Official	0%	1%	5%	2%
No One Stands Out	27%	22%	12%	6%
	n=45	n=152	n=41	n=48

Note: Percentages in all tables are rounded and do not necessarily add to 100%. The number of respondents are the same for all six tables.

Table 2
Actor Contacting Local Appointed Officials from Other Units

	1965 National Survey	1976 National Survey	Colorado Survey	Ohio Survey
City Manager	71%	84%	95%	90%
Mayor	0%	3%	2%	0%
Councilperson	0%	1%	0%	0%
Other City Official	13%	4%	2%	8%
No One Stands Out	16%	8%	0%	2%

Table 3
Actor Contacting State Elected Officials

	1965 National Survey	1976 National Survey	Colorado Survey	Ohio Survey
City Manager	31%	21%	42%	40%
Mayor	33%	35%	22%	40%
Councilperson	2%	16%	15%	8%
Other City Official	11%	9%	5%	2%
No One Stands Out	22%	20%	17%	10%

Table 4
Actor Contacting State Appointed Officials

	1965 National Survey	1976 National Survey	Colorado Survey	Ohio Survey
City Manager	53%	58%	78%	73%
Mayor	0%	9%	2%	2%
Councilperson	0%	0%	0%	0%
Other City Official	31%	15%	12%	19%
No One Stands Out	16%	15%	7%	6%

Table 5
Actor Contacting Federal Elected Officials

	1965 National Survey	1976 National Survey	Colorado Survey	Ohio Survey
City Manager	18%	26%	46%	21%
Mayor	51%	41%	32%	46%
Councilperson	2%	9%	2%	8%
Other City Official	2%	3%	2%	2%
No One Stands Out	27%	20%	17%	23%

Table 6
Actor Contacting Federal Appointed Officials

	1965 National Survey	1976 National Survey	Colorado Survey	Ohio Survey
City Manager	49%	55%	78%	63%
Mayor	0%	5%	7%	6%
Councilperson	2%	1%	0%	0%
Other City Official	22%	19%	12%	23%
No One Stands Out	27%	20%	2%	8%

was "no one stands out." However, in Colorado and Ohio the city manager was more in contact with local elected officials than in the national samples. Most of the Ohio managers and all of the Colorado managers were from smaller cities with a very limited, often symbolic, mayoral office.[6]

Interaction with local appointed officials was clearly the domain of the manager in all samples, with the percentages increasing over time.

With state officials, the pattern is less clear. Managers and mayors tend to share this duty with respect to state elected officials, while managers tend to dominate with state appointed officials. Again, managers in Colorado and Ohio are significantly more involved than were the managers in either of the national samples. A significant number of cities show a "no one stands out" pattern in the case of state elected officials while "other city officials" play a large role with state appointed officials.

Interactions with federal officials follow a pattern similar to state level officials. Colorado managers are an exception, with almost one half being the contact with federal elected officials. Perhaps this reflects the intertwining of the administration of federal grant programs among all three levels of government during the time of the two national surveys. Mayors tended to be most active with federal elected officials, though a very large group of cities indicated "no one stands out." As with state appointed officials, managers were the contact point for federal appointed officials along with "other city officials."

As noted above, managers in the Colorado and Ohio surveys evaluated the importance of intergovernmental relations by comparing it with five other activities--administrative management, policy-making, public relations, council relations and community leadership. Tables 7 and 8 note the percent of managers who rated a particular activity the "most" in terms of time spent, its contribution to program success and how much they liked it; and note the mean and modes of each activity, respectively.

The comparative ranking of intergovernmental relations provides some surprises. Among Ohio city managers, administrative management and intergovernmental relations are an interesting contrast. Most managers rate IGR as least important to general program success and spend the least amount of time doing it. Many managers enjoy doing IGR the most. (The modal rank is 1, the lowest rank, and the means are the lowest in those categories.) Administrative management is just the opposite, with many managers least liking to do it but many seeing it as important to program success and spending considerable time doing it.

Apparently, talking with officials outside of their city is therapeutic if not important or time consuming. The lack of importance may reflect the considerable discretion granted to cities under the Ohio Constitution and thus Ohio managers have little need or incentive to interact with other local units. The lack of importance of IGR may also be a consequence of federal grant programs being greatly reduced if not eliminated and/or transformed into entitlements that leave little discretion to administrators at all levels.

The reverse is true for Colorado managers. They spend the most time doing intergovernmental relations, believe these relations contribute most to program success and like doing them very much. The contrast is as clear as it is puzzling. One explanatory factor may be the existence of an active state level Department of Local Affairs. Ohio has no such counterpart agency. Also, all cities in Colorado except Denver are council-manager systems and thus an active state association can expedite discussions across local governments. Another factor may be the presence of many federal land agencies in Colorado whose policies and activities are highly salient for small independent cities. In fact, the U. S. government owns approximately 29% of the land in Colorado. In any event, Colorado city managers clearly exceed the intergovernmental roles of the other samples and the findings of most academic studies, such as Richard Stillman in *The Rise of the City Manager*.[7]

Table 7
Percent of City Managers Rating an Activity "Highest" or "Most"

	Colorado			Ohio		
	Time Spent	Program Success	Like To Do	Time Spent	Program Success	Like To Do
Administrative Management	0%	3%	5%	41%	31%	24%
Policy-making	17%	21%	16%	15%	9%	18%
Public Relations	10%	5%	14%	17%	14%	20%
Council Relations	5%	5%	6%	11%	21%	11%
Community Leadership	29%	26%	19%	9%	12%	21%
Intergovernmental Relations	37%	46%	43%	20%	27%	29%
	n=41	n=37	n=36	n=46	n=45	n=45

Note: The numbers are taken from separate questions and did not equal 100 percent. The number of respondents listed is the minimum for any of the six categories in the specific column. In most cases, categories have one or two additional managers ranking the activity.

Table 8
Mean and Modal Rankings for Selected Activities

		Colorado			Ohio		
		Time Spent	Program Success	Like To Do	Time Spent	Program Success	Like To Do
Administrative	(mean)	1.4	1.9	1.8	3.8	3.8	3.6
Management	(mode)	1	1	1	6	6	1
Policy-making	(mean)	3.7	3.5	3.4	3.8	3.6	3.9
	(mode)	2	2	2	5	3	5
Public	(mean)	3.7	3.5	3.6	3.4	3.6	3.9
Relations	(mode)	4	4	3	3	2	5
Council	(mean)	2.4	2.5	3.5	3.6	3.8	3.3
Relations	(mode)	2	1	4	3	3	3
Community	(mean)	4.6	4.3	3.8	3.2	3.3	3.6
Leadership	(mode)	6	5	4	2	4	2
Inter-governmental	(mean)	4.8	5.1	4.8	3.1	3.2	3.6
Relations	(mode)	6	6	6	1	1	6
		n=41	n=37	n=36	n=46	n=45	n=45

Note: 1 indicates lowest rank and 6 the highest.

Notes from the Administrative City

The experiences of city managers confirm the data on the importance of intergovernmental relations judged by the time they devote to it. Much of this results from the growing interdependence of units and levels of government. Conceptually, the modern city is an administrative polity. In essence, many of the traditional functions of a polity become administrative tasks and involve a variety of agencies, both public and private as well as not-for-profit organizations from many units and levels of government.

The interactions can range from checking the credentials of job applicants to joint ventures. An intriguing example of the former is the story told by Leroy Harlow, then a city manager, of hiring a chief of police in a small Oregon town. He had to travel to another city in order to learn of the dubious past of an applicant who otherwise seemed eminently qualified. The more likely involvement for most managers is among governments in a metropolitan area. Many managers have noted the increasing presence of state and national governments in what used to be purely city affairs. For example, Dave Foell, dean of Ohio city managers, doubts he would be as attracted to city management today as he was over twenty-five years ago. He lamented:

> I don't think that the profession has the same attraction. Not that the elements are not there, but it seems that either the federal government or the state government constrains our ability to react and to be service oriented.[8]

Even more pervasive is the interaction of the variety of local governments in a metropolitan area. Managers find themselves involved with cities, counties, townships, special districts, etc., in their metropolitan area. As with the "intrusion" of the federal and state governments, the necessity of interacting with other local jurisdictions circumscribes the options of a city; and it most certainly complicates the role of an appointed chief executive in the administrative city.

John Dever, a most successful city manager, summed up the nature of both internal and external relations by noting:

> ...Over the years, local governments have become very complicated to govern and therefore to manage, and you see more of an emphasis on horizontal relationships than vertical ones. What we see is more emphasis on communication and consensus building than the exercise of authority.[9]

Conceptually, city managers must begin to create and maintain internal and external interorganizational networks that provide public services and have a sensible and legitimate authority structure. Such a structure will most likely consist of shared powers, reflecting the more complicated setting of the administrative city. Intergovernmental relations will become more of a core responsibility in the administrative city and more frustrating to traditional type managers.[10]

Managing Intergovernmental Relations: Governance and Networks

The data and experiences disclose that city managers do play important roles in intergovernmental relations. They tend to meet with appointed officials at all levels of government, a not inconsiderable role in a complex administrative state which handles many classic political functions as administrative tasks. However, the importance of intergovernmental relations does not lie with particular roles around levels of government; rather the significance is how well a city manager in the role of chief executive strategizes intergovernmental relations as part of governing.

Unfortunately, the survey instrument is not sufficiently fine in its detail to ascertain the extent to which roles were assumed on the basis of their contribution to governance. Yet just such a contribution is required if the contemporary administrative city is to be governed. I will sketch briefly the importance of intergovernmental relations to governance and the probable future roles city managers must play in intergovernmental relations if they are to be "governors."

Governing a City: Network Creation and Maintenance

Governing a complex system such as a city requires the creation of networks of key actors and organizations. These actors and organizations span levels of government, local political jurisdictions and public/private distinctions. The resulting "agglomeration" must be directed if it is to be accountable to public authority and to achieve public goals. The direction of such a complex of actors and organizations is certainly a much different task than is traditional city management, and it inherently involves intergovernmental relations as a core activity.

Effective direction of networks of actors and organizations toward public goals, that is, governance, can best be conceptualized as creating viable network economies and polities. A network economy is the task relations among members and between members and external networks. Conceptually these relations can be studied as an economy, that is, an exchange system in which actors react to incentive systems. Without a viable and acceptable exchange system, relations among actors can become mainly "political," inhibiting the development of public services.

The notion of a polity emphasizes the need for a legitimate authority and power structure within a network and among networks. The power relationships among actors can be examined with many of the traditional concepts of public administration and political science, such as constitution, leadership succession, issue identification and aggregation. For example, a viable network must construct an operational "constitution" that delineates what is proper authority and the parameters to the exercise of power. Similarly, the system must be able to identify issues, especially those beyond the capacity of any one organization to manage, and decide how these are to be mutually managed.

Intergovernmental relations within metropolitan America are often struggles for survival. Failure to construct legitimate network polities and viable network economies has embroiled many local governments in a divisive political quagmire. In these quagmires, there are few agreed upon rules on how to settle extra-organizational issues that span units of government. Cooperation occurs only voluntarily when it meets the immediate political needs of a polity. For example, small political entities within a metropolitan area can sometimes stall a much needed area-wide program, perhaps extracting "quid pro quo's" for their acquiesce. The concept of a metropolitan "constitution" is indeed quaint for most metropolitan areas.[11]

40

These dynamics help explain the rise of special districts. In essence, special districts are a network approach to a single policy area, creating a polity and economy beyond the boundaries of traditional local units. The use of special districts greatly complicates local governance. A typical metropolitan area will have school districts, several special districts such as for libraries or mass transportation, counties, townships/villages, and cities. Most public problems span the boundaries of these units, but few linkages among various programs exist. Thus, effective governance demands that local chief executives be actively involved in highly complex and often politically convoluted negotiations.

City managers, by their training and experience, are ideal chief executives for such a complex urban world. Managers are trained to interact with political actors over whom they have little if any formal control.[12] They understand how to organize and focus staff while insuring that services are efficiently and equitably provided. Few political actors have such training and thus allow politics to eclipse the effective provision of public services, a cruel Gresham's Law, in which politics drives out services.[13]

Horizontal Intergovernmental Tasks

Within the typical metropolitan area, the local chief executive must strategically handle networks within and without her/his city. The horizontal intergovernmental tasks of a city manager are:

1. the creation of interorganizational networks within her/his city that tie all organizations vested with a public purpose into functioning economies and polities efficiently providing public services in legitimate ways;
2. the creation of interorganizational network economies and polities beyond the city within other units of government (cities, counties, townships, etc.) and among levels of government;
3. coordination of the interorganizational networks within and without the city.

The creation and maintenance of such networks are no easy tasks. Professional management is definitely necessary regardless of the form of government. Similarly, transformational type politics are also necessary, though that is beyond the scope of this paper.[14] Transformational politics require significant actors to focus on concerns of the polity in general. In contrast, most urban political actors participate in transactional politics, exchanging favors and other considerations for favors and considerations from others.[15] American public administration will be unsuccessful in professionalizing local government if it does not understand the importance of the pattern of local politics as well as the organization of administration.

In addition to the heroic requirements of network creation and maintenance within the local government complex, city managers must also participate in intergovernmental relations with other levels of government. The conduct of vertical relations is at least as complicated as horizontal relations. The key to governance is not only to conduct horizontal and vertical intergovernmental relations effectively, but to integrate these strategically.

Vertical Intergovernmental Tasks

The last generation has witnessed some pervasive and rapid oscillations in the relationships of levels of government. Deil Wright describes the bewildering mosaic quite well, noting that a key feature is the switch from federalism to intergovernmental relations, that is, the switch from a system in which the levels of government are relatively separate to one where the levels are intertwined in program administration.[16]

Two dimensions of this transformation are particularly important for city managers. First, intergovernmental programs differ in their organization and dynamics. Thus, strategic handling of vertical relations will differ from program to program. Secondly, the role of the national government will continue to decrease.

The study of intergovernmental relations has produced a rich variety of metaphors if not a productive research stream. Researchers, captivated by the ever changing scene, created phrases such as "marble cakes" and "picket fences." One of the roots for this variety is the fact that the federal government tended to create separate programs for each public problem. The programs often required the creation of separate state and local agencies. By the mid-1970s we saw a proliferation of intergovernmental programs and a mounting concern for their coordination.[17]

For city managers, the proliferation demanded the creation of strategies that effectively garnered a "fair share" of the intergovernmental largess without becoming entangled in the regulations of the program administration. Conceptually, managers needed, and still need, to recognize program differences in ways relevant to creating and implementing strategies of governance. Interorganizational network analysis provides such a tool.

The second concern is with the withdrawal of the national government from local programming. Unfortunately, the withdrawal is often from program funding, not mandating. The national government, and in a growing number of programs, state governments, mandate an activity and sometimes even the manner in which it must be conducted but provide little, if any, funding.

The loss of funding can be significant. Some cities were highly dependent upon federal funds with more than a quarter of the total revenues coming from that source.[18] One result has been increased funding by the states, though the revenue from states has never approached the amount from the national government.

The national fiscal withdrawal from cities may require local government to raise more revenue. Contrary to the rhetoric about government in general, most people appear to support a rather broad array of public programs. The aversion to taxes apparently does not equate with a lack of support for programs; however, tax aversion does complicate raising revenue. At the same time, activities such as economic development can reduce short term revenues by providing incentives such as tax abatement to developers. In the short term, cities will be faced with the prospect of supporting a broad array of public programs with little or no support from the national government; a continuing anti-government rhetoric; and economic development programs utilizing tax reductions for specific projects.

Conclusions

A probable response to the need to increase revenue will be more intergovernmental cooperation among local units. This will place a premium on network creation and maintenance. At the same time, state and national governments will continue to place mandates upon local governments. The combination will reward professional governments which can create interorganizational networks within the city that economically and effectively provide a broad array of public services and which can interface with external networks. City managers in the administrative city must be chief executives of appropriate interorganizational network economies and polities.

Notes

1. The specific rates of return are: 98%-1965 national survey; 65%-1976/77 national survey; 95%-1981 Colorado survey; and 71%-1985 Ohio survey.

2. The returned questionnaires were matched to specific cities by zip codes. This retained the anonymity of the respondents yet facilitated more acute analysis. However, the last survey in Ohio ruefully disclosed some spillover effects from Post Office reform. Most city managers in Ohio are in suburban cities and in many cases these received a "generic" zip code representing the metropolitan area. Thus it was not possible to match returned surveys from Ohio managers to their cities and therefore the Ohio dataset lacks information about each city.

3. The survey does not capture actual behavior obviously and therefore it is more precise to conceptualize role preferences as predispositions rather than actual performance. City managers as professionals who share a common educational background and experience may have a higher congruence between predispositions and behavior than other types of public administrators. Normatively, one would expect this and, in fact, anything less would seem to imperil governance. Empirically, however, the congruence of predispositions and behavior needs to be measured not assumed.

4. The lack of concern is understandable, as early in the century most American urban areas were highly compact and nearly coterminous with the boundaries of the central city. Also, state and national governments had little programmatic or funding influence on cities. As a result, little or no tradition has evolved around the conduct of intergovernmental relations, which complicates the sorting out of roles in our contemporary metro-complexes.

   For early accounts see Harold Stone, Don K. Price and Kathryn Stone, *City Manager Government in the United States: A Review After Twenty-Five Years* (Chicago: Public Administration Service, 1940); Leonard D. White, *The City Manager* (Chicago: University of Chicago Press, 1927) (Reprinted by AMS Press, 1971); and more recently, Richard J. Stillman, II, *The Rise of the City Manager*, (Albuquerque: University of New Mexico Press, 1974). These accounts are remarkable for an almost total lack of concern with intergovernmental relations.

5. The initial analysis of the 1965 national sample is in Deil Wright, "Intergovernmental Relations in Large Council-Manager Cities," *American Politics Quarterly* 1:151-188.

6. In fact, a critical problem with all types of municipal governments is to attract people with executive talents to public office. The problem can be acute for smaller cities which have a limited pool of qualified potential candidates.

7. Stillman found that managers reported they spent 5 to 10% of their time on intergovernmental relations. However, he covered only vertical relationships, that is, those with state and federal governmental agencies. Richard J. Stillman, II, *The Rise of the City Manager* (Albuquerque: University of New Mexico Press, 1974), pp. 80-81.

8. John Nalbandian and Raymond G. Davis, eds., *Reflections of Local Government Professionals* (Lawrence, Kansas: Department of Public Administration, University of Kansas, 1987), p. 55.

9. Ibid., p. 15.

10. See comments of managers in *Reflections* and some of the recent letters in *Public Management*. A key need for the profession will be to make the complicated structures work while coping with the demand for elected executives.

11. In some metropolitan areas, local governments have been consolidated, such as in Nashville and Indianapolis. In others such as greater Los Angeles, extensive contracting with the county for basic services has more rationally organized both local public economies and polities. However, these methods of rationalization are still relatively rare and often do not approach a broader "constitutional" resolution of how public authority and power are to be handled throughout the area.

12. In many cases managers develop considerable power over political actors. For example, by controlling information managers can exert influence over city councils far beyond the formal authority created by the charter.

    Unfortunately, managers can become far more powerful than the plan contemplated and other actors can feel manipulated. Yet, the manager may be relatively invisible to the public. This undercover accumulation and practice of power has endangered the system in many localities.

13. Gresham's Law can be reformulated for the public sector to note that political considerations will drive out service needs unless actors are trained to handle both. One of the strongest arguments for the council-manager system is the training of city managers to handle politics without sacrificing public services.

14. See the December 1988 issue of *Public Management*, especially the article by William Hansell. Also see the January 1989 issue of the *Civic Review* on leadership. The former addresses the need for a more publicly focused politics while the latter delineates a more appropriate leadership methodology. Together these constitute an excellent foundation for contemporary urban leadership within complex metropolitan areas.

15. The concept of transformational politics is from James McGregor Burns, *Leadership*. He underscored the necessity of transformational leadership if a polity was to be effectively directed.

16. Deil Wright, *op. cit.*

17. Much of the demand for coordination appeared to ignore the purpose of intergovernmental programs to achieve national goals, not just to enhance local governments generally. Constitutionally, the national government must possess the authority to offer the program if it could create a grant-in-aid effort. Later, many programs evolved toward financing local government rather than implementing national goals.

18. Cleveland at one time had 40% of its operating revenues in federal funds. Many cities channeled much of the federal funding into capital projects, cushioning any diminution in the future.

    Federal funding of local activities did skew political responsibilities but it also tended to make taxation more progressive. Until the tax revision of 1986, the federal income tax tended to be more progressive than most state and local tax structures.

Response

Buford M. Watson, Jr.
Lawrence, Kansas

The council-manager form of government is synonymous with the administrative city outlined in Keller's paper. He indicates the council-manager system, as originally founded, has made a difference to the cities of our country. The paper discusses the role of the city manager and the mayor in intergovernmental relations and uses a number of surveys to determine the levels of interaction by the appointed administrator and also by the elected mayor.

Keller points out that the surveys were submitted to professional city managers in larger cities and that the statistics generally are the predispositions of the manager's perceived role for the elected mayor. He further indicates that intergovernmental relations is one of the most complex areas of the American government system and that public administrators interact with a variety of governmental and non-governmental actors.

In general, I have found the paper to be quite perceptive of the roles of managers as they see themselves and as they work in the larger intergovernmental playing field. During the past three decades, we have seen a number of changes in intergovernmental relations. Obviously, some states such as Kansas have adopted a home rule constitutional amendment which allows more local autonomy and relieves the city of some interaction with the state legislature. However, the survey results might have been somewhat different if smaller cities had been included. ICMA reports that a large proportion of the manager members are in cities under 25,000 population.

Under the Reagan administration, the federal government has retrenched from making specific grants for projects in cities and has eliminated general revenue sharing. even with this retrenchment, however, the complexity of federal-city relations is unchanged because the federal government still imposes regulations which complicate city administration.

Today it is necessary for the city manager, mayor and the council to develop a legislative plan to be taken to the state legislature. Generally these legislative plans are defensive in nature and respond to pending bills or carry-over bills. The city may also seek to introduce legislation dealing with financial matters that are supported by the mayor and council. The state legislators, in many instances, are responding to citizens who are asking them to take more restrictive action against the cities and to eliminate authority given to the cities on certain subjects. Because of these divided constituencies, the city manager and the mayor play a very important role in contact with state legislative committees. Generally, the city manager would prefer that elected officials or the mayor appear before committees and deal with state legislators. The city manager must play a dual role in providing information to the council and to the legislators. In our case, legislators often call and ask for research on a given subject prior to action in Topeka. To accommodate this, the City of Lawrence assigns one administrative assistant as a registered lobbyist to work on behalf of the City of Lawrence.

Another intergovernmental relationship is with state regulatory agencies. Most recently we have been working to utilize a city-owned strip of land along the river for a retail development. Eight state agencies must review any request for changes along the river. This includes agencies such as Water Resources, State Health Department, Fish and Game, State Agriculture Department, etc. It is necessary for the city manager to deal with these different regulatory agencies. Because of these relationships, the city manager and staff when developing programs must be very alert and aware of regulations that are in place.

As Keller has suggested, the city manager also may contact federal officials who play an important role in approving projects. For instance, the Corps of Engineers, the Coast Guard or the Federal Emergency Management Agency have parallel jurisdictions. Outside the political realm, all reviews must be coordinated by the city manager. However, if political connections are needed, the city manager would contact the mayor who would then contact elected officials. All of these examples would appear to confirm the findings in Keller's paper. The mayor tends to be the point of contact between other elected officials and the city manager, who is in contact with other appointed officials. I agree with Keller that interaction with federal officials follows a pattern similar to state officials.

There have been considerable changes over the past decade in federal-city relations, as mentioned earlier, because of decreased availability of grants. In past decades we have received grants for a sewer treatment facility, water works facility, urban renewal projects, community development block grant programs, park and open space projects, and many others, including law enforcement assistance and highway transportation. As the federal government has begun to retrench, contact at the Washington level has been minimized. The contact on special projects, such as a highway project, may require special federal assistance and in such cases the elected officials and the city manager would be in contact with the U.S. senator's office and U.S. congressman's office to seek funding. The elected officials, both council and mayor, would make contacts with the federal elected representatives, while the city manager and staff would be in contact with state officials who are administering highway funds as well as with the Federal Highway Administration. An additional federal requirement, the environmental impact review, is a long and tedious process that is carried out by contact between appointed officials and the local appointed city manager. To allow the project to proceed, the city manager plays a lead role in making certain that all the requirements have been met from the regulatory agencies. I would confirm Keller's finding that mayors tend to be more active with federal elected officials while appointed officials are the main contact by the city manager.

Keller indicated that contact with other city officials may be therapeutic and managers enjoy that portion of their job. I believe that coordinating problems for legislative support or building interconnection between the cities is most important. It can be quite important to managers who have similar problems with agencies or need support with legislation.

Keller explains the dynamics of the administrative city. The survey examines the role of the mayor and the city manager in proposing and promoting policies. The city manager is a very important actor in proposing policies that are expected due to the change in elected officials. The manager has the institutional memory to help the new officials to work through a change in policy while promoting the policy with the public. Recent elections in Lawrence changed policies concerning retail development and it was necessary for the city manager to aid and assist in developing a policy which was acceptable, even though many of the new actors on the council were quite suspicious of the administration.

I question the Ohio manager sample which indicates that both the mayor and the manager have dominant and strong roles in policy development. My experience would indicate that managers play a significant role in all policy areas. I do, however, disagree that managers are less involved in economic policy. One of the roles expected of the city manager is to aid and assist in the development of the community and to save jobs or create new jobs when obsolete industries have moved or closed. Three basic industries have left the City of Lawrence and it is necessary to replace those with new kinds of industries and jobs. Although we are growing consistently, the obsolescence of jobs continues and must be dealt with by the administration. I have worked on development of an industrial base to diversify the university-type community and to assist in the development of retail facilities for our community. Of the employed population in Lawrence, 46% are public employees. I personally have played a lesser role in social policy other than retention of housing stock in the older areas and implementation of affirmative action programs.

In conclusion, I would generally agree with Keller that forms of government do make a difference and that professional chief executives abiding by and building traditions of government do facilitate interdependence among complex governmental units. The days of federal dominance in city affairs are probably over. However, the importance of state and local leadership provides the challenge of the future. We must continue to be innovative and willing to initiate change to achieve the missions and goals of the city and county governments in our country.

Discussion

Cassella: Last night I realized I was the participant who had been around the longest. I was beginning to think that I was the institutional memory for a lot of things. Since I had known Richard Childs and Leonard White and Luther Gulick and most of these people who were being quoted in these papers, I have to represent them. Even though they were ardent in their advocacy, they had vibrancy and a willingness to adapt to local situations. This doesn't always come through now. To suggest that they were concerned only with the great value of efficiency and economy is to oversimplify. Childs always blurred policy and administration. He was incapable of making the distinction. In this session we will talk about the state of the council-manager plan.

King: Buford Watson has pointed out the role of administrator as negotiator or implementer of the "foreign policy" of the city. You decide to do something; then you have to make the rounds of the various federal government agencies to do it. There is another element that the paper alluded to that causes me the most confusion. This particularly pertains to a city that is close to other cities in a small metropolitan area and certainly pertains to cities in a metropolitan area. Increasingly, through joint-power authorities or other formal relationships besides government, a council member is appointed to represent a city on a policy-making board for the local or regional bus system, a joint insurance agency, councils of governments, or a transportation spending program. We have difficulty keeping up with the various council members appointed to individually represent the city.

It raises questions of coordination. They vote on behalf of the city and often the council doesn't even know what they're voting on, what they're voting about, and do not get a chance to endorse that particular position. But it stands as the city's position nonetheless. A council person who spends time on these activities outside the community rarely gets local political credit for them. Some of the most important intergovernmental issues are the demands on council time and council authority to represent the city.

McIntyre: I was interested in Larry Keller's concern about the re-reform movement and whether it was really undercutting the original concept of what this reform was all about. Twenty years ago I would have shared that concern and said that that was not the right thing to do. But having lived through fifteen years in this position when we have gone from city-wide elections to district elections and having become a very activist community, I'm an advocate of having a separately elected mayor when you have single district elections. The politics get very complicated in a nonhomogeneous community, which ours is.

The other issue that hasn't been analyzed here is the public's expectation of the role of the council, mayor, and manager. In an age when nobody knows what reformed government means, people have no base to build on except what's there now. Their idea of democracy is vague. They expect the council to be much more activist and the manager to have a much lower profile than we might traditionally have found appropriate.

Keller: I don't think it's the presence of the mayor or any of those formal things that concern me, it's the powers given to that office. I see a mayor as very useful making the council work together and giving them a lot of powers. If you have a separation of power between mayor and council, however, and begin to introduce that as if it were a council-mayor system of government, then eventually the city manager becomes just a chief administrative officer. I think a manager's role really does get eclipsed and threatened in that situation.

Cassella: It seems to me that one of the things that Childs foisted on us was his contention that there was no role for a mayor as mayor in the council-manager plan. During the early period of the plan, no one really addressed the issue of the mayor in the council-manager plan. Jim Svara said he thinks the least understood local official in American government is the mayor in the council-manager plan. It seems to me that what we have to do with the model is to reformulate the concept of the mayor in the council-manager plan as a nonexecutive mayor. In other words, the mayor has a role that is consistent with the unitary system of government and that overtly rejects separation of powers. It's our contention in the new model we're working on that if the powers are properly understood and stated, the mayor in the council-manager plan can be one of the great strengths of the plan. Then the manager, as the professional, can concentrate on the things that he can do best and avoid the kinds of things--such as overt political actions--that have gotten the manager in trouble.

The mayor can be an enormous assistance to the manager. They can be mutually supportive, and, in fulfilling different roles, they can make an effective form of government. One of the advantages is having the elected official out front talking to state legislators and congressmen. One of the professional responsibilities of the manager is to provide support for the elected mayor and council.

Svara: In thinking about the mayor's role, one of the perspectives has identified the mayor as a key external link with other local and state governments. Norman King suggests that may be a task that is not going to be handled by the mayor alone. Is that too big a task, particularly for cities in metropolitan areas, for any single elected official to handle? Is this going to be scattered among a number of officials?

King: In our city it definitely is. It can't be the same person; time just won't allow it.

Svara: So speaking in a consistent, coherent voice to these outsiders is a new kind of problem.

Novak: Our city council members may serve on seven different regional boards, and they very seldom speak to each other about the subjects that they cover.

Toregas: I want to raise the information technology issue, which is presented in several papers. The mayor and council members are encouraged to see whether the city has a consistent position before they take a stand. In my [later] paper I mention indexing as a skill of the manager. If you're on a council and you deal with an issue on the transportation board for the region, you have to be able to index it with four specific things that are objectives of the council. Forget that the issue is regional--how does it impact locally?

Information technology might present us with an opportunity that we're not set up to use. Information technology now is just computers and screens. We're not yet thinking about how to diffuse it to provide a consistent voice.

King: I would say at this point voice mail is the fairly soft technology that works the best. The other is a mechanism to have the managers within our subregion meet on an ongoing basis. In our agenda we deal with these issues that the councils respond to separately.

Gleason: I've always felt that the essential ingredient was that the power of the city rests with the council; it doesn't rest with the manager and it doesn't rest with the mayor. It's technically vested in the will of the council, which is ephemeral and dynamic. If the mayor does not represent the collective majority of the council and you support the mayor, then you are opposed to the essential ingredient of the council-manager form.

Cassella: If we perceive the mayor as a central policy leader in the community and he turns out not to be, then the manager must be cautious about developing too close a relationship with the mayor as distinguished from his relationship with the council. The revised model charter emphasizes that the power of city is in the council. That means the council majority. We define the mayor as a member of the council. Some people advocate taking the mayor out of the council. That is ridiculous in terms of trying to maintain this unitary form of government with the power vested in the council. Proponents of a council-elected mayor have a persuasive argument: the mayor is elected by the council to this important role. Thus, he is the leader of the council. That follows the parliamentary model. In America we think people like to vote for the mayor. I believe in slates and in having in the nominating process the mayor as the leader of a team, of a slate. In New York state, where we elect on a political-party basis and a mayor always runs separately, then it's always perceived as the mayor and the mayor's team. In counties there's a very different situation because of a different tradition.

Denton: What the mayor is expected to do usually increases as we increase the compensation of the mayor. The question is, Should the mayor make as much as the manager? The mayor is going to have to earn the salary. If this salary increases to a certain level, he has to work full-time. If he makes 25, 40, or 50 thousand dollars and only comes in once a week, he's not earning his pay. Does that increase the pay of commissioners or council members? If you pay them very much, they also have to come in every day.

Hansell: I'd like to go back to a point in Larry Heller's paper on intergovernmental relations. I spent two years as a state municipal league director. Intergovernmental relations is about putting your side ahead. You want to win. In his response, Buford Watson affirmed what Larry was saying, which was that elected officials deal with elected officials and appointed officials deal with appointed. It's not quite that simple. You really trade with two kinds of currency in intergovernmental relations. Knowledge, skill, and information comprise one kind; and the other is political currency. As a state league director, I wanted a manager when the currency was knowledge and information, even if that was in dealing with a state senator or congressman. I wanted an elected official when the currency was political power. The people who deal with orchestration of intergovernmental relations, the state league directors, are the people who say, "Let me trade in the right kind of currency pragmatically."

Cassella: And you may want both of them in the same room.

Policy and
Administration in
Modern City Management

Dichotomy and Duality
Reconceptualizing the Relationship between Policy and Administration in Council-Manager Cities

James H. Svara
North Carolina State University

For almost 100 years, those interested in public affairs have grappled with the perplexities of the relationship between policy and administration. Woodrow Wilson's formulation, simplified over time as the dichotomy of policy and administration, defined the terms for discussing the relative roles and proper contributions of elected officials and appointed staff in policy making for half a century. Since 1945, the model of separate spheres of authority has been attacked, rejected, and seemingly destroyed. The challenge has been three-pronged: conceptual, with redefinition of the key terms accompanying the behavioral movement in political science; empirical, as the evidence mounted of extensive contributions of administrators to policy; and normative, expressed most dramatically in the New Public Administration which proclaimed that administrators should make policy to promote values rarely advanced by elected officials. Yet, despite the challenges, the dichotomy model has persisted for two reasons. First, it is partially accurate in describing the relationship between elected officials and administrators. Second, the model provides a normative base, rooted in democratic theory, for assessing the appropriateness of behavior. Alternative formulations either have not provided such prescriptions or contradict democratic theory. It is necessary to recast the policy-administration dichotomy in a form that is normatively and empirically tenable.

The purpose of this paper is to reconceptualize the relationship between policy and administration in council-manager cities. References will be made to research on other levels of government and other institutional forms in cities, but the primary data source is interviews with elected and administrative officials and citizen leaders in the five cities in North Carolina with population over 100,000--Charlotte, Durham, Greensboro, Raleigh, and Winston-Salem.[1]

In the interviews, mayors, councilors, and administrators described their roles in traditional terms which presumed a dichotomy of functions. A majority perceived separation and asserted its value to the operation of the system, yet they frequently referred to instances that deviated from that division, and 41 percent of the respondents indicated that there was some form of "mixture," either staff in policy or councilors in administration.[2] Several explanations for these findings are possible. Perhaps the majority ignored the deviations of practice from their preferred conceptual model. Perhaps the theory and meaning of key concepts is so unclear that observers interpret the same phenomenon differently. Finally, perhaps there is separation and mixture at the same time. The discussion that follows suggests that each of these explanations is partially correct, and seeks to develop an alternative model that will clarify the conceptualization of council-manager relationships. The concepts "policy" and "administration" are each broken down into two component functions, and data are presented to show how councilors and managers are both involved in some functions and largely excluded from others. The new model simultaneously accommodates division and sharing of responsibility in the governmental process.

The next two sections of the paper will trace the paths that led to the new model. The first was ultimately a dead end, although much was learned along the way by reviewing the "existing" models in the literature for understanding the relationship of policy and administration. These models have the problems of either poor fit with empirical research or normative blind spots, but each contributed to the new model. The second path was the trail of evidence from the interviews that meandered over the landscape of policy and administration, ignoring any boundary lines. The new model suggests where a boundary can typically and ideally be drawn, and notes some common deviations. The concluding section will consider the implications of the model for administrative ethics, council activities, and future research.

Review of Other Models

Discerning the alternative models which guide our thinking about the activity of elected officials and administrators in policy and administration is not easy to do. Among the alternatives to "dichotomy," the activity of administrators in policy has received much more attention in the literature than that of elected officials in administration, even though both are forms of "mixture." Further complicating differentiation is the uneven emphasis on prescription and description. Prescriptive formulations stand out with greater clarity as models, because it is neater to specify how things should be than to describe how they are. Finally, only the "dichotomy" model is explicitly developed in the literature. The reader is certainly aware of the excessive license that can be exercised in specifying the implicit.

Putting these difficulties aside, four models have been delineated. To magnify the distinctions, even at the risk of distortion, each model is given a descriptive title and translated into a graphic representation showing how that model divides responsibility for policy and administration between elected officials and administrators.[3]

The *Policy-Administration Dichotomy Model* represented the mainstream of thought through the 1930s as reflected, for example, by Wilson and Goodnow, and was reinforced by Simon's value-fact dichotomy in the 1950s and Redford's concept of "overhead democracy" in the following decade.[4] It continues to dominate thinking, if not practice, about the division of roles in local government with reformed institutions. The major elements of this primarily normative model are emphasis on democratic control of government and the rule of law. Policy is made by elected officials and implemented by administrators. Under these conditions, administrative discretion is permissible and

Figure 1
Existing Models of Relationship Between Elected Officials and Administrators in Governmental Process

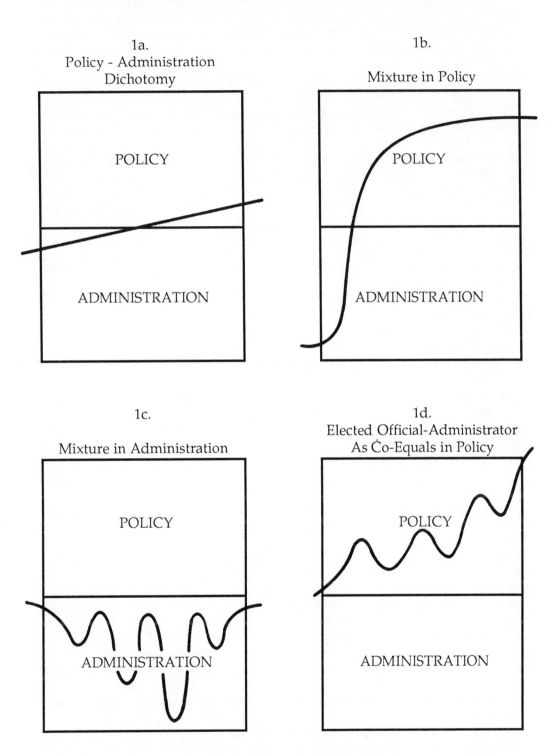

1a.
Policy - Administration Dichotomy

POLICY

ADMINISTRATION

1b.
Mixture in Policy

POLICY

ADMINISTRATION

1c.
Mixture in Administration

POLICY

ADMINISTRATION

1d.
Elected Official-Administrator As Co-Equals in Policy

POLICY

ADMINISTRATION

In each figure, the heavy line marks the boundary between the spheres of elected and appointed officials. All of the space
- above the line is responsibility of *elected officials*.
- below the line is responsibility of *administrators*.

expected--Doig has noted that Wilson stressed the need for administrators to exercise "great powers"[5]--but cannot extend to the formulation of policy. Insulation of administrative staff from elected officials is important both to eliminate corruption and also to avoid the inefficiency that results when elected officials interfere with the "details of administration." The basis for division of responsibility between elected officials and administrators, illustrated in Figure 1a, is essentially separation.

The *Mixture in Policy Model*, which emerged from the post-war behavioral revolution in political science, depends heavily on the redefinition of key terms and the shift in research on policy making that accompanied the transformation of the discipline. One cannot be certain how "The Study of Administration" would have been changed if Wilson had read Easton, Dahl, and Sayre,[6] but certainly it makes a difference to define politics as a distributional process in which administrators, among others, make value choices and allocate resources. With this reconceptualization, the scope of what constituted policy behavior was broadened considerably at the same time that the scale of governmental activity and the size of the bureaucracy were also expanding greatly. This model emphasizes "policy mixture" because insulation of administration is carried over from the "dichotomy" model, but policy is viewed as the mixture of efforts by elected officials and administrators with the latter sometimes dominant. Administrators have extensive opportunity to set policy--initiating proposals, exercising discretion, manipulating expertise, writing budgets, and determining the delivery of services--and through implementation they shape policy formulated by elected officials.[7] Administrators have considerable resources which give them power in dealings with elected officials, and, indeed, it is a common theme that neither the legislature nor executive is capable of controlling the bureaucracy.[8] Thus, there is a complete intermixture of roles in policy but virtual autonomy of administrators within their sphere is presumed, as illustrated in Figure 1b. In contrast to the first model, this one largely ignores normative issues, although, as Schick notes, legislative meddling has been proscribed in the quest for "administrative purity."[9]

The *Mixture in Administration Model* is the logical antithesis to the former as another alternative to the "dichotomy" model. It emphasizes activity by legislators in administrative affairs. The relationship is portrayed in Figure 1c, which shows legislative probes into the depths of administration, such as influence over hiring or the award of contracts. The logic of the model, but not the extreme interference, is reflected in the recent reassertion of legislative prerogatives and increased activity in administration through measures such as oversight and legislative vetoes designed to curb the presumed excesses of an "uncontrolled bureaucracy."[10] Although the model does not address normative issues, it is conceivable that one could make the case for limited, positive involvement by legislators in administration.

The *Elected Official-Administrator as Coequals in Policy Model* shares many of the characteristics of the "policy mixture" model, but adds a normative dimension. As formulated by the New Public Administration movement,[11] this model asserts the ethical obligation of administrators to promote the values of equity and participation and to oppose actions by elected officials which would be adverse to the interests of the politically powerless. The movement sought to address the deficiencies in the policy process that result from unrepresentative legislative bodies and the uneven level of political organization and participation among citizens by expanding the role of professional administrators. The presumed legitimacy of administrators as political actors was a "radical break" from traditional democratic theory,[12] and thus stands in stark contrast to the dichotomy model with respect to responsibility for policy. Not only is administrative insulation expected, but also administrators are urged to construct mechanisms for policy making and administration which by-pass elected officials and establish direct linkages between governmental staff and the public. The illustration of this model in Figure 1d, therefore, features administrative intrusion in policy but no reciprocal control by elected officials. Although support for this model has waned with the decline in political activism and shrinking budgets, the underlying logic of administrators as the driving force in government persists.[13] Furthermore, the ethical commitment of administrators to protect the public interest even without the prodding of elected officials has endured.[14]

Assessing the Models

The models can be assessed in terms of their consistency with evidence from other studies and their utility in handling normative questions concerning the proper division between elected officials and administrators. The "dichotomy" model, as noted in the introduction, ignores the accumulation of evidence that administrators do make policy and value choices of great consequence. The "mixture in policy" model, however, suggests greater administrative control than is warranted. Ripley and Franklin argue that bureaus are weak in agenda setting: "Very rarely will they join the debate over what the government should or should not address at the broadest level."[15] Also, legislators maintain much tighter control over some areas of policy than others,[16] and administrative influence over middle range policy decisions concerning budgeting and service delivery may be misinterpreted as broad policy making authority. Kaufman has dismissed the supposed rising power of the uncontrolled bureaucracy as a "raging pandemic," and controls over bureaucracy by elected officials have recently become more salient, indicating that the degree of administrative autonomy may be overdrawn.[17] Further, this model as well as the dichotomy model ignore that legislators may take part in "administrative" decisions and have a legitimate role to play in examining how policy is translated into programs. The "mixture in administration" model is, of course, contradicted by the high--if somewhat exaggerated--level of administrative insulation from legislative intrusion resulting from institutional changes in American government and the increased power of administrators. The model also fails to specify the proper limits of legislative activity in the administrative sphere. Finally, the "elected official-administrator coequal" model shares the shortcomings of the "policy mixture" model with respect to empirical fit. It does provide normative guidance to administrators as policy makers, but its prescriptions do violence to democratic theory and the rule of law. Furthermore, it slights the significance and extent of the formal authority of elected officials.

Beyond these empirical and normative problems, we are burdened with such imprecise definitions of the central concepts that distinctions between office and function are difficult to make. One cannot conclude, as Meier does, that the only distinction between "policy" and "administrative" decisions is who makes them.[18] It is essential to the task at hand to discriminate precisely among functions in the governmental process without presuming who discharges them.

The New Model

The first task in elaborating the new model is to consider the nature of policy and administration. They are intertwined yet can also be viewed as linked to more general elements in the governmental process which are distinct. Deciding what to do entails determining mission and detailed policy, on the one hand, and getting the work done involves administration and management, on the other. Whereas the responsibility for the "extreme" functions of mission and management is largely dichotomized, responsibility for policy and administration is shared and the activities themselves are difficult to separate. These concepts will be defined and operationalized for council-manager city governments, illustrated with findings from the study of cities and occasional references to other forms and levels of government.

Mission

Mission refers to the organization's philosophy, its thrust, the broad goals it sets for itself, and the things it chooses not to do. It is the determination of "what government should or should not address at the broadest level" to use Ripley and Franklin's phrase again.[19] In city government, aspects of mission include the scope of services provided, philosophy of taxation and spending, policy orientation, e.g., growth versus amenities, and constitutional issues, such as charter changes, annexation, and relations with other local governments. Mission may be explicit or implicit, resulting from significant decisions or nondecisions.

It is the responsibility of elected officials to determine mission. This is clearly the normative requirement of democratic theory, and, although exceptions are common, practice usually follows theory. City managers, despite their influence over policy, "find themselves," Loveridge observes, "regardless of personal choice, responsive and accountable to major community demands, interests, and values" translated in large part by the city council.[20] The manager's recommendations and advice about what a city can do surely influence councilmanic conclusions about what it should do, but in the cities studied, the council still determines the city's basic purposes. Naturally, it is the elected officials who occupy the public and adversarial roles associated with setting mission goals, because, as Lynn observed in national politics, shaping broad policy and the struggle over ends "is played in the open rather than behind the scenes and entails a willing involvement in controversy and the power to persuade and dramatize."[21] In this arena, professional administrators are uncomfortable and ineffective actors, unless the council has endorsed the initiative under consideration.

This is not to suggest that administrative staff are either absent from or powerless in setting mission. A great deal of the planning and analysis of trends done by staff is directed toward mission questions, if the government maintains a proactive stance and undertakes comprehensive administrative planning.[22] The manager and staff can also exert a negative force to resist change in mission. An extreme form of this influence--the "bureaucratic veto" described by Lupsha[23]--was not observed in the North Carolina cities. Still, in several cities, some respondents noted that the manager's resistance to program expansion into nontraditional human services represented an obstacle that partially prevented council initiatives in these areas. Thus, the manager is not powerless, but mission is largely the sphere of the council.

Policy

Policy refers to middle-range policy decisions, e.g., how to spend government revenues, whether to initiate new programs or create new offices, and how to distribute services at what levels within the existing range of services provided. Interaction is common in policy, as administrators give advice and make recommendations to elected officials. Staff discretion, influence over the budget, and determination of formulae for distributing services are extensive, and councils are sometimes viewed as mere rubber stamps of managerial decisions about initiation or elimination of programs. Examination of each of these manifestations of staff activity in policy making, however, reveals a pattern of sharing: the council is not alone in making policy but neither is the manager uncontrolled.

The extent of managerial discretion was considered to be appropriate--neither too great nor too limited--by most of the respondents in this study. Only 20 percent felt that the manager had too much discretion overall, and only 10 percent felt that the manager acted with too much independence in program creation or elimination. Program change has clear policy implications, and managers do not take liberties in this area by acting without councilmanic direction.

Opinions concerning the extent of council involvement in a variety of areas, including responsibility for shaping service distribution and the budget, are presented in Table 1. Staff influence over setting the formulae for allocating services, i.e., who and what areas of the city get how much of a service, is extensive in the North Carolina cities, just as has been observed in other cities. Only 21 percent of the respondents viewed the council as being very involved in this activity, and slightly more felt that the council was not very involved. The remainder--57 percent--felt the council was involved to some extent. Councilors argued

Table 1
Council Involvement in Governmental Activities

| Area/Rank* | How Much Involved (%) | | | | |
	Very	Some	Not Very or None	Don't Know	Total
A. Budget formulation/5	14	33	52	0	99
B. Budget review and approval/1	88	7	5	0	100
C. Service delivery/6	9	53	36	2	100
D. Hiring or promotion decisions about staff/7	2	7	90	2	101
E. Determining formula for allocating services/4	21	57	22	0	100
F. Handling complaints from citizens/2	45	43	10	2	100
G. Handling complaints from employees/8	0	26	67	7	100
H. Developing policies for internal management/3	33	41	24	2	100
n=58					

*Rank is determined by the proportion responding "very much" involved.

that they had a hand in service allocation in other ways, at the time of program creation or major change, through budget review, or in their follow-up of citizen complaints. Still, answering the essential political question of "who gets what" is largely a staff endeavor within the parameters set by and under the watchful eyes of the council.

Similarly, subject to review and ratification of the council, the budget is set by administrative staff, although the extent of their latitude should not be overstated. Only 14 percent of the respondents felt that the council was very involved and over half said the council was not very involved in budget formulation, i.e., preparing the budget proposal. This is a significant finding, because once the budget is constructed, the extent of change by the council is very small. Almost all of the respondents considered the council to be very involved in budget review and approval. The size and complexity of the document, however, and the pressure of time to approve it give whoever prepares the budget considerable influence over the conduct of city affairs for at least the upcoming year.

These considerations support the view that budgeting is a staff function but several forms of control exercised by councils make budgeting more a joint enterprise than is often concluded. First, most councils set budget limits, particularly a mandated tax rate, which served as a powerful constraint for administrators in preparing the budget. Second, approval of new or expanded revenue sources had to come from councils, and staff sought guidance from councils early in the budget process about whether such changes would be acceptable. Third, several of the councils set goals for the year in January which provide the framework for staff in preparing the budget document. In addition to specific directions, the shape of the budget is largely determined by prior programs in particular and the city's mission in general.

Thus, the pattern that emerges is a mixture of responsibility for policy usually involving determination of general form or limits by council and the specific content of policy by staff. Conclusions that stress either council or staff dominance or exclusion are not supportable in these cities.

Administration

Administration refers to the specific decisions, regulations, and practices employed to achieve policy objectives. As one would expect, administration is largely the domain of the bureaucracy. There are, however, four aspects of legislative action in administration: specification of techniques to be employed, implementing decisions by legislators, intervention in service delivery, and legislative oversight.

First, much attention is given to the vagueness of some legislation which leaves administrators free to set policy, but other legislation spells out in detail how a program is to be implemented. Lynn observes that congressional committees are sometimes "as much concerned with how their purpose was to be achieved as with the purpose itself," and Schick classes the trend toward lengthier and more detailed laws as one of the manifestations of a "resurgent" Congress trying to reestablish control over the bureaucracy.[24] In the study cities, similar practices were used to provide more detailed directions to the city manager about program content and execution, especially over controversial issues or matters of great interest to councilors.

Second, some specific implementing actions are carried to legislative bodies for final decision, such as application of a zoning ordinance to a particular case or approval of locations for scattered site housing. Council members choose to take a hand in others. Planning, zoning, housing, and development activities commonly involved the council in detailed examination of particular cases. Further, administrative actions may be "appealed" to legislative bodies. The congressional veto, which permitted legislators to step into the administrative process, has been prohibited by the Supreme Court, but city councils have frequent opportunities to participate in implementation of programs, particularly through their committees. Although these actions are carried out by legislators, they are essentially "administrative" in character.

Third, there are a variety of acts of intervention by individual councilors and the council collectively. Less than 10 percent of the respondents saw the council as being very involved in service delivery, but over half considered it to be somewhat involved. The most common example of intervention is handling citizen complaints. Almost half the respondents felt that councilors were very involved in complaint handling (the second highest rank among the eight areas covered), and only 10 percent viewed this as an area in which there was little councilmanic involvement. Councilmanic intervention was only rarely considered to be necessary to secure an adequate staff response to inquiries coming directly from citizens. Still, many councilors felt that their attention to the matter could make a difference especially by influencing "close calls" by staff in interpreting rules. Whether their help is needed or not, however, councilors are increasingly adopting an ombudsman role, acting as a consumer advocate for constituents to assure fair and sensitive treatment for citizens in dealings with staff. As one manager put it, councilors feel "a strong sense of responsibility for services and the way they are delivered." Complaint handling was viewed as a way to make administrative behavior more "responsive" and citizen-oriented.

Fourth, legislators in the oversight function examine the conduct of programs to determine whether implementation is consistent with policy, whether programs are being administered appropriately, and what results are being accomplished. Oversight is typically associated with state legislative or congressional activity, where the amount and depth of oversight is increasing.[25] The councils in the study cities, in contrast to their state and national counterparts, do not undertake much formal oversight activity. Although councilors typically indicated that they engaged in oversight through their other responsibilities, a third of the respondents did not consider oversight to be adequate. Although one manager replied "Lord yes!" when asked whether there was sufficient oversight, another indicated that the council could not fulfill this function because they lacked clear standards to use in measuring program performance.

In sum, although program implementation is largely a staff responsibility, the strong policy implications of administration produce a lively interest and wide ranging involvement by elected officials. In some areas, councilors may be too involved, especially when they make implementing decisions and act as ombudsmen, and in another area, i.e., oversight, not active enough. Nonetheless, involved they are in the administrative sphere.

Finally, management refers to the actions taken to support the policy and administrative functions. It includes controlling and utilizing the human, material, and informational resources of the organization to best advantage. It also encompasses the specific techniques used in generating services. Management is largely devoid of policy, even though management systems are not neutral in their effect on internal distribution of resources in the organization. Management is the province of the manager. The council is, however, involved in this sphere to some extent. It ratifies some management changes and occasionally initiates others.

Rarely does the council interfere with details of management, in contrast to their interest in the details of administration. Whereas who gets services is a legitimate question for councilors to ask, who gets a job or a contract is not. Almost all agreed that the council keeps out of staff hiring or promotion decisions, and 63 percent indicated little involvement in handling employee complaints. Typically, this activity was limited to passing employee concerns to the manager without taking sides. Staff respondents indicated that councilors also stayed out of purchasing and contract procedures, and when required by state statute to approve large purchases, tended to follow staff recommendations.

The council is quite interested, however, in questions of management "policy" and in the performance of the manager and the organization. Over a third of the respondents indicated that the council was very involved in developing policies for internal management, such as affirmative action and salary programs, and three quarters felt that the council was at least somewhat involved. Thus, management policy was the third highest ranking area of council involvement. Councils were also quite active in initiating study or prompting the manager to make changes in management areas, such as merit pay plans, staff reorganizations, grievance procedures, zero base budgeting, and minority hiring and purchasing procedures in city contracts. The council respects managerial prerogatives, and they rely on the manager's proposal as the basis for action, tending to withhold approval and seek revisions rather than substitute their own version if the manager's proposal is not acceptable. Although they do it, councilors are hesitant to enter the area of management. Making suggestions is common, but some councilors view the need to propose management changes as an indication that the manager is not doing his job and is failing to innovate. The council is most comfortable acting on its interest in management style, organizational structure, and operations in its appraisal of the manager's performance, usually in closed sessions held annually.

With some variations, all the study cities have strong management and smoothly functioning, efficient operations. For the most part, the boundary between elected officials and administrators in handling management is clear. Councils do act in the management area in the ways described. There could be wider recognition, however, that the city council can play a legitimate role in reviewing management, supporting improvements, making suggestions, and acknowledging organizational accomplishment, while still leaving the manager free to manage.

The Model

Mission, policy, administration, and management are the four functions of the governmental process. Although each blends into the other to form a continuum from "pure" policy to "pure" management,[26] each function has been distinguished conceptually. The division of responsibility between elected and administrative officials can be represented graphically by marking a line through a diagram similar to those used earlier but with the addition of zones for mission and management. The patterns observed in the study cities are summarized in Figure 2. The legislative body dominates mission formulation although the manager plays an advisory role in developing proposals and analyzing conditions and trends. In policy, the manager has a slightly larger space than the council because of the large amount of policy advice and policy setting by administrators, but the larger "quantity" of managerial policy making does not alter the council's ultimate responsibility for all policy. Staff has the much larger role in administration, although the council makes a substantial contribution to this sphere. Management is the sphere of the manager with council contributions limited to suggestions and assessment through appraisal of the manager. Thus, conceptually and in these cities empirically, there is a dichotomy of mission and management, but policy and administration

Figure 2
Mission-Management Separation with Shared Responsibility
for Policy and Administration

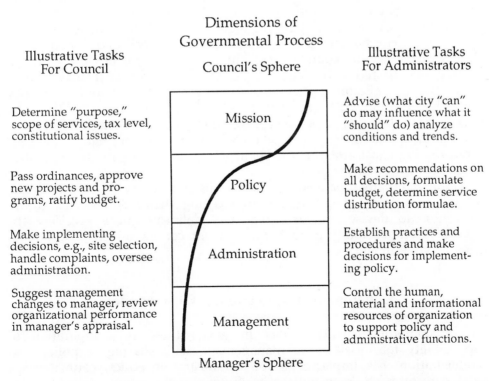

The curved line suggests the division between the Council's and the Manager's spheres of activity, with the Council to the *left* and the manager to the *right* of the line.

The division presented is intended to roughly approximate a "proper" degree of separation and sharing. Shifts to either the left or right would indicate improper incursions.

are intermixed to the extent they are a duality, distinct but inseparable aspects of developing and delivering government programs.

The diagram suggests the "average" division among the five cities, which can be regarded as "typical," and, for reasons to be discussed below, represents a hypothetically "ideal" division of authority. The size of the spheres is not based on absolute values at this stage in the development of the model, but rather is intended to be suggestive of tendencies in council-manager relations. One can make relative distinctions and compare different jurisdictions or note shifts of responsibility in a single city over time.

The variations among the five study cities are marked, although the differences fall within a narrow range that does not fundamentally shift authority for any function. Four patterns can be abstracted from the research. The "Strong Manager" pattern is suggested by Figure 3a, in which the boundary line is shifted to the left, and the manager's space for action is larger in all functions. The council becomes a "board of directors" which relies on the manager's advice concerning mission and grants him extensive discretion in all other areas. The opposite is the "Council Dominant" pattern in Figure 3b, in which the line is shifted to the right. The "Council Incursion" pattern, illustrated in Figure 3c, results from a council that probes more deeply in all areas than in the typical model, yet is not consistently assertive in all areas. The incursive council makes administrators wary of offering any proposals concerning mission and is unpredictable in its reactions to policy recommendations from staff. It accepts many recommendations but in some cases undercuts extensive staff preparations and sets off to make its own policy decision. The council probes persistently but somewhat haphazardly into administrative matters, and dabbles in management. Thus, the boundary line is "ragged" in this situation. The "Manager-Council Standoff" pattern, illustrated in Figure 3d, is produced by a strong manager and assertive council who check and contain each other with neither the council establishing clear control nor the manager securing the discretion he feels he deserves. The manager may play a larger role in mission--particularly in a veto capacity--and in policy where his recommendations are presented in such a way that the council has difficulty not accepting them, even though they feel uncomfortable doing so. The council, on the other hand, imposes administrative constraints on the manager in order to gain some control and probes into management.

These alternative patterns illustrate the variability of relationships, and the usefulness of the model in charting them. A task for future research is to devise measures that will delineate more precisely the division of responsibility in each function for council-manager and other forms of government.[27]

Conclusion: Implications of the Model

The dichotomy-duality model in which there is a separation of responsibility for mission and management, with sharing of policy and administration, has implications for administrative ethics, council roles, and future research. Each will be briefly explored.

The ethical precepts suggested by the model could be called the Neo-Traditional Public Administration, because they combine elements

Figure 3
Deviations from Typical Division

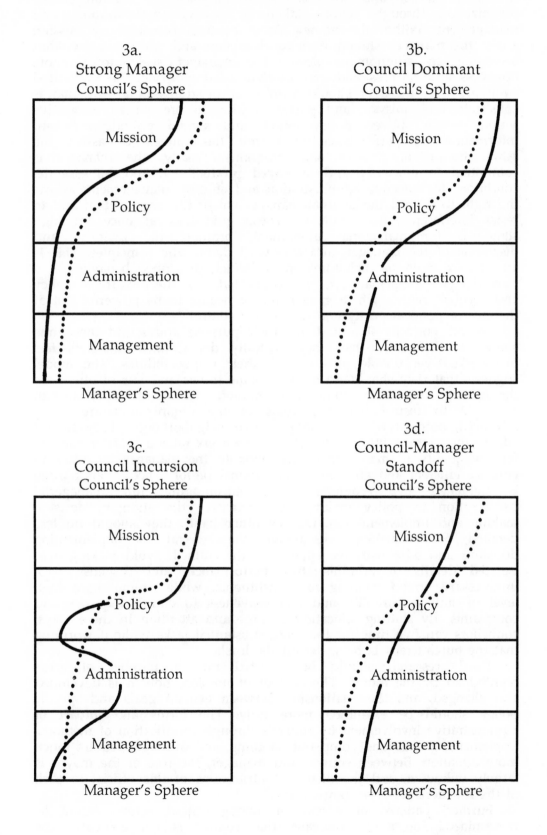

3a.
Strong Manager
Council's Sphere

Mission

Policy

Administration

Management

Manager's Sphere

3b.
Council Dominant
Council's Sphere

Mission

Policy

Administration

Management

Manager's Sphere

3c.
Council Incursion
Council's Sphere

Mission

Policy

Administration

Management

Manager's Sphere

3d.
Council-Manager
Standoff
Council's Sphere

Mission

Policy

Administration

Management

Manager's Sphere

of the long-standing as well as the new emphases in the field. Administrators should recognize the authority of elected officials to determine mission and are obligated to advance the mission of the organization through actions taken in policy, administration, and management. Within the framework of controls provided by mission goals, the manager should exercise discretion and can do so without becoming an autonomous actor. The manager seeks to promote openness and fairness and assures that existing services are allocated equitably. The manager should administer programs in a way that is consistent with mission and policy, seeking to prevent administrative actions which subvert policy intent, and should provide sufficient information on performance to permit the council to assess the administration of policies and programs. Finally, the manager is committed to efficiency and improved productivity, and, as essential conditions for effective administration and efficient management, asserts the right to control the internal management of the organization and to resist interference from outside. These guidelines at once set high standards for managerial attainment, promote the integrity and discretion of the manager, and safeguard democratic principles. This is an advance over the dichotomy model which prescribed behavior for a pure but powerless manager, on the one hand, or the mixture in policy and coequal models which gave manager license to be powerful but at the cost of political purity and democratic control.[28]

Second, councils should define their purpose and spend their time somewhat differently than they typically do. Council members feel overworked yet unable to fulfill all their responsibilities. The model suggests that they should do more of some things and less of others. In the former category is attention to mission and broad policy and to oversight to insure that the goals of the organization are being advanced, both citywide and in particular neighborhoods. They should add to their strong interest in holding down tax rates a broader concern for the quality of management and look to the manager for ways to enhance efficient and effective organizational performance. Their burden is lightened by recognizing and encouraging full managerial participation in policy making and extensive discretion in decision making and implementation. On the other hand, they should do less detailed policy making, discourage the referral of implementing decisions and administrative appeals to the council, avoid picking over isolated details of administrative performance, and dispense with unnecessary errand running for constituents, while promoting a high level of staff accessibility and responsiveness to citizen inquiries and complaints. By shifting allocation of time and attention in these ways, councilors can free time for the more substantial tasks without worrying that the bureaucracy is being let off the leash.

Third, research should be directed into a number of areas highlighted by the model. The content of mission, how it is developed and changed, and the relationship between general goals and specific policy should be examined more fully. The forms and impact of administrative involvement by councils through specification of methods, implementing decisions, complaint handling, and oversight require much more attention. Between council and manager, the role of the mayor is largely unknown, and the distinct contributions of this official to each of the functions deserves more study.[29]

Further, patterns of interaction among official actors should be reexamined. The model indicates that conflict is not inevitably the underlying condition of city government. Although the view is widespread that contentious promotion of self-interest by all participants dominates the urban political process,[30] it is possible for officials to interact positively within a framework that balances discretion and control for both councilor and administrator. When the ideal division of responsibility is found, the situation more closely approximates a cooperative model of urban governance than the conflict model which has dominated the conceptualization of city politics. It is possible for city governments to develop policies that anticipate problems instead of merely generating "political resultants" in reaction to crisis. Administration and management can make the policy making process "work" in the sense that the political will of elected officials is faithfully translated into programs and services that are provided equitably and efficiently to citizens. Thus, the "manageable" city is as much a possibility in theory and practice as the "ungovernable" city, and we should carefully examine the conditions associated with each.

In conclusion, there is not a complete separation of policy and administration as the discredited but tenaciously surviving traditional model had held. Nor is their a complete intermingling of the two which precludes the division of responsibilities between elected officials and administrative staff and obviates the possibility of maintaining democratic control over the governmental process. There is a clear division between the formulation of mission and broad policy for the organization by elected officials, which creates a framework of goals within which all other activities take place, and the management of the organization by administrative staff. The manager must be free to create and maintain a system of rational management practices that direct staff and resources toward the accomplishment of the city's goals to insure both efficient and effective operation. Between mission and management, detailed policy making must be a joint concern and councilors should recognize and encourage the full contribution of staff to policy making. The execution of policies requires the experience and expertise of administrative staff and should be primarily their concern, but councilors must direct attention to the way policies are being translated into action through general oversight. The dichotomy of mission and management with shared responsibility for policy and administration provides, therefore, not only for the division of responsibility that makes best use of the distinctive talents and resources of councilors and administrators but also insures that the conditions for democratic government are preserved.

Notes

1. In each of the cities, interviews were conducted with the mayor and a sample of councilors chosen to balance at-large and district members and socio-economic and racial characteristics of constituents; the manager and assistant manager for operations, and the directors of budgeting and planning; and leaders who would have an opportunity to observe council-manager relations--the presidents of the League of Women Voters and the NAACP, the staff director of the Chamber of Commerce, and the local government reporter from the major daily newspaper. The total number of respondents was 65.

2. Respondents were asked, "Considering experience in [city,] would you say that the council is responsible for policy and the manager is responsible for administration, or is there some mixture of responsibility?"

3. The boundary between spheres in the alternatives to the dichotomy model is indicated with a curving line intended to suggest a pattern of division in the absence of more precise measurements.

4. Woodrow Wilson, "The Study of Administration," *Political Science Quarterly* 2 (1887) [reprinted in Jay M. Shafritz and Albert C. Hyde, Eds., *Classics of Public Administration* (Oak Park, Ill.:

Moore Publishing Co., 1978), pp. 3-17; Frank J. Goodnow, Politics and Administration (New York: MacMillan, 1900); Herbert Simon, *Administrative Behavior, Second Edition* (New York: MacMillan and Company, 1957); Emmette S. Redford, *Democracy in the Administrative State* (New York: Oxford University Press, 1969). Paul P. Van Riper, "The American Administrative State: Wilson and the Founders--An Unorthodox View," *Public Administration Review*, 43 (1983), pp. 478-479, questions the direct influence of Wilson on the work of scholars before 1950.

5. Jameson W. Doig, "'If I See a Murderous Fellow Sharpening a Knife Cleverly...' The Wilsonian Dichotomy and the Public Authority Tradition," *Public Administration Review*, 43 (1983), pp. 292-304.

6. David Easton, *A Systems Analysis of Political Life* (New York: Wiley, 1965); Robert A. Dahl, "The Science of Public Administration," *Public Administration Review*, 7 (1947), pp. 1-11; Wallace S. Sayre, "Premises of Public Administration: Past and Emerging," *Public Administration Review*, 18 (1958), pp. 102-105.

7. For examples of administrative influence through budgeting, service delivery, and professional expertise in local government, see John P. Crecine, *Governmental Problem-Solving* (Chicago: Rand McNally, 1969); Kenneth P. Mladenka, "The Urban Bureaucracy and the Chicago Political Machine: Who Gets What and the Limits to Political Control," *American Political Science Review*, 74 (1980), pp. 991-998; Robert S. Lineberry, *Equality and Urban Policy* (Beverly Hills: Sage Publications, 1977); and Melville C. Branch, "The Sins of City Planners," *Public Administration Review*, 42 (1982), pp. 1-5.

8. For a review of the literature of bureaucratic control, see Kenneth J. Meier, *Politics and the Bureaucracy* (North Scituate, Mass.: Duxbury Press, 1979).

9. Allen Schick, "Congress and the 'Details' of Administration," *Public Administration Review*, 36 (1976), p. 517.

10. Ibid.; Sundquist, James L., *The Decline and Resurgence of Congress* (Washington: Brookings, 1981)

11. Frank Marini, Ed., *Toward a New Public Administration: The Minnowbrook Perspective* (New York: Chandler Publishing Co., 1971); H. George Frederickson, *New Public Administration* (University, Ala.: University of Alabama Press, 1980)

12. Lewis C. Mainzer, *Political Bureaucracy* (Glenview, Ill.: Scott, Foresman and Co., 1973), p. 72.

13. B. Guy Peters has attempted to determine whether "the bureaucracy was capable of providing a viable government--meaning both policy direction and routine management--for a society" in "The Problem of Bureaucratic Government," *Journal of Politics*, 43 (1981), pp. 56-82 (quotation p. 65.)

14. Rayburn Barton, "Roles Advocated for Administrators by the New Public Administration," *Southern Review of Public Administration*, 3 (1980), pp. 463-486. Both the National Association of Schools of Public Affairs and Administration in its guidelines for masters programs and the American Society for Public Administration have shown strong interest in elevating professional ethics.

15. Randall B. Ripley and Grace A. Franklin, *Bureaucracy and Policy Implementation* (Homewood, Ill.: Dorsey Press, 1982), p. 32.

16. Meier, Ch. 4.

17. Herbert Kaufman, "Fear of Bureaucracy: A Raging Pandemic," *Public Administration Review*, 41 (1981), pp 1-9.

18. Meier, p. 49.

19. Ripley and Franklin, p. 32; Laurence E. Lynn, Jr., *Managing the Public's Business* (New York: Basic Books, 1981), p. 146, calls the resolution of such issues the "high game."

20. Ronald O. Loveridge, *City Managers in Legislative Politics* (Indianapolis: Bobbs-Merrill, 1971), p. 173.

21. Lynn, p. 147

22. John K. Parker, "Administrative Planning," in James M. Banovetz, Ed., *Managing the Modern City* (Washington: International City Management Association, 1971), Ch. 10.

23. Peter Lupsha, "Constraints on Urban Leadership, or Why Cities Cannot Be Creatively Governed," in Willis D. Hawley and David Rogers, Eds., *Improving the Quality of Urban Management. Urban Affairs Annual Reviews*, 8 (1974).

24. Lynn, p. 18; Schick, pp. 525-526

25. Joel D. Aberbach, "Changes in Congressional Oversight," in Carol H. Weiss and Allen H. Barton, Eds., *Making Bureaucracies Work* (Beverly Hills: Sage Publications, 1980), pp. 65-87.

26. Paul Appleby, *Politics and Administration* (University, Ala.: University Press, 1949); John B. Richard, "Politics In/And/Or/But Administration," *Public Administration Review*, 35 (1975), pp. 647-651; and Cheryl Miller Colbert, "An Empirical Analysis of Policy in Administration: Bureaucratic/Administration Participation in Policy Process," paper presented to the Southern Political Science Association, 1982.

27. The model should be applicable to mayor-council systems as well. Political executives would play a much larger role in the formulation of mission and policy, and would be extensively involved in administration and management, although in the latter two areas, the boundaries between the executive and administrative staff are difficult to establish. A second boundary line could be added to mark off the sphere of the mayor, who would take responsibility from both councilors and staff. As a consequence, the scope of responsibility for legislators would be substantially smaller than in the council-manager form.

28. The standards seek, as Warwick does, to strike a balance between what he calls "administrative Darwinism" and "Weberian Idealism." Based on the observations in the North Carolina cities, the standards are attainable. See Donald D. Warwick, "The Ethics of Administrative Discretion," in Joel L. Fleischman, Lance Leibman, and Mark H. Moore, Eds., *Public Duties: The Moral Obligations of Government Officials* (Cambridge: Harvard University Press, 1981), pp. 93-127.

29. For exploratory research in this area, see James H. Svara and James W. Bohmbach, "The Mayoralty and Leadership in Council-Manager Cities," *Popular Government*, 41 (1976), pp. 1-6. [Note: see Svara, "Mayoral Leadership in Council-Manager Cities: Preconditions versus Preconceptions," *Journal of Politics*, 49 (1987), pp. 207-227.]

30. Douglas Yates, *The Ungovernable City* (Cambridge: MIT Press, 1977)

Policy and Administration
City Managers as Comprehensive Professional Leaders

James H. Svara
North Carolina State University

The council-manager plan has been promoted from its beginning as a form of government which separates policy from administration. Careful examination of concepts about government and politics in the late nineteenth and early twentieth centuries would probably show that what the early reformers had in mind by separation was not antithetical to an active administrative role for the council nor a policy role for the manager. For example, Woodrow Wilson--a noted proponent of separation--thought that the Congress should greatly strengthen its oversight of administrative performance.[1] Managers, for their part, should have "large powers and unhampered discretion."[2] The dichotomy model as originally conceived did not presuppose a narrowly constrained role for administrators.

Still, the idea of separation and the exclusion of the manager from politics and policy took on a life of its own. As a guarantee that appointed officials would not usurp the authority of elected officials, the blanket claim was made that the manager was not a policy leader. Over the seventy-five years of the manager association, this position has posed normative dilemmas for the profession as well as conceptual and empirical problems for scholars. This paper deals largely with the latter two areas. A review of the literature on the behavior of the city manager demonstrates that the issue has never been in doubt: managers *are* policy leaders. The problem has been to reconcile this evidence with conceptualizations of the form of government. The first section of this discussion summarizes previous attempts to describe and explain the manager's role. The second section examines data from a survey of city managers in North Carolina and Ohio that measure the extent and range of the manager's contributions to the governmental process. The final section touches briefly on the normative implications of comprehensive leadership by professional managers in city government.

Assessing the Manager's Role

The council-manager form of government has always divided the roles of the council and the manager in order to keep the council out of administrative affairs and to maintain democratic control of the manager. Superficially, the roles were mutually exclusive. Henry Toulmin, explaining the new form in 1915, asserted that the "spheres of action" are "wholly distinct and separate."[3] Still, the manager was seen at the time as an advisor to the council who could recommend "any measures that he may think expedient."[4] Expecting managers to attend to the problems of the city and to exercise discretion in policy execution introduced ambiguities about the limits of the manager's contributions from the inception of the form.[5]

Some early managers, "given virtually a free hand in both the initiation and execution of public policy," not only reorganized their governments but also attacked the social problems of the community.[6] In the first years of the managers' association, there was disagreement about the focus and scope of the managers' policy considerations. Managers at their 1916 meeting affirmed the prerogatives of the council, although their active involvement in efforts to persuade the council and community of the need for action to meet pressing problems "revealed clearly" to Leonard White "that the managers were far from practicing the doctrine" they had supported.[7] In 1917, Richard Childs suggested that the "great managers of tomorrow will be those whose ideals stopped at no line of dogma or tradition, but who pushed beyond the old horizons and discovered new worlds of service."[8] At the convention the next year, his advocacy of broad managerial leadership was even clearer:

> Some day we shall have managers here who have achieved national reputation, not by saving taxes or by running their cities for a freakishly low expense per capita, but managers who have successfully led their commissions into great new enterprises of service....[9]

Despite these sentiments, Childs was always a strict adherent to the doctrine of separation. His view was that the manager's job was to "administer" and not to "govern" and should not seek to impose his values on the council.[10] Presumably, if the council chose to follow the manager's lead into great new enterprises, the norm of separation was preserved. The nature of the role in Childs' thinking, however, has appropriately been described as "elusive," and this comment is probably apt for other early observers of council-manager government.[11]

White identified two schools of thought concerning the manager's involvement in policy and the extent to which the manager was a community leader, as opposed to an administrative technician.[12] White himself argued that one of the "hazards" to the manager movement is the "adventuresome spirit of many managers, especially those new to the game."[13] The issue was not settled with the Association's first Code of Ethics in 1924. Although managers were proscribed from taking an "active part in politics," other provisions permitted a contribution to determining policy and supporting and promoting policies adopted by the council. Schiesl concluded that in the early 1920s managers already viewed themselves as participants in resolving community issues and conflicts: "managers continued to participate in the making of public policy with little immunity from political considerations."[14] Managers recognized, as H.G. Otis put it in 1926, that "one of the most delicate tasks of the city manager is to educate his council without their knowledge."[15] White observed in his field study that "the office of the city manager has become the great center of initiating and proposing (but not deciding) public policies as well as the sole responsible center of administration." He did conclude, however, that "the behavior of most managers, most of the time, is not the behavior of the community leader."[16]

As an issue of philosophy within the city manager association, the matter was settled for a time with Ridley and Nolting's *The City Manager Profession* and the 1938 Code of Ethics. Stillman characterizes the former as summarizing "the orthodox scientific management ideology as it applied to city managers."[17] Not only was a clear separation between policy and administration asserted by Ridley and Nolting, but even the manager's advisory relationship was carefully circumscribed. The manager provides facts and technical assessment of consequences only: "at the request of the council, the manager may make his recommendation, but he urges the council to decide upon the policy in the light of the facts and the needs of the people."[18] The manager should not "let himself be driven or led into taking the leadership or responsibility in matters of policy" nor is the manager expected to take criticism for decisions of the council. In general, the manager should stay "out of the limelight as much as possible."[19] The 1938 Code of Ethics seemingly closed the door on a policy role: "the city manager is in no sense a political leader."

Every empirical study of the manager's roles since this reassertion of the orthodox position, however, has found policy involvement, and there have been recurring efforts to square practice and norms. In a major field study published in 1940, Stone, Price, and Stone concluded that it was "generally impossible for a city manager to escape being a leader in matters of policy."[20] Indeed, in cities where the manager and council had a positive relationship, "so long as the council could have the last word on any proposal [the manager] might make, it wanted him to take the initiative."[21] They distinguish between "community leadership" and "political leadership," i.e., partisan or electoral involvement, exchanging council support for rewards, or appealing over the head of the council to the voters. Managers eschew the latter, but are active in the former. Managers are not secure by being anonymous and emphasizing the administrative rather than the community leadership approach. When managers were attacked, management practices, e.g., elimination of patronage, were more likely to be the source of controversy than policy issues. Whether policy recommendations produced resentment had more to do with the local political traditions than with the manager's initiative per se. "To ask a city manager to avoid incursion into policy would be to set up an impossible distinction between policy and administration; it would be, in effect, to ask him not to be a city manager."[22]

The idea of community leadership found supporters within the ranks of managers as well. C. A. Harrell of Norfolk, in his presidential address in 1948, identified the "ideal manager" as a "positive, vital force in the community." As a "formulator of action and a planner," the manager "visualizes broad objectives, distant goals, far-sighted projects."[23] The distinction between political and community leadership permits the manager to assume these "aggressive functions" and still be nonpolitical. A broader sense of responsibility was emerging. "We owe it to our communities to exercise more imagination and vision in initiating policy proposals for action by the council. We have the best interests of the community at heart." Ridley concluded after surveying managers in 1958 that the "city manager by the very nature of his job acts as a policy formulator."[24] Managers take an active part in seeking to improve their communities, although they respect the ultimate authority of the council and do not care to be "designated as leaders of their communities."

In the same year, Adrian reported from observations of three cities that managers take on policy leadership but avoid "taking a public role of policy innovator, except at the specific request of the council or in cases involving matters on which he could be considered a technical expert."[25] Bosworth dropped the veil completely by proclaiming "The Manager *Is* a Politician."[26] As a "policy researcher" the manager is a "city-statesman" who brings his knowledge of urban affairs and awareness of best practice to guide the progress of his own community. He also serves as community leader aware of groups and sources of power in the city and in regular contact with state and federal government officials. "Let us think of managers," Bosworth concluded, "as officers of general administrative direction *and* political leadership, for that is what they are."[27] The research of Kammerer and her associates in ten Florida cities found managers who were involved in all aspects of policy making. "They were right in the heart of politics, in the broadest sense of that term."[28] The professionals among the managers (approximately a quarter of the managers who had served in these cities between 1945 and 1960) are particularly likely to assume a policy leadership role. Since they are usually outsiders who have no political base in the community, they are unlikely to have groups to which they can appeal "either for support of [their] policy proposals or for help in blocking [their] removal." These circumstances contribute to shorter tenure for the activist, professional managers, but all managers were involved in policy to some extent. In further analysis of the findings, Kammerer echoed the conclusion of Stone *et al.*, that administrative decisions are as likely to get a manager in trouble as policy activity, "*if either type of decision involves defiance of the clique dominant in the council.*"[29] In half the case study cities, managers exercised limited to extensive discretion in all decisions, whereas in the other half virtually no discretion was permitted by the council. Thus, managers may be active in policy but the latitude of their activities is shaped by the council and the political context in which they work.[30]

Research based on a national survey of managers in 1965 added to awareness of the manager's contributions. Wright uses the same categories of activities used by Bosworth and substantiates Bosworth's conclusions. Managers combine "preponderant authority in the sphere of administration"--the managerial role--with influence over agenda setting and policy formulation in the policy role. The manager is the "dominant policy initiator in most manager cities."[31] Furthermore, the manager is a "prominent representative *of* the city" in dealings with groups in the community and officials in other governments--the political role. They are limited, however, in their ability to make commitments or determine direction. The manager's "political role is narrowly circumscribed when analyzed in terms of speaking *for* a composite of community interests on policy matters."[32] To Wright, the manager is a politician in the sense of "achieving a workable balance among role behaviors." Indeed, handling the wide range of roles makes him "*more* than a politician."[33] The constraints on the manager's decisions by the general sentiments of the council, the activity of the mayor, and the previous commitments of city government make the manager a leader within boundaries.

Loveridge also stressed the policy behavior of managers in his research which compared attitudes of managers and council members in the Bay Area of California. Managers support behaviors which constitute activism and policy leadership. Over half viewed their position as that of political leader. Council members, on the other hand, defined the role narrowly. Over eighty percent viewed managers as administrative specialists.[34] Loveridge accepted as a given that the manager was a policy leader, reflecting previous research and the behavioralist orientation in postwar discipline of political science, but he also detailed limitations on the manager's leadership.

Since managers have extensive resources and see themselves as policy leaders, why do they not have even more power than they do? Because of the constraint imposed by council attitudes, managers are limited to safe areas. "The manager cannot introduce major policy decisions onto the civic agenda that do not have the implicit approval of the city council."[35] Furthermore, the council expects that the manager will reflect their orientation to policy questions, "not the abstract values of the public interest or of the city management profession." Ironically, Loveridge's study provides substantial support for the idea of council control even though it is usually cited--appropriately--as making a strong case for the manager's policy leadership. His work, along with that of Kammerer and Wright, provides evidence that the council limits the activities of the manager. This theme, which was partially consistent with the traditional view of roles in the council-manager form, however, attracted less attention than the evidence which seemed to contradict that view.

Mulrooney and Banovetz in 1971 further supported the acceptance of activist city managers. Mulrooney surveyed expert opinion on the question whether council-manager government can respond to the social and economic problems of cities. Most agreed not only that it can but that managers may be particularly adept at doing so. As one respondent, urban scholar Norton Long, put it, the manager's "membership in a national profession with great career mobility both emancipates him, if he is able, from parochial inhibitions and job security anxieties and gives him a wide, enlightened professional reference group to provide him standards of action and critical appreciation."[36] Banovetz, reflecting sentiments expressed in the New Public Administration movement, felt that managerial responsibility had evolved in the sixties and that managers sought to "promote the American ideals of equal opportunity, tolerance, [and] understanding, and improve the quality of community life."[37] The role of the manager necessarily was changing as well from that in earlier periods when managers concentrated on bringing "business-like efficiency" to corrupt city governments or attended to the physical needs of rapidly growing cities. As a consequence, managers are "increasingly impelled to assume the burden for advocating change and by implication stimulating controversy in order to foster community-wide social and economic well-being."[38] He argued that managers need to offset the weak representation of lower income groups and minorities on the city council. Both observers suggested that it was a liability to the manager profession and to the council-manager form to be invariably linked to other reform institutions, particularly at-large elections. Stillman found from a 1971 survey that managers differ in cities of different size in the relative emphasis they place on policy matters, planning, council relations, and community leadership as opposed to dealing directly with the line operations of city government. (No specific mention is made of staff functions.) In the largest cities, the emphasis is on the former and in the smallest, on the latter. Managers in medium-sized cities and suburban communities handle both. Among the special problems that managers face is finding ways to achieve recognition of and acceptance for their "vital contribution to the local policy-making process."[39] The continuing view that there is a sharp dichotomy between politics and administration "may at times inhibit managers from realizing the full potentialities of their important policy-making roles in community affairs." Indeed, the individual manager is the "prisoner of a peculiar form of government, the council-manager form, and he must accept its reformist emphasis on the separation of politics from administration and its middle-class, suburban, and nonpartisan biases."[40] Stillman suggested a new self image that accommodates expertise and training with involvement in the political affairs of the community.

Huntley and Macdonald, drawing on a 1973 survey of managers and CAOs (the latter were 8% of the respondents), find that virtually all managers always or nearly always participate in the formulation of policy and set the council agenda (89% and 90%, respectively).[41] Most initiate policy (64%) and play a leading role in policy making (62%). These activities are not restricted to large cities. Although small town managers may be preoccupied with service delivery, they are also most likely to set council agenda and play a leading role in policy making. Echoing Loveridge's conclusions, managers perceive that the council does not expect them to provide political leadership. Still, when policies were adopted on establishing affirmative actions for women and minorities, the policy was taken with initiative from the manager in 84 percent of the cases. Managers are active in their policy and administrative roles, but they also involve the council extensively. Slightly more than half of the managers always or nearly always consult with the council before drafting the budget and before appointing or removing department heads. Bringing the council into managerial decisions is more likely in the largest cities (over 250,000), least likely in those between 100,000 and 249,999, and then increases in likelihood again as city size declines.

Fannin develops a range of managerial roles that vary in the reliance on professional criteria and the degree of independence in decision making.[42] He examines the preference of managers for using these roles in various problem situations. There is overwhelming preference among managers and council members for managers to apply professional expertise to policy making. If there is little "political competition" contained in the situation and it is amenable to use of analytical techniques, both sets of officials accepted independent action by the manager. More common, however, was the expectation that the manager participate in policy making by offering recommendations, information, and analysis to the council. The "political activist" at one extreme and the "policy non-actor" role at the other extreme were accepted by less than ten percent of the managers and council members.

Browne, in a survey of managers in Michigan, examined attitudes about policy initiation and identified the considerable contributions of the manager. Almost three-quarters of the managers consider their leadership to be very necessary, and only three percent considered it to be unnecessary or inappropriate.[43] Managers had high success rates in securing acceptance of their proposals. This activist style is presumably acceptable, because nearly all the managers felt that their relationship with the council was excellent or good. He conceded that Michigan may be unusual in the high level of managerial policy leadership.

Green, however, reports similar findings from another national survey conducted by ICMA in 1984.[44] Response options to questions do not match those of Huntley and Macdonald and results include managers in counties and councils of governments as well as cities. Thus, direct comparison of the results from the two surveys is not possible. The patterns, however, are very similar. Over ninety percent of the managers always or sometimes play a leading role in policy making, initiate policies, and participate in policy formulation. Only fifteen percent never speak on controversial issues or refuse to work through influential community members to achieve policy goals. On the other hand, over eighty percent at least sometimes consult with the council on budget and personnel decisions, maintain a neutral stand on some divisive issues, and occasionally confine their actions to administration, leaving policy matters to the council. The balance of independence and control is reflected in the results. Being a policy and community leader does not mean that the manager is either an autonomous professional actor or a politico.[45]

Not only are managers policy leaders, they are inclined to act on the basis of their own sense of what is right. Many managers--half in a national sample conducted by Wirth and Vasu--would make a considerable effort to shift the priorities of the council in a direction that reflects the manager's value preferences if the council took an opposing position.[46] The priorities that managers hold are related to their ideology, the geographic region in which they work, and their level and field of education.

Finally, Newell and Ammons report that mayors and managers spend their time in quite similar ways among three roles used by Bosworth and Wright: "management," "policy," and "political." Mayors spend almost as much time on management as city managers (except in cities over 100,000) and managers spend roughly half their time in policy, including council relations (32%), and political matters, including community leadership but excluding partisan involvement (17%), in cities of all sizes.[47] They devote relatively more time to policy and less to political activities than executive mayors, but they are active in all areas. There is a change in assessments of the role most important for job success from Wright's 1965 survey. As before, fewer than two managers in five in cities over 100,000 population identify management as the key to success. The number who choose the policy role has jumped from 22 percent to 56 percent. Correspondingly, the political role has declined from 33 percent to 6 percent.[48]

The authors suggest that managers are now more involved in policy than previously, but a different interpretation that stresses continuity is possible. Most managers report in both surveys that the internal demands of the job, i.e., those arising within the organization, are not the most critical; external leadership is necessary for success. There has been a shift in the external focus but both community leadership and council relations presumably bring the manager into consideration of issues and provision of leadership. At the same time, relations with state and federal government--another aspect of the political role--are probably relatively less important now than they were in the grantsmanship era of the sixties. It seems likely that the changing characteristics of city councils and the new burdens with which officials are grappling make dealings with the council the critical forum rather than interactions with community leaders. Council relations are also "political" and dealings with the broader community and other levels of government involved managers in shaping "policy." Thus, these results indicate continuity along with shifting emphases in the focus of managerial leadership but also suggest that managers differ in the extent to which they are engaged in the policy or political role. A sizable minority still identifies management as its key area of activity.

This array of findings from studies over the seventy-five year history of the manager profession provides overwhelming evidence that managers do what traditionalists say they shouldn't do. How does one deal with the contradiction between formal role definition and reality? One response has been to argue that the manager has always been active in policy but we have not recognized it, as Bosworth did, or that managers have always been active in policy initiation but the range of policy concerns has gradually expanded over the years, as Nolting argued, making this role more apparent.[49] Bollens and Ries, wishing to cut loose the "intellectual and emotional baggage loaded on to" the manager's role reveal some frustration in not being able to do so. Taking part in the policy process as well as managing the operations of the city *was, is, and will continue to be the unique contribution of the profession.*[50] "Call it what one will," they argue, "the position of the manager permits him a share--ranging from minor to dominant--in policy, politics, and leadership. Such has always been the case." The roles of the manager are stable but the myths about the position change as do cities. Adrian long ago dismissed the debates over separation as "tempests created in academicians' teapots." The issue has had little interest to managers who "must have discovered the necessary interrelationship of [politics and administration] about the time that the first manager was appointed in 1908."[51]

Not all practitioners, however, have resolved the issue. Although acceptance of the policy role appears to be taking hold of the profession, there is ambivalence among managers as they think about the future. Stillman found that managers responding to a 1981 ICMA survey were evenly divided between a "Back-to-the-Fundamentals School" and a "Forward-to-the-New-Horizons School."[52] Approximately half the managers surveyed in three states express a preference for acting as an administrator and leaving policy to the council, and Green reports that most at least sometimes actually do behave this way.[53] Thus, some managers may accept the doctrine of separation, and others may hold onto it as rhetoric while they blithely engage in policy anyway.[54]

Because the issue has not been resolved, it is periodically rediscovered. Policy activity is treated as if it were new, produced by forces not found in cities at an earlier time, or associated with change in the characteristics of persons entering the field. For example, Banovetz reveals that a "candid job description for a city manager would differ considerably from a comparable document drafted 30 years or so ago."[55] Stillman argues that "modern managers" who are becoming more professionalized than earlier ones "tend to take a far more aggressive role in policy leadership."[56] In a recent example, Ammons and Newell debunk the idea that city managers do not make policy as "A Lie; Let's Face It." Reality, they argue, departs from the typical view of executive mayors as political leaders and city managers as administrators; their findings suggest a "clear break" from established images.[57] New conditions make it necessary for managers to be "more than mere technocrats."

Reconceptualizing the Manager's Roles and Responsibilities

My own views are that discussion about this topic persists because it raises serious issues--not mere "tempests in teapots." The empirical evidence produces conceptual and normative dilemmas. Presenting the problem as new and emerging is one way to redirect attention from issues which are still unresolved. There are three reasons why the policy role of the manager has been hard to assimilate and why the dichotomy model endures.

First, the dichotomy model accurately describes part of the relationship between elected officials and administrators. As we have seen, elected officials exercise tight control over managers in certain situations and impose general constraints in virtually all cities. Although managers exert influence, there is no pattern of managerial dominance of the governmental process, despite some unsubstantiated fears that the council-manager form leads to bureaucratic control.[58] For their part, councils also respect the manager's prerogatives in certain decisions in the administrative sphere--the other half of the dichotomy model which should not be discarded--although councils are no more totally divorced from administration than managers are from policy.

Second, the model provides a normative guidepost for administrators to determine whether behavior is appropriate. Despite their considerable contributions, managers should not govern. It is a mark of the integrity of the profession that managers want such guidance. Third, there has been no alternative formulation which is both consistent with democratic and administrative theory and is empirically sound.

Based on research in the large cities in North Carolina, I have suggested that manager-council relations be examined along four dimensions which are produced by subdividing the vague concepts of policy and administration. Mission refers to determination of the purpose, goals, and constitutional structure of city government as distinct from policy, the plans and programs undertaken to achieve mission. Administration refers to service delivery and implementation; it is the translation of policy into action and as such is difficult to distinguish from policy. Finally, management is the coordination and control of the resources of city government. It represents the utilization of resources for the accomplishment of the city's purposes but is essentially free of policy content.

The dichotomy-duality model for dividing responsibility between elected and administrative officials in these four dimensions retains elements of separation while recognizing sharing among officials. The council determines mission by decision or nondecision with advice and with analysis of conditions typically being offered by the manager. In policy, the manager makes a greater overall contribution because of the large amount of policy advice and policy setting by administrators, although the council is ultimately responsible for all policy. Staff are highly active in administration, although the council is interested in service delivery and citizen complaints regarding services, in specific choices involved in implementation, and potentially in oversight and evaluation. Management is the sphere of the manager. The reformist goals are met when councils keep out of the details of management, but they can make management "policy" and examine management performance through appraisal of the manager. Thus, both conceptually and empirically in large North Carolina cities there is a "dichotomy of mission and management, but policy and administration are intermixed to the extent they are a duality, distinct but inseparable aspects of developing and delivering government programs."[59]

The continuing reality appears to be that managers have accepted that initiating proposals for the council, providing leadership in the community, and paying attention to popular issues are important, as are capable service delivery and sound management. The norms of democratic control are met if the actions of the manager are consistent with the mission of city government determined by elected officials. Although there have been many changes externally (e.g., shifts in intergovernmental relations), in city government (e.g., more directly elected mayors), and within the profession (e.g., managers are becoming better trained), managers have been essentially the same from the beginning. What is still unclear is the precise nature of the reality of manager contributions. The dichotomy-duality model offers a research framework for measuring what managers do and how they relate to elected officials in making different kinds of decisions.

Measuring Contributions and Roles

In order to measure the dichotomy-duality model with more precision and depth, a questionnaire was developed to assess the involvement of both council members and managers. Most of the research findings reported here are from surveys of managers in the states of North Carolina and Ohio with occasional references to responses from council members and department heads in six pairs of council-manager and mayor-council cities.[60]

Four features of the questionnaire design should be noted. First, to avoid vague and value-laden general terms in measuring involvement, specific decisions or activities are used as indicators of the four dimensions instead of terms like "policy" and "administration." In initial field work in the six pairs of cities, twenty-nine activities were used. In the questionnaire used in North Carolina and Ohio, there were seventeen activities chosen from the larger number included in the first stage of the research. (The activities are listed in the Appendix to this article.)[61]

Second, the logic of the model suggests that the involvement of both council members and administrators be measured separately. Part of the confusion in interpreting existing research is uncertainty over whether decision making is a zero-sum activity. Demonstrating that the manager's contributions are extensive does not necessarily mean that the council's role is diminished.[62] Thus, respondents were asked to provide separate ratings of involvement by the council, on the one hand, and the manager and staff, on the other.

Third, it was important to determine whether the actual levels of involvement matched officials' preferences. This distinction between actual and preferred involvement would illuminate both the degree of council constraint of the manager's behavior and also the manager's acceptance of democratic control.

Fourth, the concept of involvement has been operationalized to stress the extent of initiation displayed in the generation of ideas in decision making. A five-point scale is used that ranges from (1) no involvement in a decision or activity to (5) handling that decision entirely. In between are (2) low involvement through minimal review, (3) moderate involvement through advising another actor or reviewing the proposal of someone else, and (4) high involvement indicated by initiating or intensely reviewing and revising a proposal. (The index as explained on the questionnaire is presented in the Appendix to this article.) The level of involvement by one actor is independent of that of another; for example, both may be high or both low. As noted above, separate ratings are made of the council and the manager.

Previous research would suggest four alternative patterns of relative contributions from the council and the manager. The expected involvement of each set of officials using the scale numbers may be summarized as shown in Figure 1. In the Dichotomy Model, the council is minimally involved in administration and management and the manager's activity in mission and policy is limited to an advisory role. The modest involvement of the manager is assumed because the traditional formulations of the manager's role and the restrictive 1938 Code of Ethics allowed the manager to offer assistance to the council in making policy decisions of all kinds. The Dichotomy-Duality Model incorporates a higher level of manager initiative in mission and policy decisions and greater council involvement in administration and management than the Dichotomy Model.

The polar extreme models are provided to offer a broader perspective on possible relationships. There is little evidence in the literature to show that either will be found in council-manager cities as a general rule. These are not implausible scenarios, however, in city government. In comparisons among the six pairs of cities with different forms of government, strong mayor cities are close to the Executive Dominance Model and the weak mayor-council city approximates the Council Dominance Model.[63]

The issue of managerial roles and relationships must be addressed at two levels--collective and individual. We shall first examine the overall levels of actual and preferred involvement of managers and council members for specific activities and the extent to which involvement approximates the four models. Divergence between managers in North Carolina and Ohio will be examined to determine whether the relationships vary by region. Deviation by individual

Figure 1
Four Models of Council and Manager Involvement

		Mission	Policy	Administration	Management
Council Dominance Model	Council	4	4	3.5	3
	Manager	2.5	3	3.5	4
Dichotomy Model	Council	4	4	2	1.5
	Manager	3	3	4	4.5
Dichotomy-Duality Model	Council	4	3.5	3	2
	Manager	3.5	4	4	4.5
Executive Dominance Model	Council	3	3	2	1.5
	Manager	4	4	4.5	4.5

(1=no involvement; 5=total involvement)

managers from the general patterns will also be checked. Generalizations should not be permitted to mask differences based on the characteristics of the manager or the local setting. On the other hand, a high degree of uniformity in managers' attitudes would be an indicator of the professionalization of city managers.

Involvement in Activities and Models of Relationships

The ratings provided by city managers of involvement by themselves and the council are presented in Table 1. Ratings of the council's actual involvement range from a high of 3.9 to a low of 1.4. Only on changing governmental institutions and approving the budget do council members receive a rating from managers of 3.4 or greater. In all the other mission and policy decisions, council members are seen to be reviewers of managerial proposals. In Ohio, the ratings of the council's involvement in mission decisions are lower than in North Carolina. In fact, the distinction between mission and policy decisions based on differing degrees of generality and importance would not be evident upon examination of the Ohio data alone. Council members are actually less involved in mission than in middle-range policy decisions. Council members in North Carolina make a greater contribution to mission than to policy decisions, although the difference is slight. Other items in the questionnaire (not in the table) reinforce both the general picture of modestly active councils and the slightly lower contributions from councils in Ohio. Over 60 percent of managers in both states feel that the council is more a reviewing and vetoing agency than a leader in policy making, and approximately 70 percent feel that the council focuses too much on short-term problems and gives too little attention to long-term concerns. Still, 70 percent of managers in North Carolina feel that the council provides sufficient direction and overall leadership to city government versus 50 percent of managers in Ohio. With regard to administrative decisions, the ordering of involvement is the same in both states although the overall level is lower in Ohio. The tendency is the same in management. The major difference is disproportionately greater involvement by council members in personnel matters in North Carolina.

The managers' ratings of their own involvement is higher than that of council members with only two exceptions (institutional change and budget approval). In mission and policy, managers display moderately high to high levels of involvement in both states.[64] They are somewhat more inclined in mission as against policy decisions to act in an advisory rather than in an initiating capacity. Across all four dimensions, the manager ratings in Ohio are modestly higher. There is a markedly lower involvement rating in North Carolina on initiating/canceling programs, developing annual program goals, and formulating the budget in the mission and policy dimensions. Presumably, these ratings signify a somewhat greater degree of consultation with the council on these matters by managers in North Carolina. The managers in both states do not display as much independence in administration as in management, but there are variations in the level of manager activity between the states. Ohio managers have higher ratings in specific decisions regarding service delivery and in implementing decisions than their counterparts in North Carolina. The differences are also greater in handling personnel matters

81

Table 1
Rating by City Managers of Council and Manager/Staff Involvement in Governmental Activities

Dimension: Activity	Manager Actual		Council Actual		Mgr-Counc. Actual[a]		Council Prefer		Counc Pref-Actual[b]	
	NC	OHIO	NC	OHIO	NC	OHIO	NC	OHIO	NC	OHIO
Mission										
Analyzing Future Needs[c]	3.85[d]	3.98	3.21	2.88	.64	1.10	3.79	3.67	.58	.79
Developing Strategies	3.71	3.91	2.99	2.85	.72	1.06	3.85	3.49	.86	.64
Changing Institutions	3.13	3.12	3.65	3.42	-.52	-.30	3.89	3.65	.24	.23
Initiating/Cancelling	3.50	3.96	3.28	2.79	.22	1.17	3.50	3.06	.22	.27
Determining Purpose	3.74	3.70	3.26	2.85	.48	.85	3.91	3.56	.65	.71
--Mission: Average	3.59	3.73	3.28	2.96	.31	.78	3.79	3.49	.51	.53
Policy										
Developing Annual Goals	3.82	4.24	2.73	2.78	1.09	1.46	3.50	3.45	.77	.67
Planning/Zoning Decisions	3.48	3.65	3.30	3.28	.18	.37	3.40	3.27	.10	-.01
Formulating Budget	4.34	4.49	2.45	2.28	1.89	2.21	2.73	2.63	.28	.35
Budget Review	3.70	3.70	3.89	3.65	-.19	.05	4.04	3.84	.15	.19
--Policy: Average	3.84	4.02	3.09	3.00	.74	1.02	3.42	3.30	.33	.30

Administration										
Operational Decisions	4.02	4.29	2.65	2.51	1.37	1.78	2.53	2.32	-.12	-.19
Citizen Complaints	4.09	4.25	2.98	2.84	1.11	1.41	2.64	2.59	-.34	-.25
Implementing Decisions	3.69	4.06	3.15	2.81	.54	1.25	3.25	2.81	.10	.00
Evaluating Programs	3.80	3.96	2.82	2.55	.98	1.41	3.36	3.11	.54	.56
--Administration: Average	3.90	4.14	2.90	2.68	1.00	1.46	2.95	2.71	.05	.03
Management										
Hiring Dep't. Heads	4.22	4.62	2.47	1.89	1.75	2.73	2.05	1.68	-.42	-.21
Hiring Other Staff	4.16	4.60	1.85	1.36	2.31	3.24	1.60	1.16	-.24	-.20
Contracting	4.05	4.26	2.47	2.13	1.58	2.13	2.43	2.04	-.04	-.09
Management Practices/Organz	3.91	4.02	2.96	2.62	.95	1.40	3.02	2.78	.06	.16
--Management: Average	4.09	4.38	2.44	2.00	1.65	2.38	2.28	1.92	-.16	-.09

a. Manager rating minus council rating.
b. Preferred rating for council minus actual rating.
c. For full wording of each activity, see Appendix to this article.
d. Mean rating of involvement on a five-point scale (1=not involved) by city managers.
   See Appendix for definition of points on scale.

n=131 North Carolina city managers; 56 Ohio city managers

and contracts. Still, overall ratings are similar--and a bit closer than those for councils--and shift in the same direction across the four dimensions. The overall picture is one of managers actively involved in all activities of city government, tending not only to advise but to take the initiative in mission and policy. Their involvement levels are slightly higher in administration and management. Since the councils' involvement recedes across the dimensions (across the last three dimensions in Ohio), the manager is left ever more fully in charge in policy, administration, and management.

Based on actual levels of involvement alone, the relative contributions of the council and manager would fall between the Dichotomy-Duality Model and the Executive Dominance Model. The Ohio cities are closer to the latter than the former. Clearly, neither matches the Dichotomy Model both because of the council's low ratings in mission and policy and the manager's high ratings. Furthermore, the council is more active in administration and in management (especially in North Carolina) than that model would predict.

The preferred levels of involvement shed a different light on interpretations of relationships. First, managers are satisfied with their current level of involvement. The managers' preferred ratings are not included in Table 1 because they are virtually identical to their actual ratings. The average ratings never deviate by more than one tenth of a point on the scale. When council members are surveyed, their actual and preferred ratings of the manager's involvement are also the same.[65] Managers, therefore, are comprehensively active officials, and both they and council members like it that way. Managers would prefer, however, greater contributions from the council particularly in mission and to a lesser extent in policy and less involvement in management. The overall direction, amount, and ordering of change is very similar in the two states. Managers would like council members to be highly involved in analyzing the future needs of the city, developing strategies for future development, and determining the purpose of city government, as they have been in changing governmental institutions. Managers prefer that the council be somewhat more active in response to the manager's recommendations about initiating or canceling programs. In policy, they would like more direction from the council in setting annual program goals and objectives. In administration, the preferences cut both ways: managers would like more council evaluation but less participation in service delivery and specific implementing decisions. Managers would like the council to reduce its modest involvement in personnel matters and, to a lesser extent, in contracting.

The overall contributions of the council and the manager in each dimension are presented in Figure 2. The preferred level of involvement is consistent with the Dichotomy-Duality Model--more so than are the actual levels of involvement. The greatest change would come in the council's performance in mission and policy where the managers desire more leadership by the council without wanting to diminish their own active role. They accept an advisory role by the council in administration and acknowledge the need to keep the council informed about management. Managers would prefer greater involvement by council members to strengthen democratic control over the purposes, programs, and performance of city government and the structure of the municipal organization. At the same time, managers oppose council involvement in specific administrative activities and interference with management systems and practices. They are not at odds with council

Figure 1
Rating by City Managers of the Actual and Preferred Involvement of City Council and Manager*

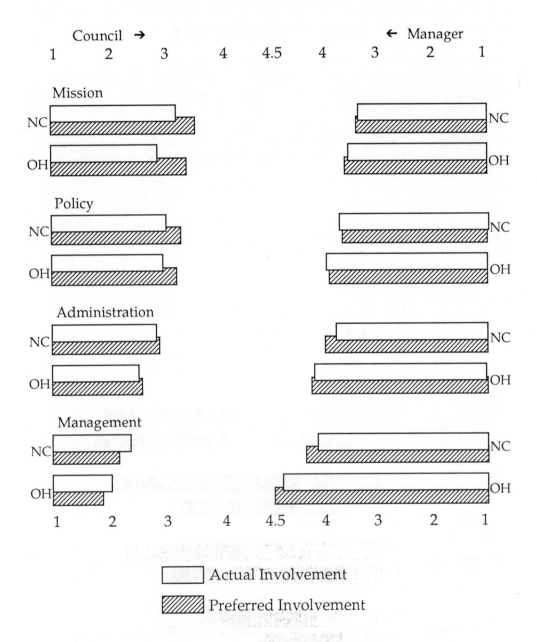

Actual Involvement

Preferred Involvement

*Graphic presentation of average ratings for each dimension of governmental process from Table 1.

members on these points and both would prefer to more fully achieve the division of responsibilities described by the Dichotomy-Duality Model. Managers acknowledge the substantial contributions they make to all aspects of the governmental process. They would also like to strengthen the leadership provided by elected officials.

Variations Among Managers

That most managers are active participants in all kinds of city government activities does not mean that all are. Generalizations may understate the involvement of some and overstate that of others. Figure 3 presents the distribution of managers by level of involvement for each dimension of the governmental process. If an average rating of "4" is treated as the dividing line between activist managers who take the initiative on all or almost all of the activities in a dimension,[66] then approximately half of the managers in the two states can be called activists in the mission dimension. (If moderately high involvement is the test of activism in this dimension, i.e., a rating of 3.5, then approximately 70 percent meet this criterion.) In policy, over 70 percent are highly involved. On these dimensions, North Carolina has a larger proportion of managers that rank moderate to low in involvement (at a

Figure 3
Percentage Distribution of City Managers
by Actual Level of Involvement

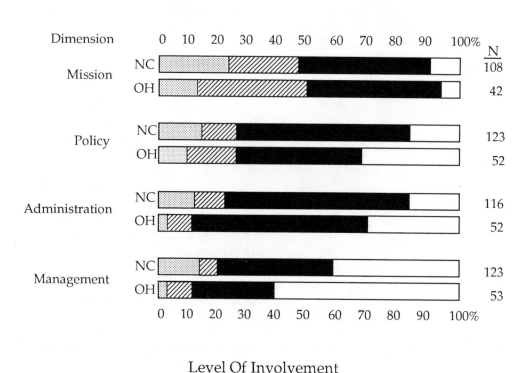

Level Of Involvement

▦ =Moderate (rating of 3.25 or less)
▨ =Moderately high (rating of 3.3 - 3.7)
■ =High (rating of 3.75 - 4.25)
☐ =Very high (rating of 4.3 or higher)

86

level of 3.0 or lower), and the proportion who rate their involvement in policy as very high is greater in Ohio. In administration and management, the proportion of activists climbs to over 75 percent in North Carolina and 90 percent in Ohio. The proportion who exercise substantial independence in decision making in administration, i.e., 4.5 or higher, is 16 percent in North Carolina and 29 percent in Ohio. In management, the very highly involved climb to 41 percent in North Carolina and 60 percent in Ohio. In general, the responsibility for management is lodged with the city manager, and this tendency is even more strongly established in Ohio (reflected as well by the lower council involvement scores.) In North Carolina, more managers are only moderately involved even in management, and it is more common for managers to take the lead while sharing information and providing the opportunity for reaction from the council.

Whether this slightly greater council involvement in administration and management in North Carolina is forced on the manager by an incursive council or allowed by the manager is not clear. The evidence from the questionnaire is mixed. On the one hand, 40 percent of the managers in Ohio feel that the council is too involved in administration, as opposed to 26 percent in North Carolina. Almost 60 percent of the latter feel that the council's appraisal of the manager's performance is adequate in depth and frequency, versus 42 percent in Ohio. In over 60 percent of the North Carolina cities, council members encourage citizens to refer complaints directly to staff rather than submitting them through council members, whereas this happens in only 40 percent of the Ohio cities. These indicators suggest a more balanced division of responsibility for administration and management supported by more positive attitudes among officials in North Carolina. On the other hand, fewer managers in Ohio report any conflict with the council over personnel matters, so perhaps clearer demarcation of roles reduces tension in the relationship. One might have speculated that the greater diversity in governmental form in Ohio and the example of conflictual relations among officials in mayor-council cities would have made the council more aggressive in dealing with the manager than in North Carolina where virtually all local governments utilize the appointed executive form. This does not appear to be the case; in fact, the opposite seems to be true. Perhaps the greater aggressiveness and insistence on prerogatives by executive mayors in Ohio affects both the expectations of councils and the behavior of managers. Councils may expect a smaller sphere of activity, and managers may be less inclined to encourage councils to expand their involvement.

Still, too much should not be made of the differences between the states. Despite substantial divergence in political culture and local government structures, managers have remarkably similar attitudes about themselves and their relationship with elected officials. The Dichotomy-Duality Model describes the general division of responsibilities among officials better than any alternative formulation. Looking at individual managers, 70 to 90 percent, depending on the dimension and the state, manifest a level of activity that corresponds to the manager's roles in the Dichotomy-Duality Model.

One might object that some managers take on more responsibility for initiating and handling decisions in mission, policy, and administration than is stipulated by the model. A level of activity that is "too high" for a particular dimension might have the effect of depressing the council's contribution. The correlation between the manager's level of involvement, however, and that of the council's level is consistent with the model.[67] Taking both states together, there is no relationship between the manager's and the council's rating in mission. The council's involvement in determining the direction and purpose of their city is apparently not affected by the manager's activity level. In policy and administration, there is a moderate inverse relationship. Extensive involvement by the manager reduces somewhat the council's involvement. In management, there is a strong inverse relationship. When managers are active, councils are virtually excluded. Managers, by their own behavior, do not shape the council role in mission. They modestly alter the council's activity in policy and administration, and they affect it greatly in management.

Insofar as managers want to see changes in the council's behavior, they desire fuller involvement by the council in mission and policy without deprecating or seeking to diminish their own extensive contributions. Over 80 percent of managers in both states report that they have a good working relationship with the council, but they would like to see more leadership from the council in governance.

Thus, it is not what managers do that distinguishes them from other city government officials. They are virtually as active as executive mayors in mayor-council cities, and most are involved in mission and policy to a greater extent than council members in their own cities. Rather, it is who they are and how they fill their roles that makes them different. Furthermore, how they do it cannot be divorced from the context in which they operate. The absence of separation of powers in the formal governmental structure promotes cooperative relationships among officials. A cooperative pattern of interaction in turn is conducive to the utilization of the manager's broad ranging expertise in city government. Managers can be effective despite the lack of political resources and a local power base. Thus, the influence of the manager in governance does not signify the subversion of elected officials. They have complementary rather than conflicting roles.

Implications

City managers are professional leaders who make contributions to all dimensions of the governmental process. The expansive role of the manager is not new but recognition of the implications of the manager's leadership does not fully match the extent of that leadership. There has been positive change, as the Code of Ethics has been brought more in line with the practice of city management. The Declaration of Ideals approved by ICMA in 1982 gives voice to the aspirations of the profession in many aspects of the manager's activities. These statements do not, however, go far enough in describing the responsibilities of the manager as a comprehensive professional leader in city government. As an organization or perhaps even better as individuals, city managers should elaborate a full list of responsibilities that will guide their extensive involvement together with council members in mission, policy, administration, and management.[68]

That the manager is active in "policy" and "administration" is beyond dispute. Managers offer professional leadership in all aspects of government to complement the politically accountable leadership of the council. To maintain the complementary relationship, however, and to achieve high levels of effectiveness, the manager must provide responsible leadership that is supportive of the council and responsive to the needs of the entire community. If managers start to take as much leadership as the council will allow or if they manipulate the council, they may expand their influence but weaken both the form of government and their professional heritage of responsible leadership. Given the continuing sensitivity of the management profession to the issue of respective roles, one may expect that city managers will continue to strengthen democracy in city government rather than to threaten it.

Notes

I would like to express my appreciation for the cooperation of the North Carolina City and County Management Association and the Ohio City Management Association and for the assistance provided by graduate assistants Lynette Ball, Joseph Koury, Donna McNeill, John Ogburn, Christopher Raths, and Timothy Storey. Funding for the survey was provided by the Research Council, University of North Carolina at Greensboro.

1. Woodrow Wilson, *Congressional Government* (New York: Meridian Books, 1956 [1884]). On the other hand, Wilson opposed Congress' "habit of investigating and managing everything" and subjecting "even the details of administration to the constant supervision, and all policy to the watchful intervention, of the Standing Committees."(50)

2. Woodrow Wilson, "Politics and Administration," *Political Science Quarterly*, vol. 2 (1887), p. 213.

3. Henry A. Toulmin, Jr., *The City Manager: A New Profession* (New York: Arno Press, 1974 [1915]), p. 53.

4. William B. Munro, *The Government of American Cities* (New York: MacMillan, 1919), p. 390.

5. See Richard S. Childs, "The Theory of the New Controlled-Executive Plan," *National Municipal Review*, vol. II (January, 1913), pp. 76-81. Toulmin, *The City Manager*, p. 84, observed, however, that the manager's powers were so extensive that the "term 'controlled-executive' is hardly applicable any more. One thing is evident. His methods of achieving results are uncontrolled. The end, not the means, is the objective of these modern instruments of government."

6. Martin J. Schiesl, *The Politics of Efficiency* (Berkeley: University of California Press, 1977), p. 185. The author discusses Ossian E. Carr of Dubuque and Louis Brownlow then of Petersburg specifically.

7. Leonard White, *The City Manager* (Chicago: University of Chicago Press, 1927), p. 188.

8. Ibid., pp. 188-89.

9. Ibid., p. 143.

10. Richard S. Childs *et al.*, "Professional Ethics in the New Profession of City Manager: A Discussion," *National Civic Review*, vol. V (April, 1916), pp. 195-210.

11. John P. East, *Council-Manager Government* (Chapel Hill: University of North Carolina Press, 1965), pp. 84-87.

12. White, *The City Manager*, pp. 182-198.

13. Ibid., p. 300.

14. Schiesl, *Politics of Efficiency*, p. 188.

15. Quoted in White, *The City Manager*, 198; Ronald Loveridge, *City Managers in Legislative Politics* (Indianapolis: Bobbs-Merrill, 1971), p. 108, makes the same point without explicitly noting the timelessness of observation.

16. Ibid., p. 225.

17. Richard J. Stillman II, *The Rise of the City Manager* (Albuquerque: University of New Mexico Press, 1974), p. 51.

18. Clarence C. Ridley and Orin Nolting, *The City Manager Profession* (Chicago: University of Chicago Press, 1934), pp. 13.

19. Ibid., p. 30.

20. Harold A. Stone, Don K. Price, and Kathryn H. Stone, *City Manager Government in the United States* (Chicago: Public Administration Service, 1940), p. 243.

21. Ibid., p. 242.

22. Ibid., p. 247.

23. C. A. Harrell, "The City Manager as a Community Leader," *Public Management*, 30 (October, 1948), pp. 290-294.

24. Clarence C. Ridley, *The Role of the Manager in Policy Formulation*, quoted in Stillman, *Rise of the City Manager*, p. 59-60.

25. Charles R. Adrian, "Leadership and Decision-Making in Manager Cities—A Study of Three Communities," *Public Administration Review* vol. 18 (1958), p. 209.

26. Karl L. Bosworth, "The Manager Is a Politician, *Public Administration Review*, vol. 18 (1958), pp. 216-222.

27. Ibid., p. 222.

28. Gladys M. Kammerer, Charles D. Farris, John M. DeGrove, and Alfred B. Clubok, *City Managers in Politics* (Gainesville: University of Florida, 1962), p. 83.

29. Kammerer, "Role Diversity of City Managers," *Administrative Science Quarterly*, vol. 8 (September, 1964), pp. 433. Italics in original.

30. See also Oliver Williams and Charles Adrian, *Four Cities* (Philadelphia: University of Pennsylvania Press, 1963), for discussion of the variation in the policy leadership of the manager depending on the leadership and role of the city council.

31. Deil Wright, "The Manager as a Development Administrator," in Robert T. Daland, Ed., *Comparative Urban Research* (Beverly Hills: Sage Publications, 1969), pp. 224-225.

32. Ibid., p. 232.

33. Ibid., p. 242.

34. Loveridge, *Managers in Legislative Politics*, pp. 52 and 88. The sharp divergence in views may have been overstated because of the way that survey items were constructed and compared. See my *Official Leadership in the City* (New York: Oxford University Press, forthcoming 1989), ch. 6.

35. Ibid., p. 109.

36. Keith F. Mulrooney, "Prologue: Can City Managers Deal Effectively with Major Social Problems?" *Public Administration Review*, vol. 31 (January/February, 1971), pp. 10-11.

37. James M. Banovetz, "Environment and Role of the Administrator," in Banovetz, Ed., *Managing the Modern City* (Washington: ICMA, 1971), pp. 84.

38. Ibid., p. 83.

39. Stillman, *Rise of the City Manager*, p. 103.

40. Ibid., p. 110.

41. Robert J. Huntley and Robert J. Macdonald, "Urban Managers: Organizational Preferences, Managerial Styles, and Social Policy Roles," *Municipal Year Book 1975* (Washington: ICMA, 1975), pp. 149-158.

42. William R. Fannin, "City Manager Policy Roles as a Source of City Council/City Manager Conflict," *International Journal of Public Administration* 5 (No. 4, 1983), pp. 381-399. Some of the role titles chosen obscure the nature of the behavior. The "administrative craftsman" makes ad hoc decisions independently from the council. The "administrative technician" makes professional decisions independently. The "expert advisor" provides professional information and recommendations to the council. The "political activist" creates coalitions and generates a power base. The "policy non-actor" does not participate in policy making, leaving it entirely to the council.

43. William Browne, "Municipal Managers and Policy: A Partial Test of the Svara Dichotomy-Duality Model," *Public Administration Review*, vol. 45 (September/October, 1988), pp. 620-622.

44. Roy E. Green, "Local Government Managers: Styles and Challenges," *Baseline Data Report*, vol. 19 (March/April, 1987), pp. 1-11.

45. Svara, *Official Leadership*, ch. 6.

46. Clifford J. Wirth and Michael J. Vasu, "Ideology and Decisionmaking for American City Managers," *Urban Affairs Quarterly*, vol. 22 (March, 1987), pp. 454-474.

47. Charldean Newell and David N. Ammons, "Role Emphasis of City Managers and Other Municipal Executives," *Public Administration Review*, vol. 47 (May/June, 1987), pp. 246-252. Using a measure of involvement to be explained further in this paper, I have also found that city managers and strong mayors in eleven moderately large cities have similar levels of involvement. See "The Complementary Roles of Officials in Council-Manager Government," *Municipal Year Book 1988* (Washington: ICMA, 1988), pp. 23-33.

48. Ibid., p. 252.

49. Orin Nolting, *Progress and Impact of the Council-Manager Plan* (Chicago: Public Administration Service, 1969), 37-38.

50. John C. Bollens and John C. Ries, *The City Manager Profession: Myths and Realities* (Chicago: Public Administration Service, 1969), pp. 5, italics in original, and 35.

51. Adrian, "Three Communities," p. 209. Stillman, *Rise of the City Manager*, pp. 60-61, also offers evidence that managers were not concerned with these abstract issues.

52. Richard J. Stillman II, "Local Management in Transition: A Report on the current State of the Profession, "*Municipal Year Book 1982* (Washington: ICMA, 1982), p. 172.

53. In my surveys of managers in North Carolina and Ohio, 52% and 46%, respectively, agreed with this position. In Oklahoma, 53% did so. See Michael W. Hirlinger and Robert E. England, *City Managers and the Legislative Process: The Case of Oklahoma* (Norman: University of Oklahoma Bureau of Governmental Research, 1986). Green, "Local Government Managers," p. 3, found that 85% of the managers at least sometimes behaved in this way.

54. A cynical view is that academicians have preserved the dichotomy model as a convenient strawman. One can always kick around the manager as administrator myth.

55. Banovetz, "Environment and Role," p. 82.

56. Stillman, *Rise of the City Manager*, footnote 8, pp. 143-44.

57. David N. Ammons and Charldean Newell, "'City Managers Don't Make Policy:' A Lie; Let's Face It," *National Civic Review*, vol. 57 (1988), pp. 124-132.

58. Robert L. Lineberry and Ira Sharkansky, *Urban Politics and Public Policy*, 2nd edition (New York: Harper and Row, 1978), p. 164, assert that "municipal bureaucracies have more power and autonomy in reformed systems, and elected decision makers have correspondingly smaller bases of power." I examine the evidence on differing impact of form of government in *Official Leadership*, ch. 3.

59. Svara, "Dichotomy and Duality: Reconceptualizing the Relationship Between Policy and Administration in Council-Manager Cities, *Public Administration Review*, vol. 45 (January/February, 1985), pp. 221-232 (also reprinted in this volume).

60. The surveys were administered to all city managers in North Carolina in 1987 and in Ohio in 1988. Cities with vacancies in the manager's position or acting managers were excluded. There were 131 responses from 216 managers surveyed in North Carolina (61% response rate); and 56 responses from 76 managers surveyed in Ohio (73%). The twelve city study is described in "Conflict, Cooperation, and Separation of Powers in City Government," *Journal of Urban Affairs*, vol. 10 (No. 4, 1988), pp. 357-372.

61. The choice of activities and wording was made with advice from an advisory committee of the N.C. City and County Management Association chaired by Wendell White, City Manager of Charlotte.

62. Stone *et al.*, *City Manager Government*, p. 246, noted that "one kind of leadership enhances the other." In contrast, Glen Sparrow, "The Emerging Chief Executive: The San Diego Experience," *Urban Resources* 2 (Fall, 1986), p. 6, has described power as a hydraulic system "whereby decrease in the manager's power would result in increased mayoral power."

63. Svara, "Complementary Roles," Table 3/1.

64. 62 versus 50 percent of the managers in North Carolina and Ohio, respectively, agreed that the manager should consult with the council before drafting the budget.

65. Svara, "Complementary Roles," p. 25. Council members are also satisfied with their own involvement which is not true in strong mayor cities.

66. The breaks in the scale for each individual's aggregate score for the items in the dimension are based on 3 of 4 or 4 of 5 items with a rating of 4 as the high category; if at least three items were 3 or lower (and none were 5), the rating was considered to be moderate.

67. The correlations between the manager's rating and the council's are the following: Mission .03; Policy -.26*; Administration -.20*; Management - .59*. Significance under .01 signified by asterisk.

68. For analysis of these existing statements and a tentative statement of the manager's responsibilities, see my "The Responsible Manager: Building on the Code and the Declaration," *Public Management*, vol. 69 (September, 1987), pp. 14-18.

APPENDIX

Measuring the Level of Involvement
by Officials in Governmental Activities

Level of Involvement Index:

1--Very Low: Not Involved
Handled entirely by someone else, who may report on what has been done.

2--Low: Minimum Review or Reaction Appropriate to Situation
Examples would be giving a routine OK to someone else's recommendations, providing the opportunity to react as courtesy, or making comments.

3--Moderate: Advising or Reviewing
Examples include making suggestions, reviewing recommendations, seeking information or clarification, ratifying proposals.

4--High: Leading, Guiding, or Pressuring
Examples are initiating; making proposals; advocating, promoting, or opposing; intensely reviewing and revising a proposal.

5--Very High: Handle Entirely
No one else directly involved but others may be informed of actions taken.

Activities for Which Involvement is Rated:

Mission

1. Analyzing Future Needs of the City

6. Developing Strategies for Future Development of the City

10. Changing Governmental Institutions or Revising the Charter

12. Initiating or Cancelling Programs

14. Determining the Purpose of City Government and the Scope of Services Provided

Administration

7. Operational Decisions About Provision of Services

8. Resolving Citizen Complaints

9. Specific Decisions that are Part of Larger City Government Projects, for Example, Site Selection, Facility Design

13. Evaluating Accomplishments of Specific Programs

Policy

2. Developing Annual Program Goals and Ojectives

5. Specific Decisions Concerning Planning and Zoning Applications

15. Formulating the Proposed Budget

16. Budget Review and Approval

Management

3. Hiring Decisions about Department Heads

4. Hiring Decisions about Employees Below the Department Head Level

11. Contracting and Purchasing

17. Proposing Changes in Management Practices or Organization, e.g., Adding Assistant Manager, Changing Budgeting System

*Number in margin indicates the order of the activity in the questionnaire.

Response

Larry J. Brown
Hillsborough County, Florida

James H. Svara's well-researched and thought-provoking paper focuses on how city managers (or county administrators) can be effective despite their lack of political resources and a local power base.

From my observation, however, it is more to the point to stress that managers will be more effective *because* they lack political resources and a local power base.

Mark Pastin, who led a workshop called "Executive Power for Managers" at the ICMA conference in Charlotte, N.C., explored the subject of power with a great deal of insight. Power, as Pastin perceives it, is the ability to accomplish things and the ability to have others act in conformity with your wishes.

The quintessential public manager, therefore, manages the power he doesn't really have--the power of others. The title to power almost always has someone else's name on it.

An Objective and Unbiased Player

The great value of a professional manager is that he can be an objective and unbiased player who exercises professional expertise and processing skills when public policy is being developed and debated. In a political arena filled with elected officials who have their own constituencies and their own philosophies and values, there is a great likelihood of arriving at an acceptable consensus with the help of a manager whose only desire is to do the best professional job possible.

A professional manager working in the political arena doesn't have to worry about accumulating political power for himself in order to do the job. He accepts the distribution of power as it exists and tries to accommodate the differences by keying in on common ground.

Another expert in the field--Ronald Heifetz, who teaches at Harvard's Kennedy School of Government--approaches the subject from the perspective of leadership. Leadership, he says, is an activity, not a set of personality characteristics. The activity of leadership becomes the "mobilization of the resources of a people or an organization to make progress on the difficult problems it faces."

As Heifetz notes in an interview in INC. magazine (October 1988), "The exercise of leadership ... requires the orchestration of competing factions. That doesn't simply mean sitting back passively and saying, 'You work it out,' because organizations have ways of avoiding that work."

With the rise of single-issue candidates and the emphasis on citizen participation, it is becoming more difficult for any one person to effectively represent a collective majority in an electoral sense. It is also hard to find elected officials with any depth of experience in the many complex issues facing local government. In these circumstances, leadership comes through a professional manager who is able to develop a broad range of community policies by facilitating participation of all the players.

The balancing act a professional manager performs in this politically charged arena is to manage the power of others without merging himself in the power base in a way that would challenge the elected governing body.

An individual, Heifetz says, exercises leadership by orchestrating the process of getting factions with competing definitions of the problem to start learning from one another. That's different from exercising authority, which Heifetz says involves maintaining the equilibrium, keeping things on an even keel.

Arlington County Vs. Hillsborough County

I think of this often in comparing my experiences in Arlington county and in Hillsborough County. During my tenure in Arlington, the community knew precisely what it wanted to do, knew precisely where it was going, and wouldn't tolerate any major deviations from that clearly marked path. With such a consensus public policy, my role in Arlington was more of an authoritative stabilizer as we moved toward that common goal.

In Hillsborough county, there is no consensus. The community isn't clear about where it is going. People who made community decisions 20 years ago are no longer as effective as they once were. The base has broadened, roles have changed, people have changed. The community is experiencing about a 25 percent in and out migration annually, meaning that many potential community leaders do not stay long enough to play a key role in the development of community policies.

In this situation, the professional manager must become a major player in policy development. This means more than running the water and sewer system, keeping potholes filled, making sure work crews have enough shovels and firefighters have enough fire hoses. It means doing as much as possible to put the community in a posture to lead itself--through facilitating, through identifying issues, through processing.

This doesn't impose the professional manager's outcome. Rather, it defines the issues, sets an agenda and sets in motion a process whereby the community can reach its own conclusions. Once this happens, the professional manager has clear marching orders to marshal resources and direct them at the decision reached by the community.

After all, who has a better potential for delivering the goals of a united public policy consensus than a professional administrator has? The voting process rotates elected leaders, different community issues bring different spokesmen to the forefront at different times, and a highly mobile environment creates a pattern of shifting community leaders. What remains steady is consistent professional leadership that has expertise in organizational dynamics, financial systems, political realities, and personnel decisions. Pastin would say that this gives public managers power based on two factors: providing information from all sources, and continuity so as to exercise decisions over time.

Finally, when examining power and leadership in public management, there must be an overriding principle of integrity, guided by clear statements of ethical behavior and an adherence to the highest professional standards.

Frustrations Bring About Temptations

Everyone, from citizen to elected official, shares responsibility for making society work. It is tempting, especially in frustrating situations, to look for someone with the answer, some savior to show the way. The temptation is for the professional manager to step into this role, or for the community to delegate authority to an elected manager. That creates a situation which destroys a public forum and any ability to arrive at a consensus on complex issues which require the efforts, wisdom, hard work and differing points of view of all people.

Discussion

King: This paper contains the implicit assumption that there is a certain amount of political leadership to go around and that therefore the fundamental issue is to figure out who has what share of it. I think the more proper perspective is that if there is strong manager involvement in policy development, there will also be strong council involvement. I think all of us agree that the best of all worlds is to have a strong manager and a strong council. In analyzing a manager's time, if a greater percentage of my time is being spent on policy development this year than last year, it's because the council also is spending more time in that area. That's the way it should be.

Frederickson: Henry Reining commented on city management this way: "The best city managers carefully practice the art and science of politics and policy but always use the language of management and administration." Reining mapped a kind of semantic theory that gets at the dichotomy model. Maybe it even describes John Nalbandian's laying out of values. We ought to be better at developing a theory. John ties his to a conception of democratic government. I'm not sure how to characterize yours, Jim.

Svara: I'm not sure the managers do talk in management and administrative terms. In many cases the managers are talking in policy and political terms and are posing issues and talking about important choices that communities have to make.

Gleason: I've had the experience in two situations where the charter said the manager participates in discussions but doesn't have a vote. Why are you sitting at the table and participating in discussions, if you're not participating in the policy process?

Toregas: I had a question about the excellent charts that are included in the paper. If I'm a council member, I want to be involved. If it's not one of these four areas (mission, policy, administration and management), which is it? Are you giving me an inadequate universe from which to choose? I'm a human being with desires and aspirations for my community. If these four don't capture a four or five (4.5 was highest rating on scale from 1 to 5) is there a list of other things that might score fours and fives?

Svara: Of course, you need to look at the specific item and not the four broad areas because they were given specific choices. On some items their scores are higher. There is variation based on city size. Council members could look at a score--perhaps for determining development strategies for large cities. At the level of four, they would be highly involved. These, by the way, are managers' opinions about the council's involvement.

Toregas: Would there be additional areas, other than policy, administration mission, and management? Would you suggest fifth, sixth, and seventh areas in which the council would get a 4 and 5? Or is this the universe of activity of manager and council in their mind?

Svara: That is the universe.

Toregas: I would reject that. How can it be that if a participant in our process does not feel involved?

Svara: What do we expect councils to handle entirely without the manager's involvement? That's what it would mean to chose a five. Choosing a four means very actively involved; there would be a high level of initiation and interaction, but it would not be exclusive. If councils say, "Aren't there things we want to do all by ourselves?" that probably says something about their relationship with the manager.

Banovetz: I would love to see a confrontation between Larry Brown and Norton Long on the question of power. I'm particularly attracted by Larry's notion that managers are more effective if they lack power than if they have power. That provides a much more useful framework for looking at the role of the manager in relationship to the council. The manager is not somebody who has power but who brokers others' power. Using that concept of brokerage to describe political activity may enable us to legitimate a role for the manager in the political system that still promotes the notion of democratic theory and the primacy of the council.

Frederickson: Doesn't brokering power mean to have power?

Banovetz: No. People broker stock money without ever having it. They're using other people's money.

Frederickson: I'm not sure you can parse out power.

Banovetz: Sure you can. There's another way to look at it too.

Brown: Maybe this is the professional management version of the poor old country boy from North Carolina. You know, "I'm just a poor little country boy in the big city trying to make a living." Watch your pockets.

Kerrigan: Professional practitioners say there's no split between policy and administration. That's been settled. Keep in mind that administrators have to eat too. When the city of New York has a shortage of water and somebody decides to bring an iceberg from Alaska to the city, that's a policy decision. When it starts to flood and comes over the curbs, that calls for an administrative response. Maybe the issue is policy versus policy and administration. Maybe it is the view of the well-trained educated administrator versus the policy-administration perception of the individual on council, who grows up with values of the society and that community and doesn't have the broader picture. What I mean by policy and what you, the city manager from Pasadena, mean by policy may not be the same. My democratic values may be different from your democratic values. I would go back to Alexis de Tocqueville to understand the idea of democracy. Some of his perceptions might sharpen a discussion.

Hansell: Last week a reporter from the *Toledo Blade*, which is leading the charge to abandon the council-manager plan in Toledo said, "You fellas running your cities all have cases when the council can't reach a decision. Doesn't that create a problem for you? How do you deal with it?" Lou Fox (San Antonio, Texas) handled it brilliantly. He said, "I tell you how I do it, I count to six. If I don't have six, I make six and I keep working at it until I get six, until the policy alternative focuses, sharpens, is defined." Now that produces end products as opposed to process. I think that is the legitimate role of the manager. I guess I have a clear understanding of where Jim Svara is coming from because I've seen the research and I've seen the model. I think it really works. It begins to break down the question of what is policy and what is administration, more finely so that you can begin to define them. I have a problem, John Nalbandian, with the model that you're laying out in your [later] paper, because it's based on the assumption that the council doesn't have legitimacy; therefore, you give legitimacy to the manager. I'm not sure that's going to work.

Nalbandian: You all talk about training councils and increasing the political focus of councils. I don't hear a council saying that. Councils are saying, "We really need to develop ourselves into a good policy-making group and we need to develop consensual techniques. And what we're really lacking in this community is political leadership." Is that what you hear councils saying?

Questioner: Do you hear the citizens saying that?

Nalbandian: The council itself is struggling because it doesn't have legitimacy in the community. So how can you seek legitimacy for what you're doing in the council?

Hansell: I would like to emphasize the words of John Gray, who is a powerful and sharp city manager at Christchurch, New Zealand. In the debate at the ICMA board about recognition and whether managers could appoint all department heads, there was a hang-up about power. John observed that in America we're very hung up on power. He said, "I have absolutely no power, I have influence." It makes all the difference in the world. That issue of brokering is very significant.

Watkins: I'm not afraid to use the "P" word. I thought that was a good comment. We get into this business to get something done or we wouldn't be here. I think we're grappling with a theoretical validation of what to do, which is probably reason for at least ten more years of papers. The governing body as a board of directors pays big bucks to hire people like us. They demand of us recommendations and identification of needs. Doesn't that in itself validate what we do? I think the easiest course I've ever had in this business is to sit around and wait for policy directives and do nothing. It's incumbent on me to identify issues and to take those issues to the governing body, to help sell these issues. They can either buy or reject them. But one of the responsibilities that we have as professional managers and people trained in urban issues is to identify these problems. I can't see how that contravenes democratic theory.

City Manager Roles in a Changing Political Environment

Charldean Newell
University of North Texas
James J. Glass
University of North Texas
David N. Ammons
University of Georgia

Proponents of local government reform saw council-manager government as the ideal form. Other elements included in the reform package were nonpartisan, at-large elections separated from state and national elections, merit systems, and the initiative, referendum, and recall commonly referred to as direct democracy. In contrast, an elected chief executive, with power centralized (the "strong mayor" form) or shared with the council (the "weak mayor" form), election of city council members by ward or district, and partisanship are characteristics associated with unreformed government.[1]

The orthodox model of council-manager government featured a small city council of five members elected at large on a nonpartisan basis for staggered terms and vested with all legislative and policymaking authority. The model further stipulated that the mayor should be selected by fellow council members or, alternately, be designated on the basis of whichever council member received the most popular votes. In either case, the mayor was to be merely the city council's presiding officer with no greater formal authority than any other council member.[2] Implicit in the model, which called for administrative authority to rest with a professional city manager, is an "amateur" council whose members devote their time and talent as a means of fulfilling civic duty rather than as an investment in achieving some political ambition. Richard S. Childs, regarded as the father of council-manager government, continued to promote the virtues of at-large council elections and selection of the mayor by the council a half-century after the introduction of the plan.[3]

In practice, electoral arrangements in council-manager cities vary considerably. Although many practices do conform to the prescriptions of Childs and other advocates of the reform model, mayors of council-manager cities are sometimes elected directly by the citizens and council members are elected under a variety of systems. Some council members represent a ward or district and are elected by voters from that district. Others run for seats reserved for specific geographic districts but are elected at large. Still others are chosen under a system that specifies some district seats and some at-large seats. About one-tenth of council-manager cities have partisan elections. Just as reformed cities have adopted various unreformed practices, unreformed ("political") cities have often adopted reform practices such as at-large elections.[4]

Since the council-manager plan was formalized in 1908 by Staunton, Virginia, not only have electoral systems become more diversified, but the roles performed by city managers also have changed. Many reformers advocated a clear separation of politics and administration, favoring an arrangement in which elected officials would have exclusive claim on political matters and leave administration solely to administrators. In the council-manager plan, they found what they thought was the perfect vehicle to institute that separation. The so-called politics-administration dichotomy continued to be of interest to theorists of council-manager government, and was reflected in concerns initially about whether administrators *should be* involved in politics and subsequently about the extent to which they *are* involved.[5]

Observation of managers in action led to the inevitable acknowledgment of the political role of the manager.[6] Managers themselves often describe their work in terms that differ sharply from earlier stereotypes. William Donaldson, who served as manager of three cities, has said of the contemporary manager: "Managers live their lives in the world of politics, and their success as managers is based on their ability to deal with this world."[7] City Manager Donald Blubaugh added,

> Now, approximately 70 percent of an urban manager's time is spent developing local policy, encouraging cooperation among policymakers, and coordinating efforts with other government jurisdictions . . . . This is new turf for those of us in the professional urban management business.[8]

Modern depictions of the relationship between council and manager roles are more likely to feature degrees of overlapping domain, with the council exercising primary, though not exclusive, authority in some facets of governance, and the city manager exercising primary, though not exclusive, authority in others.[9]

In a 1965 survey, Deil Wright found that city managers in cities of 100,000 population or greater regarded their role as community leaders--in essence, a political role--to be almost as important to their job success as the traditional administrative role of the manager.[10] Thirty-three percent of the city managers designated the political role as most important while 37 percent designated the management role as most important. Twenty-two percent placed highest priority on the third role in Wright's typology, the policy and council relations role. Replicating Wright's study 20 years later, Newell and Ammons found that by 1985 city managers perceived the political role to have diminished significantly: only 6 percent regarded it as most important. In contrast, a dramatic increase was registered in the percentage of responding city managers who reported the policy role, including council relations, as most important to their job success (56 percent). The percentage who rated the management role as most important (38 percent) showed little change from 1965.[11]

What accounts for the shifting perceptions among city managers regarding the relative importance of various roles? A tempting answer is provided by a variety of structural changes introduced in many council-manager cities over the past two decades. As more cities have departed from the prescriptions of Childs and his colleagues, have they materially altered the roles and relationships of city managers? Do city managers who serve cities with directly elected mayors, council members elected by districts, larger city councils, concurrent rather than staggered council terms, reasonably well-compensated mayors and city councils, or legislative staffs perceive their roles differently or pursue their duties differently than do their colleagues in cities that conform more closely to the reform model? Do more heterogeneous councils, which are viewed here as a likely byproduct of the presence of unreformed elements in council-manager government, result in city manager role behavior that differs from that in orthodox council-manager cities? Perhaps more fundamentally, do increased politicization and expanded mayoral and councilmanic involvement, especially in policy and political matters, allow the city manager to concentrate somewhat more intently on internal administrative matters, as some would suspect, or do politicization and expanded involvement actually draw the manager further and more deeply into matters of policy and council relations? These questions arise from our working hypothesis that unreformed elements lead to a greater emphasis on the policy role.

Methodology

A survey of municipal chief executives and their principal assistants in United States cities of 50,000 or more population was conducted during the spring of 1985 in order to examine executive time allocation. Only that portion of the responses involving council-manager cities and city managers is incorporated into this study. A total of 153 city managers, or 62 percent, responded. In 1988 a second survey of the same 153 cities was conducted and included structural characteristics of the municipalities. Thirteen cities did not respond, leaving 140 cities for which both role and structural data were available. The information gathered in the 1988 structural survey included how the mayor is selected, how council members are elected, the dates when unreformed elements (if any) were introduced into the city, whether council terms are staggered or concurrent, partisan/nonpartisan elections, council size, council composition by gender and ethnicity, the availability of staff for the mayor and council members, and mayor and council compensation. The structural survey gathered data both for 1985, to allow comparability with the 1985 data set, and for 1988, to determine changes in the intervening three years.

Following the schema of Wright, the 1985 time allocation survey defined the management role to include such activities as staffing, budgeting, and supervision, including reporting relationships; the policy role to include control over the council agenda and policy initiation and formulation; and the political role to include relationships with nongovernmental groups and individuals within the city as well as intergovernmental relations. Respondents were asked to indicate the percentage of time actually devoted to each role, the percentage of time they would prefer to devote to each role, and which role they considered to be most important to job success.

Bivariate analysis was the primary analytical method used to draw a general picture of the structural characteristics of the surveyed cities. It was also the method used to examine variations in city manager roles regarded as most important and, to a lesser extent, variations in actual and preferred time allocations to management, policy, and political roles within the context of the political environment. Because actual and preferred time allocations reported by the responding city managers were virtually identical, the reported analysis includes only the actual. In the analysis of the effect of political environment on managerial roles, observed percentages are reported, and reference is made to the size of the difference between and among certain response categories. Tests of significance are not reported for the bivariate analysis, however, because those who chose to respond to the survey are technically not a random sample of the total population of council-manager cities. Correlation techniques were used to identify explanatory variables relevant to differences in actual time allocations.

Findings

The following summary of findings is organized into three sections, beginning with the structural characteristics of responding cities. The second section describes city manager roles within the municipal political context, with emphasis on perceptions of the most important role, while the third offers explanations for variances in the time allocated to the management, policy, and political roles.

Structural Characteristics of Council-Manager Cities

For respondent cities with populations of 50,000 or greater, the presence of unreformed characteristics is more common than not. More than three-fifths of the cities reported having direct election of the mayor; in cities of 100,000 or greater, four-fifths had direct election (see Table 1). Most of the cities reported that direct election was instituted in 1975 or earlier.

More diversity was present in structural formats for council elections. The majority of the respondent cities (62 percent) had at-large elections, and only 16 percent had purely district elections. However, among larger cities--those with 100,000 or greater population--the percentage of cities with at-large elections dropped to slightly below half (49 percent) while the percentage electing all council members by district rose to 24 percent as did the percentage using a mixed electoral system. Among all cities that had adopted a system including district elections, 54 percent reported doing so prior to 1975. Few cities surveyed used a system of district nominations followed by at-large elections. One-fifth of the cities had concurrent rather than staggered terms for council members. However, one hallmark of traditional council-manager government scarcely had been breached: only 13 cities reported holding partisan elections.

Typically, the orthodox model recommended a five-member council as the ideal size. In this analysis, cities were divided into two groups: those with five-member councils, the classic size, and those with councils of more than five members. The survey revealed seven as the modal number in 1985, with larger cities tending to have councils with more members. In cities under 100,000 population, 59 percent had councils with more than five members, compared to 80 percent of cities with at least 100,000 population having councils with more than five members. City councils with memberships twice the prescribed size or greater are not unusual. In exchange for representational advantages, large councils undoubtedly present logistical and consensus-building challenges. One city manager serving a 10-member council wryly notes the need for a refresher course in arithmetic every couple of years. "I

102

Table 1
Structural Characteristics of Council-Manager Cities, by Percentage

Characteristic	Cities less than 100,000 pop. (N=88)	Cities of 100,000+ pop. (N=52)	All Cities (N=140)
Election of Mayor			
Within council	46.8	20.0	37.1
By voters	53.2	80.0	62.9
Council Election System			
At Large	69.3	49.0	61.9
At large, nom. by dist.	5.7	3.9	5.0
Mixed at large & dist.	13.6	23.5	17.3
District	11.4	23.5	15.8
Council Terms			
Staggered	85.2	73.1	80.7
Concurrent	14.8	26.9	19.3
Council Size			
Five	40.9	20.4	33.6
Six or more	59.1	79.6	66.4
Staff Support			
Mayor:			
None	6.9	3.9	5.8
Shared	80.5	53.9	70.5
Independent	12.6	42.3	23.7
Council:			
None	8.0	7.7	7.9
Shared	80.7	63.5	74.3
Independent	11.4	28.9	17.9
Salary			
Mayor, less than $10,000	81.2	44.2	67.0
Mayor, $10,000+	18.8	55.8	33.0
Council, less than $7,000	80.6	47.4	68.6
Council, $7,000+	19.4	52.6	31.4
Diversity			
Female 20% or less	62.1	51.0	51.5
Female 20% or more	37.9	49.0	48.5
Ethnic min. 20% or less	83.9	52.9	68.8
Ethnic min. 21% or more	16.1	47.1	31.2

Note: Totals do not always equal 100.0% due to rounding.

learn to count to six all over again, in a hurry, after each election."[12]

Survey items on staff assistance and compensation for the mayor and members of the city council were designed to elicit information on the extent to which the ideal model of a part-time "amateur" council was abrogated by the presence of a support system that might contribute to a more professional legislative body. While the majority of all cities reported that the mayor had only staff assistance shared with or provided by the city manager or another administrator, considerable differences in staff support existed according to city size. The mayors in only 13 percent of the smaller cities had a separate staff independent of the city administrator while 42 percent of the mayors in larger cities had an independent staff. In both smaller and larger cities, staff assistance for council members was most frequently provided by the city manager or other city administrator. In a small number of cities, no staff assistance was provided to either the mayor or city council.

Most mayors (81 percent) and council members (76 percent) were salaried rather than compensated on a per-meeting basis or not compensated at all. For purposes of analysis, mayoral salaries were divided into two groups: those below $10,000 and those $10,000 or more. Council salaries also were divided into two groups: those below $7,000 and those $7,000 or more. The divisions were based on a natural

103

break in the range of salaries reported by the cities. Although the median salary for mayors was $8,400 a year, salaries ranged up to $50,000 annually in 1985 ($60,000 in 1988). The median salary for council members was $6,912 a year, with the highest salary reported as $40,000 ($45,000 in 1988).

As might be expected, mayor and council salaries were higher in cities with 100,000 or greater population than in smaller cities. In large cities, the majority of mayors (56 percent) and council members (53 percent) received salaries above $10,000 and $7,000 a year, respectively, in contrast to less than a fifth of the mayors and council members in smaller cities.

The turbulent 1960s brought changing attitudes toward governmental authority and representation on all levels. Bob Kipp, former city manager of Kansas City and past ICMA president, summarized the post-1960s era and its effect on council representation this way: "the traditional mix of people in elective office changed, and therefore we now have a much more diverse mix in city government."[13] In this study diversity is measured by the proportion of female and ethnic minority council members. Larger cities, which presumably are also the most heterogeneous, showed a greater diversity in council composition than did cities with populations under 100,000. Almost half of the larger cities reported a council membership comprised of more than 20 percent women and almost half reported more than 20 percent ethnic minorities. Less than two-fifths of the smaller cities reported as high a proportion of women and barely a sixth reported as high a proportion of ethnic minority members.

Differences in diversity appear to be related to a city's method of council selection. White male candidates seem to be favored in the orthodox reform model's at-large system. The proportion of cities with at-large election systems having more than 20 percent female was 39 percent; for cities with district elections, 48 percent. With regard to ethnic minority membership, 21 percent of the cities with at-large council elections had at least 20 percent ethnic minority council members; for cities with district elections, 38 percent.

In summary, despite the urgings of local government reformists, unreformed elements are clearly a part of the "real world" of council-manager government. Direct election of the mayor, district elections or mixed district and at-large systems, council sizes of seven or more, and fairly substantial council and mayoral salaries are now commonplace in council-manager cities with 50,000 or greater population. Independent staffs are still a minority phenomenon, but most mayors and council members do receive some staff assistance. Historically, city councils in council-manager cities tended to be comprised predominantly of white males, but council diversity with regard to female and ethnic minority membership is evident. City population is related to structural differences, with larger cities showing a greater tendency to have unreformed elements than cities of less than 100,000 people. The political environment in which contemporary city managers work differs from the purported ideal type. What effect has this changing political environment had on city manager roles?

Political Environment and Roles

To determine whether any relationship existed between city manager roles and the political environment described in the previous section, we examined actual time allocations to and assessments of the importance of management, policy, and political roles. Actual time allocations to and assessments of the importance of the roles are often at odds, indicating perhaps that some time-consuming tasks may not be seen as among the most important to job success.

Factors involving the mayor's office are discussed first, followed by a description of the council variables. As this section will show, the greatest differences occur with regard to assessments of which managerial role is most important rather than with regard to actual time allocations, and the differences are accentuated along population lines for many of the variables. The working hypothesis in the research design was that the policy role--including council relations--would increase in importance in the presence of unreformed elements in the governmental structure.

When the mayor was selected from within the council, 39 percent of the city managers perceived the management role as most important; the perception was 33 percent when the mayor was elected by the voters (see Table 2). When the mayor was directly elected, 63 percent of the city managers designated the policy role as most important, and 4 percent, the political role. When the council selected the mayor, 59 percent of the managers noted the policy role as most important, and 2 percent, the political role. In cities of 100,000 or greater population, the tendency to name a role other than management as most important was even more evident. In those cities, when the mayor was directly elected, the management role was regarded as most important by only 27 percent of the city managers while the percentage naming the political role increased to 9; the percentage of city managers reporting the policy role as most important was 64 percent, very similar to the percentage for cities as a whole. These findings modestly support the hypothetical contention that unreformed characteristics enhance the policy role.

The effects of staffing and compensation patterns, on the other hand, appear to have an indeterminate relationship with managerial attitudes toward the importance of the policy role. Among survey respondents, the policy role was seen as most important by only 17 percent of the managers in cities where the mayor had no staff support,

Table 2
City Managers' Most Important Roles, by Political
Structure of Mayor's Office, by Percentage

| Structural Characteristic | Role | | | N |
	Management	Policy	Political	
Election of Mayor				
Within Council	39.0	58.5	2.4	41
By Voters	32.9	62.9	4.3	70
Staff Support				
None	83.3	16.7	0.0	6
Shared	28.7	67.8	3.5	87
Independent	43.8	53.1	3.1	32
Salary				
Less than $10,000	31.3	65.7	3.0	67
$10,000 or more	45.5	51.5	3.0	33

Note: Totals do not always equal 100.0% due to rounding. The city managers were asked to respond to the question of which role is most important: management, policy, or political.

by 68 percent in cities where the mayor had a shared staff, and by 53 percent when the mayor had an independent staff. In contrast, the management role was seen as most important by 83 percent of the managers in cities with no mayoral staff, by 29 percent in cities with a shared staff, and by 44 percent when the mayor had separate staff support. Staff support in any form, rather than an independent staff, appears to be the more important factor. The existence and nature of staff support has only a modest effect on time actually devoted to the various roles. For example, actual time allocations to management reveal differences of only 3 percent, with more time devoted to the management role when the staff was shared. City managers reported a 56.5-hour actual workweek; 3 percent would amount to less than two hours a week difference.

Differences in the perceived importance of the policy and management roles are also associated with mayoral salary. In cities with less than 100,000 population, 60 percent of the city managers reported the policy role as most important when the mayor's salary was under $10,000, compared to 67 percent when the mayor's salary was $10,000 or higher. In larger municipalities, city managers imputed more importance to the management role when the mayor's salary was $10,000 or greater. While 81 percent of the big-city managers in municipalities where the mayor's pay was less than $10,000 identified the policy role as most important, a slight majority (52 percent) of their counterparts in cities in which mayoral pay was $10,000 or higher designated the management role. The Dallas manager exemplifies the mere 6 percent who identified the management role as most important despite only nominal mayoral pay. City Manager Richard Knight, known as "Mr. Fix-it" for his emphasis on a smooth-running city hall, has declared: "I'm not a politician. I'm not an elected official. I'm not running for any city office. I'm an administrator."[14]

Despite the greater stress on the management role's importance, reported actual time allocations for the management role were lower in cities where the mayor was paid more than $10,000: the 6 percent reported difference amounts to slightly over three hours a week. One possible explanation is that, in the larger cities, the mayor who is better paid and who has staff support, shared or independent, assumes a greater burden of policy development and council relations, with a corresponding increase in the importance of administrative performance on the part of the city manager regardless of time spent. In situations where salaried mayors have more time and assistance to develop policy positions, city managers more nearly see the management role as their *raison d'etre*. Conversely, in smaller cities the manager may find that a better-paid mayor has time for policy development but simultaneously puts more pressure on the city manager to assist in the policy development process.

Four methods for electing council members were reported: at large, at large with nomination by geographic place, a mixed at-large and district system, and district elections. Only five cities reported the at-large by geographic place system, rendering this category too small for analysis. What effects do the other three methods have on managerial perceptions of role importance? Unfortunately, no clear pattern exists upon which to formulate an answer. For example, the policy role was seen as the most important by 72 percent of the city managers in cities with district elections (unreformed), compared to 62 percent of the managers in cities with at-large elections (reformed). In cities with a mixed system, only 52 percent of the city managers identified the policy role as most important (see Table 3).

Actual time allocations for the management role were somewhat higher in cities with at-large elections, 52 percent compared with 46 percent in district systems. Actual time allocations for the policy role increased only slightly in the presence of an unreformed election method, from 33 percent in cities with at-large elections to 37 per cent in cities with district elections. Apparently, unreformed elements are only modestly associated with some movement away from the traditional management role to the policy role when actual time allocations are considered: a 4 percent difference amounts to slightly more than two hours a week.

The policy role was perceived as most important by 63 percent of the managers in cities with staggered council terms as compared with 54 percent of the managers in cities with concurrent council terms. The proportion of city managers rating the policy role as most important was 69 percent in cities with five-member councils and 57 percent in cities with larger councils. Neither of these findings supports the notion that unreformed elements lead to a greater emphasis on the policy role since the unreformed characteristics were assumed to be concurrent terms and larger councils. However, the practice of city managers,

Table 3
City Managers' Most Important Roles, by Political Structure and Characteristics of City Council, by Percentage

Structural Characteristic	Role			N
	Management	Policy	Political	
Council Election System				
At large	35.4	62.0	2.5	79
At large, nom. by dist.	60.0	40.0	0.0	5
Mixed at large & dist.	39.1	52.2	8.7	23
District	27.8	72.2	0.0	18
Council Terms				
Staggered	34.3	62.8	2.9	102
Concurrent	41.7	54.2	4.2	24
Council Size				
Five	28.6	69.1	2.4	42
Six or more	39.9	57.3	3.7	82
Staff Support				
None	70.0	30.0	0.0	20
Shared	31.5	65.2	3.3	92
Independent	37.5	58.3	4.2	24
Salary				
Less than $7,000	32.8	64.1	3.1	64
$7,000 or more	43.3	50.0	6.7	30
Diversity of Council				
Women members:				
None	31.8	68.2	0.0	22
20% or less	26.5	67.3	6.1	49
21% or more	47.2	50.9	1.9	27
Ethnic minority members:				
None	41.3	58.7	0.0	46
20% or less	37.8	60.0	2.2	45
21% or more	27.3	63.6	9.1	33

Note: Totals do not always equal 100.0% due to rounding. The city managers were asked to respond to the question of which role is most important: management, policy, or political.

expressed in terms of time actually devoted to the three roles, is for a higher percentage of time to be allocated to the policy role when council members have concurrent terms (37 percent) than when they have staggered terms (32 percent), a difference in actual time of almost three hours a week.

Paralleling the findings in the case of staff support for mayors, although with smaller differences, city managers more frequently perceived the policy role as most important when the council had either independent or shared staff support than when it had no staff support at all. Modest differences were also reported in actual time commitments. For example, reported time allocations to the management role were greater when staff support was shared between the administration and the council (51 percent) than when the council had separate staff support (47 percent), a difference of about two-and-a-half hours a week. Results with regard to council compensation were not so distinct as those for mayoral compensation. In smaller cities, almost identical percentages of city managers perceived the policy role to be most important when council members were paid $7,000 or more (62 percent) as when pay was lower (60 percent). In larger cities, however, the results paralleled those for mayors. Higher council pay was associated with the perceived primacy of the management role. Where council salaries were less than $7,000, almost three-fourths of the big-city managers (73 percent) regarded the policy role as most important, but where council members were paid higher salaries, a slight majority (53 percent) opted for the management role as most important.

Reported time allocations for management were greater in cities where council members were paid less than $7,000 a year. A speculative explanation similar to the one regarding the relationship between role importance and mayors' compensation may be applicable here. Better-paid council members, particularly those with staff support, may take the lead in policy development, with a corresponding increase in the importance of administrative performance on the part of the city manager regardless of time spent.

While council memberships that include women and ethnic minorities do not defy the conventional model of council-manager government, more heterogeneous councils do tend to be the products of unreformed elements, particularly larger councils with mixed or district elections. The research expectation is that greater diversity would result in a more "political" (conflict-oriented) council and that, correspondingly, the city manager would have enhanced responsibilities for the policy (council-relations, policy formulation) role.

When one examines the role perceived by city managers as most important in the context of female membership on the city council, the observed percentages are opposite of what was expected. As the percentage of women on the council increased, managers were less likely to identify the policy role as most important. This finding contradicts the assumption that diversity would result in a higher proportion of managers choosing the policy role as most important. Actual time spent on the policy role by managers serving councils of different gender compositions followed an erratic pattern.

The percentage of managers reporting the policy role as most important to their job success increased only slightly as the percentage of ethnic minority council members increased. In cities with no minority council members, 59 of the city managers selected the policy role as most important; in cities with 20 percent or less minority council membership, 60 percent of the managers chose the policy role; and in cities with 21 percent or more ethnic minority membership on the council, 64 percent of the managers selected the policy role. The percentage of managers selecting the political role as most important also increased as the percentage of ethnic minority council members grew. Reported time allocations by managers serving councils of different ethnic compositions followed no consistent pattern.

Thus, ethnic diversity of the city council appears to have only a slight effect on city managers' selecting the policy role as most important while gender diversity may have an opposite effect. For both diversity variables, controlling for city size and for method of council selection provided no further insights.

Explanatory Variables

The general research question of this study concerned the relationship between structural variables and city managers' designation of their most important role. However, because the "most important role" variable is not continuous, the emphasis shifted to reported time allocations among the three roles in an attempt to identify potential explanatory variables. Eleven variables were examined for their relevance to percentage of time allocated to each of the three roles: (1) whether the city population was less than 100,000 or 100,000 or greater, (2) whether the mayor was selected by the council or by the voters, (3) whether the city council was elected at large or by a mixed or district system, (4) whether city council terms were concurrent or staggered, (5) city council size, (6) percentage of the council that was female, (7) percentage of the council that was ethnic minority, (8) whether the mayor had no staff/shared staff or an independent staff, (9) whether the council had no staff/shared staff or an independent staff, (10) annual salary of the mayor, and (11) annual salary of council members. The procedures of analysis of variance and multiple regression using forward selection were run (Tables 4 and 5). Although the multiple regression technique did provide an explanation for a higher percentage of variance, missing values resulted in the deletion of 61 of the 140 cases from the analysis.

Three variables were found to explain 14 percent of the variance in percentage of time devoted to the management role by city managers. These were staggered council terms, percent of female council members, and direct election of the mayor. However, only one of these relationships was significant at the .05 level: percent of female council members and time devoted to the management role.

Three variables were found to explain 15 percent of the variance in percentage of time devoted to the policy role: percent of female council members, staggered council terms, and direct mayoral election. Once again, the only statistically significant relationship was between percent of female council members and the policy role.

Four variables were found to explain 16 percent of the variance in percentage of time devoted to the political role: staggered council terms, absence of ethnic diversity on the council, lack of independent mayoral staffing, and small population. Only one relationship was statistically significant: absence of ethnic minority diversity among council members and the political role, a rather startling finding.

Analysis of variance had the advantage of including 128 to 130

Table 4
Summary of Explanatory Variables Identified through Forward Selection
Regression for Time Allocation Variance among City Managers
(N=79)

Dependent Variable	Independent Variable	C(P) Sign (+/-)	Partial R²	Cumulative R²	F	Significance
Percentage of	CCTERMS	+	.485	.049	3.93	.051
Time Devoted to	PCTFEM	+	.053	.101	4.47	.038*
"Management Role"	HOWELEC*	-	.038	.139	3.28	.074
Percentage of	PCTFEM	+	.098	.098	8.37	.005*
Time Devoted to	CCTERMS[b]	+	.029	.127	2.51	.117
"Policy Role"	HOWELEC	-	.025	.152	2.20	.142
Percentage of	CCTERMS	+	.048	.048	3.92	.052
Time Devoted to	PCETHNC	-	.064	.113	5.49	.022*
"Political Role"	MAYSTAFF[c]	-	.030	.142	2.60	.111
	POP80	-	.020	.162	1.79	.185

*Significant at the .05 level.

*HOWELEC variable is coded "1" for selection by council and "0" for election by voters.
[b]CCTERMS variable is coded "1" for staggered terms and "0" for concurrent terms.
[c]MAYSTAFF variable is coded "1" for separate staff and "0" for no staff or shared staff.

Table 5
Summary of Significant Explanatory Variables Identified through Analysis
of Variance for Time Allocation Variance among City Managers
(N=128 to 130)

Dependent Variable	Independent Variable	R²	F	Significance*
Percentage of	PCTFEM	.109	2.48	.027
Time Devoted to	CCSAL	.068	7.10	.009
"Management Role"	MAYSAL	.043	4.60	.034
	CCTERMS*	.042	5.67	.019
Percentage of	PCTFEM	.102	2.31	.038
Time Devoted to	MAYSAL	.037	3.92	.050
"Policy Role"				
Percentage of	CCSAL	.047	4.70	.033
Time Devoted to	MAYSTAFF[b]	.035	4.62	.033
"Political Role"				

*Significant at the .05 level.

*CCTERMS variable is coded "1" for staggered terms and "0" for concurrent terms.
[b]MAYSTAFF variable is coded "1" for separate staff and "0" for no staff or shared staff.

cases for each variable. Four statistically significant relationships were found to explain variation in the time devoted to the management role: percent of female council members (11 percent), council salary (7 percent), mayoral salary (4 percent), and staggered council terms (4 percent). Two statistically significant relationships were found to explain variation in the time devoted to the policy role: percent of female council members (10 percent) and mayoral salary (4 percent). Two statistically significant relationships were also found to explain variation in the time devoted to the political role: council salary (5 percent) and mayoral staff (4 percent).

Conclusions

The key research question raised in this study was, "Why did city managers shift their emphasis from the management and political roles in 1965 to the management and policy roles in 1985?" The assumption behind the research was that the changing political environment of the city, particularly changes in governmental structure affecting the mayor and the city council, could be a contributing factor to the shifts in managerial role emphases.

Clearly, council-manager cities of 50,000 or greater population included in this study have deviated from the classic ideal of a small council elected at large and headed by a mayor chosen from within the council. It is commonplace to see unreformed characteristics incorporated into the political structure, particularly direct election of the mayor, district or mixed systems of electing council members, and compensation and staff support for elected officials. District elections were shown to be associated with the diversification of councils along gender and ethnicity lines. Unreformed elements are more common in cities over 100,000 than in cities of 50,000 to 99,999 population.

Wright found that 33 percent of the 1965 managers perceived the political role as most important, but in relation to the characteristics included in this study, the highest proportion of managers selecting that role as most important was 10 percent in large cities with a council comprised of at least 21 percent ethnic minority members. Little change has occurred over time in perceptions of the importance of the management role. Therefore, displacement of the political role has been in favor of the policy role. As the political environment of council-manager cities has changed, city managers have apparently relinquished the mantle of community leadership to elected officials while not only spending more time on but regarding as more important the policy role, which encompasses policy development and council relations.

The "professionalization" of elected officials appears to influence city manager roles. The management role is more likely to be perceived as most important when the mayor and council have more than token salaries but no staff. Higher salaries allow the mayor and council to become more involved in policy leadership, perhaps shoving the manager from that role or perhaps simply permitting the manager to concentrate on the management role. The policy role is more likely to be perceived as most important when the mayor and council have a staff, whether shared or independent, but only a token salary. If the mayor or council have staff assistance, those staff members are unlikely to be occupied with management issues because they have no direct responsibility for management functions. Instead, the staff will be occupied with policy matters, heightening attention in that arena and making it a more crucial area for the city manager whether he (or she) spends more time there or not.

Council diversity seems to have an effect on managerial roles, although the percentage of ethnic minority council members permits an easier explanation for role variation than does the percentage of female council members. A higher percentage of ethnic minority council members may produce a more politicized council. The city manager serving such a council may well see the policy and political roles as crucial to job success, but when possible may attempt to avoid more involvement in the sensitive political role than absolutely necessary and focus instead on administrative tasks and council relations. Having more women on the city council results in managers spending more time on the policy and political roles, although the management role is viewed as the most crucial to job success by almost half the managers serving councils with the greatest gender diversity. A higher percentage of female council members appears to create the greatest role dissonance for city managers.

A more politicized version of council-manager government than that envisioned by the form's early theorists now exists, which increases the complexity of the environment in which the modern city manager works. Changing political environment and changing city manager perceptions regarding city manager roles are related, though not so strongly as some might expect. The policy role has displaced the political role in terms of its perceived importance while the management role has not diminished in importance since 1965. However, neither direct election of the mayor nor district election of council members--the two most obvious structural changes in council-manager cities in the past 20 years--proved to be so potent in explaining variance in city manager behavior as did the degree of support, in terms of salary and staff, for the mayor and council and the diversity of council membership.

Notes

The authors acknowledge financial assistance from the Faculty Research Committee, University of North Texas; research assistance from Victor M. Boyer, Nancy Moffitt, Larry Van Stenberg, and Carissa Chandler; and computer assistance from Jimmie R. Naugher and Jim Hardy.

1.   See, for example, Robert B. Boynton, "City Councils: Their Role in the Legislative System," *The Municipal Year Book, 1976* (Washington, D.C.: International City Management Association, 1976), pp. 67-77.

2.   The ideal model of council-manager government can be found in the *Model City Charter* (New York: National Municipal League, 1915).

3.   Richard S. Childs, *The First 50 Years of the Council-Manager Plan of Municipal Government* (New York: National Municipal League, 1965).

4.   James H. Svara, "Unwrapping Institutional Packages in Urban Government: The Combination of Election Institutions in American Cities," *Journal of Politics* 39 (February 1977): 166-175.

5.   The evolution of city manager roles can be traced through the work of the historians of the profession. See, especially, Richard J. Stillman II, *The Rise of the City Manager: A Public Professional in Local Government* (Albuquerque: University of New Mexico Press, 1974); Harold A. Stone, Don K. Price, and Kathryn H. Stone, *City Manager Government in the United States: A Review After Twenty-Five Years* (Chicago: Public Administration Service, 1940); Clarence E. Ridley and Orin Nolting, *The City Manager Profession* (Chicago: University of Chicago Press, 1934); Leonard D. White, *The City Manager* (Chicago: University of Chicago Press, 1931); and Childs, *The First Fifty Years of the Council-Manager Plan.*

6.   See, for example, Norton E. Long, "Politicians for Hire--The Dilemma of Education and the Task of Research," *Public Administration Review* 25 (June 1965): 115-120; Karl A. Bosworth, "The Manager *Is* a Politician," *Public Administration Review* 18 (Summer 1958): 216-222; James M. Banovetz, "The City: Forces of Change," Chapter 2, and David Welborn, "The Environment and Role of the Administrator," Chapter 4, in *Managing the Modern City*, James M. Banovetz, ed. (Washington, D.C.: International City Management Association, 1971).

7.   William V. Donaldson, "Continuing Education for City Managers, *Public Administration Review* 33 (November/December 1973): 505.

8.   Donald A. Blubaugh, "The Changing Role of the Public Administrator," *Public Management* 69 (June 1987): 9-10.

9. James S. Svara, "Dichotomy and Duality: Reconceptualizing the Relationship Between Policy and Administration in Council-Manager Cities," *Public Administration Review* 45 (January/February 1985): 221-232; "Sharing the Load of Governance: The Manager's Responsibilities," *Public Management* 67 (July 1985): 16-19; and "Political Supremacy and Administrative Expertise," *Management Science and Policy Analysis* 3 (Summer 1985): 3-7.

10. Deil S. Wright, "The City Manager as a Developmental Administrator," Chapter 6 in *Comparative Urban Research*, Robert T. Daland, ed. (Beverly Hills: Sage Publications, 1969), pp. 203-248. The percentages reported by Wright on most important roles do not add to 100.

11. Charldean Newell and David N. Ammons, "Role Emphases of City Managers and Other Municipal Executives," *Public Administration Review* 47 (May/June 1987): 252, and David N. Ammons and Charldean Newell, *City Executives: Leadership Roles, Work Characteristics, and Time Management* (Albany: State University of New York Press, 1989).

12. Jane Mobley, "Politician or Professional? The Debate over Who Should Run Our Cities Continues," *Governing* 1 (February 1988): 48.

13. Ibid., 46.

14. James Ragland, "Quiet Efficiency Earns Gold Stars for Knight," *Dallas Morning News*, December 28, 1988, p. 16A.

Leadership in
Council-Manager Cities
The Institutional Implications

Greg J. Protasel
Idaho State University

The traditional view of mayors in council-manager cities as only the titular heads of government has changed. Mayors in council-manager cities are exercising leadership as members of council-manager teams.[1] Some council-manager cities are even witnessing their mayors emerge as chief executives who rival their city managers for power and who have essentially transformed the council-manager system into a skewed version of the strong mayor system with a chief administrative officer.[2] In addition, approximately 65% of the over 2,500 council-manager cities in the United States now have mayors directly elected by the people.[3] This institutional change in the council-manager plan has moved these "reformed" cities closer to their "unreformed" counterparts by giving the mayor an electoral base for exerting leadership.[4]

At the same time that mayors are beginning to assert their leadership roles in council-manager cities, the role of the city manager has evolved. The time is long past when city managers once distinguished "politics" from "policy" in order to justify their participation in policymaking. Studies of city managers' policy orientations indicate that many managers view themselves as political types who should innovate and take the lead on policy matters, in contrast to more traditional administrative types who see their policy role in neutral terms and who reject involvement in community politics.[5]

This paper assesses the institutional implications of leadership in council-manager cities. The first part of the paper recounts the origins of the council-manager plan and graphically depicts the leadership gap in the traditional plan. In the second part, patterns of leadership are identified which have filled the leadership gap in the council-manager plan. Finally, an examination is made of the institutional impact of promoting leadership by allowing voters to directly elect the mayor in council-manager cities.

The Leadership Gap in the Council-Manager Plan

The council-manager plan evolved not out of historical necessity, but was created for ideological reasons. Along with the many other reforms of the progressive era of American politics, council-manager government is usually viewed as a reaction to corruption and inefficiency.[6] In the litany of "good government," city management occupies a place alongside the initiative, referendum, nonpartisan elections and at-large elections.

The council-manager plan was the third in a series of progressive reforms around the turn of the century. First, in 1898, the newly formed National Municipal League recommended the strong mayor form of government as a way to decrease the power of political machine bosses.[7] The strong mayor form concentrated executive powers in the mayor. These powers had previously been dispersed among councilmen, committees, and elected administrative officials. The mayor was to make administrative appointments without legislative interference. The power of the legislature was to be concentrated in a unicameral council elected at large.

Secondly, while the National Municipal League reformers backed the strong mayor form of government, business interests throughout the country began to support the commission form of government (which originated in Galveston, Texas in 1901) because of how it organized city government along the lines of a business corporation.[8] By discarding the separation of powers and checks and balances and unifying power in a board of commissioners, the commission plan copied the private corporation.

It was this feature of the commission plan which caught the attention of the National Short Ballot Organization which had been founded in New York in 1909 by Richard S. Childs with the active support of the president of Princeton University, Woodrow Wilson.[9] The Short Ballot Organization looked upon the commission form of government as a more promising municipal reform than the strong mayor system recommended by the National Municipal League because the commission form of government granted all authority to a single small governing body. By giving voters the opportunity to concentrate their attention on electing a few important officials, the commission form of government would supposedly hold them responsible, as in a Parliamentary system, for the policies and administration of government. By the time the National Short Ballot Organization officially endorsed the commission plan in 1911 it had already spread to more than 160 cities. The primary objective of the National Short Ballot Organization was to strengthen the linkage between voters and their representatives. The underlying premise of the short ballot movement was that "popular government" would lead to "good government." However, supporters of the commission plan soon began to realize that the reform suffered from a major fault--it fragmented administrative functions among the elected commissioners. Not completely satisfied with the commission form, Richard S. Childs literally invented the commission-manager form of government (later to be called the city manager or council-manager form of government) combining the commission plan idea of unification of powers and a short ballot with the idea of concentrating administrative authority in a general manager to supervise the departments.[10] In 1915 the National Municipal League revised its model city charter to incorporate the council-manager plan.

Like so many inventions, the council-manager plan took on a life of its own and overran the Short Ballot movement in terms of its national significance. Concentration of administrative authority in a city manager became the hallmark of the council-manager plan leading to seemingly endless debates about the actual and proper relationship between policy and administration. The fact that the council-manager plan was created as an intellectual afterthought to improve the commission plan has probably contributed to the confusion.

Early proponents of the council-manager plan praised it for separating policy from administration, which would supposedly enable city managers to efficiently dispatch administrative duties and render service to the public.[11] The council-manager plan became a revered political institution and an established political doctrine.

After World War II, however, evaluations of the council-manager plan became more critical. The most common criticism of the council-manager form of government attacked the basic assumption of the plan--the dichotomy between policy and administration.[12]

One recent attempt to reconceptualize the relationship between policy and administration in council-manager cities sets forth a model of dichotomy and duality (see Figure 1).[13] According to this model, there are four functions of the governmental process (mission, policy, administration, management) which blend together to form a continuum from "pure" policy to "pure" management. By studying the relationships between elected officials and administrators in selected council-manager cities, a "typical" and "ideal" division of authority between the city council and city manager was mapped out. The resulting diagram indicates that conceptually and empirically in council-manager cities, "...there is a dichotomy of mission and management, but policy and administration are intermixed to the extent they are a duality, distinct but inseparable aspects of developing and delivering government programs."[14]

If the dichotomy/duality model is an accurate conceptualization of the relationship between policy and administration in council-manager cities, it is possible to graph the council's and manager's spheres of activity on the same set of axes to illustrate why the exercise of policy leadership has been so problematic in council-manager governments (see Figure 2). The separate and shared responsibilities of the council and manager appear quite distinctly when the council's and manager's spheres of activity are oriented to the same axes.

Two aspects of the council-manager relationship in policy and administration are clearly illustrated in Figure 2. First, the manager exercises more separate responsibility than the council. This accords with the often perceived imbalance of executive-legislative relations in the council-manager plan. Second, the council and manager share most responsibility in policy, but the overall level of policy activity of the manager doesn't match the levels found in the other functional areas of the governmental process. The implication is that the traditional council-manager plan contains a leadership gap in policymaking.

Because we live in an age when demands for local governmental leadership in policymaking are increasing, the leadership gap in the traditional council-manager plan is perhaps its greatest flaw. Nevertheless, several patterns of leadership have been found to emerge in council-manager cities and by analyzing these leadership patterns, the potentials of the relationship between the mayor and the manager come into sharper focus.

Leadership Patterns in Council-Manager Cities

Four leadership patterns stand out from previous studies of council-manager cities (see Figure 3). First, there is the *traditional*

Figure 1
The Dichotomy/Duality Model

Dimensions of Governmental Process

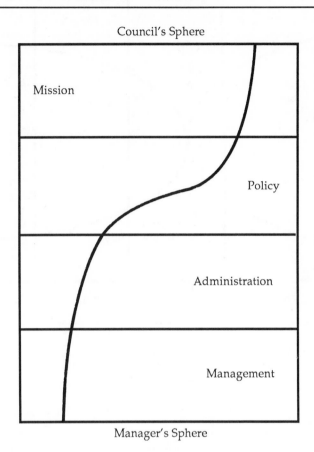

Council's Sphere

Mission

Policy

Administration

Management

Manager's Sphere

Source: James H. Svara, "Dichotomy and Duality: Reconceptualizing the Relationship between Policy and Administration in Council-Manager Cities," *Public Administration Review*, Jan/Feb 1985, p. 228.

council-manager role where policymaking power is formally vested in the city council and where administrative power is concentrated in the city manager.[15] Secondly, a *dominant-manager* pattern can be identified when the chief executive officer in charge of the bureaucracy also emerges as the main policymaker.[16]

It is sometimes difficult to discern the differences between these two patterns because they are both likely to be found in relatively smaller, stable political communities. The main difference between these two leadership patterns is the location of political leadership. The traditional council-manager leadership pattern focuses political leadership within the formal structure of government in the council as a whole. In contrast, in the dominant-manager pattern political leadership is located outside the formal structure of government.

The traditional leadership role has probably turned out to be the least frequently found pattern in council-manager cities. However, the idea that the city manager would assume the role of community leader and become the dominant policymaker was completely unanticipated by the "good government" reformers who sought to insulate the city

117

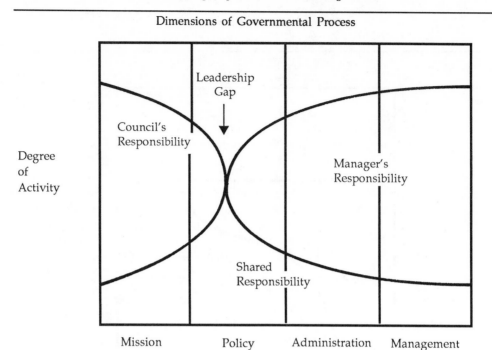

Figure 2
The Leadership Gap in the Council-Manager Plan

Dimensions of Governmental Process

Leadership
Gap

Council's
Responsibility

Manager's
Responsibility

Degree
of
Activity

Shared
Responsibility

Mission   Policy   Administration   Management

Figure 3
Leadership Patterns in Council-Manager Cities

Type of Political Government

		small city/ stable	large city/ unstable
Location Of Political Leadership	within formal structure	Traditional Role	Governing Role
	outside formal structure	Dominant Manager	Strong Mayor

manager from the political realm. The role of dominant community
leader seems to have been thrust upon city managers by the
circumstance of having to deal with amateur city councils which looked
to the professional city manager for expert advice--an indication of the
leadership gap in the council-manager plan. However, the traditional
council-manager plan did not provide any institutional basis for the city
manager to close the gap and exercise policy leadership. In theory, the
city manager was supposed to be a neutral administrator, not a policy
leader--hence the need to go outside the formal structure of government

to exercise leadership. Yet, when the city manager assumed the mantle of community leader and exercised political leadership his actions ultimately created a crisis of legitimacy because the location of political leadership lay outside the formal structure of government.

The dominant-manager pattern appears to be a paradox. The demands upon local government and the leadership gap in the traditional council-manager plan required that political leadership be exercised, but when the city manager did this it was risky political business. As Banfield and Wilson have pointed out:

> An experienced manager knows perfectly well that his council will use him for its political purposes if it can. For the sake of good relations with the council, he is usually willing to be accommodating and play its game--up to a point. As a rule, he stops short of getting into a position that would jeopardize his job or his professional standing. Sometimes, however, through a mistake of judgment or through wanting to accomplish something of importance, he goes beyond the point of safety, and takes responsibility for something that, according to the orthodoxy, should be in the council's sphere. This, when it succeeds--but only then--is called "providing leadership."[17]

The third and fourth types of leadership patterns found in council-manager cities have arisen from the changing role of the mayor in larger communities with less stable political environments. The *governing-team* pattern features the mayor working with the manager in the policy process.[18] The manager's executive leadership is complemented by the mayor's non-executive leadership. In this pattern the mayor works within the formal structure of government to become a guiding force in city government even though the manager continues to function as the chief executive officer.

By taking advantage of his strategic location spanning bureaucratic, legislative and public arenas, the mayor in council-manager cities fills the leadership gap in the council-manager plan by fashioning a political "executive" team.[19] This governing-team pattern is probably the most frequently found pattern in council-manager cities. Indications are that mayors in council-manager cities will always be expected to assert non-executive leadership as a regular responsibility of their position. An observer remarked about the mayor's job description: "strong leadership from the mayor, at least as a coordinator and preferably as a director, is no longer optional in light of the increasing demands on city governments. If these activities are not undertaken by the mayor, a serious vacuum exists."[20]

The fourth pattern of leadership found in the council-manager cities is the *strong mayor* pattern. In this pattern the mayor in the council-manager city acts as if he were located in a strong mayor-council system. The mayor reaches outside the formal structure of government for a political leadership base. Thus, the strong mayor in a council-manager city becomes the community political leader by depending upon political and extragovernmental resources. Furthermore, the strong mayor acts as a countervailing force to the manager in the policy process, thereby decreasing he manager's power. The leadership gap in the council-manager plan coupled with demands for conflict resolution in large growing cities seems to be primarily responsible for the emergence of the strong mayor leadership pattern. As the recent experience in San Diego with the city manager system has indicated, "the city manager is losing power, not because he or she is not a valuable actor in the city, but because of limitations of the system."[21]

Promoting Leadership in Council-Manager Cities through Direct Election of the Mayor

The traditional council-manager plan was based on two principles. First, executive and legislative authority was unified in the city council. Second, policymaking was separated from administration by concentrating administrative authority in the hands of the city manager. Over the years, as experience under the plan accumulated, the practical limits of these principles began to be recognized. Unification of executive and legislative authority within the council often relegated the mayor to a ceremonial role, while the idea of separating policymaking from administration proved to be unrealistic as amateur city council members frequently deferred to the expert city manager in policymaking matters. The major weakness of the council-manager plan was thus identified as the lack of an institutional focal point for political leadership--hence the leadership gap in the council-manager plan.

The recent Model Charter Revision Project of the National Civic League reflected a wish to fill the leadership gap by establishing a new institutional base for political leadership in council-manager cities.[22] By providing council-manager cities with the option of directly electing the mayor, the new charter codified what had already become an adaptive institutional response by the majority of council-manager cities. The ICMA's 1986 Form of Government Survey indicated that 65% of council-manager cities had mayors who were directly elected by the voters.[23]

Certainly, mayors in council-manager cities--whether they were directly elected or not -- have always had the potential to exercise non-executive leadership roles such as ceremonial spokesman, communicator, organizer, promotor, etc. which were not dependent upon new formal institutional arrangements.[24] However, promoting leadership by revising the council-manager plan to allow for direct election of the mayor is significant because it formally overcomes the major institutional weaknesses of the plan, while at the same time, it upholds the principles upon which it is based. A directly elected mayor provides a clear focal point for political leadership on the council, which restores the policymaking balance between the council and the manager. Furthermore, abandonment of the council-manager plan might be forestalled since the lack of a directly elected mayor has been shown to be a characteristic of the small number of cities which abandon the plan each year.[25]

While the option of directly electing the mayor enhances the council-manager plan, many council-manager cities in their quest for political leadership have actually weakened the plan by going one step further and adding an element of separation of powers. Analysis of the data for ICMA's 1986 *Form of Government Survey* reveals that directly elected mayors in council-manager cities are beginning to function separately from the council. In council-manager cities where voters directly elect the mayor, 40% of the mayors can vote in council meetings only in a tie, and 21% have the authority to veto council-passed measures. This is in contrast to council-manager cities where mayors are selected from among the council members. There, 3% of the mayors are restricted to vote in council meetings only in a tie, and just 2% have any type of authority to veto council-passed measures.

These statistics seem to reflect a view that mayoral leadership in council-manager cities can be promoted by following the separation-of-powers example of the mayor-council form of government. Mayors in mayor-council governments cannot vote in the council except in the case of a tie, and they frequently have veto power over the council. But, to incorporate these features from the mayor-council system into the council-manager system threatens to weaken the plan, not strengthen it. While mayors in mayor-council cities are chief executives, mayors in council-manager cities are non-executives. To separate a non-executive mayor from the council and to give a non-executive mayor veto power is to create a new form of government--a mayor-council-manager form of government--which undermines the council-manager plan while exacerbating the weaknesses of the mayor-council form of government.

Injecting the idea of separation of powers into the council-manager system would seem to put the directly elected mayor on a collision course with both the council and the city manager. Policymaking deadlock--a continual threat in mayor-council systems--could be expected to occur periodically as conflicts between a politically ambitious mayor and council erupt. In addition, tensions between the mayor and manager might arise should the non-executive mayor who, because of his separation from the council, may begin to view himself as a chief executive and the city manager as a chief administrative officer (CAO). It is, after all, mayoral control that distinguishes the job of CAO from that of city manager.[26] Attempts by a mayor to direct a manager would surely provoke charges of administrative interference.

In summary, the idea of promoting leadership in council-manager cities through direct election of the mayor appears to be a sound one and has been adopted in almost two-thirds of council-manager cities. What is alarming is that the good accomplished by this institutional change is being undermined because in many of these same cities mayors have been separated from their councils in the hope of promoting the type of strong political leadership found in mayor-council cities. It seems likely that the resultant hybrid mayor-council-manager form of government will create more leadership problems that it resolves.

Notes

1. Nelson Wikstrom, "The Mayor as a Policy Leader in the Council-Manager Form of Government: A View from the Field," *Public Administration Review*, vol. 39 (May/June 1979), pp. 270-276.

2. Glen Sparrow, "The Emerging Chief Executive: The San Diego Experience," *National Civic Review*, vol. 74 (December 1985), pp. 538-547.

3. International City Management Association, *1986 Form of Government* survey.

4. David A. Booth, "Are Elected Mayors a Threat to Managers?" *Administrative Science Quarterly*, vol. 12 (March 1968), pp. 572-589; Robert Paul Boynton and Deil S. Wright, "Mayor-Manager Relationships in Large Council-Manager Cities: A Reinterpretation," *Public Administration Review*, vol. 31 (January/February 1971), pp. 28-36.

5. Ronald O. Loveridge, *City Managers in Legislative Politics* (New York: The Bobbs-Merrill Company, Inc., 1971).

6. William Bennett Munro, *The Government of American Cities* (New York: The Macmillan Company, 1920).

7. Harold A. Stone, Don K. Price, and Kathryn H. Stone, *City Manager Government in the United States* (Chicago: Public Administration Service, 1940).

8. Ernest S. Bradford, *Commission Government in American Cities* (New York: The Macmillan Company, 1919).

9. Stone *et al.*, *op. cit.*

10. Ibid.

11. Leonard D. White, *The City Manager* (Chicago: The University of Chicago Press, 1927).

12. John East, *Council Manager Government: The Political Thought of Its Founder, Richard S. Childs* (Chapel Hill: University of North Carolina Press, 1965).

13. James H. Svara, "Dichotomy and Duality: Reconceptualizing the Relationship Between Policy and Administration in Council-Manager Cities," *Public Administration Review*, vol. 45 (January/February 1985), pp. 221-232 (also reprinted in this volume).

14. Ibid., p. 227.

15. Boynton and Wright, *op. cit.*, p.32.

16. Ibid., p. 33.

17. Edward C. Banfield and James Q. Wilson, *City Politics* (New York: Vintage Books, 1963), p. 176.

18. Wikstrom, *op. cit.*, p. 275.

19. Boynton and Wright, *op. cit.*, p. 35.

20. James H. Svara, "The Mayor in Council-Manager Cities: Recognizing Leadership Potential," *National Civic Review*, vol. 75 (September/October, 1986), pp. 271-281; 305.

21. Sparrow, *op. cit.*, p. 546.

22. Model Charter Revision Project, "Working Paper IV" (New York: National Civic League, Inc., 1987), p. 2.

23. The author obtained the 1986 *Form of Government* survey from ICMA.

24. James H. Svara, "Mayoral Leadership in Council-Manager Cities: Preconditions versus Preconceptions," *The Journal of Politics*, vol. 49, 1987, pp. 207-227.

25. Greg J. Protasel, "Abandonments of the Council-Manager Plan: A New Institutionalist Perspective," *Public Administration Review*, vol. 48 (July/August 1988), pp. 807-812 (also reprinted in this volume).

26. David R. Morgan, *Managing Urban America* (Belmont, Calif: Brooks/Cole Publishing Co., 1989), p. 51.

Response

Norman King
Palm Springs, California

I think the statement that the leadership gap in policy making is perhaps the greatest flaw of the council-manager form of government could be made of any form of government. Policy making is the greatest flaw of any government. I have a question as to whether that is a structural issue or whether it is primarily influenced by the people who are elected, whether they are mayors or council members. My approach to that issue is to look at other factors rather than structure.

Another statement, "In theory, the city manager was supposed to be a neutral administrator, not a policy leader--hence the need to go outside the formal structure of government to exercise leadership," raises issues regarding reformation. In theory, as a city manager, I am supposed to be active in the policy process, and I react negatively to statements that say I'm acting improperly in doing that. We are in the policy business, so we should stop trying to talk about what may have been in the past. Among these papers there is a disagreement about what was really happening forty years ago. It's not a matter of adhering to any particular past form. Howard Tipton has talked about it when he mentioned "arranging the stage." How we arrange that stage constantly changes, given the characters we're dealing with and our particular structure. How we arrange the stage changes week by week; therefore, the responses that I give to a researcher's questionnaire will change depending on what the people I work for are dealing with that week. It has nothing to do with the structure of our government; rather it is the personalities that are important.

The paper also suggests that direct election of the mayor may forestall abandonments. I think that is a valid conclusion. And it may also lead to better governed cities. In Palm Springs, we have changed in the time I've been there from council-elected mayor to a directly elected mayor. The first mayor to serve a four-year term is Sony Bono, who was elected last April. I think that the emphasis here and in the paper is on the relationship between the council and the manager. That's important. What is lacking in some of these papers is a description of the relationship between the mayor and the council in a given context. Until this is done, there is no way to figure out what the manager should be doing in that situation.

Let me just raise quickly some of the issues that come to my mind when we deal with the implications of a directly elected mayor.

First, it introduces a different interpersonal dynamic with the council that complicates the policy process in certain situations. The mayor who is elected directly by the people may not be the person who would be elected by the council to be the mayor. In those situations where both groups would have made the same choice, you have the best of both worlds. You have political leadership that is recognized in the community; you have a council that defers willingly to the mayor to formulate and carry out policy. In those situations where that's not the case, it is difficult to put together unified policies because the person who should be doing this is not necessarily the leader of the council.

123

The leader of the community and the leader of the council in this case are different. Such a situation can create conflict in policy making.

Secondly, regarding the issue of council specialization, I think we are seeing a trend toward having council members elected for specific reasons. They have their own agendas. That's not necessarily bad, but it means they're primarily interested in carrying out certain issues. If the manager or mayor gets in the way of allowing individual council members to express their own issues and to lead to their resolution, it is going to create difficulties with the council.

Thirdly, the issues of unequal communication with the mayor and the rest of the council and confidentiality take a great deal of time. How can the manager help a mayor, who would not have been elected mayor by the majority of the council, bring issues to a point where they can be talked about with the council? This situation makes the policy development process much more difficult, and often places the city manager in a tenuous position. Other council members may resent the city manager helping the mayor, especially if the mayor's agenda is different from theirs. In any case, the manager's coordination role is amplified. In contrast, the city council, which has elected its own mayor, will likely tolerate, and even welcome, the manager's differential attention to the mayor because such assists the policy making process. In summary, the irony is that the "leadership gap" can be widened by having a directly elected mayor who would not have been the council's choice as "their" mayor.

The issue of getting public attention is important for some of the council members who have aspirations for higher office. It is increasingly difficult to focus on teamwork when council members want individual attention.

Now we have council members who are less concerned about promoting an efficient, businesslike approach to government. We're dealing with councils that just don't appreciate the time necessary to run an efficient organization. The rewards that were there previously--for example, the recognition that you have an efficiently operating sewer plant--are lost. I think we somehow have got to deal with that. Otherwise we're going to lose sight of the importance of high quality service.

Discussion

Blubaugh: The best mayor that I have ever worked with happened to be in Palm Springs before they had a directly elected mayor. He was elected by the council. The worst mayor that I ever worked with was a mayor in a city where all the council members were elected by district, but the mayor was elected at large. He did not have the ability to work as a policy leader with other members on the council. The structure doesn't guarantee success.

We're not talking about living in a time where things are becoming much more heterogeneous. We have different types of people on the council and lots of conflict. Nowhere is there training for that. On our own council in Walnut Creek, we have a system of electing the mayor on a yearly rotation. It may sound horrible but it works. One mayor came to me and asked, "How do I learn how to be a mayor? How do I become an advocate for policies?" There is no place to send individuals to learn these skills. As a profession we don't train managers in interpersonal dynamics, and we're certainly not providing this training for elected officials. We keep talking about the need for consensus decision making in our communities. I'm beginning to wonder after eight or nine years of being dedicated to consensus decision making, whether it is antithetical to the political process. Elected officials don't perceive themselves getting reelected by standing before the voters saying, "I work in collaboration with four other people at city hall. Look what we did."

Pokorny: I would take issue with something Don Blubaugh said and build on his comments. I think a great deal of leadership training is going on--however one defines it. I don't know whether it is going on in the kind of places where we're living. It is happening in strange places because the universities have not paid much attention to it. Harvard may be one exception. There they bring administrators and elected officials together in some of their short seminars on the policy process. I think a lot of training is taking place in local communities. I look around at my colleagues and the people I talk to, and they're running workshops on how to function as effective council members. They may not call it that. They probably don't call it training, because that's deadly. Elected officials resent being "trained." We talk about a whole lot of things--for example, goal setting and orientation--with inadequate theory and inadequate materials because the formal institutions haven't done much to address these issues. We've been focusing a lot on structures. I think we need to spend a lot more time on leadership theory and on leadership training.

The second thing that is happening in a lot of communities is community leadership efforts. I think it's an adaptive response that goes beyond the idea of leadership as limited to council members or mayors. These leadership efforts are often based in the business community. They are a response to frustration at dealing with great diversity and the fact that a lot of the old structures we took for granted are no longer there. So there's a need to run broadly based leadership programs. Those are coming back fairly strongly, at least in Oregon. I don't know what's happening around the country, but in my area there is reawakened interest in that kind of effort. I think we ought to be aware of and encourage these programs.

Svara: These comments show the importance of recognizing structures. But there is no simple structural solution to the problems we're talking about. If it meant the council electing a mayor who reflected the majority view of the council and that person remaining mayor as long as he or she was an effective spokesman for the council, that would be one thing. But actually council election may be rotating. The mayor may be the highest vote getter, so in effect you have direct election. There may be several other variations, but the important thing about direct elections is that we tell the mayor, "We sanction your political leadership. We expect it." There is a crying need for training for mayors, for better materials describing to mayors their role. The only models mayors have are based on their counterparts in executive mayor systems. They ask, "How do I achieve the same kind of visibility and take on the same role?"

Blubaugh: I'm not convinced that structural change along the lines of the model you're talking about, where you don't create an executive, is understood by other elected officials on the council. When I worked in

Hayward, the mayor was directly elected by the people; so were all the council members. The council members resented the mayor pushing what was perceived to his/her agenda.

Svara: A lot of the training of the mayors has to stress the facilitative dimension of the mayor's role. If the mayor doesn't start by knowing the council, by knowing what the council is trying to accomplish, and then building on that collective leadership, then the mayor's not going to be effective. It is also part of the way I've described the role. That job description stresses the facilitative mayor as opposed to the executive mayor.

Kerrigan: Listening to the managers it seems to me that there's an "ought" issue here. I suspect that there should be a formalization of what I would call the informal process that you talked about. I'm not so sure the structure is as important as the informal processes. It is useful to use a retreat to clarify the expectations for the manager, and the role of mayor--whether the position is elected by the council or by the citizens.

Anderson: One of the things that we need to do is to recognize the difference the structure makes but also to recognize the role models that we have within those structures. In talking about this with my council and in talking about a directly elected mayor, I would use Henry Cisneros in San Antonio as a model for the simplicity of the structure and how well the structure can work.

Novak: To answer John's question by analogy, I think I'm a much better city manager after several years of marriage counseling.

Newland: Often charter commissions tend to look for structural differences in the mayor's role and suggest separation of powers arrangements in which the mayor won't be part of the council.

My second point refers to Norm King's comment. More important than the structure is the quality of the leadership, the capacity for leadership. When we have pressure for abandonments, it is usually because the person who is in the role of mayor is weak. We can teach some of those weak people to be more effective.

Gleason: The mayor's position in Eugene is separately elected, has veto power, can only vote in a tie, but is a strong position. It doesn't challenge the manager's role at all. The strongest mayor we have ever had is the one we have right now. The weakest one we ever had was one of those that came from the council. The thing that seems to make a difference is the mayor's salary. When the mayor starts getting a certain level of income there is an ethic--that comes out of the Midwest, I suspect--that says, "I gotta work for this." Work means taking an executive role as opposed to contemplating policy. All of a sudden, they're mucking around with stuff they shouldn't be mucking around with. For a mayor, having a separate staff is an Achilles' heel. As soon as they have a separate staff, the staff has agendas. The staff starts having relationships with the mayor and/or council.

The third thing is proximity. If the mayor and/or council--particularly the mayor--is there all the time, it is a natural gravitation for issues to end up there. Power gravitates to the office.

Ammons: The conversation has focused on the mayoral role and whether the mayor is performing adequately. I wonder if there is an entirely different perception by mayors regarding city managers. For example, when Richard Knight was appointed city manager of Dallas, some of the published commentaries from council members indicated that this would be a good appointment because Richard Knight understands his role.

Hansell: I want to pick up on a point that Don Blubaugh made about the difficulty of achieving consensus in a competitive system. People who run for council don't say, "We did"; they say, "I did." Couple that with open meetings in which you expose yourself to the world if you're going to run for elected office and think in public. Council members may seek money reward. The council member's agenda is not necessarily in the broad public interest. One of the things we're struggling with is trying to adapt structure to that political reality. Bill Cassella has made a point about the lack of leadership model training for mayors in council-manager cities, and he is absolutely right. Some of the worst feedback has been on the Harvard program for mayors. On the positive side, people have talked in the last several years about Cisneros. I don't think we have ever been in a better position than we are today, in terms of role modeling for mayors in council-manager cities who are national leaders. Every officer of the National League of Cities is from a council-manager government. Most of the strong leadership on our executive committee comes from mayors in council-manager cities. The mayors in mayor-council cities are buried in day-to-day administration, and they are not able to provide political leadership. We need to research how mayors in council-manager cities are evolving, how they are doing their jobs, how they are finding time to develop national visibility, and why they are selected by their peers as political leaders.

Denton: If you have a chance to get someone to pay the $5000 for you, you ought to go. Harvard is influential; we ought to try to change Harvard's point of view if possible. One way is by going to the summer courses for managers if you can find the time. Then we can try to condition the Harvard leadership.

McIntyre: My experience with city council staffs has been positive. We've had separate staff for council members. We call them field representatives. When they were first appointed about ten years ago, I predicted they would be a disaster. We have had in ten years only one person who didn't work out. They've acted as good PR people; and they've worked well with staff. The council appoints them. They work for the council. We do not want them to be city staffers.

Schilling: In San Jose, I wouldn't say they have been a strong addition to the system, but they have not been strongly negative either. Each department spends time with them educating them and then they become outreach persons.

Borut: On council staffing there are mixed perspectives. When the managers of large cities get together, there have been heated debates. Indeed, the current city manager of San Diego argues that the independent staffing has increased the knowledge base of the elected official and that they are much more effective than in the past. In Phoenix, the manager appoints the staff and they are assigned to the elected officials. That system works well. There have been managers from some of the East Coast cities who were opposed to this system of staffing. It is a factor of the culture of the community and the political environment. There is no rule for the issue of staffing.

Toregas: I want to make one quick point because we talked so much about structure. One of the most successful programs at Public Technology, Incorporated (PTI) has been on strategic planning. Cities and counties--more counties than cities--seek us to provide unstructured approaches for involving county commissioners, professional staff, and business leaders simultaneously. Sometimes people are not so anxious to preserve a form of government as they are to help their community. Sometimes it's helpful to initiate new patterns and permutations and cross boundaries. Sometimes activities don't fit a particular structure or particular process.

Cassella: I heard a number of managers at Charlotte for the International City Management Association (ICMA) meeting comment on the positive local government environment in North Carolina. An important reason for that is the Institute of Government at the University of North Carolina. Elected officials go to the Institute to attend programs that have been going on for years. This opportunity gives them the kind of assistance that they need. Through this institute the state provides a support system for local officials. I think that more of our universities should provide support systems for local government like North Carolina does. As Woodrow Wilson said when he was at Princeton, "Princeton is a university in service of the nation." When you talk to mayors in North Carolina, you get a different response than you do in many other states.

Denton: It's done frequently through the state leagues of cities. In Kansas Ernie Mosher of the League of Kansas Municipalities has done that for many years.

The Roles,
the Work, and
the Values of the
City Manager

Role Emphases
of City Managers and
Other Municipal Executives

Charldean Newell
University of North Texas
David N. Ammons
University of Georgia

How city managers spend their time, how they ought to spend their time, and how they prefer to spend their time have been issues of both controversy and curiosity in public administration.[1] That the discipline remains interested in such issues is not surprising since they emerge from the fundamental nature of council-manager government and reflect the evolution of reform government in the United States.[2] Only slightly less attention has been directed toward similar questions regarding mayors as chief executives in cities with mayor-council government.[3]

The council-manager form of government was introduced in part to secure expert administration through the appointment of a chief executive with requisite managerial skills. The assumption at the outset was that the city manager would devote attention to the management function, generally refraining from policy or political involvement.[4]

Council-manager government is a product of its political time. Conceived in an era of dual concerns over blatant political influence in government and the desire to find the "one best way" to carry out the activities of government, council-manager government was at once the progeny and victim of the myth of the politics-administration dichotomy. Early proponents justified the new plan either as a vehicle for the application of Taylorism[5] and other management techniques in local government or as a means of achieving a desired separation of politics and administration. Later observers acknowledged the policy implications and political nature of city management, but some still debated their appropriateness. Modern students of council-manager government, with more "science" and less "prescription," have examined the roles played by city managers, mayors, and council members, and have detected considerable overlap,[6] as well as conflicts between elected and nonelected officials arising from role dissonance.[7]

Although early notions of the manager as a technician, devoid of political or policy responsibilities, have been modified,[8] if not discarded, the mere acceptance of a broader set of roles reveals little about the dimensions or priorities of those roles. Deil Wright's pioneering work on the role perceptions of city managers in 1965 exposed the extent of executive involvement beyond the "management role"[9] and set the stage for this inquiry, which re-examines city managers on a broader scale and compares their role perceptions with those of other key municipal executives--mayors and mayoral assistants in mayor-council and commission cities and assistant city managers in council-manager cities.

Wright's 1965 data provide a baseline for comparison of city manager role perceptions after 20 years.

The relevance of issues pertaining to the role perceptions of executives themselves and role expectations held by other local government actors, constituents, and scholars suggests a series of research questions about changes in managerial perceptions as council-manager government has evolved over the years and about contrasts between the perceptions of city managers and other municipal administrators. Do chief executives and their assistants acknowledge "policy" and "political" roles, as well as a management role? What role dominates the time of city managers? What role do they see as most important? What role do they prefer to play? How do the roles and preferences of assistant city managers, mayors who serve as administrators of non-manager cities, and the chief assistants to those mayors differ from those of city managers?

Methodology of 1985 Managerial Time Allocation Study

A survey of 839 chief executives and principal assistants in the 418 U. S. cities having a 1980 population of 50,000 or greater was completed during the spring of 1985. This survey population represents a much larger segment of the total universe of municipal executives than that surveyed by Wright, who examined only city managers in cities of greater than 100,000 population. In council-manager cities, questionnaires were mailed to the city manager (or to the city manager equivalent in a given city--e.g., municipal manager, village manager) and to one or more assistant city managers or persons of similar title (e.g., deputy city manager, assistant village manager, assistant to the city manager). In mayor-council and commission cities, questionnaires were mailed to the mayor and to the person identified as the chief appointed official or the mayor's principal assistant (e.g., chief administrative officer, city administrator, deputy mayor, assistant to the mayor). Although each official was encouraged to respond personally, the instructions acknowledged the likelihood that some questionnaires would be completed by aides and simply requested that such aides identify themselves in a space provided on the survey instrument.

Responses were received from 559 officials (66.6 percent), but 32 were identified as having been completed by aides. The remaining 527 responses (62.8 percent), reportedly completed by officials personally, provide the data for the analysis presented here; the 32 responses from aides are excluded.

Among the time allocation dimensions explored in the survey were the perceptions of city officials regarding their allocation of time to the three role categories introduced by Wright in his study. In a series of three questions, respondents were asked to indicate the approximate percentage of time that they devote to the management role, to the policy role, and to the political role; the approximate percentage of time that they would *prefer* to devote to each of the three roles; and which of the three roles they believe to be most important to the successful performance of their job. In order to parallel the Wright study, the management role was associated parenthetically on the questionnaire with administrative activities; the policy role was clarified to include council relations; and the political role was associated with community leadership.

Wright's perception of the management role includes such functions as staffing, budgeting, and supervision, including reporting relationships. The policy role includes control over the council agenda and policy initiation and formulation, while the political role includes relationships with nongovernmental groups and individuals within the city and intergovernmental relations.

Although some ambiguity exists in the role distinctions suggested by Wright, the ambiguity is modest compared to the degree of apparent consensus on the principal components of the three roles. Popular perceptions regarding the management role normally include such activities as staffing, directing, evaluating, counseling, coordinating, preparing budgets, and executing policy. The policy role is typically thought to include the development of proposals for future city policy, contacts and individual meetings with the mayor or members of the city council, council meetings, responding to special requests of council members, the orchestrating of controversial issues on council agendas, and managerial defense of or opposition to ticklish budgetary items. Perceptions of the political role normally include all actions taken to enhance influence with officials of state, federal, and other local governments, nongovernmental groups, and individuals, as well as public relations encompassing meetings, speeches, and ceremonies. The analysis that follows relies on the existence of a general consensus regarding Wright's role distinctions, as the questions were asked without benefit of elaborate definition.

Findings

Analysis of the 1985 data has three foci: time allocation differences among city managers, assistant city managers, mayors, and mayoral assistants; identification of explanatory variables of relevance to differing allocations of managerial time; and a comparison of the 1985 data with Wright's 1965 findings.

Differences among Municipal Executives and Assistants

City government chief executives and their principal assistants work much more than the standard 40-hour week (Table 1). Mayors and their assistants in mayor-council and commission cities report average workweeks of 66.4 and 59 hours, respectively. City managers and their assistants report average workweeks of 56.5 and 52.7 hours, respectively. Each of these means differs significantly ($p < .05$) from each of the other three position means. Mayors and their assistants in non-council-manager cities tend to spend more hours per week performing their functions than do city managers and their assistants, presumably because the former must both manage and provide overt political leadership. Generally, but not uniformly, the number of hours worked increases as city size increases.

All four groups of city officials tend to devote a more substantial portion of their time to the management role than to the policy role or the political role (Tables 2, 3, and 4). Only mayors as a group spend less than half of their time on the management role--though at 44.2 percent that role still commands the lion's share of mayoral time. Mayoral and managerial assistants report greater percentage time allocations to the management role than do their bosses, suggesting municipal evidence of a dyadic relationship reported in the private

Table 1
Mean Weekly Working Hours of Municipal Chief Executives and Primary Assistants

		Position			
	Mayors	Mayoral Assistants	City Managers	Assistant City Mgrs.	Mean
Jurisdiction Population (1980)	Hrs. (N)	Hrs. (N)	Hrs. (N)	Hrs. (N)	Hrs. (N)
50,000-74,999	64.8 (28)	55.2 (25)	55.6 (61)	51.8 (72)	55.5 (186)
75,000-100,000	67.6 (14)	57.5 (20)	55.0 (29)	53.0 (42)	56.3 (105)
Greater than 100,000	67.4 (28)	61.3 (53)	58.2 (59)	53.2 (83)	58.2 (223)
Mean	66.4* (70)	59.0* (98)	56.5* (149)	52.7* (197)	56.8 (514)

*Mean comparisons (t-tests) for the four positions are significant at the 0.05 level.

Table 2
Mean Percentage of Time Devoted to the "Management Role," by Position and 1980 Population of Jurisdiction Served

		Position			
	Mayors	Mayoral Assistants	City Managers	Assistant City Mgrs.	Mean
Jurisdiction Population (1980)	% (N)	% (N)	% (N)	% (N)	% (N)
50,000-74,999	48.6 (29)	61.7 (27)	51.7 (57)	62.6 (73)	57.0 (186)
75,000-100,000	48.8 (13)	54.0 (20)	49.5 (29)	63.1 (43)	55.9 (105)
Greater than 100,000	37.8 (29)	52.6 (53)	50.6 (56)	57.7 (82)	52.0* (220)
Mean	44.2* (71)	55.3* (100)	50.8* (142)	60.7* (198)	54.6 (511)

*Mean comparisons (t-tests) for the four positions are significant at the 0.05 level. The mean of the largest population group differs significantly from both other groups, although the small and intermediate population group means are not significantly different from one another.

sector literature "in which the chief executive concentrates on the external roles (figurehead, liaison, spokesman, negotiator), leaving much of the responsibility for the internal roles (leader, disseminator, resource allocator, disturbance handler) to his second in command."[10]

Comparison of the two types of chief executives reveals that city managers spend significantly more of their time on both the management role (50.8 percent) and the policy role (32.2 percent) than do the mayors (44.2 percent and 25.6 percent, respectively), who spend almost twice as much of their time on the political role (30.2 percent compared to 17 percent for the city managers). Given the historic rationale for mayor-council government in larger cities, namely that it provides strong political leadership, this difference in allocation of time is not surprising insofar as the management and political roles are

Table 3
Mean Percentage of Time Devoted to the "Policy Role,"
by Position and 1980 Population of Jurisdiction Served

	Position				
	Mayors	Mayoral Assistants	City Managers	Assistant City Mgrs.	Mean
Jurisdiction Population (1980)	% (N)	% (N)	% (N)	% (N)	% (N)
50,000-74,999	24.6 (29)	22.4 (27)	30.1 (57)	24.4 (73)	25.9 (186)
75,000-100,000	24.2 (13)	29.6 (20)	34.1 (29)	23.6 (43)	27.7 (105)
Greater than 100,000	27.2 (29)	28.4 (53)	33.4 (56)	28.5 (82)	29.6 (220)
Mean	25.6 (71)	27.0 (100)	32.2* (142)	25.9 (198)	27.8 (511)

*Mean comparisons (t-tests) between city managers as a group (32.2) and other three positions are significant at the 0.05 level. No other position-to-position comparisons are significant at that level. Only the comparison of the means of the 50,000-74,999 population group as a whole (25.9) and the 100,000-plus population group (29.6) yielded a t-test significant at the 0.05 level.

Table 4
Mean Percentage of Time Devoted to the "Political Role,"
by Position and 1980 Population of Jurisdiction Served

	Position				
	Mayors	Mayoral Assistants	City Managers	Assistant City Mgrs.	Mean
Jurisdiction Population (1980)	% (N)	% (N)	% (N)	% (N)	% (N)
50,000-74,999	26.8 (29)	15.9 (27)	18.2 (57)	13.0 (73)	17.2 (186)
75,000-100,000	26.9 (13)	16.4 (20)	16.4 (29)	13.3 (43)	16.4 (105)
Greater than 100,000	35.0 (29)	19.0 (53)	16.0 (56)	13.8 (82)	18.4 (220)
Mean	30.2* (71)	17.6 (100)	17.0 (142)	13.4* (198)	17.5 (511)

*Only mayors as a group and assistant city managers as a group have means that differ significantly (t-test, 0.05 level) from all other groups.

concerned. The extensive involvement of city managers in policy matters, however, clearly contradicts an early assumption of that form of government.

The municipal official's position (i.e., mayor, city manager, mayoral assistant, or assistant city manager) and the population of the jurisdiction served explain 25.8 percent of the variance in working hours per week among the respondents and 22.4 percent of the variance in percentage of time devoted to the political role (general linear models F=15.90 and 13.06, respectively; p=.000). Those variables, however, account for only 15.1 percent of the variance in percentage of time devoted to the management role (F=8.07; p=.000) and 8 percent of the variance in percentage of time devoted to the policy role (F=3.97; p=.000).

Table 5
Mean Percentage of Time Devoted to Specified Roles and
Preferred Allocation, by Position

	N	Management Role	Policy Role	Political Role
Mayors	71			
Actual		44.2	25.6	30.2
Preferred		40.4	29.4	30.2
Difference		-3.8	+3.8	0.0
Mayoral Assistants	100			
Actual		55.3	27.0	17.6
Preferred		50.6	30.7	18.6
Difference		-4.7	+3.7	+1.0
City Managers	142			
Actual		50.8	32.2	17.0
Preferred		50.7	32.1	17.2
Difference		-0.1	-0.1	+0.2
Assistant City Mgrs.	198			
Actual		60.7	25.9	13.4
Preferred		57.5	27.9	14.6
Difference		-3.2	+2.0	+1.2

Most officials appear to be generally satisfied with their allocation of time to the three roles. Differences in mean responses by position to the questions of actual time allocation and preferred time allocation were modest--especially for city managers (Table 5).

Examination of Explanatory Variables

Responses of chief executives--mayors and city managers--were examined in greater detail in an attempt to identify potential explanatory variables of relevance to differences in working hours and percentages of time devoted to the management, policy, and political roles. Eight variables were examined for their relevance to executive working hours through the step-wise regression technique: (1) population of the jurisdiction served, (2) age of the chief executive, (3) whether the chief executive was a mayor or a city manager, (4) whether the executive held a master of public administration (MPA) degree, (5) number of years the executive had been employed in the current position, (6) percentage of time allocated to the management role, (7) percentage of time allocated to the policy role, and (8) percentage of time allocated to the political role (Table 6). Only the position and age of the official were found to be significant at the 0.05 level, explaining 20.6 percent of the variance in working hours per week. The likelihood of longer working hours increased if the official served as mayor rather than city manager and decreased as the age of the official increased.

A similar process was used to explore possible explanatory variables for percentage of time devoted to each of the three executive roles. Six potential explanatory variables were examined: (1) population of the jurisdiction, (2) age of the chief executive, (3) whether the executive was a mayor or city manager, (4) whether the executive held an MPA degree, (5) working hours per week, and (6) years employed in current position. Four significant variables combined to explain 13.3 percent of the variance in percentage of time devoted to the management role. Not surprisingly, city managers were more likely than mayors to devote greater percentages of their time to the management role. Older executives and those serving smaller populations were also more likely

Table 6
Summary of Significant Explanatory Variables Identified through Stepwise
Regression for Working Hour and Time Allocation Variation among Mayors and City Managers
(N=205)

Dependent Variable	Explanatory Variable	B-Value sign (+/-)	Partial R^2	Cumulative R^2	F	Significance
Working Hrs.	MAYOR[a]	+	.184	.184	45.6	.000
Per Week	AGE[b]	-	.022	.206	5.6	.019
Percentage of Time						
Devoted to	MAYOR[a]	-	.040	.040	8.5	.004
"Management	MPA[c]	-	.040	.080	8.8	.003
Role"	POPULATION[d]	-	.025	.106	5.7	.018
	AGE[b]	+	.02	.133	6.4	.012
Percentage of Time						
Devoted to	MAYOR[a]	-	.066	.066	14.4	.000
"Policy	AGE[b]	-	.039	.105	8.8	.003
Role"	POPULATION[d]	+	.034	.139	7.8	.006
Percentage of Time Devoted to						
"Political	MAYOR[a]	+	.242	.242	64.9	.000
Role"	MPA[c]	+	.015	.258	4.1	.044

[a]MAYOR variable is coded "1" for mayors and "0" for city managers.

[b]AGE variable is coded "1" for 35 or younger, "2" for 36 to 50, "3" for 51 to 65, and "4" for 66 or more.

[c]MPA variable is coded "1" for master of public administration degrees or equivalent (e.g., MGA); "0" for other degrees or levels of education.

[d]POPULATION variable is the 1980 census population.

Notes:
(1) Variables included in the analysis of the dependent variable "working hours per week" were: years employed in current position, percentage of time allocated to the "management role," percentage of time allocated to the "policy role," percentage of time allocated to the "political role," and the four variables described above--mayor, age, MPA, and population.
(2) Variables included in the analysis of the dependent variables dealing with percentage time allocations were: working hours per week, years employed in current position, and the four variables described in footnotes a-d.
(3) Only variables significant at the 0.05 level are included in the models.

to devote greater portions of their time to administrative activities. Furthermore, officials holding MPA degrees tended to devote lower percentages of their time to the management role than did those without such training. Such a finding is surprising if one considers the MPA to be a professional management degree narrowly construed, but much less surprising when one considers the vehemence with which many modern public administration scholars have refuted the notion of public executives as mere technicians.[11]

Three significant variables were found to explain 13.9 percent of the variance in percentage of time devoted to the policy role among mayors and city managers. City managers, younger officials, and those serving larger populations were likely to devote greater percentages of their time to the policy role.

Two significant explanatory variables accounted for 25.8 percent of the variance in percentage of time devoted to the political role among chief executive respondents. Mayors and officials holding an MPA degree were more likely than their counterparts to devote greater percentages of time to the political role.

Table 7
Municipal Officials' 1985 Designation of Most Important Role Compared with
Wright's 1965 Findings (Populations Greater than 100,000)

Role perceived as most important to job success	Wright's Study of City Managers 1965[a,d]	City Mgrs. 1985[a]	Mayors 1985[b]	Assts. in Council-Mgr. Cities 1985[a]	Mayoral Assts. 1985[b]
Management Role (administrative activities)	37%	38.5%	23.1%	75.0%	75.5%
Policy Role (and council relations)	22%	55.8%	34.6%	25.0%	18.4%
Political Role (community leadership)	33%	5.8%	42.3%	0.0%	6.1%
N	45	52[c]	26[c]	80[c]	49[c]

[a]Council-manager form of government.

[b]Mayor-council or commission form of government.

[c]Missing data and ties are omitted from computations.

[d]Deil S. Wright, "The City Manager as a Development Administrator," Chapter 6 in *Comparative Urban Research: The Administration and Politics of Cities*, Robert T. Daland, ed. (Beverly Hills: Sage Publications, 1969), p. 236. While this chapter appeared in 1969, the data were gathered in 1965. The Wright table does not add to 100 percent.

Comparison with Wright's 1965 Findings

Wright found that 37 percent of the respondents in his 1965 survey of city managers perceived the management role as being most important to job success. The political role was identified as most important by 33 percent of his respondents and the policy role by 22 percent. Wright's findings are compared in Table 7 with the responses of the four groups of city officials included in this study. Since Wright's data were drawn only from officials serving cities of greater than 100,000 population, the responses of officials serving smaller jurisdictions in 1985 were omitted from the tabulation.

The percentage of city managers in 1985 perceiving the management role as most important is remarkably similar to the 1965 response--38.5 percent in 1985 compared to 37 percent in 1965. In contrast, only 23 percent of the mayors perceived the management role to be most important to job success, while 75 percent of the managerial and mayoral assistants perceived it to be their most important role.

The most striking contrast between Wright's 1965 findings and the 1985 responses is the dramatic increase in the proportion of city managers perceiving the policy role to be most important and a correspondingly dramatic drop in the percentage perceiving the political role as most important. While 22 percent of Wright's respondents deemed the policy role most important and 33 percent the political role, 55.8 percent of the 1985 city managers regarded the policy role as most important and only 5.8 percent so designated the political role. Among these respondents, only the mayors accorded the degree of preeminence to the political role granted by Wright's city managers.

Conclusions

The classical theorists of council-manager government were correct in their assumption that form does make a difference. Although scholars may debate the degree to which form influences policy and service, form of government does influence the activities and role emphases of key officials. City managers and mayors, both of whom serve as chief executives, clearly differ as to how they allocate their time, how they prefer to allocate it, and which role they see as most important to job success. Furthermore, level of executive responsibility--as well as form of government--prescribes differences between the emphases of chief executives and their assistants. Most assistants are appointed primarily to assist with managerial functions, and their responses so indicate.

Perhaps more important than distinctions deriving from different positions and forms of government are perceptual changes among persons filling a particular executive post--changes made evident among city managers in this case by Wright's 1965 baseline data. The job of the city manager has evolved over time, with fewer managers perceiving community leadership as their key role and more according policy initiation and council relations that priority. One may speculate that these differences have been propelled, at least in part, by the trend beginning in the 1970s for council-manager cities to amend their city charters to provide for direct election of the mayor and council elections by districts. Direct mayoral election more clearly established an official with a mandate to fill the high-profile community leadership role and to perform public relations duties, while district election of council members simultaneously created a greater need for, but more difficulty in gaining, consensus for public policy. Thus, it is no wonder that the modern city manager emphasizes the policy and council relations role. Richard Childs and other early advocates of a separation of politics and administration could at least be pleased with the nominal de-emphasis by city managers of the overtly political role.

The results of this study suggest that researchers hoping to account for major portions of the variance in executive time allocation in local government are likely to be challenged greatly. The variety of factors impinging on the executive post and its incumbent defy simple explanation. Henry Mintzberg, a noted authority on executive roles and time allocation in the private sector, posits a contingency theory of managerial work that holds that an executive's actions are influenced by four complex variables: the environment, the job, the personality and style of the incumbent, and the situation.[12] Surely, the determinants of municipal executive work are no less complex. Considered in this light, models such as those presented here that account for 26, 21, or even 13 percent of the variance in executive time allocation using only two, three, or four executive and community characteristics are less remarkable for how little they explain than for how much.

Notes

Data collection for this paper was supported by a Faculty Research Grant from North Texas State University. The authors wish to acknowledge the assistance of Victor M. Boyer in the initial stages of the project.

1. An excellent example of the debate remains the symposium found in *Public Administration Review*, vol. 18 (Summer 1958), pp. 208-222.   The politics-administration dichotomy underlay

this series of articles, although earlier writers had demonstrated the flaws in the concept. See, for example, Paul Appleby, *Policy and Administration* (University: University of Alabama Press, 1949).

2. The classic examination of reform versus nonreform government can be found in Robert L. Lineberry and Edmund P. Fowler, "Reformism and Public Policies in American Cities," *American Political Science Review*, vol. 61 (September 1967), pp. 701-716.

3. See, for example, John P. Kotter and Paul R. Lawrence, *Mayors in Action: Five Approaches to Urban Governance* (New York: John Wiley and Sons, 1974).

4. See, for example, Richard S. Childs, *The First 50 Years of the Council-Manager Plan of Municipal Government* (New York: National Municipal League, 1965); John Porter East, *Council-Manager Government: The Political Thought of Its Founder, Richard S. Childs* (Chapel Hill: University of North Carolina Press, 1965); and Richard J. Stillman II, *The Rise of the City Manager: A Public Professional in Local Government* (Albuquerque: University of New Mexico Press, 1974), especially pp. 5-27.

5. See Frederick W. Taylor, *The Principles of Scientific Management* (New York: Harper and Bros., 1911).

6. James H. Svara posits the existence of a four-category continuum depicting both the sharing and separation of responsibilities. Elected officials dominate "mission," share responsibility with managers for "policy" and "administration," and yield "management" to the managers. See Svara, "Political Supremacy and Administrative Expertise," *Management Science and Policy Analysis*, vol. 3 (Summer 1985), pp. 3-7, and "Dichotomy and Duality: Reconceptualizing the Relationship Between Policy and Administration in Council-Manager Cities," *Public Administration Review*, vol. 45 (January/February 1985), pp. 221-232. See also Edward B. Lewis, "Role Behavior of U. S. City Managers: Development and Testing of a Multidimensional Typology," *International Journal of Public Administration*, vol. 4 (No. 2, 1982), pp. 135-165; Frank Aleshire and Fran Aleshire, "The American City Manager: New Style, New Game, " *National Civic Review* (May 1977), pp. 235-239; and Neil Wikstrom, "The Mayor as a Policy Leader in the Council-Manager Form of Government: A View from the Field," *Public Administration Review*, vol. 39 (May/June 1979), pp. 270-276.

7. Among the many citations that might be provided are Gladys M. Kammerer *et al.*, *City Managers in Politics: An Analysis of Manager Tenure and Termination*, University of Florida Monographs, Social Sciences, No. 13 (Gainesville: University of Florida Press, 1962); Jeptha J. Carrell, "The Role of the City Manager: A Survey Report," *Public Management*, vol. 44 (April 1961), pp. 73-78; John C. Buechner, *Differences in Role Perceptions in Colorado Council-Manager Cities* (Boulder: Bureau of Governmental Research and Service, University of Colorado, 1965); Ronald O. Loveridge, *City Managers in Legislative Politics* (Indianapolis: Bobbs-Merrill, 1971); and Robert J. Huntley and Robert J. Macdonald, "Urban Managers: Organization Preferences, Managerial Styles, and Social Policy Roles," *The Municipal Year Book* (Washington: International City Management Association, 1975), pp. 149-159.

8. Modification of the concept of the city manager began early, as was evident in Harold A. Stone, Don K. Price, and Kathryn H. Stone, *City Manager Government in the United States: A Review After Twenty-five Years* (Chicago: Public Administrative Service, 1940). Clarence Ridley's changing views can be traced in Clarence E. Ridley and Orin Nolting, *The City Manager Profession* (Chicago: University of Chicago Press, 1934), and Clarence E. Ridley, *The Role of the City Manager in Policy Formulation* (Chicago: International City Managers' Association, 1958).

9. Deil S. Wright, "The City Manager as a Developmental Administrator," Chapter 6 in *Comparative Urban Research*, Robert T. Daland, ed. (Beverly Hills: Sage Publications, 1969), pp. 203-248.

10. Henry Mintzberg, *The Nature of Managerial Work* (Englewood Cliffs, NJ: Prentice-Hall, 1980), p. 131. *The importance of a good second in command in the case of mayors is noted in Kotter and Lawrence, Mayors in Action, pp. 234-236.*

11. Among the many illustrations of the growing complexity of the city manager's job, including policy and political responsibilities are the following: David Welborn, "The Environment and Role of the Administrator," Chapter 4 in *Managing the Modern City*, James M. Banovetz, ed. (Washington: International City Management Association, 1971), pp. 77-107; Richard J. Stillman II, "Local Public Management in Transition: A Report on the Current State of the Profession," *The Municipal Year Book* (Washington: International City Management Association, 1975), pp. 161-173; and David R. Morgan, "Managing the Urban Future," Chapter 12 in *Managing Urban America*, 2d ed. (Monterey, CA: Brooks/Cole, 1984), pp. 312-326.

12. Mintzberg, *The Nature of Managerial Work*, p. 102. Using Mintzberg's framework, Alan W. Lau, Arthur R. Newman, and Laurie A. Broedling found similar complexities in the work of federal executives; see "The Nature of Managerial Work in the Public Sector," *Public Administration Review*, vol. 40 (September/October 1980), pp. 513-520.

The Values
of City Management

Edward G. Schilling
Stone & Youngberg
San Francisco, California

America's progressive era, covering roughly the first two decades of the 20th century, was a period of revolutionary ideas in literature, art, architecture, religion, sociology, economics and government. The changes which progressives brought to the institutions of American government were profound and long-lasting, born primarily out of middle class reactions to the negative by-products of rapid urbanization and the rise of big business. Scientific management and public administration are related aspects of a general movement of the early twentieth century to extend the method and spirit of science to a widening range of society's concerns. Dwight Waldo and others have identified both movements with a philosophical point of view closely related to August Comte's "positivism." Both movements seek a growing range of indisputable fact, an extension of rule by law, and the substitution of science and measure for metaphysics.[1]

The council-manager form of local government was developed under the influences of both the progressive movement and scientific management. While the council-manager form of government encompasses conflicting values from its mixed parentage, early city managers appear to have favored scientific management techniques and values over the more moralistic and democratic values of progressivism. This preference was not unique to city managers. Economy, efficiency, and other quasi-scientific concepts superseded the moralistic approach as the blueprint for improving all levels of American government. As a result the rallying cries of the progressive movement, "fidelity," honesty," and "national pride," were superseded by the managerial values of "economy," "efficiency," and the "one best way."[2]

The contemporary city manager, educated in government and public administration, is likely to have adopted many of the traditional values which underlie the creation of the council-manager plan, along with other key values from the study of administrative theory and organizational behavior. These professional values, and related personal values, have been reinforced and/or modified through municipal administrative experience.

The objective of this study was to complement the existing literature on city managers with a detailed examination of city manager values. The study included an extensive analysis of existing literature about city managers and the council-manager plan, and a survey of California city managers which was conducted in 1983. The study and its research methodology followed values research on public executives completed by Edwards, Nalbandian and Wedel[3] in the late 1970s and preceded similar work which was published by Schmidt and Posner[4] in the mid-1980s.

How Manager Values Influence the Organization

City managers hold influential positions in cities, towns and villages across the United States and in other countries around the western world. This key group of urban administrative leaders and policy advisors affects the organization and interaction of city employees by prescribing or interpreting personnel rules, recruiting new personnel, defining training objectives, and allowing or disallowing the development of internal group interests.[5]

Chester Barnard describes the distinguishing mark of executive responsibility as the creation of a "moral code" for others. "This is the process of inculcating points of view, fundamental attitudes, loyalties to the organization or cooperative system, and to the system of objective authority, that will result in subordinating individual interest and the minor dictates of personal codes to the good of the cooperative whole."[6]

Values are implicit in administrative designs, management theories and various applications of technology. Additionally, the way in which values are reflected in the design and operation of social organizations plays an important role in creating community values by influencing the individual values of those who come in contact with those organizations.[7]

At its most basic level, a primary role of government is the resolution of community value conflicts. As the most important professional advisor to elected council members, the city manager frequently defines the nature of questions brought before the council, and generally makes a recommendation which provides a starting point for the decision-making discussion. The city manager's values will be both visible and influential in this process and will often play a larger role in the outcome of a decision than the values of any individual council member. Even if the values asserted by a manager are associated with efficiency, effectiveness and economy, which are virtually inseparable from the definition of professional management, these values may be at odds with other community and council held values such as equality, freedom of choice, and the right to use one's property as one would choose.

Survey Methodology

In 1983, 213 California city managers (57.6% of the 370 city manager positions occupied at the time) responded to a value survey. The survey instrument invited respondents to rank, according to their personal sense of importance, 54 values divided into three categories of 18 each: terminal values, instrumental values, and managerial values. Each respondent was also asked to complete a short list of demographic questions.

The results of the value survey were analyzed to determine how city managers as a professional group differed from members of the general public, from other occupational groups, and, based upon demographic subgroupings, from one another. The responses were also factor analyzed to determine if there were underlying clusters of values which could describe the range of value preferences more succinctly than the 18 values in each list.

The overall value rankings and basic descriptive statistics associated with each are described in Tables 1, 2, and 3.

Based on an analysis of the value rankings one must conclude that city managers in California are concerned primarily with getting a job done well, through their own actions or through the work of others. The values of effectiveness, achievement, capability, and sense of accomplishment are among the top choices in the three value lists. The managers' strong sense of personal responsibility for the work of their municipal organizations is reflected in their placement of the values accountability and responsibility near the top of their respective lists, and in their ranking of the value administrative leadership as the highest of the management values.

The fact that city managers hold themselves and others to high standards of personal and professional behavior is reflected in their concern for the values honesty, courage, and fairness. The importance of

Table 1
Comparison of Terminal Value Responses

Terminal Values	1983 City Managers		1968 Adult Americans		1968 Americans $15,000+	
A Comfortable Life	11.36	(11)	9.0	(9)	13.40	(14)
An Exciting Life	9.88	(9)	15.3	(18)	14.25	(16)
A Sense of Accomplishment	4.58	(2)	9.0	(10)	6.08	(5)
A World at Peace	12.63	(13)	3.3	(1)	3.47	(1)
A World of Beauty	14.71	(16)	13.6	(15)	12.57	(13)
Equality	12.53	(12)	8.5	(7)	7.46	(6)
Family Security	3.92	(1)	3.8	(2)	4.09	(2)
Freedom	7.29	(5)	5.5	(3)	5.00	(3)
Health	5.21	(3)	*		*	
Inner Harmony	8.40	(6)	10.5	(13)	9.20	(9)
Mature Love	9.30	(8)	12.5	(14)	11.75	(12)
National Security	15.55	(17)	9.5	(12)	11.33	(11)
Pleasure	13.72	(15)	14.6	(17)	15.20	(18)
Salvation	16.41	(18)	8.8	(8)	13.25	(15)
Self Respect	5.25	(4)	7.7	(5)	7.75	(7)
Social Recognition	12.81	(14)	14.4	(16)	14.55	(17)
True Friendship	10.89	(10)	9.3	(11)	9.38	(10)
Wisdom	8.85	(7)	8.0	(6)	5.55	(4)

*See note, Table 2.

living in a manner which is consistent with those values is demonstrated in their concern for self-respect and inner harmony.

In spite of the emphasis placed on ethical behavior, city managers are not rigidly idealistic. They rate the value of practicality highly, while assigning the value of idealism to the bottom third of the management values list.

City managers rate the value of family security at the top of the terminal values list, and include the value of health close behind. They also demonstrate appreciation for the autonomy which their chief executive position offers by ranking the values of freedom and independent in the top third.

In spite of the relatively high percentage of managers who are members of the International City Management Association (ICMA), the value of professionalism is accorded a relatively low standing in the management value list. Other management values which are clearly out of favor for the majority of California city managers are consensus, rationality, political leadership[8], and independence (freedom from political interference).

Table 2
Comparison of Instrumental Value Responses

Instrumental Values	1983 City Managers		1968 Adult Americans		1968 Americans $15,000+	
Ambitious	9.14	(8)	6.5	(2)	6.38	(3)
Broadminded	9.44	(9)	7.5	(5)	7.00	(4)
Capable	5.36	(3)	9.5	(9)	8.81	(8)
Clean	16.43	(17)	8.7	(8)	14.35	(17)
Courageous	8.70	(6)	7.8	(6)	7.20	(5)
Forgiving	12.53	(15)	7.2	(4)	10.69	(12)
Helpful	10.53	(11)	8.2	(7)	9.08	(9)
Honest	2.84	(1)	3.3	(1)	3.00	(1)
Imaginative	8.64	(5)	15.4	(18	11.40	(15)
Independent	8.61	(4)	10.5	(13)	8.25	(6)
Intellectual	10.95	(12)	13.0	(15)	8.56	(7)
Logical	8.75	(7)	14.2	(17)	10.94	(13)
Loving	11.96	(14)	9.7	(11)	9.81	(10)
Loyal	10.47	(10)	*		*	
Obedient	17.10	(18)	13.3	(16)	15.29	(18)
Polite	14.46	(16)	10.8	(14)	13.19	(16)
Responsible	4.78	(2)	6.7	(3)	5.85	(2)
Self-Controlled	10.96	(13)	9.6	(10)	9.92	(11)

* The earlier version of the Rokeach Value Survey included two values which are not part of the instrument used for this survey. The Terminal value of Happiness and the Instrumental value of Cheerful have been replaced respectively by the values of Health and Loyalty.

144

The relatively low ranking which managers assigned to the terminal value of equality also demands attention. City managers in 1983 ranked this value significantly lower than did members of the general public in 1968. While some of that difference can be explained by the heightened sensitivity toward race-related issues in the late 1960s, it is nevertheless alarming that governmental leaders who have as much influence as city managers appear to have become casual about the importance of guaranteeing equal rights for all persons. The actions of ICMA leaders in recent years to enhance opportunities for minorities and women in local government management demonstrates that concern for equality is a part of the professional organization's agenda for change.

While the value survey method used for this study provides no way of measuring the intensity with which values are held, the author's close acquaintance with city managers over sixteen years prompts the observation that most managers have a strong sense of personal value priorities and confidence in their own sense of what is right in situations where value choices are required. This characteristic is communicated to others through the sense of self assurance which most city managers project.

Table 3
Management Value Responses

Management Values	1983 City Managers			
	Median		Mean	Standard Deviation
Accountability	6.68	(3)	6.97	4.77
Achievement	7.47	(5)	7.84	5.23
Adaptability	10.11	(11)	9.63	4.30
Administrative Leadership	4.50	(1)	5.35	4.31
Challenge	9.45	(8)	8.93	4.60
Consensual	13.37	(15)	12.17	4.46
Creativity	9.25	(7)	9.20	5.02
Dignity	9.86	(10)	8.82	4.67
Effectiveness	5.08	(2)	5.67	3.78
Efficiency	11.25	(12)	10.37	4.30
Fairness	7.43	(4)	7.56	4.30
Idealism	12.39	(14)	11.01	5.33
Independence	14.23	(17)	12.46	4.88
Political Leadership	15.82	(18)	13.62	4.64
Practicality	8.83	(6)	8.70	4.62
Professionalism	12.19	(13)	10.91	4.90
Rationality	13.73	(16)	12.46	4.37
Service	9.62	(9)	9.25	5.17

The picture of the city manager reflected in the survey's value rankings reinforces the characterizations which informed observers have sketched over the seventy-five years that city managers have been at work. A description of city managers from Stone, Price and Stone's 1940 *City Manager Government in the United States* illustrates this fact:

> There was no typical city manager. Nevertheless managers possessed some common characteristics. They were in general *capable* administrators with a *professional* attitude toward their work. They were well-educated, *practical* men, experienced in some phase of public or private administration. In general they possessed a serious bent of mind and great enthusiasm for their work. They were men of *direct action* who could make decisions and could stick to them. They were *honest* men. They were, in fact, so bluntly honest that they often caused discomfort to others in public life.[9] (emphasis added)

Because of the diversity of value profiles which exist among the respondents, the aggregated median, mean and standard deviation statistics on the entire sample can convey only a skeletal outline of the value structures of contemporary city managers. The important questions about how city manager values relate to the dynamics of the city manager job and what contemporary value preferences might mean for the future of the profession can only begin to be answered with the individual responses and the aggregated statistics. To facilitate a more meaningful analysis, responses were also subjected to factor analysis with rotation of factors to a final solution according to the Varimax criterion (see Table 4).[10]

The "managerial values" are effectiveness, efficiency, practicality and rationality. Based on survey results, the managers who are most likely to favor the "managerial values" include those from southwestern states, those who have an average tenure of six years or more in their present position, those who are unmarried, and those who express a preference for Republican politics. Thirty-four respondents ranked the four "managerial values" at or above the median. Their average age was 47.3 and the percentage who had completed a masters degree was 59 percent.

The "humanist values" are dignity, fairness, idealism and service. The survey results identify as managers who tend to favor the values of humanism those with a preference for Democratic or non-traditional politics, those who are currently employed in an urban area, and those who are married. Thirty-three managers fit the humanist "ideal type" profile. The average age of that group was 43.6 and the percentage with a masters degree was 70 percent.

The "entrepreneur values" are achievement, challenge, creativity, and adaptability. The profile of city managers who tend to favor "entrepreneur values" include those who were raised in an eastern or northeastern state and those who majored in a liberal arts field as an undergraduate. Thirty managers fit the entrepreneur "ideal type" profile. The average age of that group was 42.7 and 67 percent had completed a masters degree.

The leader "ideal type" category was weakest of the four in terms of factor analysis loadings. The "leader values" are political leadership, challenge, idealism, and service. The group of values which resulted from the factor analysis was not predicted by the author as were the

Table 4
Four City Manager "Ideal Types"

Factor 2		Factor 1	
Manager		*Entrepreneur*	
Effectiveness	.25	Achievement	.35
Efficiency	.30	Challenge	.43
Practicality	.58	Creativity	.40
Rationality	.46	Adaptability	.33
Humanist		*Leader*	
Dignity	-.41	Political Leadership	-.24
Fairness	-.49	Challenge	-.46
Idealism	-.39	Idealism	-.23
Service	-.45	Service	-.19

other three groups, but is supported by conclusions described by Warren Bennis and Burt Nanus. Their analysis identified four areas of competency which are characteristic of effective leaders. Placed in parentheses after three of the four areas in their study are the values from the management values list in this study.

- Attention through vision (idealism)
- Meaning through communication (political leadership)
- Trust through positioning and persistence; and
- Positive self regard and faith in a positive outcome (challenge)[11]

Survey respondents who indicated a preference for "leader values" include those who are under 40 years of age and those who are female. Twenty-four survey respondents matched the leader "ideal type" profile. Their average age was 41.8 and 79 percent had completed graduate school.

The author assumes that the 92 managers whose responses did not fit them clearly into one of the four "ideal types" represent a combination of types, or are inclined toward one of the types but missed being included in the groups because their ranking of at least one value was below the survey median.

Key Values for Managers of the Future

It is interesting to compare managers' stated value preferences with the values implicit in the work of the 1980 ICMA Committee on Future Horizons of the Profession. The ICMA Committee concluded that managers would have to develop four particular skills to succeed: negotiating ability; empathy with elected officials; an understanding of sophisticated management techniques and an awareness of their own personal needs.[12] Each of these skills incorporates one or more values which will have to be "valued" by managers before they can be put into practice. Looking at the four skill requirements in greater detail and comparing the implicit values of each with the author's assessment of the values of contemporary city managers provide several interesting results.

1. *Negotiating Ability*

> Brokering and negotiating may be the prime talents of the successful manager of tomorrow. Managers will be required to listen carefully, interpret ideas, empathize with many people, and defer personal ego needs. Managers will need great patience and great faith in people's ability to reach agreement and understanding.[13]

In considering this point, it is useful to refer back to Richard Stillman's 1974 book *The Rise of the City Manager* in which he suggests that city managers study the training and perspective of the professional foreign service diplomat as a model for future development.

> A diplomat in the classic sense is a professional with expertise and training which he brings to bear upon the highly political environment of international affairs in order to achieve workable agreements and mutual accommodations between nations for the benefit of both the nation he serves and its allies. A diplomat's duty is not to solve world problems with technical solutions but to engage in the continual process of negotiations with the more limited goal of attaining or maintaining peaceful relationships between countries....The image of the city manager as a professional diplomat on the urban scene with specialized skills in human relations, negotiations, compromise, and accommodation seems to strike an excellent balance between the practical realities of managers' jobs and the ideals toward which they can grow and contribute in a meaningful professional way in the development of their communities.[14]

Former ICMA President and Long Beach City Manager John Dever described the same phenomenon:

> Over the years, local governments have become very complicated to govern and therefore to manage, and you see more of an emphasis on horizontal relationships than on vertical ones. What we see is more emphasis on communication and consensus building than on the exercise of authority.[15]

The relatively high ranking for the instrumental value of independent and the low ranking for the management value of consensus suggest that California managers as a group do not currently reflect the values which would suggest their ability to become effective negotiators and brokers in the sense described above. Although a lower ranking for the value of independent and a more positive reception for the value of consensus were demonstrated by women managers and managers in sub-urban cities, a change from the primary role of expert administrative leader to facilitator is likely to be difficult for many contemporary city managers.

2. *Empathy with Elected Officials*

City managers will be required to have great sympathy, understanding, and an intuitive affinity for the needs of elected officials. They will have to think like political leaders and be sensitive to their career, personal, ego and financial needs. To an extent consistent with ethical standards, managers should be able to help elected officials satisfy these needs--in the very same way elected officials should assist managers.[16]

City managers ranked the value of political leadership *last* of the eighteen management values. This is the most troubling response of the entire survey and suggests that managers do not rate highly the importance of effective elected officials. If this is true, it is unlikely that current managers will make an extraordinary effort to develop empathy for their council members. The "we" versus "they" attitude which is readily apparent between many local government elected officials and their appointed staffs should be a concern to both groups and to the communities they serve, and is likely to be perpetuated unless the value of political leadership grows in importance to city managers and members of their staff.

Many progressive managers recognize this denial of political leadership as a problem of significant concern for the council-manager plan. David Mora, City Manager of Oxnard, California, expressed the following candid thoughts on the subject:

The plan is not as responsive as future councils will demand. We must recognize demands of elected officials as legitimate demands even if they may not make the most professional sense. That is the real problem...City managers are going to govern their own destiny, and the profession is going to govern its own destiny. We have got to adapt. It's as simple as that. If ICMA is going to continue as an effective force for municipal leadership, we've just got to adapt to a changing environment. The change may be that we're not going to be city managers. We may be chief executive officers or chief administrative officers.[17]

A hopeful sign for the future is the fact that city managers under 40 years of age rated the value of political leadership significantly higher than their more veteran peers.

3. *Managerial Understanding*

The challenges of [the year] 2000 will require sophisticated management techniques. These will be the successors to zero-base budgeting, management-by-objectives, and many others of recent vintage. The challenges also will require vast amounts of knowledge--the application of technology to social problems; information and data processing and transmission; and uses of sophisticated behavioral science.
Do not expect the manager of tomorrow to be able to implement these techniques personally; . . . look instead for a

sophisticated consumer of management analysis and service delivery technology--look for someone who can manage others with the specialized skills.[18]

The survey results suggest that today's managers will have little difficulty dealing with the demand for technological understanding. Managers rated the value of creativity relatively high, and the value of effectiveness second only to administrative leadership. It is noteworthy, however, that the instrumental value of intellectual was rated relatively low consistent with the thoroughgoing pragmatism which has been a hallmark of the city manager profession from its inception. This raises the question of how current managers will accommodate the new management sciences and evolving technologies given the considerable demands on their daily schedules.

4. *Awareness of Personal Needs*

The manager of the future cannot afford to be involved in work to the exclusion of everything else. The manager of the future cannot neglect the familial, spiritual, and physical needs of a complete person.[19]

Survey respondents rated family security as their highest ranking terminal value. By contrast, the values of mature love and true friendship were ranked eighth and tenth respectively. These relative rankings, along with the fact that the value responsibility was ranked second among the instrumental values, suggest that the high family security ranking could be reflecting a strongly developed sense of responsibility generally, as opposed to indicating a willingness to put personal needs above job demands. The value of inner harmony was ranked sixth among the terminal values, suggesting that managers are critically aware of the conflicts which are inevitable in their jobs, and that they recognize the importance of finding peace within themselves as a way of dealing with job stress. Significantly, manager respondents aged forty and under rated the values of inner harmony and mature love somewhat higher than the group which was fifty and over.

Managers holding a master's or a doctoral degree ranked the value of mature love significantly higher than did the managers without graduate degrees, while the managers without graduate degrees ranked the value of family security significantly higher. Women managers ranked the value true friendship much higher than their male peers, suggesting that they may be more aware of the importance of relying on friends to help meet personal and professional needs.

The results indicate that city managers find greater satisfaction in their jobs than they do in leisure or personal relationships. Since the age of manager respondents appears to make a significant difference in how personal need satisfaction is valued, it may be that those entering the city management profession today will be more concerned about recognizing and satisfying their personal needs than today's veterans have been.

Conclusion

The values of city management are as varied as the values in society at large, but their priority rankings reflect the unique nature of

150

these men and women and their vocation. While the dominant city management values were forged in the reformist zeal of the early 1900s, those values have been augmented, complemented and sometimes contradicted by the values of developing management science and of a changing society. One of the strengths of council-manager government has been its ability to adapt to the differing needs of cities across the country and to the changing demands of society. Through those changes managers have been guided by their strongly favored values of responsibility and honesty, their interest in providing effective administrative leadership to the cities they serve, and their adherence to the ICMA Code of Ethics.

The future success of council-manager government is dependent upon city managers' abilities to critically examine and to modify as necessary the priorities of key management values as the city management profession responds to the changing demands of communities and elected officials.

The immediate danger for city managers is that they will "lock in" outdated definitions (and related value preferences) of the city manager's role which do not acknowledge the legitimacy of more active involvement by elected officials. By doing so they will find themselves increasingly at odds with the city councils they serve. The city management profession is challenged, therefore, to critically examine the viability of the prevalent city manager role definition and its attendant values, and to change both as necessary. Changing to meet the demands of more politically active communities and city councils while retaining the basic belief that professional management is the key to effective government will ensure that city management continues its tradition of making cities the best they are capable of being.

Notes

1. Dwight Waldo, *The Administrative State: A Study of the Political Theory of American Public Administration* (New York: The Ronald Press Company, 1948), p. 47.

2. Ibid., p. 192.

3. J. Terry Edwards, John Nalbandian and Kenneth Wedel, "Individual Values and Professional Education: Implications for Practice and Education," *Administration & Society*, Vol. 13, No. 2, August 1981, pp. 123-143, and John Nalbandian and J. Terry Edwards, "The Values of Public Administrators: A Comparison with Lawyers, Social Workers and Business Administrators," *Review of Public Personnel Administration*, Fall, 1983, pp. 114-127.

4. Warren H. Schmidt and Barry Z. Posner, "Values and Expectations of Federal Service Executive," *Public Administration Review*, September/October, 1986, pp. 447-454; and "Values and Expectations of City Managers in California," *Public Administration Review*, September/October, 1987, pp. 404-409.

5. Philip Selznick, *Leadership in Administration* (New York: Harper and Row, Publishers, 1957), p. 57.

6. Chester Barnard, *The Functions of the Executive* (Cambridge: Harvard University Press, 1938: reprint ed. 1976), p. 279.

7. F. E. Emery and E. L. Trist, *Towards a Social Ecology* (New York: Plenum Publishing Company, 1975), p. 69.

8. This surprising and disturbingly low ranking is discussed in more detail below. Several city managers familiar with the survey and the low ranking given to Political Leadership suggest that respondents may have reflexively reacted to the value as representing a role which is inappropriate for city managers to assume. Consequently, they ranked it low on the list.

Arguing against that interpretation is the fact that this value was accompanied by an elaborating subscript which reinforced its meaning as valuing "effective elected officials."

9. Harold A. Stone, Don K. Price and Kathryn H. Stone, *City Manager Government in the United States* (Chicago: Public Administration Service, 1940), p. 71.

10. Norman H. Nie, *SPSS*, 2nd Edition (New York: McGraw-Hill Book Company), pp. 468-487. Results of the Management Value List factor analysis were used to relate individual city manager value profiles to four Management Value "ideal types." Each of the values included in the following "Ideal Type" matrix had a factor weighting of at least .19 (+ or -) on its particular factor. Together, the two factors account for 23.2% of the total variance of the Management Values list based upon the original, unrotated principal components iteration. While the factor analysis results suggest a logical grouping of responses and respondents, there are obviously other important variables which, taken together, have affected the value rankings even more significantly.

    To determine the fit of the city manager responses to the four "ideal types," the survey results were sorted to determine which managers rated each of the four values in each "ideal type" set at or above the median score. The results of this selection process were then analyzed to determine that population's age and educational level so that the four "types" could be compared to the entire group of respondents based on those two categories.

11. Warren G. Bennis and Burt Nanus, *Leaders* (New York: Harper and Row, Publishers, 1985), pp. 19-75.

12. Laurence Rutter, *The Essential Community: Local Government in the Year 2000* (Washington, D.C.: ICMA, 1980), pp. 125-137.

13. Ibid., p. 133.

14. Richard J. Stillman, II, *The Rise of the City Manager* (Albuquerque: University of New Mexico Press, 1974), pp. 110-112.

15. John E. Dever, *Reflections of Local Government Professionals*, edited by John Nalbandian and Raymond G. Davis (Lawrence, Kansas: Department of Public Administration, University of Kansas, 1987), p. 15.

16. Rutter, p. 133.

17. David Mora, *Reflections of Local Government Professionals*, p.128.

18. Rutter, pp. 134-135.

19. Rutter, p. 135.

Discussion

Frederickson: I do want John Nalbandian to comment on whether he feels that the values that these city managers are identifying are compatible with his model.

Novak: I want to sound a foghorn for academics whose ship is potentially on the rocks. When you send out questionnaires like this, do not overestimate the amount of deep thought we give to filling them out. Most questionnaires are thrown into a briefcase and filled out while you're standing in line for an airplane. We don't give them so much deep thought that you can find in all those numbers a real meaning.

Keller: I find the best way to define power is dependence. I lack power to the extent I'm dependent on somebody else. What's happening in American cities is the rise of interdependence. People are not as dependent on other people as they were in the past. Power has been a prime motivator in the past because there was a big difference between professionally educated people and nonprofessionally educated people. That's getting more even. Now there's more interdependence; therefore, power is less necessary to accomplish ends. In fact, trying to recreate the independence that in the past gave people power may now turn a lot of people off.

Nalbandian: I wanted to ask Ed Schilling what his definitions were of "consensual" and "professionalism."

Schilling: "Consensual" is cooperative decision making. "Professionalism" is concern for occupational standards.

Kerrigan: Because this is based on a larger study, how do you explain in greater detail the low rankings of consensual idealism and political leadership?

Schilling: Most managers valued technical competence values: effectiveness and administrative leadership. In an aggregate of 213 respondents, the manager group in California does not find much value in working with elected officials in trying to bring about the kind of consensus and in using the brokering skills that we've talked about as important for the future. That is a troubling response. The one thing that gave me some hope was that younger and better educated managers tended to rank those values higher.

King: It just depends on the words that you choose. Political leadership is the wrong word to test the response of managers. By using "policy development," you would have had a different response.

Protasel: Ed Schilling's figures suggest that some city managers may get locked into not recognizing the legitimacy of elected officials' participation in government. Svara's figure that describes preferred involvement and actual involvement indicates that managers would prefer for council members to be more involved. You can look at that as compatible with democratic theory, or we could say that managers want more assistance or more delegation. I'm not certain what interpretation to give Svara's findings. Do they show that all the managers want more help or that they'd like more involvement from the council in terms of defining mission or getting involved in policy because it would make their jobs easier? Is it just a matter of design or is it a matter of genuine concern for community values? Is it really a concern with democracy?

Schilling: Let me give you an unbiased answer. I think that the findings do show the strong support from managers for heightened

153

council involvement, not only in handling the big issues, the hard decisions, but in evaluation.

McIntyre: Managers are concerned about doing their jobs and being responsible and effective. They are concerned about the outcome of their work--about doing effective work but not as concerned about the process. That's my perception of California managers as a group. In spite of some of the methodological problems that I pointed out, I think that is consistent with my own knowledge.

Toregas: I wonder whether we're trying to read too much into one survey.

Schilling: Initially, my intent in setting it up was to describe administrative leadership and political leadership. In one instance, the manager leads the organization through administration; in the other, he works through the city council to enhance its leadership. I wanted to see how managers would rank the two relative to one another. I found out that administrative leadership is number one.

Tracing the Changing Knowledge and Skill Needs and Service Activities of Public Managers

David W. Hinton
University of Nebraska, Omaha
John E. Kerrigan
University of Houston

Almost twenty years ago, Graham Watt, John Parker, and Robert Cantine examined the roles of urban administrators with a focus on determining the knowledge and skills required of administrators in an increasingly complex society.[1] Through a series of surveys, essays, and workshops in 1971, the researchers contacted 133 administrators and sought their views on both administration and the knowledge and skills needed in public administration education. About ten years later, John Kerrigan and David Hinton replicated the study by contacting 388 public administrators over a three-year period (1977 through 1979).[2] Kerrigan and Hinton conducted another follow-up survey of 478 public administrators ten years later (1987-88). The results of this third survey along with an analysis of change over time are presented in this paper.[3]

A primary purpose of this study is to provide data to help chart changes and future directions in the knowledge and skills bases required of the local government management profession. While individual respondents to the surveys changed, and the selection criteria used in the Watt-Parker-Cantine study differed somewhat from the first Kerrigan-Hinton study, the emphasis on occupational pressures felt by people working in the administration of local governments and their perceptions of future demands on public administrators remained central to the survey. Overall, the questionnaires were aimed at the same occupational group and the results can be viewed as an expression of the views of local government professionals over time.

Knowledge Needs for Tomorrow's Administrators

The public managers were asked to rate 13 areas of knowledge on a three-point scale, from "most important" to "least important." Results of the most recent survey are presented in Table 1 and a comparative analysis of the three survey periods is presented in Table 2.

"Urban economic development, including both public and private sectors," showed the most marked, and statistically significant, increase in importance.[4] Ranked seventh out of the 13 areas in the early 1970s, this knowledge area moved to third in importance in the late 1970s and to first in importance in the most recent survey.

Researchers have noted the increasing importance of economic development issues to local governments. Michael H. Annison's analysis

Table 1
Tomorrow's Knowledge Needs (n=478)

Types of Knowledge	No Answer	Least Important	Moderately Important	Most Important	Weighted Score a/
Urban economic development, including both public and private sector	3	14	141	320	2.64
Human relations, i.e., theories of individual and group behavior relevant to managing organizations	3	26	160	289	2.55
Causes underlying major urban problems	5	18	177	278	2.55
Values motivating the behavior of the people in urban areas	4	32	164	278	2.52
Organization principles and practices	4	24	223	227	2.43
Personnel administration, including labor relations	3	21	255	199	2.37
Principles and practices of governmental planning	5	24	259	190	2.35
Social characteristics, institutions and processes of urban areas	3	49	212	214	2.35
Political institutions and processes	3	43	243	189	2.31
Various techniques such as data processing, information systems, etc.	3	62	278	135	2.15
History and aspiration of minority and disadvantaged groups and how these characteristics are reflected in contemporary behavior	3	94	276	105	2.02
Specific services government provides its citizens: health care, welfare, model cities, etc.	4	88	291	95	2.01
Engineering principles	4	239	223	12	1.52

a/ The weighted score was obtained by valuing least important as 1, moderately important as 2, and most important as 3. This was then divided by the total number of respondents.

of the implications of our nation's changing social, economic, and political structure for economic development in the 1990s stated, "A general pattern seems to be getting clearer with regard to economic development issues: local communities and state governments will become increasingly active on a wider range of economic development issues."[5]

This shift also is consistent with the analysis of Luke, Ventriss, Reed and Reed[6] in which they trace the evolution of economic development as a major public policy objective for cities, counties, and states. The late 1970s were characterized by a diminished federal involvement in local economic development and a corresponding increase in involvement on the part of state and local governments. The first Kerrigan-Hinton study showed this shift in emphasis. Luke, et al., also

Table 2
Tomorrow's Knowledge Needs:
Changing Perceptions Over Two Decades

Types of Knowledge	1987-88 (n=478)		1977-79 (n=388)		1971 (n=133)	
	Rank	$\overline{X}$ a/	Rank	$\overline{X}$	Rank	$\overline{X}$
Urban economic development including both public and private sector	1	2.64	3-4	2.49	7	2.08
Human relations, i.e., theories of individual and group behavior relevant to managing organizations	2-3	2.55	3-4	2.49	1	2.59
Causes underlying major urban problems	2-3	2.55	1	2.61	3	2.39
Values motivating the behavior of the people in urban areas	4	2.52	5-7	2.45	2	2.40
Organization principles and practices	5	2.43	5-7	2.45	9	1.95
Personnel administration, including labor relations	6	2.37	2	2.58	6	2.10
Principles and practices of governmental planning	7-8	2.35	5-7	2.45	10	1.78
Social characteristics, institutions and processes of urban areas	7-8	2.35	8	2.28	5	2.19
Political institutions and and processes	9	2.31	9	2.21	4	2.24
Various techniques such as data processing, information systems, etc.	10	2.15	11	2.04	12	1.64
History and aspiration of minority and disadvantaged groups and how these characteristics are reflected in contemporary behavior	11	2.02	12	1.96	8	1.98
Specific services government provides its citizens: health care, welfare, model cities, etc.	12	2.01	10	2.11	11	1.68
Engineering principles	13	1.52	13	1.63	13	1.09

a/ Weighted means. The weighted score was obtained by valuing least important as 1, moderately important as 2, and most important as 3. This was then divided by the total number of respondents.

point to the 1981-82 recession as a period that pushed economic development to the top of the priority list for public administrators. Our data reflect the same conclusion. While economic analysts tell us that economic development is the word of the day, our practitioners are telling us that it is the word of tomorrow.

As Table 2 illustrates, the relative importance of the 13 knowledge areas actually changed little over time.[7] Practitioners continue to focus on understanding the "causes underlying major urban problems," "human relations," and "values motivating behavior." Overall, the survey results support the notion of the public manager as a generalist. Knowledge areas such as data processing, information systems,

Table 3
Tomorrow's Skill Needs (n=478)

Types of Skills	No Answer	Least Important	Moderately Important	Most Important	Weighted Score a/
Situation analysis, i.e., "sizing up" the community political milieu, organization, and staff	2	1	66	409	2.86
Assessing community needs	3	1	136	338	2.71
Handling interpersonal relations	2	5	129	342	2.71
Bargaining, negotiating and other consensus-seeking techniques	2	16	164	296	2.59
Delegating authority and responsibility to subordinates	2	9	180	287	2.58
Financial analysis	2	8	186	282	2.58
Audience-oriented communication, i.e., speaking effectively	2	11	197	268	2.54
Analytical thinking, problem solving and associated techniques of analysis including those employed in program evaluation	3	34	186	255	2.47
Relating to and understanding minority, disadvantaged, and other culturally distinctive groups	2	48	288	140	2.19
Organizing and writing policy statements, reports, etc.	2	57	277	142	2.18
Job analysis, i.e., assessing the requirements and responsibilities of positions	3	128	259	88	1.92
Systems design and operations analysis	2	144	273	59	1.82

a/ The weighted score was obtained by valuing least important as 1, moderately important as 2, and most important as 3. This was then divided by the total number of respondents.

engineering, health care, and welfare remain relatively low on the list of knowledge needs, both for current managers and for tomorrow's managers. Concerning techniques of data processing and information systems, however, there has been a slight upward trend in the weighted rankings.

The emphasis on knowledge areas which help to understand human behavior and broader policy issues is consistent with the literature. Daniel Barber's study of newly promoted city managers, for example, stresses the importance of a range of undergraduate educational experiences, graduate work in public policy/administration, and external management education programs that focus on general management issues.[8] Roy Green's research findings related to the allocation of work time of local government managers showed half of a typical manager's time is spent on four activities: (1) responding to crisis, (2) acting as negotiator, (3) allocating resources, and (4) managing personnel.[9]

158

Table 4
Tomorrow's Skill Needs:
Changing Perceptions Over Two Decades

Types of Skills	1987-88 (n=478)		1977-79 (n=388)		1971 (n=133)	
	Rank	$\overline{X}$ a/	Rank	$\overline{X}$	Rank	$\overline{X}$
Situation analysis, i.e., "sizing up" the community political milieu, organization, and staff	1	2.86	1-2	2.75	1	2.57
Assessing community needs	2-3	2.71	1-2	2.75	5-6	2.25
Handling interpersonal relations	2-3	2.71	5-6	2.56	3	2.42
Bargaining, negotiating and other consensus-seeking techniques	4	2.59	7	2.53	2	2.54
Delegating authority and responsibility to subordinates	5-6	2.58	3	2.68	5-6	2.25
Financial analysis	5-6	2.58	4	2.68	9	1.67
Audience-oriented communication, i.e., speaking effectively	7	2.54	8	2.44	8	2.06
Analytical thinking, problem solving and associated techniques of analysis including those employed in program evaluation	8	2.47	5-6	2.56	4	2.39
Relating to and understanding minority, disadvantaged, and other culturally distinctive groups	9	2.19	9	2.27	7	2.08
Organizing and writing policy statements, reports, etc.	10	2.18	10	2.25	10	1.53
Job analysis, i.e., assessing the requirements and responsibilities of positions	11	1.92	11	2.11	12	1.21
Systems design and operations analysis	12	1.82	12	1.93	11	1.32

a/ Weighted means used. See earlier table.

Skill Needs for Tomorrow's Public Administrators

Public managers were also asked to rate the importance of twelve skill areas for tomorrow's public administrators. The results are presented in Tables 3 and 4. The response patterns showed little change from the earlier studies with "situation analysis, i.e., 'sizing up' the community political milieu" ranking as the most important skill. The ability to "assess community needs" also remained one of the most important skills.

A significant increase in importance was discovered, however, with "handling interpersonal relations," which moved from fifth in importance in the late 1970s, to a tie for second in the 1980s. The nature of the questionnaire prevented any follow-up concerning reasons for this shift, but it is reasonable to speculate that a more complex and diverse working environment confronts today's administrator.

The two most recent surveys also point to a major change in importance in "financial analysis." Only 14% (18 of 126) of the Watt-Parker-Cantine respondents rated skills in financial analysis as most important. By 1988 this had increased to 59%. Financial considerations obviously have become more closely tied with administration over time, and today almost all local government managers are involved in the process of financial analysis. Barber's study of newly promoted city managers supports the importance of finance to today's managers. Of 16 topics for external management education programs, finance/budgeting was rated second in importance with general management being the top rated education program.[10]

The data also show a moderate, but statistically significant, decline in the importance of "delegating authority and responsibility to subordinates." On the one hand, the survey results indicate that "handling interpersonal relations" is becoming a more important skill; on the other hand, the same respondents note that the ability to "delegate authority and responsibility" is becoming less important. Some would argue that more attention given to the latter would reduce time spent on the former.

Public Service--Past, Present, and Future

Following up on the Watt-Parker-Cantine study, the survey also addressed the issue of "career-to-date" involvement in eleven public service areas and thoughts regarding the future importance of the same service categories. Results of the most recent survey are presented in

Table 5
Career Involvement by Service Category

Service	No Answer a/	Involvement			Weighted Score b/	Watt-Parker-Cantine Study
		Limited	Moderate	Extensive		
Land Use	2	42	172	262	2.46	2.13
Economic Development	2	48	164	264	2.45	2.01
Public Order	6	89	187	196	2.23	2.17
Employment	4	112	193	169	2.12	2.07
Transportation	10	119	198	151	2.07	2.10
Housing	6	180	208	84	1.80	1.98
Ecology	9	212	203	54	1.66	2.20
Race Relations	7	233	164	74	1.66	1.86
Public Health	12	286	151	29	1.45	1.64
Education	12	321	124	21	1.36	1.73
Welfare	10	391	63	14	1.19	1.43

a/ Includes unusable responses.

b/ Weighted score was calculated by weighting responses as follows: limited = 1, moderate = 2, and extensive = 3.

Tables 5 and 6. Land use and economic development were the top two service categories in terms of career-to-date involvement, followed by public order, employment, and transportation.

When administrators were asked to rate the same service categories in terms of future importance to public administrators, the results also showed some clear distinctions. More than 80 percent of the respondents indicated that economic development would become a more important service area in the future, followed by transportation, ecology, housing, and land use.

The relative ranking of career involvement by service category changed little over the two decades. One exception to this was the area of "ecology" which headed the list in the early 1970s and was seventh by the late 1980s. Other than this category, the rankings remained about the same although the magnitude of involvement did seem to change. Economic development and land use show significant increases in involvement while housing, ecology, race relations, public health, education, and welfare have diminished significantly (see Table 5).

The focus on economic development noted earlier is even more pronounced when viewed in light of the career service involvement of public administrators and especially the projected importance of the service category. Of the eleven service categories, economic development ranked sixth in terms of career involvement in the Watt-Parker-Cantine study. Economic development rated *last* in terms of the percentage ranking of the various service areas as becoming more important for "future" public administrators. In his comments on the Watt-Parker-Cantine research, Henry Reining, Jr. said:

One is really inclined to quarrel with the 133 respondents in the way in which they listed these service categories. They have education, land use, and economic development as the last three

Table 6
Future Involvement by Service Category

Service	No Answer a/	Future Involvement			% More Important	Watt-Parker-Cantine Study % More Important
		Less Important	No Change	More Important		
Economic Development	1	1	89	387	81	43
Ecology	5	14	191	268	57	88
Transportation	4	6	196	272	57	62
Housing	4	13	196	265	56	85
Land Use	4	5	163	306	56	65
Education	7	25	255	191	41	56
Public Health	6	31	282	159	34	68
Employment	3	24	311	140	29	66
Public Order	8	20	330	120	25	66
Race Relations	4	50	304	120	25	74
Welfare	4	58	311	105	22	60

a/ Includes unusable responses.

service categories in terms of future importance. And welfare comes off one position higher. Could it be that most of the respondents were city managers who were not accustomed to dealing with education, because in so many places education is under a separate school district; nor with welfare, because in so many places welfare is handled by the county? This still does not account for land use and economic development being so low, especially since the planning and zoning function is generally to be found in city halls.[11]

Given the results of the latest survey, Reining was on target. Our two top categories--economic development and land use--agree with Reining's questions concerning the low rating given these two areas in the early 1970s. While methodological differences might account for some of the variance, the Watt-Cantine-Parker study was sound and did reflect, in our view, the perceptions of urban administrators in the early 1970s. The most recent survey includes more administrators from fewer urban environs, but we are confident that differences in city size or region of the country account for little difference in response rate for most of the service categories.[12]

Given the dramatic shift in importance of economic development, it is reasonable to speculate that other areas might also change in importance in the future. Despite the low ratings, for example, of education and welfare both in terms of career-to-date involvement and in terms of future importance, all public administrators, regardless of governmental level, may well become more involved in the future.

Race relations as a service area changed little in terms of career-to-date involvement, but perceptions as to the future importance changed considerably. In the Watt-Parker-Cantine study, 74% expected race relations to become more important to future public administrators. In the most recent survey, only 25% expressed the belief that race relations would become more important. We question whether these views will hold given current demographic, economic, and social trends.

Conclusions

Since 1971, the public management profession has shown consistency concerning the knowledge and skill needs for public administrators. There have, of course, been changes, most notably the increased importance of economic development, an indication that public administrators respond to the changing needs of the community.

While public administrators seem to be excellent at predicting the knowledge and skill needs for tomorrow's managers, their ability to predict the importance of topics for tomorrow is in question. They missed on economic development and land use years ago. Today, they tend to downplay the importance of race as a determinant of behavior and expectations and of information management technology for tomorrow's administrators.

Overall, our respondents continue to show the importance of having the ability to rise above it all--to understand the values which motivate behavior and to have a knowledge of human relations; to have the skill to analyze situations; and to be able to understand the needs of the community. For tomorrow, the public manager seems prepared to deal with what Tom Peters defines as chaos. "The true objective is to take chaos as given and learn to thrive on it. The winners of tomorrow will deal proactively with chaos. . . ."[13]

Notes

1. Graham Watt, John Parker, and Robert Cantine, "Roles of the Urban Administrator in the 1970s and the Knowledges and Skills Required to Perform These Roles," in Frederick N. Cleaveland (ed.) *Education for Urban Administration*, Monograph 16 (Philadelphia: The American Academy of Political and Social Science, June 1973), pp. 50-79.

2. John Kerrigan and David Hinton, "Knowledge and Skill Needs for Tomorrow's Public Administrators," *Public Administration Review*, vol. 40 (September/October 1980), pp. 469-473.

3. The data in this paper represent the product of a mail questionnaire sent to 922 practitioners who received service award recognition by the International City Management Association. Usable questionnaires were returned from 478 practitioners; this represented a 55% return after discounting questionnaires that were not deliverable. A follow-up questionnaire was not incorporated in this study as the earlier Kerrigan-Hinton surveys showed only slight improvements in return rates and no statistically significant differences in responses.

4. Given the nature of the data, both the t-test and the chi-square test were employed to determine whether or not the changes in individual items were significant over time. An alpha of .05 was used and significant differences are mentioned only when obtained from both the t-test and the chi-square test.

5. Michael H. Annison, "New Economic Development," *Economic Development Quarterly*, vol. 1 (November 1987), p. 325. Annison is President of the Westrend Group, a business that monitors social, economic, and political change.

6. Jeffrey Luke, Curtis Ventriss, B.J. Reed, and Christine Reed, *Managing Economic Development* (San Francisco: Jossey-Bass Publishers, 1988).

7. "Personnel administration, including labor relations," however, showed a significant decline, having a weighted score of 2.58 in the late 70s and a score of 2.37 in the most recent survey. This knowledge area was lower rated (sixth) in the early 70s study, increased to second in the follow-up study, and then dropped to sixth in the most recent study. While methodological differences may account for this shift, it seems unlikely given the relative stability of the other rankings. An increased specialization within the public sector where personnel specialists are taking over more responsibilities is one possible explanation.

8. Daniel M. Barber, "Newly Promoted City Managers," *Public Administration Review*, vol. 48 (May/June 1988), pp., 649-699.

9. Roy E. Green, *Local Government Managers: Styles and Challenges, Baseline Data Report*, vol. 19, no. 2 (Washington, D.C.: International City Management Association, March/April 1987).

10. Barber, *Public Administration Review*, 1988.

11. Henry Reining, Jr., "Commentary on the Watt-Parker-Cantine Paper," in Frederic N. Cleaveland (ed.) *Education for Urban Administration*, Monograph 16 (Philadelphia: The American Academy of Political and Social Science, June 1973), p. 92.

12. John E. Kerrigan and David Hinton, "Region, City Size and Length of Service as Determinants of the Roles and Functions of City Managers," a paper presented at the Tenth Annual Meeting of the American Institute for Decision Sciences, St. Louis, October 1978.

13. Tom Peters, *Thriving on Chaos* (New York: Alfred A. Knopf, 1987), p. xii.

Response

Donald A. Blubaugh
Walnut Creek, California

My observations are based upon my own personal experience which spans twenty-four years of public service in local government and on my sense of where my colleagues are here in California.

My observations are as follows:

1. Before commenting on the rankings in the various tables, let me note that the choices on the questionnaire: 1-Low Importance; 2-Moderate Importance; 3-Most Important, lead to rank differences that are often less than a tenth of a point apart. It would be my inclination in reading this paper to look at groups of priorities rather than at pure statistical rank order. Future studies, hopefully, will provide more choices for the respondents so that a more realistic set of priority concerns can be developed, if that is indeed necessary. Notwithstanding this comment, I believe the survey analysis is helpful and the paper will be useful to practitioners in the field.

2. City managers tend to rank higher that which is of critical concern to them at any given point in time. We are masters at "rising to the occasion" and then integrating that which we have learned and experienced into our "kit bag" for future reference should the need arise. An example on Table 2 illustrates this point. Knowledge of urban economic development ranked seventh in 1971, third/fourth in 1977-79 and first in 1987-88. It is fairly obvious that in 1971 cities were growing and developing through natural market economic forces. As the economy and our cities mature, more intervention is needed if development is to occur. Further, with shrinking fiscal resources, cities are acutely concerned that growth and development produce tax and fee revenues to support service delivery systems and other governmental projects. Managers have learned quickly how to help shape the local economy and they see a continuing need to learn more in this area. Another example is found in Table 4. Skills of handling interpersonal relations and bargaining, negotiating and other consensus-seeking techniques both have moved up from the 1977-79 rankings. The "name of the game" today and in the future is getting council members, staff and community groups to work together within themselves and with each other to build lasting, workable solutions to problems. Win/lose is out because the stakes are too high. All of us in the profession are seeking more skills to help in this more demanding but critical decision-making process.

3. In their analysis, the authors say that "'handling interpersonal relations' is becoming a more important skill; on the other hand, the same respondents note that the ability to 'delegate authority and responsibility' is becoming less important. Some would argue that more attention given to the latter would reduce the time spent on the former." There are some matters one cannot delegate. Working on city council member interpersonal relationships and interpersonal

relationships of department heads who report to the city manager are matters that cannot be delegated. Further, as managers find that they can not do it all themselves and have learned to delegate, the topic area becomes of less concern. In my own case, I have found it necessary to delegate more day-by-day ongoing operational responsibility to key subordinates on my staff so that I have more time to work with council members, the community and department heads in developing consensus solutions to problems.

4. Public health, education and welfare have scored high in previous surveys, I suspect, because the sample may have included more city managers who had direct responsibility for these service areas. The last survey may have reflected a more accurate picture of city manager concerns in these particular areas. It has been my experience that responsibility for these disciplines has not fallen on city government. This is not to suggest that even though we may not have functional responsibility for these areas we should have no concern. But I am not at all surprised to see a lowering of the priorities in the areas of public health, education and welfare.

5. As to future involvement by service category on Table 6, the five top categories (economic development, ecology, transportation, housing and land use) accurately reflect what I believe to be topic areas of greatest concern to my colleagues and myself in California. For reasons stated earlier, no effort is made to follow the rank order 1, 2, 3, 4, etc. To the degree we are not consumed with the process of decision-making, these five areas demand most of our time and will continue to do so.

6. I concur with the conclusion that public administrators may not always predict the importance of topics for tomorrow but they do have a good sense of the knowledge and skill needs for the managers of tomorrow. In fact it is my belief that, as a profession, we spend so much time reacting to forces over which we believe we have no control that we have little opportunity to pause and reflect on what's on the horizon and how best to prepare for it. This is a difficult task because we cannot sacrifice the actions needed today to get ready for the future. As noted earlier, however, we do rise to the occasion, no matter what confronts us.

In conclusion, there is a role for academicians to play in working with practicing administrators in assessing where we are and what the future may hold. My advice to my colleagues in the practicing profession would be to be open to current research; there is much to be learned. To the academicians studying the profession and the forces that are upon us, I urge you to be as relevant as you can in your research, to outline implications of the findings and to suggest and propose concrete action steps (this paper does not) that should be considered. Above all continue your efforts to get our attention!

Discussion

Hansell: What we see in the future tends to be mostly here and now. Let me pose a question to Howard Tipton: What does the situation in one's community mean for the elected officials?

Tipton: I think a manager can bring experience and/or research ability to the job. Most council members don't usually have that background. There are cases where certain council members have great abilities. But assessing your community and assessing what direction you ought to be going, is the task of the team approach in the council-manager form of government.

McIntyre: I think there's a lot of ambivalence in southern California about councils saying both they want to control growth and they want more jobs. There's a lot of frustration in our area about too much traffic, too much growth, too much inconvenience to the quality of life.

Hansell: Don has brought up one conflict, growth management versus economic development and job creation. Does this take us to the edge? It involves financial analysis and other things that we're perhaps not well trained in. When we put managers so far out in front, we may create undue risks for the council-manager plan.

Gleason: I don't think it puts undue risk on the plan when the strength of the plan is its flexibility. The nature of the business is that you have to be on the outer edge of the envelope all the time--whether it's growth management or economic development or social issues. When that assessment is done by the council, the staff, or the community, or cooperatively by representatives of all these components, the expectation is that you will lead the organization and the community to an appropriate role. That role is determined by a lot of factors--some legal, some historical--in terms of the nature of the community. Some of them have to do with the social contract you have with the council and how much rope they give you. One way you can look at a council is to treat its members like a consumer focus group, with regard to their constituency contact. The constituency contacts them: they then have opinions and iterations that may be intuitively accurate but may not be put in a context that's easy to work with. My experience is that there may be frustration but councils typically are reflective of the dynamics of their community. That's why they are there.

Nalbandian: What I found really startling in the Hinton-Kerrigan research was the low priority that managers placed on race relations. In many ways I can't believe this; it is so out of sync with what I think is now in the research. The survey in Table 2 says that from 1971 to 1987 the respondents feel that race relations are less important today than they were fifteen years ago. And in the future this issue is predicted to be among the least important of these ten or so categories. I just can't believe this.

Kerrigan: The Watt-Parker-Cantine study was done in the era of the burning of the cities, and race relations was an important issue. Then, managers had to be generalists. Community economic issues have become a more important item on the manager's agenda since the 1970s. But the changing demographics in this country indicate that we'd better get very serious about this issue at the local level. Some states will go through a tremendous change in which the minorities will become the majority. So race relations, as it relates to economic development, will surface as a very important issue in the future. I think my colleague Hinton and I would say the managers have overlooked something in the race relations area.

Toregas: The titles and labels we apply to our social relationships change over time. Therefore, imagine being asked today whether race relations are important. You'd say "no" because we are not as immersed in that issue, when it is phrased that way. Perhaps we've developed different words to trigger what we do. That is a problem for the

166

academics. They must have replicability and maintain some standard categories. But I don't think we'll be able to track the fundamental shift in the way we deal with business if we can't somehow change the language.

Anderson: When I read the paper I reacted to the questions and the categories at the time. As I read the results now, I had the same reaction. When you look at the top half of Table 2 and the bottom half, what I would characterize as the general management skill categories wound up in the top half. The item dealing with theories about individual and group behavior relevant to managing organizations reflects a broad set of techniques and processes that you apply to a lot of specific situations. In contrast, engineering principles, dealing with bridges, sewers and sidewalks, are, for me, a narrow skill area. I think the things in the bottom half of the table tend to be focused around what I would characterize as fairly specific, in-depth kinds of knowledge. Those items at the top tend to deal with process issues. As a result I think the top half and the bottom half rarely change except when we have a hot issue like economic development that shoots to the top. In the late 1960s/early 1970s race relations shot to the top and then dropped back down into the pack. I think that's going to happen over time.

Hansell: Don Mendonsa from Savannah postulates that our concerns as managers in the next twenty years will essentially be human service problems, rather than traditional fiscal or economic issues.

McIntyre: I think city managers are a lot more open and know how to deal better with interracial issues than in the past. We have a better attitude and we understand better how to deal with race relations. I think younger people coming into the profession are much more open to these issues than some of us older people are. That may be the reason for the projection that this will be less an issue. I know the demographic changes are going to be enormous, particularly in the Southwest.

Nalbandian: It's my impression the racism among today's undergraduate students is startling.

Banovetz: I agree wholeheartedly with John. The degree of racism on our college campuses today is tremendous. But I think there are two different dimensions of the race problems that have to be kept in mind. The black-white dimension is becoming much more severe on the campuses. Yet my experience is that while managers are quick to identify black-white problems, they are not nearly so quick to identify problems with race relations when they involve hispanics, at least in the northern part of the country. These problems don't fit into their category of race relations. While race relations are viewed as problems in some parts of the country, they are not significant problems in the perceptions of managers in other parts of the country. Thus, when we aggregate we get a false picture. In small-town suburban America, the managers are not dealing with it now, but the problem may still be severe in the southern third of the country.

The Nature of
City Managers' Work

Martha L. Hale
Emporia State University

What do city managers do? How do they spend their work time? With whom do they interact? Why do they allocate their time and energies in certain ways? What is unique in city management work?

Henry Mintzberg[1] in studying business managers found little empirical evidence to support the descriptions and prescriptions of managerial literature. He developed a methodology for collecting and sorting data on managerial work, analyzed the data, and articulated a series of propositions about the nature of managerial work in the private sector. This paper reports on a study that examined city management work utilizing the methodology for data collection employed by Mintzberg. His method of data collection was replicated during 239 hours of structured observation of five city managers in Los Angeles County.[2] Replicating Mintzberg's method of sorting the data included creating a chronological record of what managers did and examining in greater depth the managers' primary activities. The analysis included examining the general characteristics of how the work was done as well as the purposes behind major categories of work.

What Do City Managers Do?

The simplest way to describe what city managers do is to say that they talk. Seventy-seven percent of work time was spent in conversation and 13% spent at desk work, which is primarily contact with people through reading what someone has written or writing to someone. Verbal interaction is clearly the managers' preferred mode of operation. Desk work fills in the spaces between contacts and is often interrupted. In rounded figures, a city manager averaged almost seven hours per week on the phone, spent 21 hours in scheduled meetings, 8.5 hours in unscheduled meetings and 26 minutes touring. The city managers spent 7%-30% of their work time away from city hall, touring a site, at meetings or observing while on route.

	% of work time	% of contacts
Telephone	14	41
Unplanned Meetings	18	44
Scheduled Meetings	45	13

When time committed to contacts was examined, the variety of activities in a city manager's day became more vivid. In an average day, were there such a thing, a city manager would be apt to work 9.5 hours, take 14 phone calls averaging almost 6 minutes apiece, participate in 4 scheduled meetings lasting about an hour each, have 15 unexpected meetings averaging seven minutes each, and go on one five-minute tour. In all, before addressing desk work, the city manager may have shifted mode and topic up to 44 times and dealt with up to 40 people in at least two locations. Furthermore, the manager processed an average of 22 pieces of paper a day. Desk work took less than six minutes.

While this superficial description of activity may be of interest and may answer a question about what city managers do, it does not tell much about the nature of city management work. It is necessary to go a step further and investigate the way city managers carry out their daily activities.

How Do City Managers Spend Their Work Time?

There were two general characteristics of managerial work described by Mintzberg that held true in the study of city managers. First, Mintzberg wrote that the managers work at an "unrelenting pace".[3] The chronological record of any work day observed is evidence that this statement holds true for the managers in both studies.

A true break seldom occurred. Coffee was taken during meetings, and lunchtime was almost always devoted to formal or informal meetings. When free time appeared, ever-present subordinates quickly usurped it. If these managers wished to have a change of pace, they had two means at their disposal--the observational tour and the light discussions that generally preceded scheduled meetings. But these were not regularly scheduled breaks, and they were seldom totally unrelated to the issue at hand--managing the organization.[4]

The preceding was written by Mintzberg but can also be said of the city managers. Mintzberg recorded 547 activities in 202 hours of work, the city managers logged 1,398 activities in 230 hours. The evidence in both studies is that managers work at a furious pace. Mintzberg's private managers averaged 22 minutes per activity, the city managers averaged 10 minutes per activity.

The second general characteristic of managerial work is that verbal interactions are characterized by brevity, variety, and fragmentation. In addition to working at a rapid pace, city managers shift focus often and rapidly.

In fact, "the manager actually appears to prefer brevity and interruption in his work" and to prefer the "stimulus-response environment" in which he works.[5] The five city managers reported that they liked the variety of the job. There is evidence that the city managers interrupted themselves, especially from desk work. Mintzberg concluded that this characteristic breeds "superficiality [as] an occupational hazard of the manager's job".[6] However, in the case of the city managers it would be detrimental to the process of city government for them to be involved at a greater depth. What Mintzberg referred to as superficiality, may here be recognized as overview. In public management, it is important in his administrative role that the city manager remain a court of last resort. Smaller cities with smaller staffs demand, from time-to-time, that the manager step in with greater depth, but this substitute activity takes his attention away from providing an overview. An important part of public management theory holds that the city manager not usurp the decision making role of the city council but that he gather information from a variety of sources so that he can disperse it widely.

With Whom Do They Interact?

Together the city managers had contact with close to 1,000 people in 835 contacts during the five weeks of observation. The categories of people contacted are as follows:

1. Council members
2. Citizens
   a.   local press
   b.   individuals
   c.   local organizations
3. Staff
   a.   deputy
   b.   department heads
   c.   division heads
   d.   other employees
   e.   secretary
4. Associates
   a.   developers
   b.   consultants
   c.   third sector agencies
   d.   vendors
   e.   county agencies or officials
   f.   state agencies or officials
   g.   general agencies or officials
5. Professional colleagues
6. Personal contacts

General managers may spend little time with superiors but they have frequent interaction with subordinates; Mintzberg reported that the managers in this study spent about 10% of their time with their directors. In contrasts, the city managers spent from 8%-32% of their time with city council members. City managers spent 22%-38% of their time with staff members, most of it in small segments. Longer, scheduled contacts were kept with associates, people who do business with the city only from time to time and thereby cannot be called "subordinates." One unique characteristic of the interactions in the city manager's workday is that his clientele (citizens) are supposed to have direct access to the city council, whom they, of course, elect. Unions, employee groups, or citizens can do an "end run" around an administrative decision by going to the council, by meeting with other citizens, or by threatening the council with such action. In fact, the open weekly or biweekly public council meeting is often used by citizen groups as a forum to pressure the council to pressure the city manager to pressure the staff to immediate and visible action. Or, an employee group can use the same public forum to pressure the council to make a decision that an administrator would find inefficient. On the other hand, this pattern by these same groups ensures that the voters have input into the administration of city government.

Perhaps the most distinctive trait of the culture of public management is the idea of "publicness." The observational data on the purpose underlying city managers' activities discussed later suggests a daily operating principle of *collective* responsibility for the affairs of others.[7] This principle contrasts with the more commonly assumed instrumental model of the manager who is individually responsible for guiding the organization toward its goal in the most technically efficient manner. Collective responsibility is reflected in the different style of decision making described below. City managers spent a good deal of time supplying members of the city council with information upon which public policy decisions could be made. They were consistently careful to distinguish between seeing that the council reached a decision reflecting the various interests of constituents in accordance with certain time tables (such as the annual budget cycle) and seeing that a particular decision outcome was selected. Hence, rather than being a lone decision maker, city managers are more accurately described by the term "decision facilitators."

The "publicness" of city managers' daily routines is also indicated by the frequency of their unscheduled meetings and telephone calls. When coupled with data which show more frequent interaction with "clients," these findings suggest openness of the public manager to people outside City Hall. Furthermore, the greater frequency of city council meetings (relative to meetings of corporate boards of directors) underscores the collective responsibility of the city manager through the ritual of public contact among the three principal actors in the public-sector drama: managers, city councils and members of the public.

Why Did The Managers Allocate Their Time and Energies as Described?

What were the purposes of the interactions? It is here that the divergence from the managers described by Mintzberg becomes significant. (Mintzberg reported time in terms of percentage of contact time; this study used percentage of total work time. In order to avoid misleading comparisons, time figures have not been used in listing the five most predominant purposes of contacts for each group of managers.)

Most Time-Consuming Purposes of Contacts

Mintzberg's Business Managers	*Hale's City Managers*
Receiving Information	Educate
Review	Strategize
Strategy	Explore
Ceremony	Link
Action Requests	Monitor

In order to give the reader a flavor of city managers' work and a sense of the contrast with Mintzberg's business managers, the following is a brief statement on each of the Mintzberg purpose categories followed by examples of the predominant activities found in the city management data.

Receiving information was the most time-consuming purpose of the contacts Mintzberg's business managers had with other people. Mintzberg reported that more than one-third of the information received was "gossip, hearsay, and opinion"[8] and another 28% came from more formal information he called "briefings." The city managers also received information but it was neither of these types. City management information was much more specific to a particular program or problem and therefore a part of such categories as exploring, monitoring, and to a small degree assessing. The city managers' information framework seemed to call for more specific definitions of purpose.

The term *review* has been used in both studies, but its prevalence among Mintzberg's business managers and the two larger cities of the present study suggests it is more evident in larger settings where the manager is further from direct contact with the operation.

The primary difference in the *strategy* contacts of managers in both sectors is that decision making does not reside with the city managers; for the Mintzberg managers, strategy and decision making were very definitely linked. For city managers, strategy was more often linked to carrying out decisions made by the council.

The prevalent *ceremonial contacts* for the Mintzberg managers were nonexistent among the city managers. The ceremonial activities are carried out by the mayor or other elected officials, not by the chief administrative officer.

Mintzberg included requests for authorization, for information, requests for the manager to initiate something, and attempts to influence the manager in the category called *action requests*.

On 43 occasions, the primary purpose of a city manager's contact was to *educate*--his most time-consuming work. This included explaining the city's position to a reporter, correcting information, defining a task for a department head, explaining to a developer what is politically possible for the council members, giving information by answering a question, and some types of public relations. Managers sought out reporters, took time to explain the difference between an initiative and a referendum, or the background to a current issue.

During the week of observation, one manager (designated as *Manager C* for purposes of the study) spent 17% of his time educating. The deputy city administrator for management and budget had been at his job only a short time and the finance director had recently died, so the city manager had to educate the new department head and the acting division head. He said it was his job to help the new people comprehend the whole city financial picture. It is likely that Manager C monitored the budget process more carefully during the budget team's first budget cycle.

Although it did not appear in the five observation weeks, each city manager has a method of educating new council members. In City B this includes spending a full week after each election visiting every city park and department and sharing city hall jargon with each elected official. Each weekly staff report subtly educates the council members and does not depend on prior knowledge being retained. The city managers also educate by forwarding selected written material to staff and council.

The term *strategize* is not to be confused with overall military planning or with smoke-filled back rooms. Discussion during these contacts centered on how to accomplish what the city council had directed or conversations with councilmen about how to go about reaching ends they thought desirable. Eighteen of the 24 contacts coded in this way were meetings with people from two or more of the participant groups defined earlier. The city managers from the two largest cities raised the average amount of time spent in strategy. The managers from three smaller cities spent 3%-4% of their time in contacts for this purpose, whereas managers from the two larger cities spent 12% and 16%.

The purpose of some contacts was to begin to plan the decision-making process, often by gathering information, or to *explore*. "To search through or into" described such contacts as having a conversation over lunch with a department head about how his department would cut its expenditures if it had to, listening to a political activist describe how he would handle a potentially explosive issue, holding a staff meeting to brainstorm about the upcoming budget cycle, or showing sensitivity as a department head began to solve a sticky problem. Some weeks of a city's budget cycle allow for more time spent in such preparations. City Manager E averaged almost one hour in five on such contacts during the week. Contacts coded as exploratory in purpose were the third highest consumer of time (8%). Most of the exploring was done with department heads even in cities where there was a deputy city manager.

A *link* is a "unit in a communication system." A city manager is a link between council and staff, a link to the world outside the city, to the community outside of city government, an interpreter for the "outsiders" about the city and/or its government. This includes being a conduit and passing information, bringing someone up-to-date (e.g., a councilman who was not at a staff meeting), putting a staff member in touch with a document that will answer her question, or telling the staff how to write a report for the council. In Manager A's opinion, "When you boil the job down, you're a conduit for information." City Manager D was most visibly a link with state officials when an assemblyman asked him how small cities would react to potential legislation. Eight out of Manager D's eleven contacts on the UDAG grant (his major issue) were link contacts, as he was the contact person for Washington to pass information to the council, the city attorney, and the consultant.

In addition to exploring at the beginning stages of projects, *monitoring* is needed to move an event to its next point. At least since 1945,[9] this activity has been seen as a city manager's responsibility. Keeping an eye on current issues, updating and exchanging information, reprimanding an employee, or receiving information requested earlier allows him to know the next move. "To keep track of, regulate, or control the operation of (as a machine or process)" is the dictionary definition of monitor. While most of the monitoring was done with department heads, this was also the purpose of most of the contacts with division heads, deputies and city attorneys. The budget is a device for monitoring both expenditures and programs.

The other purposes used in the coding of city managers' contacts were organizational meetings that included many of the other activities, review/preview, negotiate, touch base, represent the city, transition activities, sell a city program, supervise, mediate, follow up, scheduling, prod, assess, evaluate, delegate, decide.

Mintzberg's terms did not work for explaining the purpose of activities in the present study because city managers are more frequently involved in the initiation of action and monitoring of action rather than either decision making or final review which is the common purpose of activities for business managers. City managers appear to be brokers who initiate or stimulate action with the city council. After the council makes a decision, the city manager initiates action by the staff and stimulates the activity by monitoring. These "activity purposes" simply do not match those used commonly in business.

Conclusion

What is unique about the role of the city manager? The twenty-two purpose categories were clustered into four role categories in an attempt to draw closer to a concise statement about the nature of city management work. The roles of city managers in this study were those of brokers, information agents and administrators.

Brokers

In their role as brokers, city managers spent most of their time sharing knowledge, educating, negotiating or brokering among various groups, and instigating communication by linking people. This role consumed the highest percentage of the managers' time (37%) and accounted for just over one-quarter of their interactions.

In all of their contacts as brokers, the city managers did not operate in the forefront despite their reputations for being assertive managers. City managers are barely aware of the theory of representative government which calls for the mayor and council to make decisions and to function in formal ceremony. The city manager is not merely an administrator whose task it is to run an organization efficiently; he is an administrator who brokers for council members. We see here a fundamental distinction between private and public management. In business, managers decide and carry out. In cities, managers initiate, broker and implement.

Information Agent

The activities in the role of interactive information agent accounted for the highest percentage of the contacts (29%) but less time (21%) than brokering. One of the assumptions in the public management culture is that all parties have a right to all information. This assumption may account for the significance of the role of a city manager as an information officer. One of the earliest surprises for the researcher was the incredible openness with which these managers operated. Doors were not closed to keep information inside. The public nature of city management work was constantly evident.

The role of the city manager in policy building has been debated for many years. Data generated in this study suggest that the policy role is one of a group of invisible activities; that is, through information gathering and disseminating, managers stimulate policy based on an understanding of the directions of the city council. At the same time, information is used to stimulate council members toward implementation of an overall plan. City managers tend to form a general long-range plan early in their tenures. The implementation of that plan is not even begun unless council members are interested in moving along the same path. The speed with which city managers facilitate movement in the direction of this plan depends on their understanding of the council's abilities and needs. It is through brokering that city managers stimulate development of policy and through information transfer that they facilitate implementation of policy.

One of the interesting side views of this study was watching city managers work to get city councils to take ownership of their plans. Council members would, of course, dismiss a manager for usurping policy planning power if they thought he was doing so!

Administrative

A review of city management literature led to the expectation that the administrative role would take precedence over all others. This assumption was not confirmed; 15% of the time was consumed by 28% of contacts that were related to administration. Perhaps at the time that most of the literature was written the conventional wisdom held administration to be the city manager's primary role. Another explanation is that as community leadership and policy activities have become more evident in the literature and the rhetoric of the profession, the activities of a broker and information agent have become more acceptable and therefore more visible to a researcher in the 1980s.[10]

Though conventional wisdom may not support this argument, the efficiency desired by the early backers of the city manager plan of government has probably been realized. On most council-manager cities the usual programs for cost controls, and efficient staff deployment have been in place for many years. In addition, most cities have undergone both a sharp reduction in federal aid and local revenue limits, resulting in years of cutback management. The extraordinary diversity of the city's line of services, the complex interaction of council, citizenry, associates, staff, and manager, all covered by the press, leave the public with the impression that city government is both untidy and inefficient. It is often difficult for citizens to clearly understand the linkage between their taxes and city services. The taxpayer revolt is one result. While there are always widely varying opinions as to what the city ought to do, there is virtually no evidence that what the city does choose to do is done inefficiently. Too often, however, the debate over what the city should do leaves the impression that what is being done is not done well.

The legal guidelines under which the manager and staff operate are more than rules or principles that can be changed by administrative decision. Laws governing such administrative activities as public agency bid requirements for city contracts severely restrict administrative discretion while protecting fairness to the bidders. Public employee retirement laws are voted on by the council, they are not internally negotiable items. As local attitudes change, laws tend to remain fixed and few city councils want to tackle wholesale revision or updating. This reluctance lessens administrative flexibility for city managers in a way that business managers seldom experience or understand.

This study demonstrates that city management is unique work. While it is still a form of management and matches Mintzberg's business managers in intensity and in its general character, it is sharply different. City managers' work is more educational, more brokering in style, more information based and more democratically procedural. It is also much less visibly decisive than business management. Nalbandian's research indicates that people choose public, as against business, administration because they are more interested in professionalism, the public interest, effectiveness, equity and innovativeness. These interests surface as skills in the work of city managers. Managing both an efficient *and* a democratic city is markedly different work from managing a business.[11]

Notes

1. Henry Mintzberg, *The Nature of Managerial Work* (New York: Harper & Row, 1973).

2. Martha L. Hale, *A Structured Observation Study of the Nature of City Managers' Work.* Ph.D. Dissertation, University of Southern California, 1983.

3. Mintzberg, p. 29.

4. Ibid., p. 30.

5. Ibid., p. 51.

6. Ibid., p. 51.

7. H. George Frederickson and David K. Hart, "The Public Service and the Patriotism of Benevolence," *Public Administration Review*, vol. 45 (September/October 1985), pp. 547-553.

8. Mintzberg, p. 253

9. Richard J. Stillman, II, *The Modern City Manager: A 1971 Profile of a Public Professional in American Local Government* (Washington: International City Management Association, 1971), pp. 18.

10. Peter L. Berger and Thomas Luckman, *The Social Construction of Reality: A Treatise in the Sociology of Knowledge* (Garden City, New York: Doubleday, 1966).

11. James G. March and Guje Sevon, "Gossip, Information, and Decision-making," *Advances in Information Processing in Organizations*, vol. 1 (Greenwich, Connecticut: JAI Press, 1984), pp. 95-107.

Response

Howard D. Tipton
Daytona Beach, Florida

The tasks of city managers are many and varied. The statistical analysis presented in "The Nature of City Managers' Work" discusses why city managers spend their time in certain areas of work.

I agree that the modern city manager spends a minority of time on administration in the classic sense. Cost cutting and efficiency are important but not primary. Today the expectation of city councils is that managers will be brokers/negotiators/leaders in public/private ventures. Administrative efficiency is not as important as making the deals that build the vision of what the city wants to become. Managers are evaluated by their city councils and community groups on whether they "get things done." Therefore, managers often stimulate or initiate policy. While the final decision rests with elected officials, the manager's recommended program will often become the adopted plan of the legislative body.

Many managers are very assertive in their role of recommending policy. While they give public credit for accomplishments to elected officials, they are no less aggressive than are private managers. It is clear that those managers who are strong policy leaders spend a great deal of time with their councils, educating and briefing them on the issues at hand.

In my experience, managers spend much of their time in strategy sessions. Information is reviewed, alternatives are outlined and direction is given for implementation. The manager's relationship with the external community requires the same kind of strategy sessions.

Managers are initiators. Their experience in a myriad of city problems and issues gives them the knowledge necessary to handle many opportunities or problems. It is important for managers to maintain an overview and not get bogged down in details. Managers anticipate needs and develop alternative approaches; they do not sit back and wait for the council or the community to raise issues.

I differ with the Hale conclusion on city manager decision-making where it was indicated that strategy for city managers was more often linked to carrying out decisions. The manager must envision decisions to be recommended to the city council just as the private manager makes recommendations to a board of directors. Therefore, the manager's strategy must involve decision-making both at the policy level and at the implementation level.

The modern manager is very much involved as a broker/information agent and I believe he spends a great deal of his time in that capacity. The manager's office is an information center and the manager serves as an informed broker for the city council among competing interests.

Finally, the measure of city management activity is not broad category descriptions that result from averaging survey numbers; it is the actual effort which takes place. For example, describing managers by saying, "Seventy-seven percent of work time was spent in conversation and 13% spent at desk work" does not indicate the dynamics of city management. Therefore, my remaining words concentrate on discussing manager activities within the principal categories presented in the paper, giving life to Professor Hale's analysis.

Manager as a Broker

Managers spend the majority of their time implementing goals and objectives through negotiation or brokering. They will be found soliciting proposals for a new convention center and headquarters hotel; negotiating for parking that will help existing business; working to secure a new anchor tenant for downtown; selling the need for a new harbor development that creates a drawing for redevelopment areas; negotiating for new city golf courses so as to improve community recreation and attract high quality residential development; convincing a developer to provide a free site for a new stadium and selling the old stadium site to a university for its expansion needs; packaging a low interest loan program with local bankers to facilitate the rehabilitation of downtown buildings; negotiating the purchase of key sites that accomplish redevelopment needs; negotiating with property owners outside the city to annex their property; negotiating interlocal agreements among local governments for provision of services or distribution of revenues; and lobbying state legislators.

The above examples show the dynamics of modern city management, the activities that make the work rewarding, build a healthy city, improve the tax base, and provide new jobs.

Manager as a Strategist

While many city goals are possible, timing and support are initially important. The judgment of the manager gained from experience is the key to building a base of support from required interest groups. That judgment can also control the time sequence in order to obtain the best result.

An example is the requirement to raise taxes. The building of a base of leadership support in the business and residential community is important. Outreach meetings and media releases which explain the need for tax increase should precede any public consideration by the city council. Support group endorsements are needed as well as spokesmen from those groups who will appear at public hearings to support the tax increase.

Timing is often critical; an example is the management of the financial process so that taxes are not raised in an election year.

Manager as Communicator and Educator

The manager is in the center of information flow from city staff, city council and citizens. The use of knowledge to educate the community is a primary responsibility of the manager. Verbal, written and multi-media communication is commonplace. Briefing council members on important issues is one of the manager's required duties. No elected official wants surprises. A council member does not want to read in the morning paper that something significant happened in the city yesterday. Councils do not want to be called by the press for a comment and not know what happened.

Policy decisions are the domain of the elected official. But managers recommend policy on a regular basis and council members initiate policy. The experience and knowledge of the manager afford the council the expertise to recommend answers for the great majority of issues that come before them. Council members, as elected officials, are by nature problem avoiders. The manager can make the hard choices between competing interests in the creation of policy and present overall policy to the council for final approval.

Discussion

Hansell: One of the things that struck me was how the manager's role changes with more at-large representation. I'm not sure that's accurate; councils are tending to be elected by district. Fifty-eight percent of council-manager communities have either all district or a combination of district and at-large council members. That representation is causing a totally different focus.

Denton: Counties have always had single-member districts. When that's been the tradition, they react badly to having an at-large chairman of the county board. When counties have always had single-member districts and then become urban, they don't want to have an urban mayor. The trend in cities is to single-member districts and at-large mayors, but counties seem to be fairly comfortable with single-member districts. They like, however, to share the chairmanship. I've worked under both systems. In Dallas it worked very well to have a strong, identifiable mayor elected at large, but in the counties there's a lot of jealousy. Apparently such a model would not work at this point.

Keller: I think the issue may not be how counties elect their representatives. I see two trends. One is the decline in an identifiable power structure through which things get done in a city. The other is more democratically representative councils in which the members are not tied to the existing power structure. In my survey I find councils have more women and more blacks--people who have not previously had high-level positions in the city. Therefore, they can't easily assess the city in a useful way to the manager and they don't form traditional partnerships. Chet Newland's paper tells of the decline in civic-mindedness in cities. Leading citizens ran for councils in the past; therefore, councils became very potent. Now you don't have civic leaders on many councils. Thus, council members may not connect very well to the community in a meaningful way. I'd like to get managers' reactions to that.

Schilling: This at-large issue keeps coming up; it's got many different faces. Single-member districts in Tucson, Arizona, for example, exist at the primary election level but in the general election level you have at-large seats. That does not guarantee minority representation. So that situation is different from the situations mentioned earlier.

Watkins: Our city (Lenexa, Kansas) is fast-growing. If we were tied to the at-large concept, the new people--dynamic young people moving to town--would be excluded from the political process. There is a community south of ours with the old form of commission-manager government. Three of the five elected officials lived within one block of each other. This happened in a community that's growing geometrically from a population standpoint. In growing cities, at least, district representation will help. I think at-large representation in our city would have probably captured the old power elite of this small town. The city would have kept electing the same people.

Denton: The change toward more district representation will require a change in how managers do their work. It will enhance the importance of the brokering and the negotiating role. Although the elite that was elected at large may have worked together naturally and knew how to work together, these people from different districts representing different interests won't necessarily know how to work together to develop policy for the city. The manager and the elected mayor are the people who will carry out that responsibility.

Borut: I'd like to pick up on an issue related to the role of the manager that has only been touched on: the interpersonal facilitator role. The manager has become more of a facilitator and a broker who brings people together and builds consensus. That this is likely to become a more important role.

Anderson: I think that's accurate. We've just gone from at-large to district representation, but without an at-large mayor. The mayor is selected from the council. The people who have been elected to the council are much better representatives of their parts of the community. But they're not used to working together. It does require consensus building, and it does require that they develop themselves as new leaders in the community. The process depends on the ability of the manager in our situation to bring the council together and help them work together.

Gleason: I'd like to reinforce that. I think councils are becoming more eclectic. Yet one of the things the profession is accused of when we get challenged about a change in form is that we are representing the old power elite. District representation encourages people to be more representative but much less focused. If you're too close to the decision-making process, then you're rightly accused of manipulating. So you try to make it possible for these people to be effective and to represent their points of view and change things as appropriate and yet not dominate the process. If you don't do that, then their frustration and the community's frustration become a major impediment to getting anything done.

Toregas: I think a role for the academic is to fit the data into a model and come up with suggestions. What does the information mean? What do the numbers tell you? For example, are we teaching the students at public administration schools interpersonal skills and at what level? If we spend sixty to eighty percent of our time talking to people, then it becomes important to know how to listen and how to talk. I don't know whether we teach that in our schools.

Hansell: But to walk through the Mintzberg role relationships--particularly the categories of roles, decisional roles, external roles, and representational roles--would have been very helpful in terms of giving practitioners guidance.

Hale: You can't use Mintzberg's roles. You get stopped. You end up with zeros in Mintzberg's roles. The roles are different. That brokering role, for example, is much more dominant in the city manager study than it was in Mintzberg's. The facilitator and broker are the primary roles of city managers. Through distribution of information they are building consensus, policy and decisions.

Watson: One of the big changes has been open meetings and open records, and television. I suspect that we're talking about growing cities, but a lot of cities are not growing and don't have those same structural problems. In your survey you need to remember that a large proportion of city managers are in cities under 25,000 people. They're not having those same kinds of problems. In this city (Lawrence, Kansas) we have television right in the face of the commissioners. According to law, two of the five commissioners cannot get together and talk about what we're talking about today. If two commissioners were here today, I'd have to have it on their calendar so that the press could know about it and could be here. That has brought city managers into a broker role. You're trying to get people together and trying to bring ideas out, rather than sitting down at a meeting and talking about issues freely and openly. I don't think you can overlook these changes that have been initiated by statute.

Hansell: I remember an ICMA task force in 1968 or 1969 on the quality of the local government career service. The lead comment in each sentence in that report noted that city managers in the future were going to require tolerance for a high level of ambiguity. Your paper and others say that we've multiplied that by a factor of about fifty. When you work in the kind of environment that your paper describes, it's no wonder there are some burnout problems and people who are facing situations where they change jobs prematurely or stay too long and don't really see their own well being in relationship to the job.

Hale: An interesting thing happened after the study was done and the city managers themselves read it. Two of them said, "Now that you have described what it is that I do, what I'm doing is ok. My stress level is lower." I wonder if that's not a clue to us in terms of education. We're saying, "Yes, of course, you're fragmented, you're dealing with ambiguity, and so forth, you are not working in a straight linear pattern. You shouldn't feel guilty."

Pokorny: As I read the study, I got a picture of frenetic activity--much action and very little reflection. My question is, Where in your model did you build in time or did you find time for just reflecting and thinking about building and strategic planning?

Hale: I'm convinced that the thinking goes on in the context of action, which is one of the things Karl Weick shows in some of his work. It actually does happen. In talking things out with other people, they are reflecting--how do I know what I think until I hear what I say?

McIntyre: I think brokering is a high-risk, high-stress operation. I think that some council members would probably be very offended to think that they were being brokered, manipulated, or somehow directed behind the scenes even though that happens a lot. I doubt seriously that you feel less stress if you know that you are brokering.

Professionalism in City Management
A New Beginning

John Nalbandian
University of Kansas

The field of city management, long a standard for professionalism in public administration, finds itself at a crossroads. Once idealized as politically neutral administrators, city managers have become policy advocates, negotiators of diverse community interests, and brokers of community power. The evolution of the role attests to their skills and stature in contemporary communities. But an uneasiness exists as managers shed the mantle of neutrality in the policymaking process. For in so doing, they have gradually disassociated themselves from a supportive 75 year old philosophical and intellectual heritage.

In the changing role of the city manager we now see a crisis in legitimacy--a growing distance between the actual role of the manager and its idealization. The challenge facing those committed to professional administration of local governments requires finding a new legitimacy. We must justify, both in terms of our democratic heritage and today's political reality, a viable political role for non-elected municipal administrators.

A new kind of professionalism in city management is emerging, grounded in community values and politics. Before examining the new professionalism of city managers, I will first review what is behind the crisis in legitimacy the profession faces.

Modern City Management

For several decades city management has been evolving in ways that challenge the traditional city manager's role. First, the city manager's role reflects the trend of contemporary management away from strict lines of authority and accountability toward consensual decision making. Second, some managers are thrust into the policymaking arena by councils unable or unwilling to exercise political leadership. Third, the enhanced role of special interests in local government has thrust the manager into the role of policy negotiator and power broker.

The changing nature of management itself challenges formal accountability structures at all levels of government and in the business world as well. Some 50 years ago the manager's role was described with the acronym, POSDCORB--planning, organizing, staffing, directing, coordinating, reporting, and budgeting--where responsibilities and accountability could be clearly delineated. In contrast, Paul Ylvisaker offers a contemporary POSDCORB--participating, orchestrating, sharing, devolving, coping, responding, and battling.[1] David Foell, longtime manager of Oakwood, Ohio, expresses a similar view, "The major change [in city management] has been from the pyramidal business way of organizing to a more open, horizonal organization. I think that city managers within their own organizations have to be more like power brokers, the person who helps direct where the resources are going."[2]

John Dever, former city manager and past president of the International City Management Association, voices the frustration of the manager who has to work with a council unwilling or unable to set the direction for local government when he says:

> A major project in a city today takes 7-12 years to plan, finance and realize. How do you get people who are only interested in the next election or how good they look today to participate in this process? This takes council courage and managerial courage--sacrifice--and some communities demand it. Some cities get it through leadership by the council, mayor, or managers--or a combination. The manager must provide whatever assistance is needed, if there is political leadership. If there is none, the manager must foster it--sometimes by taking the lead.[3]

Former executive director of the International City Management Association Mark Keane identifies a third reason why managers have become more active in policy:

> The old concept of the council-manager plan, where everyone on the council would represent city wide interests, and would be immune from special interest pressures, is much less of a practical concept today than it once was. So the manager now is thrust more often into the role of negotiator and mediator... The political role of the manager now is more important and difficult.[4]

For these and perhaps other reasons, contemporary city managers are:

1) enmeshed in the policymaking process as they regulate information, influence priorities, and make recommendations;
2) respond to expectations from community interests, and administrative staff as well as the governing body; and
3) find themselves balancing and compromising demands for professionalism with demands for political responsiveness.

In short, city management has become a politically active profession even as it avoids partisan and electoral politics. Further, *the most salient politics in today's communities involve policy processes and the relationship between citizens, politicians and bureaucrats rather than the dynamics of electoral processes.*

Traditional Foundations of City Management

In contrast to this picture of the manager's role are beliefs which for 75 years have validated the manager's traditional position, providing the philosophical rationale for the council-manager form of government and for professionalism in city management. These beliefs are:

1) the work of city administrators separates them from policy formulation;
2) the city manager is accountable to the governing body alone for policy direction; and
3) efficiency and political responsiveness can be harmoniously pursued in the community.

The Separation of Politics and Administration

Municipal reformers at the turn of the century responded to corruption and inefficiency primarily by seeking to remove politics from administrative processes.

In the reformer's ideal, politics was concerned with policymaking, while administration involved policy execution.[5] Moreover, the essence of city government was seen as administrative--providing services efficiently.[6] Leonard White succinctly wrote in 1926, "The business of government in the twentieth century is fundamentally the business of administration."[7]

Removing politics from administration and placing the reins of administration into the hands of an administrative expert raised this question: How could the administrative arm of government be held accountable to the people if isolated and protected from political processes?

Administrative Accountability

The answer to the accountability question was creative and revolutionary. The reformers sought to unify the power of the legislative and executive branches, arguing that all power should flow from the legislature.[8] The executive, who would be responsible for policy implementation and administrative processes, would report to a small governing body which would concentrate on developing public policy. There would be no need for checks and balances because the structure of government would not provide the executive with independent authority which could challenge the elected body's responsibility for policy development.

Efficiency and the Public Interest

The early part of the 20th century is noteworthy for its unbridled faith in science and rationality. In scientific management, efficiency was the opposite of corruption.[9] According to Samuel Haber, "Efficiency and good came closer to meaning the same thing in these years than in any other period of American history."[10] How could anyone argue against efficiency in government when it symbolized morality?

By extension, the business community, the embodiment of efficiency, also was regarded positively. In contrast, the reformers identified politics as a source of corruption and inefficiency.[11] Richard Childs, father of the council-manager plan, deliberately adopted the title "city manager" to parallel the "general manager" common at the time in business enterprise.[12] For the reformers government was a business, thus the value of efficiency should prevail in designing its structure as well as in establishing norms of administrative procedure.[13]

Depoliticizing the City

The council-manager form extends the depoliticization of government beyond administrative processes into the sphere of electoral politics as well. Unifying powers rather than separating them assumes the community is a harmonious unit with a single purpose rather than the summation of desires and needs of special interests and constituents. This belief is reflected in non-partisan, at-large elections and the idea that governing is a part-time endeavor where political amateurs are the rule not the exception.[14] The council-manager form envisions a governing body comprised of a mayor selected by the governing body from its members--preferably business leaders--who work during the day and are willing to serve the community in repayment for their economic good fortune.[15]

Vulnerability of the Council-Manager Plan

Almost immediately, weaknesses were found in the council-manager plan which foreshadowed the present crisis in legitimacy. Foremost among them was division over the role of the city manager.

The role of the manager--policy leader or neutral administrator--was strongly debated among the first managers. They appeared comfortable in the world of action and in maintaining their prerogatives as executives, and even occasionally as reformers. They were less comfortable when reflecting on the meaning of their political responsiveness.[16] Samuel Haber observes, "On paper, the City Manager was a strict construction of Goodnow's maxims. However, in the most celebrated management municipalities, the manager soon eclipsed the elected council."[17]

A second weakness, both then and now, is the lack of political leadership on the city council. According to Leonard White, "One of the puzzling problems in connection with the city-manager position is presented by the difficulties in achieving trustworthy and competent political leadership."[18] In part, the managers were taking a more visible role in their communities because there was no active political leadership to remind them of their role. White reports, "When the Republican national convention met in Cleveland in 1924 there was displayed over the city hall a large banner, 'Welcome to Cleveland, W. R. Hopkins, manager.'" In their zeal to reduce the power of political machines, the reformers failed to acknowledge the legitimate role of politics in the community.[19]

A third weakness centers on the belief that efficiency and the public interest go hand-in-hand. A few of the early critics recognized that at-large elections, amateur politicians, and the courting of the business community would leave many citizens estranged from a city government which had been as close to them as their block worker and precinct captain.[20] Childs commented on elections in Dayton:

> In Dayton there is extra danger in the fact that the business
> men at the beginning had things too wholly their own way and

elected a handpicked business ticket. Now business men comprise but a trifling percentage of the population and live a good deal in a little social world of their own, and a good many currents of opinion can flow that business men know nothing of.[21]

While early criticisms of the plan led to concern over the job security of city managers, today these weaknesses have spawned doubts about the plan itself: that the manager unduly influences the policymaking role of the council; and that the professionalism which managers hold in esteem is pursued at the expense of responsiveness to all parts of the community.

Administration Under Attack

While city managers and the International City Management Association are justifiably concerned about these criticisms, the attack simply focuses a broader debate. Government is under scrutiny in general, and professionalism suffers in particular.

In the past several decades two major social trends have occurred which fundamentally affect politics and, ultimately, our understanding of why people criticize the council-manager plan.

Demands for More Government

Government works, therefore people have higher expectations and place more demands upon it. People know their trash will be picked up, snow will be removed, streets will be repaired, water will be drinkable, and sewers will work. If cities were unable to deliver services, citizen expectations would not continue to grow. Elaine Sharp expresses the point this way, "The more the broad mass of the population is exposed to the problem-solving capacities of urban governments' service-delivery bureaucracies, the more they develop a taste for these services which is incapable of satisfaction."[22]

Related to Sharp's conclusion that effective service delivery stimulates higher expectations is the more general proposition that political activity can make a difference in communities. It is not just through the initiative and referendum in California where citizens and special interests influence policy and politics. Nationwide, citizens and special interests exert significant pressure in rezoning cases, location of landfills, school curricula, and economic development.

As citizens realize that government works and politics can make a difference, they lobby government to regulate behavior of which they disapprove. The simplest example is the pressure to ban smoking in public places, but there are many others. Whether government prohibits smoking in public buildings, requires motorcyclists to wear helmets, sanctions or prohibits abortions, subsidizes economic development, or provides sanitized needles to drug abusers, it raises fundamental questions of legitimacy. What is it we want our government to be and to do?

186

While government itself comes under increasing pressure to justify itself, the ability of administrators and bureaucracies to do their work effectively has advanced at a much faster pace than has the ability of elected officials to do theirs. Moreover, while I believe it is far easier today to be an effective administrator than an effective politician, the importance of politics has increased not diminished. John Dever, former ICMA president, describes the importance of politics to the administrator when he says, "Behind every effective and strong city manager, you inevitably find a council willing to formulate clear and concise policies. Council members need courage too."[23]

More effective politics, not more professionalism, is needed to improve the legitimacy of city government. Nevertheless, professionalism will grow simply because today's problems require objective, sophisticated, long-term analyses. Moreover, criticism which is aimed at government in general ends up being criticism of administration because it is visible. John Schaar succinctly makes the point that while the power of professionals is increasing, their authority is decreasing.[24] Over the long haul professionalism, as we presently conceive of it, cannot overcome ineffective politics. For example, in Wyandotte County, Kansas, across the river from Kansas City, outgoing part-time commissioners voted themselves a lump sum payment of $29,500 for unused sick leave and vacation time. The payment was subsequently rescinded by the new commission, but it is doubtful that the rescission can shield any public employee of Wyandotte County from the community's view that "government officials" tried to abuse the public trust.[25]

Professionals think rationally and objectively and, in some cases, scientifically. While professionalism is essential to dealing with public problems, it cannot answer fundamental questions of individual worth, of pride in belonging, or of the relationship of citizens to their schools, churches, courts, and governments. These are fundamental questions in contemporary society which can only be answered through reflective political discourse. I think citizens and elected officials know this better than the broad array of professionals who work for municipalities or other levels of government. Furthermore, the call for stronger mayoral power in cities like Fort Collins, Dallas and Kansas City reflects implicitly citizen frustration over the lack of political dialogue and the ineffectiveness of council politics to deal with fundamental questions.[26]

A New Foundation for Professionalism in Local Government

This critique of bureaucracy and professionalism comes into focus in local governments. Compared to state and federal government, local government is where broad concerns are transformed into concrete issues. In order to lay a new foundation to legitimize the power of professionals in local government, we start with the observation that the quality of politics in our communities is not going to improve demonstrably. Recognizing the importance of politics to effective administration, how does the professional proceed to reclaim lost legitimacy? The first step is to recognize that government in general flows from community values. If professionalism cannot be legitimated within the confines of an elected city council, it must turn to the community itself. After all, the legitimacy of the council rests on community values as well.

The new professionalism portrays the community in terms of four values and focuses on governmental responsiveness to those values. Further, any community can be viewed from a value perspective; and each community emphasizes each value differently, giving communities distinct political profiles. These values are representativeness, efficiency, individual rights, and social equity.

Representativeness

Citizens who will be affected by a public decision should have an opportunity to debate that policy prior to its enactment. Elected officials represent the opinions and demands of citizens, groups of citizens, and special interests. Citizen demands and opinions are weighed one against another and against previously established policies. The more heterogeneous a community, the more importance its citizens will place on representation. Tom Downs, then chief administrative officer in the District of Columbia, noted, "Cities are complex, messy, and conflict-oriented. They are melting pots. The more diverse the city council is, the more diverse the politics. They probably better represent the real city. So, it is easier, in some respects, to deal with real problems."[27]

Efficiency

This value encompasses rational and objective analysis of public problems, cost/benefit analysis, bureaucratic norms and professionalism. As public problems become more complex, requiring more expertise, this value increases in importance. John Fischbach, city manager in Lake Forest, a suburb of Chicago, expresses the value of efficiency in the following:

> You can argue about whether Lake Forest should pick up garbage, but once you've made that decision to pick it up, there is a cost effective way to do it that a professional manager can bring to bear. I may not have anything to add to the decision of whether we pick up the garbage, other than my opinion, but once they've told me I'm going to pick it up, I can do it better with professional management than without it.[28]

Individual Rights

This value connotes legal protection and is expressed when property owners request rezoning, public employees invoke merit system or Constitutional protection, and when clients of public services seek redress for inequitable treatment. Individual rights may be expressed in the due process provisions of administrative decision making. The more that citizens perceive governmental decisions as capricious and arbitrary or want to minimize the impact of government the more likely they are to emphasize individual rights.

Social Equity

This is the last value and the most controversial. It regards the distribution of public policy outcomes rather than opportunities. Social equity is more concerned with fairness to groups than fairness to individuals. It is a highly controversial value because it frequently conflicts with efficiency and individual rights. The argument that city services should be distributed to each neighborhood equitably is non-controversial. More controversial is the idea that public jobs or government contracts should be distributed equally to racial groups or by gender.

Sylvester Murray, then city manager of San Diego, expressed the value of social equity this way:

> There are some people in the community who appreciate the importance of government and are sophisticated enough to weave it and to mold it so that the quality of their lives are enhanced. There are other people in the community who do not recognize this with the same degree of sophistication. It is the responsibility of managers in government to take the initiative to see that an individual's quality of life is not negatively affected solely because that person does not know how to use the system.[29]

To simplify my point: *political responsiveness=representativeness + efficiency + individual rights + social equity.*

All communities will reflect these four values in political debate and public policymaking, but not in the same proportions. Sometimes these values will reinforce one another. In such cases very strong public policies will emerge. However, in most cases, they will conflict. In these situations, compromise policies will result. In addition, community value profiles change over time so that at one point a community may place more value on efficiency (professionalism) and at another time on representativeness (politics). This is what I think is happening today in Dallas where there is growing community pressure to politicize government organizations.

If we take a value perspective on traditional professionalism, we find that: *professionalism=efficiency + responsiveness.*

While at first glance this formula appears acceptable, closer scrutiny suggests otherwise. Traditionally, professionals have left responsiveness to elected officials. In other words, "we will handle the efficiency aspect, you handle the responsiveness, and we will work as a team because I report to you." The logic breaks down if the community is dissatisfied with the quality of political discourse.

In short, if councils fail to provide political leadership, either because they are unable or unwilling, the legislative values of representativeness and social equity will not forcefully enter public debate. In such a case, the legitimacy of administration, if not its power, depends upon the incorporation of these values into administrative processes. Further, to the extent that individuals perceive government as an unresponsive monolith, the importance of due process--individual rights--in administrative action cannot be overstated. If the city council does not embody the community's values, the legitimacy of professionalism depends upon incorporating them independently.

City Management: The Practice of Idealism

The new professionalism recognizes the dual heritage of city management. On the one hand, managers have always been expected to act as realists, to follow pragmatic and practical lines of thinking and action. On the other hand, the history of city management is founded in idealism. The new professionalism acknowledges the realistic side of city management as it seeks to reformulate an ideal sensitive to contemporary political life in our communities.

Realism

Managers share pride in their ability to get things done and to quietly build the consensus necessary to implement complex public policies. John Dever captures the "can-do" side of management when he says, "I think the important thing is to find out what people need, to put together the resources to satisfy those needs, and to then see benefits from something you have done."[30] In a newspaper article, Richard Knight, city manager in Dallas, was referred to as "Mr. Fix-It," a reflection of the professional realist.

As a realist the manager's power stems from expertise and experience, held in check by the nature of the manager's employment relationship with the governing body. The realism of city management is captured in the saying that success is being able to count to three in a council of five. The realistic manager *must* be responsive to the council not only because it is democratically correct, but because the manager serves at the council's pleasure. In other words, legitimacy is insured by the realistic need to respond to the council in order to maintain job security.

The notion that legitimacy of the manager's role is insured by the employment relationship is so widely held among managers that to suggest otherwise is heresy.[31] The difficulty with the realist's view is that it passes questions of legitimacy from the manager to the council. That is, when managers justify their roles and actions pointing to council support, they are assuming the council's legitimacy in the eyes of the community. If the council has credibility the manager will also have credibility. However, if the council does not, there is *nothing* the realist manager can point to as an alternative or independent foundation for his/her role and actions.

The only way managers who anchor their role solely in the council can maintain independent credibility is to question the quality of elected officials. In other words, it is not the council as an institution that is the problem, it is the individual council members. Thus, it is common to hear managers criticize the quality of individual council members, "If only I had better council members!" This exclamation effectively divorces the manager from the council, but in so doing it discredits the realist manager's only potential source of legitimacy.

The manager responds by falling back upon his/her "professionalism." The problem with this response is that too many in today's communities view professionalism as a threat to responsiveness. Don Blubaugh, city manager in Walnut Creek, California, acknowledges the critique this way:

A manager today with traditional values may find himself or herself frustrated. Good professional staff work no longer "cuts

190

it." I suspect that even being labeled an efficient, professional person will not work to one's best advantage in dealing with the myriad of comments about government being unresponsive, too businesslike, and uncaring of the people it serves.[32]

While city management will always be rooted, in part, in the manager's relationship to the council, that relationship is not enough to nurture the profession of city management in the future.

Idealism

Earlier, this paper reviewed the idealism which led to creation of the council-manager plan. The essence of city management is found not only in what managers can accomplish; it is also found in their beliefs. The manager as an idealist is committed not only to an employment relationship as a vehicle of legitimacy, but also to an understanding of and commitment to community values--representation, individual rights and social equity, as well as efficiency. Commitment to these values provides an independent source of legitimacy for city managers *and* city management as a profession.

As Martha Hale's research has shown, city managers function largely as educators--of their staff, the council, and citizens.[33] As head of a stable administrative apparatus of government, the manager is a trustee of these values and fosters community education about them. The *legitimacy* of the manager as idealist is rooted in the same values which underpin legitimacy of the council--but with different emphases. This commitment is why managers sometimes take action "because they must" or "because it is right" even though the action may be unpopular with the council or with segments of the community.

The idealist side of city management is captured in these words from Sylvester Murray, former manager of San Diego and past president of ICMA:

> I have been accused of making policy or trying to make policy when I should have been just part of the administration. I have been accused of being a politician because I get out in the community. And I do make speeches, and I do talk to the citizens, and I do encourage neighborhood groups, and I do listen to them, and I do make the city bureaucracies change because a neighborhood group says that they want something. I think that I have been right all these years and that more is going to be demanded from managers who haven't been doing that.[34]

Jewel Scott, city manager in Delaware, Ohio, provides another expression of idealism in city management:

> The council-manager form says that there are some things that are right and some things that are wrong. That doesn't mean that everyone's going to live by that ethical code of conduct, but it does establish a certain expectation. High ethical standards and honesty are important for citizens to have confidence in local government. If professional managers are functioning as they should, they can delineate between the special interests and overall community needs and try to insert some balance into the way services are delivered.[35]

191

In sum, the new professionalism in city management relies on commitment to the council and commitment to community values as a renewed source of legitimacy. The new professionalism acknowledges the tension within the manager as a practical idealist. It defines this tension by regarding realism as the manager's ability to survive and by regarding idealism as the manager's continuing pursuit of the question of "survival for what?"

Consequences

A brief discussion of two of the many consequences of the approach to professionalism which I am proposing will serve as a conclusion. First, I am suggesting that professionalism in city management must focus on administrative process more than on outcomes. City management is about the creation of culture in a community, not about the design of that culture. Whatever activities are required to continually create that culture must be nested in the end values themselves. In other words, the process of searching for the community's values must be based on the same values which are anticipated. If a city is searching for its perspective on social equity, the search itself must reflect social equity. Similarly, if the community is searching for the meaning of representativeness, it must employ representative means and bodies.

Second, while effective city managers are already doing what I am suggesting in this paper, their legitimacy depends on a broader view of professionalism among the manager's key department heads. Managers are at the mercy of their department heads, they're dependent on the quality of interaction between department heads and the community as well as with the city council. For example, in a city beset by problems in police-council-community relations, Dallas City Manager Richard Knight's appointment of Mack Vines as police chief is not only a test of the manager's judgment, but a touchstone signalling a desired relationship between government and citizen in that city.[36]

The transformation in recent years of the parks and recreation function provides another example.[37] In many communities, the increased use by wealthier citizens of private fitness facilities means that city recreation programs become social services to other citizens. Recreation directors now develop programs which the community wants (representation), pay their way through fees (efficiency), insure that programs are available to all segments of the community equally (social equity), and insure that programs do not discriminate against special populations (individual rights).

In larger cities it has become common wisdom that city managers should take care of external relations while the assistant city manager concentrates on internal city operations.[38] While city managers are commonly seen as brokers, negotiators, and consensus builders in the community, similar roles internally cannot go unattended. There is not a department of city government solely concerned with internal operations. As the legitimacy of city management broadens to more fully incorporate community values, the difference between internal and external city operations decreases in importance. The key is legitimacy, both internally to the city staff and externally to the citizens.

1. Larry Lane, *Campus and the Public Service* (Washington, D.C.: National Academy of Public Administration, Fall, 1987). Summary of proceedings and commentary on the Fall, 1987 meeting of the National Academy of Public Administration.

2. John Nalbandian and Raymond G. Davis, eds., *Reflections of Local Government Professionals* (Lawrence, Kansas: Department of Public Administration, University of Kansas, 1987), p. 63.

3. Ibid., p. 19.

4. Ibid., p. 103.

5. Frank J. Goodnow, *Politics and Administration: A Study in Government* (New York: Russell and Russell, 1900). Reissued in 1967, p. 5.

6. Goodnow, *Politics and Administration*, p. 84; Clarence E. Ridley and Orin F. Nolting, *The City Manager Profession* (Chicago: University of Chicago Press, 1934), p. 2.

7. Leonard D. White, *Introduction to the Study of Public Administration* (New York: MacMillan Company, 1926), p. 24.

8. Richard S. Childs, "The Theory of the New Controlled Executive Plan," *National Municipal Review*, vol. 2 (January 1913), pp. 76-81. Reprinted in Edward Charles Mabie, ed., *City Manager Plan of Government* (New York: H. W. Wilson Company, 1918), pp. 77-84; Richard S. Childs, "How the Commission-Manager Plan is Getting Along," *National Municipal Review*, vol. 4 (July 1915), pp. 371-382. Reprinted in Mabie, *City Manager Plan of Government*, pp. 111-123.

9. Dwight Waldo, *The Administrative State* (New York: Ronald Press Company, 1948).

10. Samuel Haber, *Efficiency and Uplift: Scientific Management in the Progressive Era, 1890-1920* (Chicago: University of Chicago Press, 1964), p. ix.

11. Harold A. Stone, Don K. Price and Kathryn H. Stone, *City Manager Government in the United States: A Review After Twenty-Five Years* (Chicago: Public Administration Service, 1940), p. 27.

12. Stone, Price, and Stone, *City Manager Government in the United States*, p. 11.

13. New York Constitutional Convention Commission, *The Constitution and Government of New York* (New York: Bureau of Municipal Research, 1915).

14. This view can be seen today in Kansas City, Missouri, where the Citizens Association, successor to the civic group which successfully challenged the Pendergast machine years ago, recently proposed a two term limit on council members. The *Kansas City Star*, "Two Terms With a Change" (July 26, 1988), p. A-6 endorsed this charter revision writing, "It would reduce the power of incumbents to steamroller to victories. It would ensure turnover on the council, fresh voices from all parts of the community. Perhaps most important, it could restrict the growth of political empires at City Hall which do little for the people but plenty for the barons."

15. Stone, Price and Stone, *City Manager Government in the United States*, Part 3.

16. Leonard D. White, *The City Manager* (Chicago: University of Chicago Press, 1927).

17. Haber, *Efficiency and Uplift*, p. 104.

18. White, *The City Manager*, p. 165.

19. Ibid., p. 10.

20. Lent D. Upson, "Comment on the Dayton Charter," *National Municipal Review*, vol. 4 (April 1915), pp. 266-272. Reprinted in Mabie, *City Manager Plan of Government*, pp. 137-145.

21. Childs, "How the Commission-Manager Plan is Getting Along," p. 120.

22. Elaine Sharp, *Citizen Demand-Making in the Urban Context* (Lawrence, KS: Regents Press of Kansas, 1986), p. 173.

23. Nalbandian and Davis, *Reflections*, p. 17.

24. John Schaar, "Legitimacy in the Modern State," in Philip Green and Sanford Levinson, eds., *Power and Community: Dissenting Essays in Political Science*. Reprinted in William B. Connolly, ed., *Legitimacy and the Modern State* (New York: New York University Press, 1984), p. 126.

25. "Wyandotte County Finishing Business," *Kansas City Times*, January 4, 1989, pp. B-1 and B-2; "Wyandotte Board Promises Changes," *Kansas City Times*, January 11, 1989, p. B-3.

26. See for example, "Let's Vote For Our City's Mayor," *Coloradoan*, December 14, 1988, p. 4; Eddie Faillace, "Mayor Should Balance City Manager," *Coloradoan*, December 7, 1988, p. 6; "Mayor's Race Is Overlooked," *Dallas Morning News*, December 1, 1988, p. 30A; Henry Tatum, "There Is No 'No' Annette," *Dallas Morning News*, January 2, 1989, p. 14A; Yael Abouhalkah, "How Well Is The City Managed?" *Kansas City Star*, August 28, 1988, pp. 1D and 4D; "Veto For Mayor Makes Sense," *Kansas City Star*, November 20, 1988, p. G2.

27. Nalbandian and Davis, *Reflections*, p. 34.

28. Ibid., p. 51.

29. Ibid., p. 150.

30. Ibid., p. 13.

31. The original version of this paper placed far more emphasis on the need for managers to align themselves with community values which might conflict with council decisions. My understatement of the manager's need to respond to the council was met with vocal criticism and literally no support.

32. Donald A. Blubaugh, "The Changing Role of the Public Administrator, *Public Management*, vol. 69 (June, 1987), p. 10.

33. Martha Hale, "The Nature of City Managers' Work," presented at a conference on "The Study of City Management and the Council-Manager Plan," University of Kansas, Lawrence, Kansas, November 10-12, 1988 (also reprinted in this volume).

34. Nalbandian and Davis, *Reflections*, p. 156.

35. Ibid., p. 213.

36. See various articles in the *Dallas Morning News*. For example, "Vines Picks 3 Blacks, Hispanic, Woman for Top Posts" (November 15, 1988), pp. 1A and 8A; "Quiet Efficiency Earns Gold Star for Knight," (December 28, 1988), pp. 1A and 16A.

37. Joseph J. Bannon, ed., *Current Issues in Leisure Services: Looking Ahead in a Time of Transition* (Washington: International City Management Association, 1987).

38. David Whitlow, "The Future is Now: The Role of the Assistant/Deputy Manager," *Public Management*, vol. 69 (June, 1987), pp. 17-18.

Response

Eric A. Anderson
Eau Claire, Wisconsin

The council-manager form of government does not lack legitimacy for the role of the city manager. The prohibition from participation in electoral politics is valid, functional, and reflects the values of our citizens. The role of the manager in the policy process is also valid, functional and reflects the values of our citizens, dating from the 1938 Code of Ethics: "In order that policy may be intelligent and effective, he . . . encourages positive decisions on policy by the council instead of passive acceptance of his recommendations." The amendments to the code in 1952 recognized the manager's role as community leader explicitly: "The city manager as a community leader submits . . . facts and advice on matters of policy to give the council a basis for making decisions on community goals."

City managers have, almost from the beginning, had an acknowledged role in the formulation, recommendation and advocacy of policy. Most managers recognize that politics and administration represent the ends of a spectrum and not opposite rims of a canyon.

People who reside in council-manager cities do not typically see the policy involvement of the manager as politics. Rather, they know it is a check on the extension of electoral politics into the operation of their city government. To say to the people of my city that I occupy a "visible political role" would not be accurate because it implies that I am involved in electoral politics--they know I am not.

After separate referenda on the same ballot to change the form of council elections, as well as abandon the council-manager form, I have had a stronger political mandate than the council.

I have, briefly, visited that "paradise" of the legitimated political mandate for the manager. It doesn't work. Council leadership is destroyed and representative democracy is endangered. I offered my resignation to the new council in order to restore the proper balance of power between the council and the manager.

For the city manager to have tried to maintain a political role would have violated the symbolism citizens recognize and rely upon, symbolism that works. I am a check on politics, leavening the policy process with objective, technical, managerial information and activity. Managers cannot determine policy. Yet, without professional involvement, policy would lack objectivity and integration, as well as the technical and managerial basis needed for it to be effective. Managers are expected to be involved in policy formulation and advocacy. Most residents to not consider it a political role in the same way they define the political role of council members.

The Need for New Legitimacy

Yet, I agree that the legitimacy of the city-manager form of government is under attack. The attack, however, appears to be coming from those who feel that city councils have failed to represent their constituents. The complaint made in several of the papers prepared for this conference is that the quality of leadership and ability of council members is less than adequate. Citizens often put it differently--"I want a council member to represent me in the city government, not one who represents city government to me."

Councils are often chastised for failure to represent. Sometimes, as in Phoenix, Arizona, and Eau Claire, Wisconsin, council member elections have been changed from at-large to district (or ward). In other cases the change is more radical, and the form of government is thrown out in favor of the mayor-council structure. In other cases, a chief administrative officer is hired to fulfill the responsibilities previously carried out by a city manager. The role of the administrator in the policy process often remains the same as that of the manager.

Cities with the mayor-council form have become more professional in their operations and management. They have maintained the strength of their political decision-making and electoral process while incorporating some of the advantages of professional management. Advocates of the council-manager form have to support the incorporation of stronger political representativeness to maintain legitimacy.

The need for new legitimacy means a more viable, effective political role for the council, not to "justify . . . a visible political role for non-elected municipal administrators."

We need to recognize that political parties, apart from the evils of the patronage system, do foster and maintain effective political debate and do link the citizen to the city government through participation in the political process.

We need to recognize that, for some cities, district (or ward) election of city council members does result in more effective representation of citizens.

We need to recognize that the separately elected mayor within the council-manager form can provide a necessary focus for political debate and council leadership.

Legitimacy requires strengthening the representative nature of the electoral process and, thereby, both the real and perceived ability of the citizen to be represented in the deliberations of the council and especially in the policy decisions they make.

Summary

We are still engaged in the great democratic experiment begun over two hundred years ago. Nowhere is the experiment more important than in local government. The council-manager plan came into being to eliminate the damage that "unreformed" politicians were doing. It has grown successfully because it has repaired that damage and met the challenges for technical and managerial competence and leadership required by our society.

We must assure that the form does not become the vehicle for abandoning the experiment in our cities and towns. We need to assure that the powers of our elected officials to address the content of political debate, to set the missions of our communities, and to lead are strong and effective. We can do this by strengthening the institutional arrangements within the council-manager form that build strong councils.

Discussion

Frederickson: I'm reminded of the observation "It works in practice, but we can never make it work in theory." Does the Nalbandian theory help us explain what is going on in the practicing professional world of city management?

Schilling: I think this theory tells us what to focus on and what's important in practice. What John Nalbandian has described is accurate in terms of a way for a city manager to work with a council, learn the values of the community, and help the council and the government to express those values through a process orientation. That theory may be dangerous in bypassing the council members to gain legitimacy for the manager and his staff.

Frederickson: Have we passed the time of neutral competence as our justifying theory, as an explanatory or normative position? If we are no longer neutral, what are we for?

Novak: I'm very simplistic about this. I want to get something accomplished. That's my goal.

Frederickson: Is what you want to get accomplished what the people want to get accomplished and what the council wants?

Novak: My job is to get accomplished what the city council wants accomplished.

McIntyre: I think I heard John Nalbandian say that we are moving toward more involvement with the process. If that's the case, we've shortchanged the administration, the council, and the public.

Banovetz: I understand John to have meant process is more important than outcome. The way people view the process that was used to accomplish a goal may be more important than the goal itself. You see this in some political decision-making forums, even in national politics. The kinds of people on the Supreme Court become more important than the Supreme Court itself. The process that is used to reach decisions when you campaign becomes more important than the outcome of the campaign. You have to be sure that every affected interest base has been contacted, that everything has been done according to Hoyle. Reporters are more often critical of procedure than for achieving 80 or 90 percent of an objective.

Frederickson: Yet I hear others saying that the city manager has some responsibility for results. The city manager has to have some vision of where the city ought to go.

Banovetz: I agree that process has become very important.

Frederickson: Can that be codified in our professional training on campus?

Banovetz: I don't know how.

Tipton: I think there comes a time when we look at process and managers and say, "Now we must exclude certain elements that normally we've included in the process." When we ask leaders to make those kinds of assessments, we take a risk by leaving certain people out who might otherwise muddy the water.

Hale: It seems to me that one of the underlying themes in John's paper is the concept of professionalism. If we take professionalism to mean neutrality, I want to reject that definition. Professionalism means knowing when to take those risks; indeed, being unprofessional is not taking those risks at certain times. One of the things that may be holding back an acceptance of what John is saying is a provincial view of what professionalism has been.

Svara: The professional model has as one of its core values autonomy, which is incompatible with the values of public professionalism. What we're really groping for is a new set of values, a new set of ethical responsibilities for public professionals who consider accountability to be of central importance.

Toregas: I'm a little confused. Clearly a red button has been pushed. I don't understand John's concept. I want to ask John, "What is the significant thing that has touched off this debate?"

Nalbandian: I can't tell exactly what has touched off this debate. Terry Novak says, "I do what needs to be done," and I say, that's fine except I'm concerned with democratic theory, not with building a street. And I want to be able to justify what you do, how you go about it in terms of a theory of democracy. I can't do that because you say the justification for what you are doing is in your relationship with the council. Right? The council legitimizes what you do. I'm telling you that the council doesn't have legitimacy with the community. How can the council legitimize what you do when the council doesn't have legitimacy in the community? Therefore, you have to be in touch with the community.

Pokorny: The implication is that we shortcircuit the democratic process. If there is an imbalance, you need to strengthen the process and restore legitimacy.

King: Everything is on a continuum. At one end is what the community wants, at the other what the community needs. Often these are very different. That's one of the problems we have in cities. I recommend to the council what our staff feels the city needs. We feel that there's a body of knowledge that allows us to make those judgments. The council responds with what the community wants and then negotiation of the issues occurs.

Serna: I think I'm hearing that the changing council-manager form of government is somehow in conflict with the values of the process. I would argue that it's not. In fact, the process itself is democratic theory. We need to show that district elections have to do with representation, that neighborhood associations have to do with democracy. I have to emphasize those relationships for the people in the community when perhaps the members of my council aren't able to do that. I have to inform even members of the council about those relationships.

Newland: Normally the function of the professional manager is to facilitate the success of the council-manager government system. They facilitate success both in substance, for example, by getting streets paved. In the process there are times where the governance system is threatened, and we all become deeply involved in making that system work. The comment "Administration supersedes politics" has come to be more true as the political process in the country has deteriorated and continues to deteriorate. It has less capacity to facilitate informed self-government. Yet the administrative process has shown some gradual improvements, for example, in our automated systems.

Ruder: I'd like to follow up on John Nalbandian's last point. Part of what people are saying is, "Yes, that's right, we incorporate values, we work with the communities." John also raises the issue of the internal organization versus the external role and the extent to which the understanding of the process and community values are represented to staff. This is one of the responsibilities of the city manager. I'm in a unique position because my title is deputy city manager for finance. What that means is that I go to city manager events and to finance director events. At the California league meeting for city managers last spring in San Diego, one of the best-attended sessions involved city managers talking about why they can't find good department heads. The focus of that session was why managers can't find people to hire who understand that their role is broader than providing operational services. Managers want staff members who understand what's going on in the community and the values that the council needs to incorporate into city services. Of course, that agenda item is not regularly on the finance director's meeting schedules. Part of the problem is that city managers are now more involved in brokering in an external environment and working with all the citizen groups. They must incorporate a diversity of values and build consensus among council members. Today councils are so diverse that more time may be focused on those issues rather than informing and developing staff on those values.

For my position there was a recruitment for finance director. My boss thought those candidates were too narrowly focused. He changed the title to deputy and hired me because I had worked in city managers' offices. I was trained in the broader process, with a values strategy orientation. Now part of the time I'm a deputy and part of the time I'm running operations.

Watson: John noted that efficiency and responsiveness are not always compatible. I think this is the first time I have read the word "efficiency" in fifteen years. People today don't think in those terms. Years ago you talked about a business-like government run with efficiency and economy. Now we talk about responsiveness. It doesn't have anything to do with efficiency, because people feel that the government is efficient in many ways. So now they're being responsive to other needs. A few years ago one of our council members said, "Look, I'm not interested in the bottom line like you are, I'm interested in the process." When our city has gotten in trouble and some policy determinations have been reversed it has been when council members or officials didn't take time on the process. They didn't include others and other ideas. You have to depend on the council to be the antenna of what the community feels is responsive at the time. Less than six years ago we had thirteen candidates for the council. Every one of them ran on economic development.

Protasel: One of the things that helps me understand this paper is to look at the distinction that John makes between the creation of culture and the design of culture. You're saying that good management is about the creation of culture, not the design of culture. When we are creating culture, we are much more involved in the process and are more connected to the community. When we are designing the culture, we are more removed and are imposing on the community without really being involved.

Frederickson: City management is not a spectator sport.

Toregas: I said earlier that maybe we're using the wrong labels because of the need to have standardization. I don't think fire is a fire chief issue; fire is a community issue. I don't think streets are a public works issue; they are a community issue. It may be that we need to develop new values for our structures. People may need a different vision of their jobs.

Technology, Economic Development and Innovation in the Administrative City

Council-Manager Government's Response to Economic Development

James M. Banovetz
Northern Illinois University[1]

Long before Karl Bosworth opined that "The Manager is a Politician" in Lawrence J. R. Herson's "Lost World of Municipal Government,"[2] advocates of council-manager government were busy constructing a litany of the virtues of their favorite form of local government. Richard S. Childs, considered the father of council-manager government, observed that the objective of council-manager government "is not good government exactly, but democratic government" and asserted that "we seek...the concept of a government that will diligently cater to the sovereign people!"[3]

Even earlier, Don Stone and colleagues added their voices to the litany when they concluded, "The city manager plan, with its principles of the unification of powers and the concentration of administrative authority, has been a dynamic force in American municipal government. It has had a catalytic effect toward improvement in the administration and the politics of cities that have adopted it."[4]

Once such praise had established the legitimacy of council-manager government, the platitudes in the litany became more practical--they were the arguments of the plan's adherents who took to the stump to promote its adoption in an ever growing list of cities. Rarely committed to the formal literature, the platitudes are nonetheless well known and used. They include:

- The city manager who can't save twice his salary each year isn't worth his pay.
- Council-manager government provides a professional to help part-time elected officials manage city affairs.
- The city manager should secure enough federal grants each year to pay his salary several times over.
- City manager government eliminates patronage and raises the over-all level of integrity in government.
- The city manager brings training and experience--and knowledge derived from work in other cities--to the job of directing daily operations and solving local problems.
- The council-manager plan provides more service outputs per dollar of public expenditures. It will bring "the most bang for the buck"!
- Hiring a city manager will cut the cost of government and reduce taxes.

Repetition of the litany has secured the loyalty--sometimes blind loyalty--of council-manager government's adherents and won the support of a growing number of both citizens and elected officials. The plan has become the nation's most widely used form of government in municipalities over 10,000 in population;[5] it is gaining acceptance in a rapidly growing number of American county governments; and its use has spread to a number of other countries.

As is so often true of litanies, the validity of individual platitudes becomes questionable over time. Council-manager government may still meet Childs' concern for democracy and Stone's test of effectiveness, but there is no contemporary evidence that adoption of the plan will reduce taxes. Managers may once have been able to secure grants totaling several times their annual salary, but to impose that standard in an era of sharply diminished intergovernmental revenues is certainly threatening to the individual manager and to the plan itself.

Thus the litany needs updating. It particularly needs a recognition of the vital link between council-manager government and change itself. Within the field of public administration, the city management profession has consistently been in the vanguard of change and development. Initially tied to Woodrow Wilson's politics/administration dichotomy, the profession was the first component in public administration to formally recognize the political involvement of the public administrator.[6] The profession changed dramatically in the post-war era when the growth of cities required managerial skills more than technical and engineering expertise. Since the 1960s, it has responded well to the criticisms of the 1968 Kerner Report[7] and to the call for greater city involvement in providing "human services."[8]

While the *model* of council-manager government has remained constant, the *form* of council-manager government has also changed to meet evolving demands. Direct popular election of the mayor, election of council members from wards or districts, adoption of the form by local ordinance rather than statutory option, use of the title "administrator" rather than the title "manager," and modifications in managerial powers have all become variables in the form of council-manager government that have evolved in practice even though they represent departures from the orthodox model of council-manager government. Indeed, in Wisconsin the statutory form of council-manager government is considered nearly unworkable and all contemporary expansion in the use of council-manager government has come as a result of local ordinances. Illinois counties are not provided with a county manager option, but over a dozen counties have used ordinances to adopt some variant of the council-manager form of government.

The International City Management Association has recognized the validity of such variations and has extended its "recognition" to governments employing them. Indeed, the flexibility provided by such options--the flexibility to adapt the form of government to meet community needs and preferences while still utilizing a professional chief administrative officer--might be viewed as a requisite for the plan's survival.[9]

The last decade has seen another, different demand for change on the part of professional managers and the council-manager form of government. Contemporary public expectations now impose a major obligation on local governments to provide leadership in the field of economic development. While this obligation is not new--local governments have long been expected to be sensitive to the need for economic development as a tool for easing property tax burdens—they now face a much different, much more critical assignment: to manage the economic development process in order to shape the quality of life in the community itself.

The Hypothesis

The issue at hand, then, is threefold:

1. Have local governments operating under the council-manager form of government responded to this new service expectation?
2. Have such governments demonstrated competence in responding to economic development pressures?
3. Have local governments organized under the council-manager form of government responded better to economic development expectations than governments organized under other forms?

In short, the key question is this: does the use of a professional manager enable local governments to achieve greater success in economic development efforts?

Economic development is a complex phenomenon, one that differs in different contexts and is affected by a large number of variables, of which form of government is, at best, a minor one. To date, there has been no effort to identify a possible correlation between form of government, or the use of professional managers, and economic development outcomes.[10] Nonetheless, it is reasonable to hypothesize that form of government is a variable which has some influence on the economic development process, and that the use of a professional manager can affect the success of economic development efforts.

This paper will not attempt to establish, empirically, that forms of government using professional managers have such influence, nor will it demonstrate empirically that such governments have a better success rate in dealing with economic development concerns. What it will do, rather, is demonstrate, both rationally and with prima facie evidence, that such a hypothesis is reasonable, and it will suggest the kinds of research that are needed to test the proposition.

The Supporting Rationale

In part, the rationale linking economic development activities and professional managers is based on the nature of the economic development activity itself. Jeffrey S. Luke and colleagues, in their study *Managing Economic Development*, define the emergence of economic development as the culmination of several trends, including the growing interdependency of local economies with state, national, and global economies; the lingering impact of the recession of the 1980s; and the decline in the federal government's role in managing such problems at the local level. The result, they argue, is that "leadership for economic development now falls most heavily on state and local public executives."[11]

A major element of the rationale supporting the use of professional managers has been the assertion that such forms improve the quality of local public leadership. They do so, according to the argument, both by bringing professional expertise to the management of local affairs and by attracting more competent persons to positions of elected leadership. If economic development responsibility falls increasingly on local leadership, and if such forms do indeed improve local leadership, then it is reasonable to assume that economic development efforts should be more successful in governments with professional managers. This might be called the *leadership factor* linking economic development success to professional local government management.

There are five other factors which also support the notion of such a linkage. Like the leadership factor, each of these has historically been ensconced in the litany of the strengths and advantages of council-manager government. Some of these factors are also found in other forms of government; council-manager advocates contend that no other form achieves all these factors to the same extent or with the same consistency as council-manager government.

The *experience factor* describes the sophistication brought to the task of problem-solving at the local government level. In governments without professional managerial expertise, the primary problem-solving strategy tends to be "how did we solve this problem the last time we had it?" Such a strategy, rooted in the past, has obvious limitations, especially when applied to problems like economic development which may never have been confronted on the same scale before. Council-manager governments employ career professionals with experience working in other local governments. Such persons are employed as chief administrators and often in middle management positions as well. They bring a wide range of experience to problem-solving. They can fall back on their experiences in other cities which faced similar problems; they will be able to supplement personal experiences with their professional training and with information derived from their network of contacts with other professionals and professional associations. Thus, the range of experience which can be brought to bear on problem-solving situations, including economic development problems, should be broader and richer.

The experience factor, of course, is supplemented by the *professionalism factor*. Council-manager government is predicated on the principle that managers will have professional training as well as experience. Such training is expected to include substantial emphasis upon decision-making and problem-solving skills and technologies. From it, the professional is expected to acquire knowledge about intergovernmental relations, policy-making, economics, planning, community dynamics, and similar subjects of relevance to economic development. Indeed, the advent of economic development responsibilities has led universities and professional associations to develop pre-professional and in-service education components focusing specifically upon economic development.

Council-manager proponents also claim that professional managers offer the advantage of improved central coordination of local services. The presence of a professional manager provides a central control mechanism that can blend such disparate service professions as police, fire, public works, utilities, health, planning, and recreation into a synchronized, mutually supporting unity. From such a unity, provided by the *coordination factor*, more effective service provision can be expected.

The coordination factor is important to economic development for two reasons. First, most developers look for communities that provide good local services. Good local services can help sustain and support private investment. If local services are provided more effectively in council-manager communities, then such communities should be more attractive to developers. Second, actual development projects frequently require major adjustments in public service levels--in new or rebuilt roadways, upgraded utility services, added traffic engineering, and expanded police patrols to support new development. Such service upgrades are difficult to arrange under the best of circumstances, but they are much more difficult when the local government lacks a professional manager with central control and coordinating responsibilities. If the presence of such central coordinating capability makes development easier, then governments with such capability--council-manager governments--should have a better record of economic development.

Next is the *policy factor*. There is evidence to suggest that developers look for communities in which public policies are relatively stable over time, and thus are comparatively dependable.[12] Developers making long term investments prefer a community in which the value of the investment is not likely to be subject to abrupt changes in public policies.

Such policy dependability is a characteristic of council-manager government. The presence of a professional manager stabilizes policy in several ways. First, the manager adds a source of input, derived from a professional perspective, that is likely to be biased in favor of systems, procedures, and policies that have proven effective over time. Second, in many communities, the average tenure of a professional manager is longer than the tenure of elected leaders. Even where this is not the case, successive incumbents in a professional management position are likely to have more consistency in outlook and values than successive incumbents in elective office. Third, professional managers are likely to promote staff competency by emphasizing merit-based recruitment and in-service staff training. Middle management staff--department heads and supervisory personnel--usually enjoy longer tenure in office than either managers or elected officials. As middle-management competency increases, so too, typically, does its influence in policy-making. Combined with length of tenure, that influence provides a stabilizing effect on public policy in the community.

Finally, there is the *sociological factor*, based on the principle that people communicate most effectively with those they perceive to be most like themselves. Corporate leaders, most of whom are themselves professionally educated, can be expected to find communication with persons of comparable educational and professional background easier and more productive. Professional public administrators, whose training and background are likely to be quite comparable to professional business administrators, are more likely to be perceived as professional peers by private development officers than are elected officials drawn from a wide variety of backgrounds. While locally elected officials are sometimes drawn from business backgrounds, they are equally likely to be drawn from other backgrounds such as small town businesses (e.g. barbers, local store owners, morticians), tradesmen, craft workers, homemakers, health care professionals, teachers, and salesmen. To the extent that the sociological factor is valid, economic developers will thus be more attracted to communities with professional managers. Furthermore, because such managers devote full-time to the business of government, they are more likely to have more information readily available to use during development negotiations.

Individually and collectively, all six of these factors suggest that local governments which have a full-time, professional manager, and thus operate under the principles of council-manager government, should have a better record of success in economic development activity. It remains to be seen whether or not this apparent linkage--or correlation--is achieved in actual experience. That is the task to which this paper will turn next.

Supporting Evidence

Data for this analysis will be derived primarily from the State of Illinois, which has a 74 year history with council-manager government and in which approximately 125 municipalities and a dozen counties, including most of the larger cities and counties, employ professional managers. Not all use the formal council-manager plan--indeed Illinois counties are not legally authorized to use it--but Illinois cities and counties can informally adopt the essential core of the plan by ordinance, and an increasing number are doing so.

In addition to offering a substantial number of both professional manager and non-manager governments for comparison, Illinois offers another advantage as a source for preliminary data gathering. It also has a large number of local governments facing each of two different kinds of economic development challenges.

Economic development, as a label, covers two distinctly different kinds of service problems. In some communities, economic development means management of intense pressure for community growth and expansion; in other communities, it means efforts to generate such growth and expansion, or at least to generate new economic activity in order to minimize problems of unemployment and community deterioration. In Illinois, most communities in the six county Chicago metropolitan area face the first kind of pressure. DuPage County, immediately west of Chicago, is one of the most rapidly growing urban counties in the nation. Outside the six county Chicago area, however, the state's economy has traditionally been based upon agribusiness and the manufacturing of agricultural implements. The downstate economy has never recovered from the recession of the early 1980s and, for nearly a decade, downstate Illinois cities have suffered some of the highest unemployment rates in the nation. Illinois thus offers examples of extreme conditions in both kinds of economic development challenges.

Council-Manager Government in a Growth Environment

The use of council-manager government, and of professional managers, in the Chicago metropolitan area has paralleled the growth and development of the area's suburbs. Nearly all municipalities in the most rapidly growing sectors of the area use some variation of council-manager government. The use of professional managers is so closely linked to economic growth and expansion that it is difficult to discern whether such growth is attracted to areas employing professional managers, whether the employment of professional managers is accepted as the preferred method of managing such growth, or, more likely, some combination of the two. Regardless, the relationship between economic growth and the use of professional managers by local government appears to be clear.

Chicago's suburban economic growth has radiated outward from the city along the area's interstate highway corridors. There are five such corridors: I-94 which goes north to Milwaukee; I-90 which goes northwest to Rockford; I-88 (formerly I-5) which goes directly west toward Iowa; I-55 which goes southwest toward Springfield, the state capital; and I-57 which goes south past Champaign-Urbana and the University of Illinois. Economic growth in these corridors appears to be directly correlated to the presence of professional managers in adjacent municipal governments.

Preliminary findings from an on-going, comparative analysis of 40 such communities, half with and half without professional managers, showed that communities with such managers experienced, in the aggregate, over 300% more growth in local employment than the communities which did not use such managers. The analysis includes all major communities without professional managers; it excludes the communities with professional managers which had experienced the most rapid growth rates during that period.[13] In short, the slowest growing professional manager communities still experienced substantially more growth than the non-manager communities.

Edgar L. Sherbenou noted in 1961 that council-manager government in the region was expanding in close conformity with the region's socioeconomic structure. The form started in the affluent northern lakeshore communities and spread in a counter-clockwise fashion west and southerly to largely blue collar southern Cook County.[14] Economic development in the intervening years has followed a similar pattern. The region's growth has occurred primarily in its northern and western areas; nearly all of the region's northern and western suburbs employ professional managers. Much less economic development has occurred in the southern portion of the area, or along I-55 and I-57, the two most southern interstates. Significantly, relatively few southern suburbs employ professional managers. Even in the south, communities with professional managers have experienced higher levels of economic development activity.

From the standpoint of economic geography, the region's development pattern is difficult to understand. Suburban growth typically develops along corridors to an area's primary hinterland. If this rule applied in the Chicago area, the I-55 and I-57 corridors should have experienced a greater percentage of the area's growth.

It is also difficult to explain the lack of growth in the southwestern portion of the region, in the area between Aurora (in southeastern Kane County) and Joliet (in western Will County). The area is close to the National Accelerator Laboratory and the R&D development along the I-88 (formerly I-5) corridor, yet it has experienced little growth until very recently. It is an area lacking professional managers: Aurora, until recently, had an old-style partisan mayor system; Joliet operates under the council-manager form, but its managers have received little support, resulting in a "revolving door" of managers. In between, there are no incorporated communities and the intervening county, Kendall County, does not employ a professional manager.

On the other hand, the northern and western development can be explained, in considerable part, by the proximity of the region's major airport. Faced with growth pressures stemming from O'Hare Field, municipalities in the area have nearly all employed professional managers to provide leadership for their development programs. The Village of Bartlett, for instance, adopted the plan for that reason, and hired, as its first manager, a woman who had extensive economic development experience in the downstate city of Decatur. Even very small communities, such as Burr Ridge, Country Club Hills, and Indian Head Park have employed professional managers to help them control growth. As Mayor Sonya Crawshaw of Hanover Park commented, "Our community development efforts weren't getting anywhere until we hired a manager who could develop a plan and then hold the village to that plan."[15]

Perhaps the importance of a manager in responding to development pressures was best portrayed in a *Chicago Tribune* story on economic development pressures in McHenry County, located in the extreme northwest corner of the metropolitan area:

> In McHenry County, Crystal Lake is the standard by which all other towns are measured. It is not only the largest community and the county's commercial center, but is the most developed, with a city manager and a professional staff. City Manager Joe Misurelli spends much of his time on the telephone with officials of other towns explaining to them how things are done. He is the county's professional expert on municipalities.[16]

Such evidence from Illinois suggests that there is some correlation between the use of professional managers in local government and successful economic development efforts. The State of Ohio offers similar evidence, comparing Cincinnati and Cleveland. The City of Cincinnati uses the classic council-manager form; professional managers are also widely used in the city's suburban communities. A large percentage of the state's development is occurring in the metropolitan area. The City of Cleveland, on the other hand, uses a mayor-council form of government. Such government also predominates in Cleveland's suburban communities. The Cleveland area, by comparison, has experienced high unemployment and economic recession for most of the past decade.

Much of the evidence is admittedly impressionistic and episodic in nature. It is not offered as proof that the employment of professional managers assures greater success with economic development, or that council-manager governments as a group are more successful in providing economic development services. It does, however, suggest that a correlation may exist between the use of professional managers and economic development. Whether such a correlation, if it in fact exists, is causal or spurious is a question requiring further inquiry.

Council-Manager Government in Depressed Economies

Similar evidence supporting the correlation between professional managers and economic growth is provided by analyses of cities located in downstate Illinois.[17] The correlation is suggested both by impressionistic and empirical information as well as by downstate Illinois' use of municipal home rule powers. Both will be examined.

As noted earlier, the downstate Illinois base for this comparison is particularly appropriate because the last decade has been one of severe economic decline in the region. Downstate Illinois' economy has been heavily dependent upon agriculture, both as a farming region and as a world center for the manufacture of agricultural machinery and implements. Most of the region's major cities--Bloomington, Champaign, Danville, Decatur, East Moline, Galesburg, Moline, Normal, Peoria, Rockford, Rock Island, and Urbana--have been adversely affected;[18] some, such as Peoria, Rock Island, and Rockford, have competed for the dubious honor of suffering the nation's highest unemployment rate. It has been a region where economic development efforts have been of critical importance and in which the rate of governmental success in responding to the economic development challenge has varied substantially from community to community.

These economic development challenges, in turn, have provided a hard core test of the adaptability and workability of Illinois' home rule system. That system, adopted in 1971, has been termed the nation's most liberal system of home rule[19] because it represents the nation's most complete implementation, in actual practice, of the home rule provisions contained in the model charters and codes recommended by the National Municipal League and the Advisory Commission on Intergovernmental Relations. As such, the economic development challenge in downstate Illinois has provided a real acid test of the workability of those provisions.

Downstate Illinois' Economic Development

An overview of the record suggests that the downstate municipalities which use professional managers have a better over-all track record in economic development than those which do not. Of the largest downstate cities which have suffered most from the recession of the 1980s--Bloomington, Danville, Decatur, East St. Louis, Galesburg, Peoria, Rockford, and the Illinois Quad Cities (East Moline, Moline, and Rock Island)--those which have the best recovery in progress are the council-manager cities. The most progress has been made in Bloomington-Normal and Peoria, communities which have professional managers in both their city and county governments. Bloomington-Normal has attracted a major new automotive factory; Peoria has redeveloped its downtown and its major employers are now recalling workers.

The next best rate of progress has been made by Danville, Decatur, and Galesburg. Decatur and Galesburg are council-manager communities; Danville has shifted from a commission form to a mayor-council form during this period.

The least recovery progress has been made in East St. Louis, Rockford, and the Illinois Quad Cities. East St. Louis and Rockford operate with mayor-council governments (although Rockford employed a professional manager as an administrative officer during 1981-87). Two of the three Illinois Quad Cities have a professional manager. East St. Louis is on the brink of bankruptcy; Rockford lost its commercial base to its suburban communities before 1981 and has not recovered lost jobs; the Quad Cities similarly have not been able to offset the loss of jobs. Perhaps the outstanding example of economic development success in Illinois occurred in Bloomington-Normal. In direct competition with several other cities, including Rockford, the Town of Normal made a concerted and successful effort to bring Chrysler Motor's new Diamond Star plant to the community. Under the leadership of the town's manager, who worked in concert with the manager of the City of Bloomington and the administrator of McLean

County--both professional managers--intergovernmental agreements were made with the state to secure financial enticements, a McLean County Enterprise Zone was established, a "metro zone intergovernmental agreement" was reached between Bloomington and Normal under which the two communities shared revenues and expenditures in connection with the development, and Normal's manager was authorized by his council to buy, sell, and trade property on behalf of the town in order to acquire land needed for the new factory.

Communities with professional managers also score well in comparison with non-manager communities in the use of one of the newest weapons in the economic development arsenal: the tax increment financing (TIF) district. Illinois has 143 such districts; 65, or 45%, are located in communities with a professional manager.[20] Since only 31% of Illinois' cities over 2500 population have a professional manager, cities with such an official are disproportionately represented in the use of this development tool.

The Home Rule Connection

Home rule was not established by the state of Illinois as a local government economic development tool; nevertheless, it has been used by municipalities primarily to promote economic development.[21] This is not surprising in light of the extremes of growth pressures or recession which face the state's communities; economic development concerns have held top priority on the agenda of policy concerns confronting Illinois cities and villages for more than a decade. Home rule has proven to be critically important in addressing economic development problems, and it has been used most extensively and creatively in communities which employ professional managers.

Under the Illinois home rule system, municipalities over 25,000 automatically become home rule governments; municipalities under 25,000 can acquire home rule powers through referendum. There is no

Table 1

Use of Home Rule

in Manager/Administrator and Non-Manager Municipalities

Reported uses	Non-Manager	Manager*
Number	6	9
Total Home Rule Uses	44	108
Average Home Rule Use per Municipality	7.3	12
Median	7	11
Number of Innovative Uses**	3	8

* Includes the City of Moline, which uses a mayor-council government with a chief administrative officer.

** Innovative uses are defined as home rule applications not previously used by other governments.

evidence that municipalities with professional managers are more likely to adopt home rule powers.

There is, however, evidence which suggests that communities with professional managers make more extensive and creative use of their home rule powers. That evidence is drawn from a comparison of home rule applications in larger (e.g. over 10,000 population) Illinois communities located outside the Chicago and St. Louis metropolitan areas. Nineteen of 21 such communities were studied:[22] ten have governments which employ professional managers; eight have mayor-council or commission governments; and one, the City of Moline, has a mayor-council government with a chief administrative officer (CAO) who is a member of the Illinois City Management Association.

Fifteen of the 19 municipalities responded to surveys in 1983 and 1986 on their use of home rule powers. A compilation of the results is presented in Table 1.

The data in the table suggest that municipalities with professional managers make both more varied and more innovative use of home rule powers. One statewide Illinois study cited thirteen municipalities for innovative use of home rule powers for economic development purposes; twelve of those cited were municipalities using professional managers.[23]

Summary

Downstate Illinois cities which employ professional managers clearly have a record of greater activity and innovation in their efforts to recover from economic recession. On average, such communities also appear to have experienced a better rate of recovery. Again there is an apparent correlation between the use of a professional manager and economic development success.

A Concluding Overview

The Illinois experience supports the rationale that local governments using a professional manager should have a better track record of success in economic development activity. Specifically, the evidence presented herein demonstrates that:

1. Local governments operating under the council-manager form of government have responded constructively to the contemporary demand for economic development.
2. Such governments have demonstrated competence in this response. They have been active in generating economic development programs and they have been creative in designing innovative solutions to economic development problems. There is also prima facie evidence that they have been successful in such efforts.

It is more difficult to determine empirically whether council-manager governments have been more successful than other forms of government in providing economic development services. The evidence presented herein suggests there is such a correlation, but that evidence is not based on empirical proof.

That proof will require more elaborate and detailed research. Economic development is a phenomenon influenced by many considerations:

the global economy, national and state economic conditions and forces, geography, labor market characteristics, transportation facilities, local educational facilities, development capital, the local availability of lifestyle amenities, local public services, and local leadership.

In such an array of variables, the form of government is not likely to be a major consideration, but such an observation does not eliminate it as a factor of consequence. Form of government might be related to economic development in two ways: it might influence economic development indirectly by the effect it has on local public services and lifestyle amenities; and it might directly influence the quality of local leadership or the development and implementation of local economic development strategies.

Empirical determination of such an effect will require three kinds of inquiry. First, additional case studies and situational studies are needed in order to identify with more precision the variables which are likely to influence the correlation between form of government and economic development efforts.

Second, measures of economic development success must be established. A simple measure, such as the change in employment levels, will not suffice; all communities do not share common development objectives. Indeed, some communities prefer development strategies designed to limit or reduce commercial and industrial activity.

Third, careful research which controls for the influence of the many other variables affecting economic development will be needed before the correlation between form of government and successful economic development can be made clear.

In the interim, however, there clearly is prima facie evidence which suggests that the use of professional managers in local government does improve community performance in providing economic development services.

Notes

1. This paper was prepared with the help of Carol B. Zar, William Syversen, and NIU Center for Governmental Studies.

2. Karl Bosworth, "The Manager is a Politician," *Public Administration Review*, vol. 18 (Summer 1958), pp. 216-22; and Lawrence J. R. Herson, "The Lost World of Municipal Government," *American Political Science Review*, vol. 51 (June 1957), pp. 330-45.

3. Richard S. Childs, "The Coming of the Council-Manager Plan," *Civic Victories* (New York: Harper & Brothers, 1952), Ch. 15. Reprinted in William J. Murin, *Classics of Urban Politics and Administration* (Oak Park, IL: Moore Publishing Co., 1982), pp. 80-87 at p. 81.

4. Donald K. Stone, Douglas Price, and Kathryn Stone, "City Manager Government in the United States" (1940), reprinted in Murin, *op. cit.*, pp. 88-110 at p. 93.

5. Heywood T. Sanders, "The Government of American Cities: Continuity and Change in Structure," *The Municipal Year Book 1982* (Washington, D.C.: International City Management Association, 1982), pp. 178-186. See especially Table 3/2, p. 180.

6. Richard J. Stillman II, *The Rise of the City Manager* (Albuquerque: University of New Mexico Press, 1974). See especially the recognition given to the political role of the city manager profession in the profession's 1924 code of ethics (see p. 36, 52) and its strong statement on the subject in its 1952 code revisions (p. 62).

7. *Report of the National Advisory Commission on Civil Disorders* (New York: Bantam Books, 1968), see especially p. 287.

8. Norvel Smith, "Human Development in Urban Communities," lecture delivered at the 50th Annual Conference of the International City Managers' Association, September 28, 1964. See also James M. Banovetz, *Managing the Modern City* (Washington, D.C.: International City Management Association, 1971), Ch. 2, pp. 18-43 and especially p. 33-39.

9. This paper considers the concept of a professional chief administrative officer to be the essential core of council-manager government. It will thus use the term "professional manager" to refer to such officers and all variations in form of local government which use that core, including the classic council-manager governments, but also including city/village administrator forms, county manager forms, and county administrator forms. It will also use the term "council-manager government" to refer to all the forms which use that core.

10. No references to any such studies have been found. Review, for example, the bibliography in Jeffrey S. Luke, *et. al.*, *Managing Economic Development: A Guide to State and Local Leadership Strategies* (San Francisco: Jossey-Bass Publishers, 1988).

11. Luke, *op. cit.*, p. 17.

12. See, for example, the remarks that John Philipchuck, attorney for a number of Illinois developers, made to a meeting of the Illinois Municipal Clerks Association, October, 1988.

13. This reference is to an on-going study by the author in conjunction with the Center for Governmental Studies at Northern Illinois University. It compares employment growth in suburban communities over the period 1977-86 to the form of government of such communities.

14. Edgar L. Sherbenou, "Class Participation and the Council- Manager Plan," *Public Administration Review*, vol. 21 (Summer, 1961).

15. Mayor Sonya A. Crawshaw, in remarks made to the Illinois Municipal Clerks' Association, October, 1988.

16. David Young, "Hanging Tough," *Sunday, The Chicago Tribune Magazine*, October 30, 1988, pp. 12-35 at 31-32.

17. Illinoisans use the term "downstate" to refer to all portions of the state falling outside the six county Chicago metropolitan area.

18. Some downstate cities have continued to prosper during this era, primarily because of the presence of large state institutions. Springfield, the state capital, has largely escaped the economic decline as have cities with state universities: Carbondale, Champaign, Normal, and Urbana. Some of these cities, however, have undertaken major economic development efforts in an attempt to maintain their downtown business districts.

19. William N. Cassella, Jr., "A Century of Home Rule," *National Civic Review* (October 1975), p. 448.

20. Kent D. Redfield, *Tax Increment Financing* (Springfield: Taxpayers' Federation of Illinois, 1988), Appendix C, p. 49.

21. Thomas W. Kelty and James M. Banovetz, "Economic Development Advanced by Home Rule," *Illinois Municipal Review*, vol. 64 (August 1985), pp. 19-21 at 19.

22. This analysis excludes two cities: Rockford, which abandoned home rule in 1983, and Mt. Vernon, which adopted home rule in 1986.

23. James M. Banovetz and Thomas W. Kelty, *Home Rule in Illinois: Image and Reality* (Springfield: Sangamon State University, 1987), pp. 30-31.

Response

Gary F. Pokorny
El Cerrito, California

Platitudes are like potato chips; once we begin eating them it is very hard to stop.

As a city manager, my first temptation is to want the central *implied* hypothesis of the James Banovetz paper to be true. Of course council-manager local governments are more effective at managing economic development, just as they are at most things.

The pursuit of solid evidence to support our shared belief on which most of us in this room have staked our lives that professional public administration does make a significant difference in results achieved by local government is a worthwhile endeavor. Such research has for too long been thin or absent. The comments which follow are offered in the spirit of trying to encourage that research to be stronger and more defensible. What follows is a series of reflections upon some of the issues raised by this paper which, I believe, must be effectively addressed if the pursuit of research along the lines outlined is to be as productive and helpful as it is intended to be.

Are we exploring the question of whether there is a relationship between the council-manager *form* of government and economic development results? Or, are we exploring the linkage between such results and those local governments which have a *position of professional, central administrative authority*? Shifting back and forth between the issue of form versus the presence of professional management is woven throughout the paper with the dichotomy occasionally appearing in the same sentence. The balance of the argument seems to be in favor of the professional management capacity position. But the paper does not effectively address either the expectations raised by its title or the stated purpose of the paper.

This is not a fatal flaw. I believe the second proposition is the more useful one to study and more in keeping with the mission of ICMA and of most schools of public administration: to foster, nurture and improve effective, efficient public *management*, not to narrowly support any one *form* of government. But the focus of this paper should be clarified and any subsequent research based upon it should be well focused and internally consistent.

Underlying the whole exposition of the framework for the suggested research is the hidden assumption that the form of government is an independent variable stimulating economic development. Yet, at key places, the author acknowledges that "economic development is a complex phenomenon, . . . affected by a large number of variables, of which *form of government* is, at best, *a minor one*" (emphasis added).

Elsewhere the author states that the prima facie linkage between form and economic development may even run in the opposite direction. That is to say that economic development generates pressure to professionalize: "Faced with growth pressures stemming from O'Hare Field, municipalities in the area have nearly all employed professional managers to provide leadership for their development programs." The entire section regarding success in managing economic development pressures in the Chicago metropolitan area could take on the

216

characteristic of an endlessly circular argument. Need for management caused by growth caused management to be hired which caused growth which generates need for professional management, etc., etc.

For me the six "linking factors" developed in the section on the supporting rationale are not persuasive in dealing with what I see as a serious problem with the overall assumptions about the direction of causality.

Further, the absence of an explicit discussion of such factors as the presence or absence of key community leadership cadres, underlying community values, and the fundamental community vision of itself omits critical factors which may be much more significant independent variables which affect *both* the form or structure of local government *and* success in economic development.

The paper has both a hidden assumption that all communities want more economic development (my personal experience suggests this is an assumption which ought to be tested) and an absence of any clear measure of how relative success in reaching that goal will be determined.

To compare samples of communities with and without a strong position of central administrator *without* taking into account communities' statements of their own goals in regard to economic development (as exemplified by such criteria as: community strategic plans, community goals and action plans relative to economic development, expressions of community values regarding the appropriateness of public sector involvement in economic development activities and, where such factors are present, an examination of how each community defines success in achieving its own vision of economic development) runs the risk of trying to correlate professional administration with a hopelessly global and soft definition of success.

It is clear to me that each community's commitment to vigorous economic expansion ebbs and flows with both national economic cycles and local success or lack of success in achieving economic goals over time.

As the author notes, the process of economic development is itself a complex and slow process where inputs often may not achieve results for many years. These facts make the linkage of results to stated goals an analysis which requires patience, insight and a healthy respect for the cycles of history. Indeed, both historical and statistical research, carefully coordinated, may be what we really need to test these hypotheses.

The author briefly mentions both the problem of unclear goals for economic development and absence of measures of success but, in my opinion, does not deal adequately with these issues in a way which leads me to share his confidence in his conclusions.

This point is linked to the previous one. There is a substantial body of theory and some experiential evidence that communities which have sound processes for explicitly setting goals and doing careful planning to reach these goals have far greater success in reaching their goals than communities which do not have such processes and plans. As it affects this research model, it would be worthwhile to test whether the presence or absence of effective goal setting and planning processes over time is itself a predictor of success in economic development. If it is, a second and linked line of inquiry is whether such processes are more likely to be present in local governments which have professional administrators and, if so, whether such processes are more likely to be present in local governments which have professional administrators and, if so, whether this would be a key factor for inclusion in the 'rational' model. This might be a more plausible hypothesis than several of the ones presented.

What the author calls "the leadership factor" is introduced as the first factor linking the council-manager plan to success in local economic development. The author characterizes this as an assertion without commenting on whether research supports this platitude or whether the author himself believes it to be plausible. Building research designs upon platitudes and assertions--especially ones which may be 50-70 years old--is risky business at best.

James Svara's paper and my observations both suggest that the propensity of city managers and city councils to provide leadership varies greatly and needs to be analyzed as to the type and focus of the leadership involved.

My experience leads me to believe that in at least some communities at certain times in their history the presence of a strong city manager in the local government may allow or even encourage the atrophy of local elected leadership. "Everything at city hall is going well. Why should I get involved? Let George do it." Thus the linkage based upon the leadership factor-platitude-assertion is at best a shaky hypothesis, though not identified by the author.

Similar arguments could be made with respect to each of the linking factors. In this regard, the paper, and the research model, would be stronger if a review of the relevant literature regarding each purported factor was presented.

As I have suggested earlier in the discussion of planning and goal setting, other linkages could be posited which have more surface validity in connecting management professionalism to economic development success. A search of the literature on economic development models as well as the professional management literature might be most productive in constructing a topology of such linking factors.

Finally, the underlying question the author is trying to answer lends itself more to either a comparative case studies approach or an economic history approach. A body of studies done from both of these perspectives by thoughtful, observant scholars might then suggest more narrowly focused opportunities to develop and test hypotheses about the ways in which concepts of effective public administration and success in economic development are linked. Such studies, thoughtfully designed and carefully undertaken, should greatly reduce or even eliminate the need to rely on platitudes to demonstrate the value of professional management.

Response

Karma Ruder
Concord, California

Dr. Banovetz begins his paper by stating the need to update the ways we measure the effectiveness of the council-manager form of government. He reviews some of the old "platitudes" and determines they are no longer relevant. He suggests that success with economic development activities, either in managing growth or in attracting it, is a more current measure for determining the legitimacy of a form of government:

> The last decade has seen another, different demand for change on the part of professional managers and the council-manager form of government. Contemporary public expectations now impose a major obligation on local governments to provide leadership in the field of economic development. While this obligation is not new--local governments have long been expected to be sensitive to the need for economic development as a tool for easing property tax burdens--they now face a much different, much more critical assignment: to manage the economic development process in order to shape the quality of life in the community itself.

Dr. Banovetz describes the practical difficulties of actually establishing a realistic correlation between form of government and economic development activities. He pursues a theoretical connection and then reviews empirical data to support the hypothesis that professional management improves "community performance in providing economic development services."

There are problems with clarifying the nature of the relationship. For example, Dr. Banovetz points out: "The use of professional managers is so closely linked to economic growth and expansion that it is difficult to discern whether such growth is attracted to areas employing professional managers, whether the employment of professional managers is accepted as the preferred method of managing such growth, or, more likely, some combination of the two."

Additionally I question some of the arguments discussed under the section on supporting rationale. For example, it is tenuous to state that developers identify more with professional staff, which then is a sociological factor that encourages economic development. I agree that a professionally run government is more likely to have an environment that makes development easier to manage and thus creates communities that are more attractive to developers. However, I think developers will deal with whomever will deal.

Dr. Banovetz does present a good empirical case that there is a linkage between professional managers and successful economic development activities. My concern is about the almost interchangeable use of *professional manager* and *council-manager form of government*.

A summary of the rationale offered by Dr. Banovetz to support his hypothesis is that successful economic development is related to leadership, experience, professionalism, the ability to coordinate service delivery, policy stability and the ability of the development community to identify with city officials. Dr. Banovetz describes how the council-manager form should be superior in these areas. However, he also states that these factors have "historically been ensconced in the litany of the strengths and advantages of council-manager government." One of the challenges that we face is how we evaluate and document what the advantages are for the council-manager plan compared to other forms that also use professional managers. Some of the significant challenges to the council-manager plan are from advocates of the strong mayor form with a professional chief administrative officer. Some of those advocates would be likely to suggest that these factors are not inherently part of a particular structure but rather related to the professionalism of the government.

Selecting economic development as a measure of effectiveness for the council-manager plan provides an interesting twist. While members of the profession believe that the council-manager form of government provides for the most professional structure, economic development activities are among those which cause the greatest blur in traditional roles of city managers. In promoting these private-public relationships, the need of confidentiality from the private sector often conflicts with the accountability of public process. The city manager may end up in the middle negotiating a path towards a politically acceptable solution that can be practically implemented. It is in the economic development arena that the roles of government and private sector become overlapping. Working with the city council to decide on matters of public subsidy, and to translate community values into decisions on who benefits from development and who pays, places the manager in what can be a very political role.

At the end of his article, Dr. Banovetz suggests additional research which would examine the relationship between form of government and economic development. Those are interesting research topics. I hope we would not forget the original premise, which was that we need to update the measures by which we evaluate the effectiveness of different forms of government.

It would be helpful to have some research done that would evaluate how the form of government relates to the overall quality of government and/or quality of life in a community. At the 1988 ICMA Conference, the National Civic League presented a session on conducting community assessments to evaluate the overall level of satisfaction and quality of life. What is the correlation between the council-manager plan and satisfaction with government and quality of life? Economic development is an important factor, but only one of many.

I agree with the assertion that the council-manager plan provides a structure that supports superior government services. We need to start developing data beyond the theoretical to assess whether the greatest differentiation is between forms of government or between professional and nonprofessional management. We need to examine what it is that makes certain structures work more effectively. We need to define what makes for successful governance in ways that support the choice for one structure over another. It is in these ways that we will update the basis for affirming the effectiveness of the council-manager form of government.

Discussion

Borut: We've got a highly controversial session. The subject is how is city management associated with economic development? Someone earlier had said in a paper that economic development is the most important activity of city managers.

Novak: One of the currencies we bring to the table in economic development is the perceived ability to keep a secret. People pursuing their economic projects don't think a directly elected official is likely to keep a secret. This puts the manager in the interesting diplomatic situation of explaining quietly to the city council that you have to do A, B, and C and something good will happen. That's a sort of stressful thing to do. Perhaps part of his research ought to ask whether we are perceived as able to keep a secret.

Keller: Managers were strongest in economic policy, not traditional policy. In Ohio the Japanese investment is south of Columbus and concentrated around council-manager cities. There is none in the northern part of Ohio, which is dominated by the council-mayor system. The northern part is marked by racial politics. The Japanese do not like to get involved in those cities.

Borut: The Japanese know a good thing when they see it.

Gleason: It is a rare politician who has enough experience to know the ins and outs of the infrastructure. Somebody would have to be steeped in that activity to be able to carry it out at a level in the organization where transactions can actually take place concomitant with private investment. In this situation the council-manager form of government has inherent advantages over other forms.

King: The issue of involvement in these economic decisions is beginning to have some important implications for responsiveness issues. Much of what we're talking about falls into the category of bargaining. Every case is unique and there are no bureaucratic rules for treating every case equally. That opens up a different political dynamic for councils and managers to deal with because the rules and precedents aren't helpful. You have to justify each case on its own grounds. Many of these deals have to be negotiated in secret--from the party you're dealing with and from the public. You're spending money or saying you're going to spend money to make something happen without the public knowing it until it's a deal that's resolved. The lack of understanding of why risk money is necessary to make something happen is causing increasing difficulties with the public.

Johnson: I think we have enough pieces that I see a little more clearly now. John Nalbandian's points are made from an academic's point of view. I'm concerned that as the administrator is negotiating these deals or is searching for clients that the manager is working from a set of democratic values. This raises concerns about social equity and individual rights, for example. I hope that administrators can balance those issues within the council and with the public to make clear that those have been truly considered. Is this a justification for ambiguity in the system, for measuring our performance in cutting deals? If, for example, we don't need the minority community or we don't need to take individual rights into consideration I can cut a deal with the council. Maybe we're a little idealistic on occasion because we want to consider that these tremendously significant democratic values are part of the process, and part of that process is involving all of those ideals with the participants in the community.

221

Borut: The issue you're raising is that you want to get all of the people involved, but that may mean that something doesn't happen. You're promoting participation rather than resolution.

Johnson: One example of that is the UDAG program. It helped real estate developers and businessmen tremendously, but did it really provide the jobs that were promised to the rest of the community?

Svara: A study by David Sink in Cincinnati shows that the way managers handle democratic control is qualitatively different from the way executive mayors handle this task. When council members in mayor-council cities complain about being steamrollered by a mayor, they are left out of the process. The mayor is moving fast and pushing things through and buying off council members who might be potential forces of opposition. Councils feel that they do not really have a significant role.

Another study has been done by Feiock and Clingermayer on the use of different economic development techniques. In comparing mayor-council and council-manager forms of government in larger cities, this study shows that in mayor-council cities, there's likely to be active involvement in economic development. I think it would be different from what you'd expect in smaller communities. In larger cities mayors are active in economic development whether the city needs it or not. This activity is an extension of the mayor's building his own reputation and bringing credit to himself. It is a way for mayors to put together campaign backers and financial supporters. There is a relationship in the manager cities between need indicators and economic development activities. Manager cities are less likely to be involved in these areas if there is not high unemployment or indicators of economic distress. This is evidence that managers bring a professional perspective to bear even on a highly political, volatile kind of issue.

Watkins: This paper suggests that cities should be directly involved in cutting deals and negotiating economic development. I'd like to question whether we should be doing that. In our city we contract the negotiating stage to our chamber of commerce. The city funds it and we set the parameter, but we don't get involved in the deals. I think it creates conflicts internally with your planning staff and other department heads who might speak out against a deal the manager's cut.

McIntyre: I agree that this is a very delicate issue. Four years ago we helped our council put together a $200 million project. While we thought we were keeping them informed, we weren't; so we don't do deals in secret anymore. When developers come in, we say, "Go public just as soon as you can." I think it stretches the credibility of the system too far to deal in secret for a long period of time without telling the council.

Hansell: On the contracting-out issue, I don't know who you would contract out to, quite frankly. The chamber of commerce has its own agenda. I can remember an economic development deal where the business community was bitterly against it because of labor competition. We were trying to bring in an industry that would create competition for a scarce labor pool, and local business said, "We are not interested in that." The people wanted jobs. They were good jobs but the local business said, "We're not interested." I'd be very reluctant to contract out to the chamber of commerce. That's an incredible vested interest. In my experience as a manager, when our mayor wanted a deal, he didn't really care about the issues. I would say, "We need to look at cost-

222

benefits, we need to look at the social factors." He'd say, "Look, I want the deal; I want the bottom line." I would hope we wouldn't overreact to the professionalization in mayor-council governments. They're getting better technically but if professionalization is defined to include some of the value statements in John Nalbandian's or Chet Newland's papers, I'm not sure they're getting any better. I'm not sure they're getting more professional than we are in the council-manager system.

Pokorny: Often the presence or absence of that professional is very tenuous, depending on who's in the mayor's chair.

Gleason: First, I think Don McIntyre's point is a good one. I've discovered over time that you can go public a lot sooner than you think you can. By holding issues close to the chest, you risk your credibility with the community and limit how quick you can go forward. The easiest way to go public is to go talk to the council; and then let them decide how public the discussion will be.

Secondly, I think we're defining economic development too narrowly; we could contract out some of the deal-making capacity around tax increments and similar issues, but we're not going to be able to delegate out access to the infrastructure, such as curb-cut permits and water access.

This is the essence of why we are a municipality. The professional ethic that I cling to is that we do the public's plan very deliberately and very publicly. We work the plan. The legitimacy of cutting deals has to be ground into that plan.

Pokorny: What enforces the plan is the legitimacy that the council attaches to it because of its involvement.

Kerrigan: Economic development is so complex that a couple of things are going to have to happen. First, there needs to be a greater infrastructure inside city hall. The manager's role will decrease in many ways. Maybe on the top level there still will be some contacts. There will be blurring of the cooperation of the private sector, the public sector, and the university. There will be more contracting out. Instead of using its chamber of commerce, Houston formed an economic development council. On certain issues, however, you can't give away the city's role. Economic development skills are not necessarily the managers' best role because that's not what they were trained to do.

We in higher education need to start teaching some courses in these areas. We are just starting to move into economic development in the curricula for MPA programs.

Anderson: My experience is that it's most successful in places where its value is least questioned--where people agree it's got to be done. When you've got high unemployment and empty buildings, it's much easier to do. The council-manager form has an advantage as a system because when the deal is done--whether it's early or late or public or private--it's going to be described as the council's accomplishment; it's not going to be a political credit for the manager.

Hale: I'm wondering whether economic development is today's complex issue. Terry Novak said he didn't have any courses in real estate except for twenty years of experience. The city manager has to be on the cutting edge of whatever complex issue we keep cycling through. And that's the professional part of what we're talking about. The city manager can hit an issue early with expertise, even though it's risky. For those of you who have been in this business for some time, what preceded economic development as this type of an issue?

Gleason: Housing. These issues work through cycles. There's a local cycle as well as a national one. When you land a big plant, for example, all of a sudden different dynamics come into play and neighborhoods get organized.

Hale: In terms of curriculum, are we ever going to catch up? There will always be something that the curriculum is behind on, unless we concentrate on getting in on the ground floor and being able to see upcoming issues and move with them. We need to focus on process as well as content.

Borut: That's why we're going to always have the academic-practitioner conflict.

Svara: This point raises an interesting question. We act as if managers have to be trained in MPA programs and then launched. We think we've got to put everything on the ship that they are ever going to need. That's not ever going to be realistic. What about continuing professional education? What we need to be doing differently is to bring together ideas and training in emerging areas for practitioners who are already in the field.

Romzek: That's just what I was going to address. The presumption that we in college communities should be introducing students to these concrete subject areas like economic development is faulty. By the time students get into positions where they're responsible for major development, that information is all going to be outdated. If they're lucky, they will have such responsibilities in ten years; more likely it's going to take fifteen years. We educate students to think so they can solve crises. Students say they want a budgeting class. In fact, what happens is when they start to work, they work for people who have their own way of doing the budget. There is always this sense of "Oh if I'd only had a course in this when I was in school." By the time they get there the information would be outdated. When they need the information is when they are ready to take the course. That's what executive development, continuing professional development, can help you do.

King: I want to comment on the risk that is increased in this phase. Your successes are taken for granted, but the public watches your failure much more closely. Another area related to what's missing in our background is ethics, the issue of corruption. At what point do cities and managers draw the line on putting public money into something that perhaps didn't need public money? In the competitive environment we're in, especially in a multi-city area, we're trying to lure the same auto center or the same mall. Millions of dollars that didn't need to be spent "by the public" to make something happen are being spent because of the ability of developers to go around with their hand out and find the best deal. For us to continue to say, "We need it to make things happen" is wrong.

Olson: Now people are watching their councils to make sure that we're not overextended, or we really shouldn't be putting public funds into projects.

Unidentified Speaker: Or analyzing investment. I know of a city not too far away that has committed nearly $200 million. Its return in twenty years will be less than if it had put that money in a bank.

Toregas: I want to return to what Barbara Romzek said. What do we do with the student today? Are there generalities that you can give us to test, for example, interpersonal skills?

Romzek: Yes.

224

Toregas: Are there ways to test whether the dimensions you have chosen in university sites ring true to the practitioners?

Romzek: Look at the success of your graduates. If they're successful ten years from now, you've done a good job. Can they handle themselves when they get out there in the long run?

Pokorny: So we look in the rear view mirror but glance ahead, too.

Romzek: Absolutely.

Brown: That may be relevant to the education you received in the first place. I think we're talking about the art of management, not the science or the problem solving. Knowing when to do what comes from experience.

Frederickson: Some of that is acquired on the campus. Have you ever tried to register for classes?

Glass: I think most of the MPA programs would like to take credit for the success of our graduates, but I think a lot of that success depends the intellectual ability of the person in the program. We need to be concerned with attracting the best talent into MPA programs.

Frederickson: Because of the federal tax structure, we see the rapid creation of all kinds of authorities--for example, airport authorities, research and industrial park authorities, etc. What kind of an ethical harvest are we going to reap from that? All the rules and all the details that we hold dear as city managers--the red tape that makes sure that the public's business is done right and honestly--are being bent with respect to purchasing and auditing. How much of that have we compromised in the name of economic development, either by setting up structures that are distant from us so our hands are clean, by letting the mayor do it, or in some other way?

Banovetz: I am not going to respond to that question; I am returning to some earlier educational issues. In some ways our educational curricula are like the United States Congress. They are excellent at producing a response six months after the need has passed. In the 1960s, we were involved in intergovernmental relations and grant writing. In the 1970s we were rushing grant-writing courses into our curricula after grant-writing had already been delegated by city managers to their staffs. That isn't all bad because we don't turn out city managers; we turn out people who function as staff until they work their way up to city manager. They go through these stages of doing the things the managers have passed on to them. Economic development will be delegated to staff members, but we still need to give people a conceptual framework within which to solve problems. We have to tell our students where the values and the ethics that we're teaching are going to impact.

Schilling: I'd like to underline the need for some technical skills in this area, too. Many MPA graduates just aren't prepared with the financial analysis tools that they need to handle municipal work, much less negotiations with developers who have armies of people behind them that know these issues well.

Hale: I think that's true but I'm not sure that we as practitioners or academicians know enough to integrate new issues--for example, economic development--into the classroom unless we're willing to do so with lots of ambiguity.

Banovetz: In this case, we don't need to show all the nuances of the public/private worlds. That's not as important for an analyst or a manager as being able to understand the issue with the same skills as the developer does.

Gleason: I think the philosophical framework is not in place. We are not giving students, practitioners or anybody a philosophical framework for the municipal corporations. It doesn't exist. As practitioners, we operate much like welders do. We don't know why electricity comes out the end of the electrode, but somehow metal gets imparted and something gets glued together and we keep on welding. Understanding what this institution is, the fact that it produces 110 products, and how those products relate to human beings is important. Why do human beings have to have cities? The structure for understanding these issues doesn't exist. We're much like Terry Novak says: we are going to make it work no matter what it is.

Hale: Yes, but the philosophical framework within which you make it work was a part of your education.

Gleason: What I would most want the institutions to do is to work on what the creature is. Then we can describe why it works better when it has professional management than when it doesn't. Why is one form of government preferred to another? What is it doing? What is it producing? And why would it even consider producing that? People are the principal asset that has to be connected in order to produce anything. You can't produce cars if people can't drive them on the streets. The issue of why the public has a right to that asset and who gets to use it isn't framed well.

Keller: I was trained under C.A. Harrell. The first book he had me read was *The City in History.* What happened in the structural era that Chet Newland writes about is that we replace city with management. We got involved with technology and then economic development becomes a technological issue. How do you work out deals without talking about what the city is supposed to be? What's the role of economic development in furthering the ideal city and enhancing the lives of its residents?

Borut: Let's assume that the notion of economic development is a primary activity of a large number of managers. That may be fallacious because not everybody is doing the same thing. Economic development can be an invigorating challenge but what about some of the other activities that don't get addressed because we're putting all of our energies into economic development? It may be easier and more satisfying to do something because we can achieve closure on it. We can see something happen. Many councils have made the choice to get into economic development. Have we simply followed in that direction or are we taking the lead? We ignore some other social issues because they're harder to tackle.

Tipton: When we move into economic development, we may rationalize that we are creating jobs. I could list three or four public/private ventures that did that in my community, but if I were entirely honest, I'd have to say the many of the people we thought we were going to help weren't qualified to do the jobs that were created.

Frederickson: Don Borut's question is a good one. I'm not sure that the energy given to economic development is displacing other things. But let us assume that since you can't do everything, some things are displaced. Michael Harmon describes the tendency for governments to be more effective in dealing with so-called "tame problems." We build highways, sewers, and treatment plants. We're even developing extensive ways of dealing with our solid waste. We have a whole lot more trouble, however, dealing with our "wicked problems." Is economic development the fulcrum around which most city managers presently function that enables us to avoid the wicked problems? I suspect that's the case.

Kerrigan: Let's not just pick on the managers. What about the universities? We're into economic development because it's easier to tackle than access to higher education. You cannot help the people you want to help through economic development, partly because education is not achieving its goals.

Frederickson: Harmon's argument is not about management so much as it is about government—what government is and is not doing. It goes back, I think, to John Nalbandian's paper. Are there questions about democratic theory and questions about ethics? Economic development also fits nicely with the interests of the majority. The majority elects our councils. It's very comfortable but it does not comport well with the interests of some subsets of our communities that aren't well organized, that are inchoate in their demands. These people get lost in the system. What responsibilities do we have to them?

McIntyre: We are in economic development because it's an evolutionary process that we have been involved in for a long time. We've graduated into making deals without federal help. We're doing them on our own. Proposition 13 no longer gave us the ability to fill our budget gaps with traditional property-tax increases so we look for new entrepreneurial ways to obtain revenue. In California the sales tax is the life blood of cities. We do everything that we can to create sales taxes, bed taxes, or tax increments because we have to have these revenues.

Toregas: Economic development is a label. It is nothing more than our cities living, breathing, creating, and doing things. Sometimes we rely too much on labels like economic development. I worked for a man twenty years ago who developed a theory of human settlement called ekistics. He tried to develop a cohesive theory of why and how cities live. Since his time I haven't seen a structural approach to cities to which we could relate management, policy, and administration.

Anderson: I think it's a mistake to assume that we lack an environment or a context. We just came out of a recession. That's created a series of new challenges, not only for managers but also for communities and for the city governments of those communities. I suspect that if you took today's manager back fifteen years and dropped him into a different economy and a different context, there would be a different set of issues confronting that manager. I don't think the challenge is for professional administrators or managers to sit making decisions about what they can do successfully as much as it is for those same people to grapple with the issues that are forced on them by the council, and the communities, and by trends outside the community. Few managers have ever sat down and thought, "Let's go international because the economy has changed." This decision came to us; we didn't actively seek it. It's a mistake if we separate ourselves from that context—whether we're talking theory or practice. We've got to acknowledge that context exists and plays a large role, not necessarily in the decisions but in the need for a decision.

Banovetz: Cities are like people. They have a hierarchy of needs. If your lower-level needs aren't satisfied, you're not going to worry about your higher-level needs. Man has always been willing to sell his political rights for a full belly. Cities are the same way. The retreat from the social agenda has been partly caused by poor economic times. George, while we are grappling with those lower-order needs are you

227

suggesting that individuals in the profession have an obligation to push cities to deal with needs that are not now at the forefront of their agendas?

Frederickson: No. I might argue that the economic development agenda of the 1980s has left a lot of people off the bus. For example, we create jobs but we're not able to train people to do the jobs. I'm not sure that city managers can ameliorate that much. My comment is more generally about the nature of contemporary government. In an aggressive and thoughtful city that is concerned with all its citizens, how much difference could a city manager make if he has real concern for those issues and consistently works on them? My guess is that you could make some difference. On the other hand, a banal manager out cutting economic development deals might forget about these issues. In the long run, a city will pay the price for this neglect.

Svara: I think managers do consider those concerns.

Frederickson: Many do, yes.

Svara: One question I asked in a recent survey followed up on some of the values questions that Ronald Loveridge asked a long time ago. One question asked whether managers believe they should advocate new policies to promote social equity. More than eighty-five percent said yes. Should communities ensure that equity is guaranteed in the provision of existing services? Equity has been broadly accepted by managers as a norm that should guide their actions, and they are looking for ways to promote equity. The question is, How do they do it? Do they have an independent social agenda or do they try to work with a legitimating body, the city council, to strengthen that council and enhance the ways that the council reflects the needs of the community? This interaction makes the governmental process more open and inclusive. It encourages participation. Over the last twenty years, we have seen progress on those fronts. If you make broad comparisons between mayor-council, and council-manager forms of government, there is evidence that managers support democratic governance. They support the legislative body. Mayors stress an executive leadership model that promotes the mayors themselves but really weakens the position of the legislative body. It indulges them in their lowest impulses and encourages them to seek special benefits and services for their constituents. Managers often tell councils, "I know these are your concerns, I know you have these wants but there are these needs too. We must come together to figure out where we should be going."

Brown: Maybe the reason that municipalities are involved in economic development is because they are not responsible for the primary human service delivery system. In most states this is a county, state or federal function. Many city and county administrators have no direct influence on these human services.

Newell: In answering George Frederickson's question and considering Jim Svara's response regarding social equity being a high value, I think there are some day-to-day things that managers should do. Some do these things and some don't. For example, regarding police relations and how the police department is handled, what kind of directives are given to that department on sensitive issues? That's a day-to-day thing that has much to do with social issues.

Gleason: Both of your comments are very accurate. Across the country the social service delivery system is augmented by cities but not directly delivered by cities. There are some exceptions to that, particularly in the west. One of the troublesome things that I've struggled with in my career is why we have not been able to rationalize the relationship between municipalities and counties. There is a strategic need for counties to perform certain functions, but we regularly deny this need. The reverse is also true. There are certain functions that are municipal in nature yet counties become involved in them when they have no business doing so. The inability to rationalize that creates or reinforces a lot of distrust and mistrust in the community. People say, "My God, they're wasting our money. They're not coordinated; they don't know what in the hell they're doing." Regularly, municipalities bash counties, counties bash cities. It's a "pox on both your houses" kind of discussion.

Denton: In Johnson County, Kansas, all five of my bosses are former mayors. The mayors in the county took over the county government, and the job of the county is to assist the cities. I work for 21 cities; I don't work for the county. There is an opportunity to work in social services, and that's a new challenge for me. But I'm still associated with cities and still work with mayors. Maybe that's the answer. I think it's the coming trend and it also opens up a lot of job opportunities.

Kerrigan: Just to support what Mike Gleason was saying, when Jim Banovetz brought a group together at a conference a couple of weeks ago, Dave Hinton and I presented some data on our study on the difference between the city manager and the county manager perspectives. Three areas that were of great difference were the ones you would expect: public health, education, and welfare. The county managers were much more involved in these three areas than city managers. That's probably going to continue.

Denton: That's where our performance evaluation is based.

Borut: I want to bring closure to this session and provide an opportunity for anyone else who wants to comment on the papers.

Sarah Purdy: I'm a student at the University of Kansas and I had a lot of thoughts during the discussion of the Newell, Glass, and Ammons paper, "City Manager Roles in a Changing Political Environment." We discussed changing behavioral roles because of the growing number of women in the work force and the need to be aware of cultural diversity in the work force. I heard various comments that disturbed me.

I hope to become a city manager within the next five years, and I don't think that the environment will have changed enough in that time for the things that I'm about to say to be false. As women entering this field, my classmates and I face some big issues that did not come up during the discussion. As we enter the field, we will have to deal with mobility issues, how often we're going to have to change jobs, how quickly we'll be able to move up, and whether the market is going to be open to us. Although I know that I'd like to be a city manager within five years, there are several communities where I would not even be considered. That's one thing that didn't come up. In addition to looking at city managers' roles in a changing political environment, you also have to look at whether the political environment is going to be receptive to the city manager at all. This may be a little blunt, but there are some communities that are receptive to a male city manager although not to a female or a minority city manager. I think that's too bad. I hope it changes but I don't expect it soon. Also there was some discussion of how studies have shown that female city managers and city council members tend to engage in more coalition building than male city managers or city council members. Then I heard the phrase, "the housewife background," which I guess was meant to refer to the fact that some of these people have a little more time or aren't engaged in some other activity so they have the time to build coalitions.

We all know it is not easy any more to support a family on one income. Over the last thirty years there's been a tremendous number of women who entered the workforce. I suggest that the idea of a housewife background simply doesn't apply anymore. And I want to leave you with a question that I'm going to be facing, probably for the rest of my career, which is, "How do we fit in and what behaviors do we exhibit?" Someone said that they suspected that women city managers are going to wind up acting more like men. I strongly disagree with that. If I were to behave in a manner that is not acceptable for me, I'd get run out of town. If I were to go out and cut economic development deals and be a wheeler dealer, I'd probably get fired because the council would look at me and say, "My goodness, she's not behaving the way we would want her to."

Kerrigan: I'll turn around and ask you a question. How different do you think it is in the private sector?

Purdy: I came from the private sector.

Kerrigan: I would postulate that it's not that different.

Purdy: No, you're right, it's not that different. In fact, that's one of the reasons that I've decided to change careers. I thought I stood a better chance of making it to the top in the public sector than in the private sector. I want to comment on some other discussions that have been going on this afternoon also. I think this is something that can't really be taught in school. We can get so much out of school but we can't learn how to assume a leadership role and how to assume an appropriate leadership role.

Kerrigan: That's a broad-based question in higher education. How many female university presidents do we have except Donna Shalala and a few people that we know in our own profession? It's true in higher education, it's true in private sector. I agree with you but it's a broader question than just local government.

Borut: You've stirred up a lot of folks. Let me make sure that we give other people a chance to respond to those points.

Purdy: I just wanted to make sure that my comments were on the table.

Gleason: I respect your courage to make these comments. They were very appropriate and unfortunately they're very true. I don't think anybody in this room has resolved these issues. I feel that the majority of communities in the United States would not hire female city managers. I also believe that the representation of women managers in corporations is low. The reasons for that involve the history of our culture, but a lot of them have to do with availability of trained managers. When you recruit, you still have to try to fill an experienced position with an experienced manager or you have to take tremendous risks. Our public works director is female. We had to recruit in our public works department for this major position. We had to take a chance on someone who was thirty years old and didn't have a civil engineering degree in order to put a female in that role. She's been there five years and she's outstanding, but that's a hell of a risk to take. Those kinds of problems are associated with placing people in these positions. In the final analysis, you don't serve anybody's purpose by filling a job with anything other than competency.

King: I feel that these reactions may be to a couple of comments I made. When I used the term "housewife," I was referring to my experience working for seven or eight different women as council members. None of them had their own career. They were housewives, and I say that with respect. In fact, I regret the passing of that era of housewife council members more than some of you who haven't experienced it. They have the time, the ability, and the consensus orientation that is not being replaced. That era has passed, and in the future the female who is on the council will be different. I did say that the female of the future on the council will likely be more like a male, but only because their professional backgrounds will be more similar.

Toregas: I think part of the magic of public service is that we have the ability to shape a future that does not necessarily build on the errors of the past. We in this room have a responsibility to change that. ICMA is working hard through the structures and behind the scenes to change attitudes. Sometimes we preach to the choir. We should be at the National League of Cities Conference arguing for the inclusion of women in the city managers' short list. How do you do this? We develop strategies. That is where the community in ICMA comes together. That is what it means to have an association of management, if we believe what Sarah Purdy said is true. I argue that other institutions have the same problem. It sounds exactly like the argument about blacks and Hispanics. We developed creative ways to override that and I don't think we should stop now.

Branscome: The wagon is moving. If you had sat at the head table in the assistants' luncheon at the ICMA conference with a room of 400 or 500 people and had seen the great mix of women and minorities in that group, it would give you faith for the future. You've got to have a pool of people who have the experience and the training. It may not come as quickly as we would like, but the process is in motion and once there are more female and minority assistant managers, there will be more managers.

Blubaugh: Half of the Assistants I and Assistants II in California are women now. The big issue though is the next move up.

Svara: Of concern is not the question of whether women can be hired as managers. There are obstacles but change is occurring and that's going to happen more often. Another concern is, Can a woman be herself as a manager? You said that you couldn't be an entrepreneurial manager, active in economic development. I'm not sure that's true. We need to be careful not to impose another kind of stereotype on women, one that says they have to be nurturing. Individual women will have very different management styles.

Technology
Forcing Strength into the Policy Debate

Costis Toregas
Public Technology, Inc.

" . . . In a world that is being driven onward at apocalyptic speed by science and technology, we cannot . . . give up the idea that human beings can control their political and economic policies. They must have some sense of where they are trying to go, of what they are trying to do, of what the world may look like twenty years from now...." So wrote Barbara Ward in her book *Spaceship Earth*, as she looked to a future increasingly dominated by technological change. The book was written in 1966, a time of the moon race, when the awe of gleaming metal, powerful computers and rockets projected an image that technology could do no wrong.[1]

The management profession responded to the comment: "if we can get to the moon, why can't we bring the technology to our cities and counties and pick up the garbage in a more effective way?" There was also an institutional response: ICMA's Technology Application Program was born in 1969 with a solicitation of some 200 managers from the executive director for a $500 contribution to match a challenge grant of the National Aeronautics and Space Administration (NASA). Those ICMA participants became the charter members of what was soon renamed Public Technology Inc. (PTI), an institutional response to the challenge of technology and a bid for leadership in this arena.

Many changes have occurred since those early years, but the intent of PTI has remained the same: to maintain a leadership edge in technology management for our managers and elected officials, and to strive to bring technology to a subordinate, supportive role in solution of urban problems. As more of our urban problems require sophisticated, expensive, and high risk solutions such as waste-to-energy plants, hazardous materials treatment centers, computer-aided dispatch systems or computer procurement and system installation--the price tag and frustration levels go up. Community leaders are feeling isolated from the decisions, uncomfortable with the possible impact of those technologies, and consequently resistant to technological change.

Figure 1
Levels and Activities in the Technology Policy Process.

Level in the Policy Process	Appropriate Policy Activity
I. Overall Policy Setting	Strategic Planning
II. Service Level	Decision Support System and Information Technology
III. Technology	Effective Procurement

The debate over technology procurement is going on in a policy vacuum because two pre-procurement stages have been skipped (see Figure 1). The first pre-procurement stage in technology decision is at the policy level, a stage requiring strategic planning to bring together the many decision makers who are a part of the policy process. The second pre-procurement stage is at the service level, a stage at which decision support systems and information technology are the suggested means of policy review. Once these two stages have been completed, the effective procurement of needed technology can proceed with both community support and administrative competence.

Why Tie Technology to Policy?

Cities and counties routinely make major procurement or operational decisions involving millions of dollars in a high risk, high visibility environment. Computer aided dispatch systems, cable franchise and service agreements, telephone system upgrades or switch procurements, waste to energy plant design and construction are some of the technology-dominated decisions that appear in council and commission meetings.

There is, however, a major difference with times past: these technology procurements are now front page news in the local press rather than mere administrative decisions made out of the spotlight of public scrutiny. Elected officials often become involved at inappropriate levels in the policy debate, and confuse rather than help the ultimate decision. As a case in point now, a major jurisdiction recently went through a public safety radio system upgrade, including a debate among elected officials over the distinction between 400 megahertz and 800 megahertz systems! It can be argued that a policy debate should not be framed in terms of megahertz, but rather in terms of ability to pay and support public security goals.

Lessons from Strategic Planning

Strategic planning is well established in private industry. PTI supports strategic planning and its ability to empower the multiple decision makers of today's complex public policy environment. From our six-year experience with strategic planning we draw two lessons: the importance of organizational framework and the strengths-weaknesses-opportunities-threats (SWOT) framework.

Organizationally, the most important element of a correct strategic planning effort is the mandate to the jurisdiction to establish a method that can deal *at the same time and in the same context* with internal (intraorganizational) as well as external influences. Two dominant dimensions must be managed simultaneously, and the administrative leader must sit at their congruence and appropriately move along both dimensions! On one dimension, elected officials, department heads and operating staff all have a major stake in the strategic direction of the community: they are the ones that will have to carry it out.

On the other dimension, private industry, the nonprofit sector, interest groups and the general public are all part of the resource base on which the community is built. Rather than argue for the separation between policy and administration, experience suggests that the two

Figure 2
In the eye of the hurricane

Elected
Leaders

Department   Nonprofits
Heads   The
                      Manager

Private   The
Sector   Church
              Workers
              in the
              Field

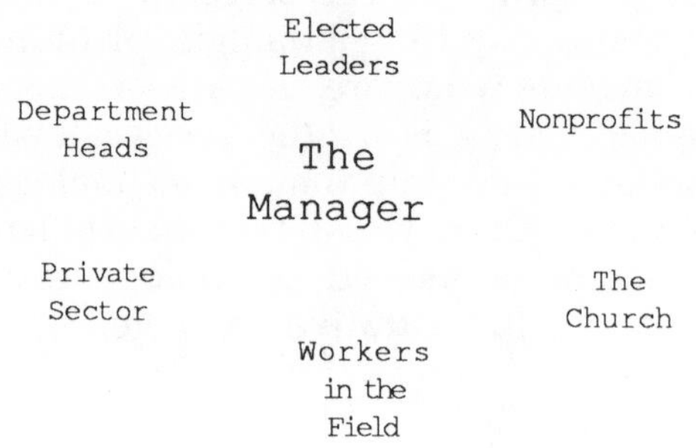

come together at the intersection of these two dimensions of strategic action. The manager, to make strategic planning work, must be at this intersection--in the eye of the hurricane (Figure 2).

One of the acronyms used in strategic planning projects is SWOT: strengths and weaknesses; opportunities and threats. These are the four dimensions along which strategies are cast and by which they are related to the environment.

Strengths are usually areas of complacency: if everyone is convinced that the city's major strength is tourism, then time has a strange way of making all city agencies assume that tourists will continue to arrive, today and forever. Forecasts of occupancy rates and revenues from room taxes begin to get that "it will be there" air of confidence. Staff efforts take on the fun direction of spending the money rather than assuring its generation. In such environments, one can see how the competitive edge may dissipate and become a weakness if every department's action is not always viewed from the aspect of supporting and regenerating that unique community strength. PTI experiences suggest that areas of strength, once identified, must be emphasized and made an active part of overall strategy.

Weaknesses are perhaps the toughest elements to define: no one wants to admit shortcomings. Yet, it is essential for the organization to know them, and to carefully build strategies around them. Once identified, weaknesses should be avoided in the near term (1-3 years), while a deliberate process is initiated to consider two options: should the city strengthen itself in those areas, or simply recognize them as weaknesses and move on? If the decision is the former, then the medium term (3-5 years) should be used as a timeframe for fixing those weaknesses in the community. If the decision is made to accept them (remember, we cannot be the best in everything), then all subsequent strategies must explicitly recognize and avoid these weaknesses.

Opportunities are very much time-dependent: they appear suddenly, and disappear swiftly. Cities must be prepared to seize those positive opportunities when they present themselves. A local government bureaucracy that can quickly respond to an opportunity may be unusual, given legal due-process and consultation requirements that serve as built-in delay factors. Cities should, therefore, consider alternate structures that might enable them to move quickly when opportunities arise.

Finally, threats are important to recognize as attacks on the competitiveness of the organization. There is a Russian proverb that describes organizational threats: "meet the wolf at the door and come back wearing a fur coat." Learning just who the wolf is (sometimes our best friend) can be difficult, but once identified, explicit strategies can be developed to fight back. And the traditional aspects of a complacent government that is kind to all and accepts all attacks with graciousness is simply no longer valid. We in public service must learn to strengthen our hand and develop our fighting tools to a sharply honed edge. In PTI, we have even looked at the tools of marketing as they are used in private business and adapted them to the public sector: perception management becomes a valid tool for hard pressed cities and counties.

Elements for the Future

Given this background, what are some elements to be used as foundations for the professional administrator of the future? I will distill PTI's own experience over the last two decades with five simple concepts. Each of these "I" words is insufficient by itself to make a difference, but the combination defines a powerful profile for managerial strength and visionary direction. And the connecting, common thread through them is that they are all human, personal skills rather than management tools acquired through analytic training. Using the "I" mnemonic, I hope to remind everyone of the importance of the individual in the increasingly complex society in which we work.

Initiate

Managing the community of tomorrow as a challenge to resource allocation skills and responding to pressures and issues as they arise has two major flaws: it does not appreciate the degree of severe economic and cultural dislocations that the nineties will bring to the public sector work environment, and it does not appreciate fundamental changes in professionalism that have occurred among the ranks of city department heads and their staffs. Increased professionalism and the ability to manage within the "big picture" context is by now an expectation of any good department staff person. It is a waste of time and scarce managerial attention to define the role of the city and county manager in those areas anymore.

Instead, the future manager must initiate change, and manage the dual dimensions (inside and outside) of governance around strategic, future oriented issues. Managers like Bob O'Neill in Hampton, Virginia, are already moving in this direction: he and his four deputies no longer spend their time on line management responsibilities over departments. They manage major council-empowered community issues, while the department heads "manage themselves" through committee structures with rotating, one-year chairs. This arrangement gives O'Neill a chance to initiate needed change at the community level and beyond.

Index

One of the toughest jobs we have as administrators is to ensure that all issues, all resources, all needs are visible and made available to problem solvers. And, contributing to the usual chaotic picture at the local level is our basic insular orientation. Fiefdoms spring up, vigorously guarded by each node of power: departments that create their own paper or electronic data bases, supervisors that have their own evaluation systems, neighborhood committees that see issues in their own orientation alone . . . the list is endless.

The administrator of the future must develop new skills in breaking down this insularity and infiltrating it with elements of common ground. And the tool that can do this might be called indexing, or orthogonal thinking, the ability to take a particular thought, orientation or information element and to project it along a dimension where there is commonality and a better fit with community needs and goals. Ted Gaebler, while managing Visalia, California, took the problem of stolen street signs and refused to classify it as a "law and order" issue that may have meant increased and costly patrols, more jail crowding and a negative impact on the community. Instead, he "indexed" it as a market opportunity! Students wanting to hang street signs on their walls suggested a far superior strategy: make signs and sell them at high school and college football games for profit! It is this ability to think orthogonally (at right angles to the way the problem comes in) that gives a new meaning to management, and a hopeful direction for the future. And it is this orthogonal thinking that is celebrated every year in PTI's Solutions awards program.

Interpret

The complexity of society today and the explosion of issues and problems at the local level will stress the ability of the manager to communicate across special interest groups. Even more importantly, the problems in society have become multi-year and multi-disciplinary, while the mechanisms and tools continue to be single year (budgets) and single dimensional (assign issues to one department).

The skill that will be in most demand will not be one of managing an issue, but interpreting that issue across time boundaries and special interests. Multi-year budgeting as exercised by Sunnyvale, California, and other communities is one tool that can help interpret current decisions across time boundaries. Procurement methods that strengthen our ability to derive performance specifications and use life cycle costing rather than low bid methods are other administrative tools that have the same result: a better interpretation of complex issues to the community we serve.

Finally, the interpersonal skills of the manager will really be tested. An ability to articulate a vision across ethnic, economic and racial classes will become an essential attribute of the administrator.

Interconnect

The success of any community will depend on its ability to network the resources at its disposal around effective and sharply focused strategies. And this networking requirement is essential as no single agency, no single group and no single leader can successfully cope with complex problems. The explosion of the AIDS epidemic, the pollution cloud over our water and air resources and the economic imbalances between the haves and have-nots are issues that have multiple impacts and cannot be rationally considered to be any one person's or institution's "problem." The role of the professional administrator in the future will be more that of a connector. Tom Moody, mayor of

Columbus in the seventies, articulated this direction well when he said that his vision of City Hall was a place where societal needs were clearly articulated and where organized responses were "packaged." He expressly rejected the notion that city government would necessarily be the provider of that organized response, but accepted a strong responsibility for the city as the locus of problem identification and the generator of solutions.

ICMA, NLC and PTI have organized and launched an electronic system called Local Exchange intended to provide the 1990s equivalent of Mayor Moody's city hall example and permit the connection of market place forces and societal needs to create organized responses to community problems. Going beyond electronic messaging to transaction services, we hope to provide a new level of linking between local jurisdictions and the public and private institutions that work with them.

International

It is clear that the boundaries of our problems may not ever again be perceived as local, or even national. Acid rain, the energy imbalance, off-shore manufacturing and its impact on local jobs and economic development trade opportunities are all reminders of the international setting in which our cities and counties currently operate. Most managers are very ill equipped to become major actors in this international arena. An ability to speak a second language is almost unheard of as a requirement in any public administration curriculum, and sensitivity towards different cultural environments and ways of thinking is still a distant dream. Some administrators now deal with issues of internationalism as their communities transform themselves into polyglot, strong and diverse organisms; this forced internationalization should be seen as an element of strength, initiating a process that should have been started long ago.

Special links with international organizations must be established, and trade opportunities aggressively pursued. The understanding and support of the local press is essential in such undertakings, as "boondoggle" is still the word most directly associated with the concept of international trips. This parochial attitude must be changed before internationalism can begin to bring dividends.

Conclusions

This conference is proof enough that academics and practitioners in public administration hear the drum rolls of distant clashes approaching. The time is right to engage in the battle of change. To do less is irresponsible toward future generations. It will require a lot of energy, stamina and risk-taking to modify both personal and professional traits in order to prepare the future manager for the rough times ahead. And technology can provide strength, when properly harnessed and used, in this assault on the status quo.

Note

1. The opening paragraphs of this paper are based on Costis Toregas, "Technology and Our Urban Communities: Who Shall Lead?" *Public Management*, May 1988, pp. 2-5.

Response

E. H. Denton
Johnson County, Kansas

The blend of policy and administration suggested by Paul Appleby and the role of science in administration urged by James McCamy now come together in the paper by Costis Toregas, who observes that the manager who would survive must act strategically in the eye of the policy hurricane while initiating, indexing, interpreting, interconnecting, and inter-nationalizing.

What does all this mean to city and county managers? It appears that the advance of technology forces managers to be futurists--to stretch their minds 20 years into the future. Yet governing bodies often are concerned more about the next election, and citizens are anxious about the next tax bill.

This means that managers must be willing to take risks with a bias for advancing technology, or else be left behind by the private sector and other more progressive public managers.

The scalpel of technology is double edged. If you initiate, but fail to index, interpret, interconnect or keep aware of universal or international trends, you may be embarrassed or perhaps dismissed. If you fail to initiate, the same fate awaits you certainly.

The Kansas City-Johnson County metro area is greatly benefited by the living heritage of L.P. Cookingham, Edwin O. Stene, and Orin F. Nolting, still personifying the triad of professional management, ethical performance, and technical competence. The people of this area expect efficiency and effectiveness in local government, as well as excellence in academic support for public management at the University of Kansas, the University of Missouri at Kansas City, as well as at nearby Park College.

The crucible of professional management is often subject to extreme heat in the process of strategic thinking and painful change. Its tensile strength must be proved not only in promoting technology, but in being sensitive to human beings and their needs for housing, health care, jobs, education and reeducation in often depressing and decaying urban settings.

Technology is a big help in meeting infrastructure and human needs. Managers must be willing to be proactive, integrated and knowledgeable. They must also be sensitive and caring. They must not abandon a strong sense of justice, ethics, and fair treatment for all. Technology must be a resourceful tool in improving the quality of life for all citizens.

Discussion

Novak: One of the job titles I haven't heard for several years is technology agent. Ten years ago a number of cities had technology agents on their staff. Has this position waned on purpose?

Toregas: Yes. Technology agents were part of a five-year experiment (1973-1978) of the National Science Foundation to take technicians, primarily from the aerospace industry, and place them in mayors' and city managers' offices. Today we don't want technology to be encapsulated, but we need it to become one of the tools of the trade. The role of the single technology agent is diminished because technology has become a tool for everyone--elected officials, appointed officials, and department heads. A newer approach is the concept of the PTI contact person in each community. This person is an agent of change, not necessarily using technological tools but managerial tools and making connections.

McIntyre: Our contact person is more of a communicator. Ours is a librarian who is a database expert. That person is not expected to be a change agent as the technology person was. If we had been more active, we would have had the agent on staff.

Novak: Part of the problem is the time pressures on the city manager. It's tough to get new technology adopted without firm pressure from the top and the clock is limited to 24 hours. I've had trouble trying to do both things.

Keller: One of the other issues that you might think about is intergovernmental as much as technological. Many of the major technology problems that we have in large urban areas are due to the fact that we can't deal with most of these tough technological problems by ourselves. Locating waste to energy plants or dumps is something that no one is prepared to deal with, even councils of governments Eventually some level of government must make those hard decisions, but it would be good if we had a governmental technology consensus, which I don't think most of us have.

One of the things that can help is the urban university planning what we'll call the library of the future. Ideally it will tie together all of our public sector databases. We collect all the housing data in Cleveland in the auditor's office and produce the annual housing report for the metropolitan area. It can then be tailored for each community. Our local university becomes a tie technologically. You could do strategic planning with public sector officials, tying their databases with university databases and with the state capital.

Hansell: Perhaps communication in decision-making technologies could help to close the gap between participatory and representative democracy. One of the reasons that we're looking for major modifications in structure is the shift from a representative democracy to a participatory democracy. As you increase the complexity, diversity, and focus of the interest groups, you seek more focused leadership; therefore, you want an elected executive. These technologies could help strengthen representative democracy in an era when there are incredible pressures to participate.

Denton: Costis Toregas's paper talks about the technology of integrated communication at the service level--the 24-hour courthouse and city hall, where more people know more. The professional staff uses technology to share information.

Schilling: Although it would break up the "I" nature of your presentation, perhaps you need to add a "C" or a "Z" to stand for "champion" or "zealot." In San Jose we found that the technologies have been advanced significantly up to the policy level and at the administrative level because we've had champions or zealots in areas like solid-waste management, water and energy conservation, and the use of computers by different departments. There are several ways you can bring these champions or zealots in. When you decide that one of those areas is critical, people will identify themselves as candidates for those roles.

Protasel: I want to follow up on Bill Hansell's idea that we may be moving from representative to more participatory democracy. In the diagram in Costis Toregas's paper about the eye of the hurricane, where do you put the general public? The general public is the resource base on which the future of the community is built. The people that determine the strategic direction for the community are the elected leaders, the manager, the staff. Do you see a role for the general community in setting the direction of the strategic planner?

Toregas: The general public is in fact the entire diagram.

Unidentified speaker: It's the hurricane.

Toregas: It's hard to pull away and say that business is not a general public, and everybody is connected with everybody else. The general public is the background of the diagram. Specific manifestations of the general public such as neighborhood groups would probably be on my horizontal scale. The vertical one is inside city hall. It is the structured process. The horizontal is other entities outside of city hall.

Gleason: Technology coming in as little capsules is not terribly useful. Technological innovation has to have not only internal champions but a champion from the policy side and possibly even from the community side. It's the constituency that keeps asking for and expecting higher productivity. Productivity is not the only reason to get involved in technological change, but it's one of the principal reasons.

Productivity has three independent variables: the capital infrastructure systems, from trucks to streets; the quality of that infrastructure; and the quality of management. The first two are the quality of the capital and the age of the capital. They are a necessary component of institutionalized and technological change, because technological change typically comes in tiny incremental improvements--the backhoe that can handle twice the dirt as the old machine, for example. The end cost is increasing because the quality of the capital is going down, due partly to its age and partly to poor maintenance. The reinvestment in the capital is not occurring. We're mining what capital is left. If you buy a new pumper truck that allows two people to operate it as opposed to three, you've still got three people sitting in the old truck. You can't invest in the new technology and yield the benefit. It doesn't accrue in the next five or six years. So we fall into a self-feeding down-cycle. We don't have enough money to buy new capital; therefore, we are not using the new technologies. The situation can only get worse. The only way I know out of that cycle is to have the community invest in a separate funding pool that is set aside specifically for capital.

We tried that three or four times and haven't been able to accomplish it, but we have more interest in reinvesting in that billion dollars' worth of assets. This makes more sense than my saying, "What I'd like to have is a new mainframe system so that I can add and subtract faster."

Toregas: You're absolutely right in terms of the lack of a capital infrastructure to move us forward. Today we buy technology just to buy the technology. When you buy technology, you shift the capital labor to a more productive state. That's what private industry does when it invests in technology.

We invest in technology just because the chief says I need a new truck. That is why we cannot recoup our investment in technology. We don't even know how to measure its efficiency. We need to advance the state of the art in measuring the performance of productivity in managers, cities, and counties. In the 1970s there was some measurement of performance in municipal government. Today nobody comprehensively assesses anything. We still don't know how to measure fire performance or solid-waste collection.

Newell: I'd like to return to something that Bill Hansell and Gene Denton mentioned about participatory versus representative democracy as they are linked to technology. We may be entering a danger zone with technology in a referendum-happy public. With technology already available through cable television, we could reach a situation where the public wants to vote on everything in a referendum format. This has many implications for governance.

King: I agree with what Costis says in his paper and the comments after it. I think that the basic perspective on technology is that it has cost cities more than it has saved. The existence of technology in our society has been one of the biggest reasons why government has had to expand in all areas. Medicine is perhaps the best example. Were it not for technological breakthroughs in medicine, the load on our entire medical system--much of which the government pays for--would be far less. The main role of technology in our society has been to induce higher costs. Those of us on the futures committee ten years ago heard Kenneth Boulding make a statement about the gravestone of our society: "Here lies the greatest civilization on earth, killed by high standards."

Technology in fact raises our standards. We don't build bridges the way we used to. It costs more to build bridges because we have the ability to build safer bridges. We have the ability to build safer cars, to prolong life, and to design buildings with all kinds of technological features. The quality of life increases, but the bottom line is that it costs us more when you mix that technological ability to do something with our legal system that says you have to do it. We have increasing pressure on government to build everything more safely, to overbuild, and to overdesign.

Hale: I'm particularly interested in what is going on in cities in information technology. Many of you have taken a look at this technology and the effect that it has on restructuring your organization.

McIntyre: One of the interesting phenomena that has occurred in our city is that a library service that is very good at providing information to other city departments has grown enormously in the last five years. One reason for its growth is that library management is greatly improved. Equally important is the fact that we have discovered that we have linked into enormous data bases that provide information that we can't get any place else. This is a resource base for almost any subject. It's a function that libraries haven't been able to perform effectively in the past.

Denton: The librarians are worried about what will happen to the book. They've got a tremendous investment in books. What if all the new books are on laser disks? If they are, we might be able to share that information immediately electronically. They think that will be a major revolution. And it will be expensive.

Gleason: I was reflecting on the academicians' problems in getting good data from managers and an earlier comment about how casually we fill out those questionnaires. I must admit I have a predilection to fill them out on airplanes. An appropriate technology transfer might be having the academicians use a focus group of managers and/or other people that varies from year to year. Information could be gathered electronically through the new Local Exchange network. This could be a way to query each other in more depth than just sending out questionnaires.

Toregas: I want to go back to the book discussion. We've got to acknowledge that technology transfer has changed, but it has not changed peoples attitudes. Therefore, promoting technology is going to take some risk taking again by the academic community. The finances are structured on top of the book form. Guess who's doing the old form? The Dutch and the Japanese. We are losing sight of knowledge dominance because we're still using books.

Brown: I think one of the issues that city and county managers have to master in information technology is to make sure they've got the appropriate technology in the hands of the people who are doing the work within the organization. As this information base goes directly to users and not through filters, interpreters, or analysts, we've got to make sure that the behavior of the individuals within the organization changes. Traditional bureaucracies award merit points based on information hoarding. That's the power base. This new information technology rewards information sharing and teamwork. The organizational systems that deal with personnel, performance evaluations, budgets, and the control elements have to be refocused because of that basic change in organizational behavior.

The second point I'd like to make is that if you share information to create a better organization in terms of productivity and output, you are investing in your human capital. Technology is a tool to increase the effectiveness of the human element within your organization. This technology will increase the ability to place decision making in the hands of the right people adequately trained to use that technology.

Schilling: One point which was made in the Future Horizons book ten years ago and needs to be underlined as part of this discussion is the importance of managers becoming more sophisticated consumers of the products of technology, particularly the information sciences. Analysts with computers available to them in medium- and small-sized cities look at data now in ways that they couldn't before. With spreadsheets it's easy to create five-, ten-, or fifteen-year models of revenues and expenditures in a city. A city manager needs to be skeptical about the information in those models. It is important that managers and their staffs can be skeptical reviewers of this information.

Keller: In Ohio nine suburban cities and Dayton linked together in a computer network tied into the university. It's a nice way to keep this exchange going electronically. One of the reasons the university promoted a long-range view is that the underclass is being kept out of these interactions. We are creating a technological society in which I can talk on line to somebody in Israel, but I can't talk to the ghetto in my own city. I think that's a critical social problem. We must build these kind of technologies of the future to provide community access to electronic networks.

Johnson: One of the things that we see in the corporate use of information technology is an inclination to research very narrow questions. That's all they pay attention to. This narrow focus can get us into trouble.

Watson: Why should we emphasize all this technology and forget about the closeness of human relationships? I've worked for 128 city council people, 30 in Lawrence, probably as highly educated as anyone. We've got a System-38 upstairs that cost $5-600,000 dollars. Every department head has a base that he could pull this information from. Yet on Tuesday night when someone is standing up here in front of the city commission, that person doesn't give a damn about that. He's shooting from the hip, counting on us to have everything done. We sometimes shortchange managers by saying, "Gee, the mayor is going to be the one who's innovative; the council members are the ones who are pushing you. That's not true. We're pulling the council into it. I think that we ought to take credit for that. I think we beat ourselves too many times by saying we're not the ones--it's someone else who is driving this. I don't believe that. I think that the managers are the leaders, and I think we will continue to be the leaders in innovation and technology.

Toregas: The most important element is humanism. You said, "I can talk to Israel but I can't talk to the ghetto." Walk there instead. You don't have to talk to the ghetto, walk there. If we can emphasize our own humanity and not permit the technology to tell us what to do, that will make stronger managers, stronger academics.

Professionalism, Innovation, and Entrepreneurship
Evolution in a Changing Society

Richard D. Bingham
Claire L. Felbinger
Cleveland State University

"Our Constitution is in actual operation; everything appears to promise that it will last; but in this world nothing is certain but death and taxes" (letter to M. Leroy, from Benjamin Franklin, 1789).

Today we can add a third certainty: change. There has been more scientific knowledge added to the world in the past ten years than the total knowledge gained in the rest of history.[1] We are truly in the heart of a technological revolution. We have the 240K dram, FAX machines, and VCRs. We can fly from New York to London in 2 hours. We can pick up the telephone and direct-dial Japan. On the other hand, we also have acid rain, AIDS, crack, a cycle of poverty we cannot break, and millions of people who are functionally illiterate. These problems, of course, are problems for the public sector.

The purpose of this paper is to examine some of the ways in which public sector professionals have dealt with problems in the relatively recent past and to identify what we see as an evolving trend-- innovation to entrepreneurship.

During the 1970s, many of the problems faced by cities were seen as productivity improvement problems. Why productivity? Three factors seem to have caused the concern: economic ill health of many cities, the rising cost of public services, and citizen rebellion against taxes-- especially state and local taxes. All of these factors put pressure on city budgets and on managers to improve productivity. Perhaps naïvely, many of the ways cities sought to improve productivity were through the adoption of technological innovations. In New York City, for example, city officials were concerned with the relationship between technology and productivity. In 1967 the city contracted with the Rand Corporation to "enlist the aid of technology and analysis to help break through New York's massive problems."[2] The term *technology* is key. One of the leading publications of the day was a short book by the Urban Institute entitled *The Struggle to Bring Technology to Cities*. Many professionals and academics believed that if cities could overcome the obstacles to adopting technology, vast productivity improvement would result.

According to the Urban Institute, the obstacles working against innovation in the city included institutional factors, political risk, budget constraints, job security requirements, distrust of industry experts, lack of accepted performance data, and lack of capability for technological evaluation.[3] Professional societies in the United States were among those working to aid municipalities to overcome these barriers.

Over a century ago, de Tocqueville wrote in *Democracy in America*, "Wherever, at the head of some new undertaking, you see the Government in France, or find a man of rank in England, in the United States you will be sure to find an association."[4] Indeed, this continues to be the case. There are over 2,000 professional and learned societies in North America. Professional associations, such as the International City Management Association (ICMA), are a part of this group. The professional association is an organization composed largely of those employed by governments in administrative, professional, and technical roles, and whose major objective is to improve the performance their members in the public service.[5]

During the 1970s these professional associations worked with cities in an attempt to stimulate interest in productivity improvement and innovations. Projects undertaken by ICMA provide examples.

In 1973, ICMA began a cooperative effort with the National Commission on Productivity and Work Quality to produce a *Jurisdictional Guide to Productivity Improvement Projects*. This undertaking produced a series of productivity improvement publications. These guides featured hundreds of projects which effected cost savings or improved services in a broad range of functional areas. Short write-ups concerning productivity improvements were listed for each area along with the name and address of local officials to contact for further information.[6] In the solid waste area, for example, Dallas, Texas

> has reduced its crew size from three to two by using a modified step-in cab, which allows the driver to load and drive in a standing position. The "telephone booth" cab and controls were designed by the City of Dallas as an inexpensive modification to their regular side loader packer trucks. The Sanitation Department saves approximately 325,000 man-hours per year through this program...[7]

In addition to the jurisdictional guide, in-depth reports on selective projects were available through ICMA's Report Clearinghouse.

Another ICMA activity of the 1970s was the "Municipal Innovations" series. The series was part of ICMA's Local Government Management Innovation Transfer Project funded by the Office of Intergovernmental Science and Research Utilization (ISRU) of the National Science Foundation (NSF). Each issue in the series was an in-depth report of an innovation in municipal government believed to have widespread applicability.

In addition, ICMA, again with federal assistance, developed projects which promoted the adoption of innovations in specialized areas. The organization disseminated information on successful criminal justice innovations through its monthly publication, *Target*. *Target* was part of the association's criminal justice project and was supported by a grant from the Law Enforcement Assistance Administration (LEAA). The association also published *Waterline* on a bi-monthly basis as part of a water quality project funded by a grant from the Environmental Protection Agency (EPA).

The federal government's interest in innovation in municipal government was not restricted to providing funds for association projects. The Department of Housing and Urban Development (HUD) and NSF were long involved in setting up organizations and networks to expand local government use of research and technology. Among the programs developed by NSF out of the ISRU Office was the Urban Technology System (UTS) program. Within UTS technology adoption patterns varied from city to city, but one common element involved placement of an experienced engineer on the chief executive's staff, whose job it was to apply new technologies to emerging city problems. These experiments generated "innovation" networks supported by NSF. The California Innovation Group, composed of a number of California cities and support groups, developed from one experiment. The Urban Consortium for Technology Initiatives funded by the Department of Transportation and NSF developed from an industry training technology coordinator on the city payroll in Tacoma.[8] During the 1970s a series of reports began linking professional associations to the adoption of innovation.[9] It was not until the late 1970s and early 1980s, however, that formal studies were undertaken which attempted to show how professional associations influenced innovations in government. Figure 1 presents a multiple element sequencing of the process whereby a professional association influences a city's movement toward an adoption decision on a given innovation.   In general, the organizational

Figure 1
Process Whereby an Executive Association Influences
the Movement Toward a Decision to Adopt an Innovation

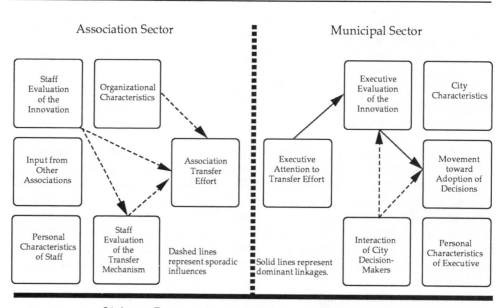

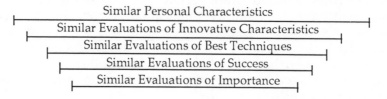

Source: Richard D. Bingham, Brett W. Hawkins, John P. Frendreis and Mary P. LeBlanc, *Professional Associations and Municipal Innovation* (Madison, WI: University of Wisconsin Press, 1981), 140.

characteristics of the association, particularly its financial resources, shape the association's innovation transfer effort. (A transfer effort might be a series of articles promoting an innovation in an association publication or demonstrations at an annual meeting.) A city's chief executive's attention to the transfer effort and his or her trust in the association influences the executive's opinion of an innovation. Research has shown that it is the chief executive's opinion which is the dominant factor in a city's movement toward an adoption decision. The city's chief executive plays the key role in these efforts, despite Herbert Kaufman's conclusions to the contrary.[10]

Innovation in the 1980s

As we look back through the 1980s, we find a dramatic change from an interest *primarily* in adopting technological innovations as a measure of local government productivity to a more general interest in innovative behavior (which sometimes includes adoption of technological innovations). If we look at ICMA today, we find that it no longer publishes a *Jurisdictional Guide to Productivity Improvement Projects*. That series has evolved into a *Guide to Management Improvement Projects in Local Government*, a quarterly publication listing executive summaries of local programs which have improved service levels or cut costs. Budget cuts have reduced staff's in-depth reports on innovations, although ICMA still acts as a clearinghouse for locally generated descriptive material. ICMA's Municipal Innovation Series (reports) has been discontinued. ICMA no longer has a local government management innovation transfer project and no longer publishes either *Target* or *Waterline*.

At the federal level the Intergovernmental Science and Research Utilization Program has been terminated. The National Science Foundation no longer supports innovation groups. The Urban Consortium for Technology Initiatives no longer exists. The U.S. Department of Housing and Urban Development is no longer active in setting up organizations and networks to expand local government capacity to use research and technology.

All of these projects received positive reviews in the 1970s, and yet they no longer exist. Why? Is innovation no longer important?

Some might answer that the Reagan administration is to blame--that these programs were the first to go in the wake of federal budget cuts. There is some truth to this. NSF did, in fact, restructure and eliminate its Innovation Processes Research unit. ICMA also lost grant funds and eliminated its innovation programs.

Overall, however, we suggest that cuts in federal funding have little to do with the demise of these programs. The innovation programs died not solely due to the Reagan cuts, but due instead to the eventual realization that it was not hardware and technology per se that would make governments more effective but an increased professionalization of management. The adoption of technological innovations has been replaced by "public entrepreneurship." Public entrepreneurs are

> individuals whose careers at managerial levels [are] linked to innovative ideas and efforts to carry these ideas into effect, often attended by some risk to their organization and to their careers.[11]

Public entrepreneurs are involved with "innovation" as opposed to adopting innovations. Under this conceptualization, innovation does not have to be a "thing" at all and need not be "technical" or "technological."[12] Indeed, some of the major innovations of our time, like social insurance, are successfully implemented ideas. In the 1980s and beyond, innovative programs and technologies will continue to be important; however, strategies of implementation will be at least equally critical.[13]

Most writers on public entrepreneurship stress that public entrepreneurs are "opportunity-focused" and proactive. Peter Drucker states that entrepreneurial innovation is work--it does not just "happen." Jameson Doig and Erwin Hargrove argue that the ability to use entrepreneurial strategies depends on factors both external to the entrepreneur and a function of internal characteristics.[14] In the external realm they believe that fragmentation and overlapping of governmental units and responsibilities offers an "entrepreneurial opportunity" for experimenting with innovative ideas. Public support, either a spontaneous ground swell or one "created" by the entrepreneur when public opinion is vague, works in favor of innovation. Of course, the rise of new technologies is still important for success, but not solely important. Finally, political support and resources from elected officials keep the process democratic.

Internally, the personality and skill of the public entrepreneur is "crucial to successful innovative actions carried out in the complex environment of a government office."[15] The skills cited are: (1) the capacity to engage in systematic rational analysis; (2) the ability to see new possibilities offered by a changing historical environment; (3) the commitment to want to "make a difference" even though the organization's and the professional's reputation might be at risk.

By way of illustration, *Inc.* magazine ran a feature article entitled "The Most Entrepreneurial City in America." Featured was a discussion of programs in Visalia, California, and of City Manager Ted Gaebler.[16] Gaebler urged city employees to think like owners, not like managers. He argued that government officials must learn to take risks and seek profits, to think "outside the box," to avoid paperwork and regulations. Managers must be given autonomy and encouragement to continually rethink their product mix. They must be willing to divest services. Since research has already discovered the importance of CEOs in the innovative behavior of organizations, the entrepreneurial behavior of a CEO can, and in the case of Visalia did, shape organizational culture.

One of Gaebler's first moves in Visalia was to adopt a budget system that encouraged entrepreneurial behavior. Gaebler adopted a new system called "executive control budgeting," which forces managers to make tough choices. He adapted a system from Fairfield, California, whereby each city department would automatically receive the same budget dollar amount every year, adjusted for inflation and population. Gaebler changed the formula for Visalia to include only half the inflation rate. A department would be allowed to keep any savings it accrued during the year, which eliminated the year-end rush to spend the entire budget in order to avoid future cuts. Department heads thus have an incentive to be entrepreneurial and to show a profit.

The police department saved money on its squad cars by developing a lease-purchase program. It also switched from a system of three officers sharing each car on revolving shifts to one in which each officer has his or her own car and can take it home. The city thus put more police cars on city streets and improved maintenance because officers felt a new sense of ownership. Cars now last an average of five years as compared to 18 months before the change.

This budget model is now spreading. Cities from Hampton, Virginia, to Pueblo, Colorado, are imitating this program. Cities in some areas have become so efficient that even the private sector cannot compete. For example, when a private company looked at the books of the solid waste system in Visalia with the hope of convincing the city it could do the job for less money, it walked away without even making an offer.

Public entrepreneurialism like this in the public sector is not of recent vintage. At the national level there are legends such as David Lilienthal of the Tennessee Valley Authority, Admiral Hyman Rickover of the "Nuclear Navy," Nancy Hanks of the National Endowment for the Arts, and Robert McNamara of the Defense Department. Local government had its entrepreneurs also--like the contemporaries Robert Moses and Austin Tobin, former director of the New York Port Authority.

Tobin is less well known than Robert Moses, but that is because of the style he used in his entrepreneurial activities.[17] Unlike Moses and Gaebler, Tobin did not operate in the limelight--he did not have a high public profile but he was very well known and respected by his political peers. He worked very much like the text book version of a traditional city manager. However, like Moses and Gaebler, Tobin was the embodiment of the entrepreneurial personality described above. He loved his work and went at it relentlessly. Even as a youth Tobin demonstrated a great capacity for coherent reasoning, discipline, and drive. An anonymous author described Tobin in his yearbook entry at Holy Cross as one of:

> only a few compelling people who become so sincerely bound up in every task to which they are assigned, that they positively fill the atmosphere with their determination. Austin is of that rare and valued type. No half-way measures for him; do it well or don't do it at all--with a vengeance. In fact, we would be inclined to smile at his earnestness, if it had not a wealth of genuine talent to justify his actions.[18]

So it was with a vengeance that Tobin immersed himself as a real estate attorney and later as general counsel for the Port Authority of New York. In addition to arranging for usual land acquisitions, Tobin orchestrated national grassroots opposition to President Roosevelt's and Treasury Secretary Morgenthal's proposal for the taxation of municipal bonds. Tobin and his colleagues won their case in the Supreme Court.

Tobin had an uncanny knack for making most of the initiatives about which he felt strongly seem like they were proposals from agencies or politicians not directly associated with the Authority. Unlike Moses, he did not publicly look as though he were empire building. Rather, others (including a friendly press which liked his regional approach) would announce publicly that a condition existed and that the Authority was the likely unit to study it. His efforts to get other units of government involved in efforts such as the municipal bond tax made it appear that the initiative had a national impact (it did) and that it was not only the wish of the powerful New York Port Authority (they only realized it first).

By the time he was 39, Tobin had assumed the top staff position in the Authority. His was an era of expansion in airports and marine terminals and container shipping terminals. He surrounded himself with the top professionals in the fields of engineering, planning, and law and paid them top salaries which made the Authority the agency of choice among professionals in the region. He encouraged employees at every level to share their ideas with him, everything from increasing quality of processes to multi-million dollar acquisitions. And he shared ideas with them. He visited with them, provided incentive bonuses for quality work, presented awards for valued service or for providing ideas which had a fiscal or effectiveness payoff. In return Tobin had an intensely loyal and effective work force which believed in what the Authority was doing and loved the man himself.

Tobin introduced other managerial innovations in his years at the Authority. For instance, he instituted the "self-supporting" criterion for Authority projects. Only projects for which it could be demonstrated that they would, in the long run, generate enough revenue to meet total operating and construction costs would be undertaken. This is quite different from the proliferation of special districts, in states like Illinois, which are set up to incur debt and provide an additional taxing mechanism.

Another innovation was one of the earliest uses of "responsibility centers" in government. By 1950/51 the Authority had grown so large and diversified that the organizational structure--planning and development in one department and operations in another, each with a director--was too unwieldy. With the help of a management consultant, Tobin reorganized the Authority into four operating departments (aviation, marine terminals, tunnels and bridges, and terminals). Each department had the long term commitment to planning, developing, and operating and the responsibility to be financially self-sufficient. Of course, they were rewarded for their ability to do this.

Tobin did not get everything he wanted. In fact, he was cited by Congress for contempt when he refused to turn over all internal files for a general investigation. He argued, with the governors of both New York and New Jersey, that his was a state agency, not one which should be the subject of a federal probe. His appeal was successful; however, the two year appeal period was taxing to both the man and his staff. Tobin resigned in 1971 with many of his projects intact. He was a consummate professional, using his public entrepreneurial drive to shape the region's economy.

Innovation exploits change. Public entrepreneurs will capitalize on opportunities by recognizing the sources of change. Peter Drucker lists what he sees as reliable sources of change:

The unexpected--the unexpected success, the unexpected failure, the unexpected outside event;

The incongruity--between reality as it actually is and the reality as it is assumed to be or as it "ought" to be;

Innovation based on process need;

Changes in industry structure or market structure that catch everyone unawares;

Demographics (population changes);

Changes in perception, mood, and meaning;

New knowledge, both scientific and nonscientific.[19]

To Drucker these items represent a hierarchy where the items from the top to the bottom represent the reliability and predictability of opportunity sources. Note that the behavior of professional managers and their professional associations in the 1970s focused on the source of opportunity which Drucker views as the least reliable and least predictable. Today successful public entrepreneurs capitalize on what is more predictable in their internal environment and exploiting change in processes and products.

Fairborz Damanpour and William Evan examined the relationship of adopting product (technical) and process (administrative) innovations and organizational performance in the public sector in the 1970s.[20] They found that the average number of technical adoptions was greater than the number of administrative adoptions. There was a higher correlation between adopting administrative innovations (or changing processes) and high performance across a range of efficiency and effectiveness measures than the adoption of technical innovations. Moreover, adopting administrative innovations lead to an increased number of technical adoptions over time. On the other hand, adopting technologies did not lead to increased adoption of administrative innovations.

The imposition of administrative innovations is a top-down activity. It is initiated by top level professionals to make a process more efficient and effective. Knowledge of technological breakthroughs is a function of more narrowly focused professional mid-level staff. It is clear that to maximize the knowledge of both sets of innovations requires the direct involvement of top management in providing the opportunity for mid-level staff to feel free to approach management with ideas, concepts, and technologies. Many of these opportunities are opened up through administrative innovations such as participative management, compensation plans, incentives, and rewards connected with organizational entrepreneurial activity. The best performing agencies are headed by public entrepreneurial professional managers.

Clearly, City Manager Gaebler fit the definition of a public entrepreneur. However, he could not have accomplished as much if he were acting on his own. Drucker points out that entrepreneurial management requires an organization which is receptive to innovation and which does not view change as a threat but as an opportunity. Gaebler's city council had a history of long term planning--that released him from a major obstacle. In addition, he kept to Drucker's principles by systematically measuring organizational entrepreneurship and instituting procedures to reward innovators.

Innovation is not an idea; it is the implementation of ideas which make sense. Innovators, Drucker continues, think with both sides of their brains. They are conceptual and perceptual. They live innovation and view the process as pragmatic, normal, steady, and continuous. Their drive is focused, not cluttered. They solve today's problems and do not predict (and are not afraid of) the future. It appears to us that the only way professional managers will be able to be successful is if they accept their new role as public entrepreneurs and view their positions as a locus for opportunity and success rather than as a job in which they solve problems.

251

1. Derek J. de Solla Price, *Little Science, Big Science...and Beyond* (New York: Columbia University Press, 1986), p. 5.

2. Urban Institute, *The Struggle to Bring Technology to Cities* (Washington: Urban Institute, 1971), p. 31.

3. Comptroller General of the United States, *State and Local Government Productivity Improvement: What Is the Federal Role?* (Washington: General Accounting Office, 1978), pp. 22-28.

4. Alexis de Tocqueville, *Democracy in America* [Reprint, 2 vols; New York: Schocken, 1966], Vol. 1, p. 129.

5. Richard D. Bingham, Brett W. Hawkins, John P. Frendreis, and Mary P. LeBlanc, *Professional Associations and Municipal Innovation* (Madison, WI: University of Wisconsin Press, 1981), pp. 12-13.

6. Ibid., p. 16.

7. International City Management Association, *Guide to Productivity Improvement Projects* (Washington: Government Printing Office, 1976), p. 59.

8. Bingham, et al., pp. 15-18.

9. Richard D. Bingham, *The Adoption of Innovation by Local Government* (Lexington, MA: Heath, 1967); Robert K. Yin, Karen A. Heald, and Mary E. Vogel, *Tinkering With the System: Technological Innovations in State and Local Services* (Lexington, MA: Heath, 1977); Irwin Feller and Donald C. Menzel, *Diffusion of Innovations in Municipal Governments* (University Park, PA: Pennsylvania State University Center for the Study of Science Policy, 1976); David A. Tansik, *An Investigation of the Adoption of Technological Innovations to Law Enforcement Agencies* (Tucson, AZ: University of Arizona College of Business and Public Administration, 1977).

10. Herbert Kaufman, *The Administrative Behavior of Federal Bureau Chiefs* (Washington, DC: Brookings Institution, 1981).

11. Jameson W. Doig and Erwin C. Hargrove, eds., *Leadership and Innovation: A Biographical Perspective on Entrepreneurs in Government* (Baltimore: The Johns Hopkins University Press, 1987), pp. 7-8.

12. These ideas are developed in Peter F. Drucker, *Innovation and Entrepreneurship* (New York: Harper and Row, Publishers, 1985) and summarized in a series of articles in *Modern Office Technology*, vol. 31, January, 1986, pp. 16-20; February, 1986, pp. 12-16; March, 1986, pp. 12-16; April, 1986, pp. 19-24.

13. Doig and Hargrove, p. 8.

14. Ibid., pp. 8-11.

15. Ibid., p. 11.

16. David Osborne, "The Most Entrepreneurial City in America," *Inc.* (September, 1985), pp. 54-57, 60, 62.

17. The material for this section is from Jameson W. Doig, "To Claim the Seas and the Skies: Austin Tobin and the Port of New York Authority," in Jameson W. Doig and Erwin C. Hargrove, eds., *Leadership and Innovation: A Biographical Perspective on Entrepreneurs in Government* (Baltimore: The Johns Hopkins University Press, 1987), pp. 124-173.

18. Ibid., p. 132.

19. Peter F. Drucker, "Innovation by Design," *Modern Office Technology*, vol. 31 (January, 1986), p. 20.

20. Fairborz Damanpour and William M. Evan, "Organizational Innovation and Performance: The Problem of 'Organizational Lag,'" *Administrative Science Quarterly*, vol 29 (September, 1984), pp. 392-409.

The Future of
City Management and the
Council-Manager Plan

The Future of
Council-Manager Government

Chester A. Newland
University of Southern California

In 1978 the International City Management Association (ICMA) Committee on Future Horizons launched a two-year examination of prospects for the profession of local government management in the year 2000. That committee studied society generally and local government in particular to gain useful insights. In an initial publication in 1979, the committee reported cautiously optimistic conclusions looking toward "new worlds of service."[1] The focus of the anticipated service challenge identified by the committee was highlighted a year later in the ICMA book, *The Essential Community: Local Government in the Year 2000*. That focus was on the neighborhood level, where, the committee said, "everything comes together."[2]

That optimistic focus of a decade ago provides useful points of departure to assess prospects for council-manager government in the year 2000. The added experience of the past ten years and the shorter span of time to the turn of the century make the present effort considerably less ambitious than that of the Horizons Committee.

Like the earlier ICMA project, this assessment examines past and current developments as bases for thinking about and creating the future. It accepts the Horizon Committee's premise that the future is in part conditional: it can be created to some extent by deliberate actions, and it should be. In short, the chief purpose of futures study is not simply to project what may be but to provide bases for actions to bring about desired future circumstances.

This analysis consists of three parts. Initially, the work of the Future Horizons Committee is summarized and briefly placed in two contexts: first, that of the longer history of council-manager government and then, that of futures disciplines practiced by professional local government managers. In the second part, structural issues of council-manager government are highlighted first and then roles of the council, manager, mayor, and other key officials are discussed. Many of these old and current concerns were passed over lightly by the Horizons Committee, but their importance has grown during the past decade. In the concluding part, the future prospects of local government in the United States are briefly assessed. Future assessment constituted much of the work of the Committee in 1978-1980, and some of its projections were impressively on target, while others have turned out to be wrong or irrelevant.

Kenneth Boulding cautioned ICMA conferees in 1979 that futures

257

study is the most celestial of celestial sciences. It is like looking into a cloudy crystal ball. Some clouds of the 1970s have dissipated over the years; other old ones are closer; some large, dark, unpredicted clouds have moved over the horizon, seeming to dominate today's scene. Bases for much optimism about professionally managed local government are now present, however, as many were a decade ago. As then, some of the most sustaining grounds for hope for the future stem from an idealism which has deep roots in American culture. The committee in 1979 quoted Richard Childs' 1918 advice: "The great city managers of tomorrow will be those who push beyond the old horizons and discover new worlds of service."[3]

That ideal of public service and its twin discipline of democracy, civic duty, are fundamental to the dynamic balance of council-manager government. Purposes and processes of constitutional government must also be sustained in the larger environment of American society, or that delicate balance is unlikely to survive at the local level. That is much of the challenge as the United States moves toward the year 2000. That challenge, most evident in the widespread growth of transactional politics and the decline of transformational politics, is even more evident today than it was in the exchange environment of government that became dominant nationally by the 1960s.

Past Experience and Futures Disciplines

Experience with council-manager government during its first three-quarters of a century is briefly defined here in terms of four successive periods, three with relatively clear contours plus the current period in which diversity makes definition difficult. Conclusions and disciplines of professional urban managers as futurists, particularly as highlighted by ICMA's Horizons Committee, are then discussed.

Past Clarity; Growing Diversity

For purposes of "futures assessment," the three most easily defined past periods of council-manager history are these:

- *The Political Reform Period* from the early Progressive Era into the 1940s.
- *The Structural Orthodoxy Period* from the late 1940s into the 1960s.
- *The Social Activism Period* from the 1960s through the 1970s.

The Political Reform Period which gave birth to council-manager government was, to a significant extent, a time of transformational politics. From the years of the nation's Constitutional Centennial to the Sesquicentennial, reformers used politics to attack spoils, inefficiencies, and related governmental problems. The Centennial gave occasion for many to reflect on how the United States, born out of the transformational idealism of the closing years of the Enlightenment, had shifted course since the 1820s. American governments had become objects and instruments of a market-type exchange for private gain; politics had degenerated into transactions for personal gain. Opposition to that corruption and dismay over the loss of American idealism ushered in a new period in which transformational politics sometimes prevailed again, as in the incremental creation of council-manager government nearly halfway through the reform era.

In terms of problems of the 1970s and 1980s and projections through the 1990s, it is worth reiterating that development of council-manager government and related reforms were not initially attempts to escape from politics. Reform was aimed at displacing the corruption of transactional politics with the idealism of transformational politics. Council-manager government in its early decades was designed as a *political* means to facilitate a civic culture of integrity and informed accomplishment.

The Structural Orthodoxy Period from after World War Two into the early 1960s came to be dominated by strict tenets of public administration. Two doctrines prevailed: executive aggrandizement and the politics-administration dichotomy. The latter doctrine *in that period* can be described as one of attempted escape from politics. But in terms of issues of the last two decades of the twentieth century, it is principally the public administration doctrine of the powerful executive that altered perceptions of council-manager government during the 1940s, 1950s, and 1960s that generated later pressures for political reform of what some came to see as a detached or neutral form of government. At its creation, this form was routinely known as COUNCIL-manager government, and it was perceived as a *political* reform plan, anything but detached or neutral. By the 1950s, it was referred to in public administration circles as the CITY MANAGER form. Engineers who, as city managers, had earlier reported as subordinates to politically superior councils were increasingly displaced by MPA's who had been taught to value executive power and to disdain politics and politicians. Structures of executive power became inviolate in "The Plan." The manager's budget became a bastion of executive power, barely subject to council modification. The manager came to have a near monopoly on information, subject only to inquiry by the council as a whole. Councilmember contacts with operating officials other than the manager became virtually impossible, often illegal. Appointed managers prospered in power, but the old politics of reform gradually withered, and, by the late 1960s, that greatly expanded executive power lacked the authority of popular support. The structural disciplines of "The Plan" undermined councils as vehicles of authoritative government, threatening the future viability of this governmental form.

The Social Activism Period that erupted during the 1960s challenged both professionally managed and politically dominated governments. Some professional managers, schooled in what later came to be called New Public Administration thinking, responded vigorously with proposals of "new worlds of service." Keith Mulrooney, then city manager of Claremont, California, for example, along with others, filled a symposium in the *Public Administration Review* with challenges for managers to provide needed policy leadership to deal with urgent social conflicts and needs.[4] That orientation remained one of managerial dominance, consistent with experience of the structural orthodoxy period, but it resulted in newly visible managerial involvement in issues of nonconsensus politics. Conflicts characterized many issues of the 1960s, leading to a period of political dissensus in America that still persists.[5] By the late 1970s, this new political environment led to a period of concerns among professional managers, civic leaders, and others about the future of professionally managed local government. These concerns, leavened with positive idealism, resulted in formation of the Future Horizons Committee, appointed in 1978 by ICMA President Bob Kipp, city manager of Kansas City, with George Schrader, city manager of Dallas, as the committee chair. That development acknowledged what informed professionals in local government had long understood: council-manager governments were functioning under increasingly diverse forms and varied processes in efforts to satisfy changing definitions of effectiveness while subject to new pressures for economy and efficiency. It was time to search the horizons for new directions.

Diversity and Futures Disciplines

By 1978, professionally managed local governments could best be characterized by diversity. The orthodoxy of "The Plan" was not simply challenged but already significantly eroded: councilmember election at large was increasingly displaced by single-member districts, council staffs were being created and expanded; mayors were exercising strong leadership, even dominating some governments while relying on professional managers as deputies; some managers were employed under contracts with severance provisions; hierarchical control over information and some operations had been reduced; and forms of popular participation had greatly expanded. The mayor-council form of government also continued to be popular in both the biggest cities and smallest towns. Those developments were continuing issues from the past, and they were scarcely touched upon by the Future Horizons Committee. A decade earlier, the International City Managers' Association had become the International City Management Association. By 1978 another name change--substituting "local" or "urban" for *city*-- was informally considered and rejected.

Orthodoxy had ceased to be the discipline of many professional local managers. "Futures studies" filled the gap for some. For ICMA, the Horizons Committee recommended disciplines of lifelong learning and professional action as crucial, including:

∘ Study of the known and the unknown--to attain a mature balance of confidence and humility in the face of changes.
∘ Awareness of situations and diversity--to appreciate both the positive science of "the one best way" and the open inquiry of contingency management.
∘ Practice of values and processes of constitutional democracy--to facilitate popular self governance and the rule of law.

The Horizons Committee stressed the conditional character of history: that probable and possible futures can be changed. The Horizons Committee concluded that the chief responsibility of professionally expert managers as futurists is to facilitate a continuing search for reasonableness in public affairs--to facilitate constitutionally based self governance, firmly grounded in values of transformational politics: human dignity and the rule of law. As practical futurists professional managers can make a difference.

Practical strategies were also recommended by the committee to contend with expected conditions of the 1980s, and five assumptions about the future turned out to be largely accurate:

> . . . learn to get by modestly, regulate the demand for local government services, be skeptical of federal dollars and the dependencies they cause, emphasize decentralization over regionalization of services, look at new services needed as a result of the [changing] population.[6]

While the Horizons Committee projected a future in which managers would need to "be even more idealistic," much of the focus was on realism about future challenges.

Structural Issues

Twenty years after ICMA's examination of structural and related issues in council-manager government and ten years after the Future Horizons Committee, developments in professionally managed local government have resulted in sustained concerns about structures of urban government. Projections into the future require assessment of these concerns and the structural issues behind them. This assessment first deals with conflicting doctrines and dynamics over roles of the council, the manager, the mayor, and other officers. It then discusses these roles as related to both charter provisions and changing urban dynamics. This part concludes with a summary of these issues in terms of three sets of contrasts between the council-manager and mayor-council forms of city government.

The Council--Control of Purposes and Resources

It is a part of the orthodoxy that the city council in professionally managed government has ultimate authority over purposes and resources. Beyond that, many differences exist about councils. Three sets of practical issues of varied scope seem certain to persist:

Elections: At-large/District/Partisan? Two issues are most important in terms of "the plan": (1) council election at large or by district and (2) nonpartisan or partisan elections.

The first issue has been driven by court orders to elect councilmembers from single-member districts to facilitate minority electoral power in ghettoized communities.[7] Clearly, district election enhances neighborhood power. "The Plan" rejected districts for precisely that reason, favoring a "community at-large" orientation. Generally, such at-large election results in selection of councilmembers with higher educational and occupational status; also, they are usually Anglos. But changed media and electoral dynamics may be redefining the nature of the at-large/district controversy. Community wide media coverage--particularly cable television and local commercial television news--may be an effective force to heighten shared awareness of some public matters. It is clear, for example, that television coverage of council meetings encourages councilmembers to "play to the bleachers." When elected from districts, the results are enhanced power of neighborhood interests over those of the community at large. Expanded media influence and national political dynamics have resulted in escalating costs of many local elections. At-large campaigns commonly cost much more than district campaigns, making them more subject to special-interest financing; district elections, in turn, may become relatively invisible, making them victims of special-interest manipulation.

One result of these pressures has been heightened, conflict-oriented politics, whether or not community-wide or neighborhood issues are involved. Television, a medium that plays community-wide or, more often, nationwide has become a force of dissensus by focusing on 15 to 90 second bites of mostly conflict-oriented or sensational events. Local news reports give vastly more time to homicides, auto accidents, bar-room brawls, and comparable political shenanigans than to broader or deeper political matters.

Partisanship has been on the rise in council elections, although many jurisdictions formally continue nonpartisan forms even when high partisanship informally dominates elections. The trend toward partisanship is linked to the national trends noted above, and it seems destined to continue at least into the near future.

Several other pressures also account for heightened politics. Consensus about roles of government has declined. Party competition has spread nationally, greatly reducing regions of one-party politics, as in the former "Solid South" and the Republican Midwest. High costs of media politics have forced renewed dependence on some party apparatus for financing elections, with renewed linkages through computerized donor and voter lists from precincts through city, state, and national levels. Special interests have formed parallel networks from precinct through national levels. Individuals who aspire to offices beyond local government see council election as a springboard to "higher office." All of these developments are linked to a general trend from the late 1960s through the 1980s toward partisan politicization and deinstitutionalization, as in abandonments of civil service commissions and council-manager government.

Council Size, Terms, and Compensation. These three issues are interrelated in practice. "The Plan" favored small, unremunerated councils, with members generally serving limited terms.

Recent trends favor slightly larger councils, particularly following population increases, although tendencies have not been to such large councils as in strong-mayor cities of comparable size. No signs suggest much change from modest growth in council size in the near future.

Terms for councilmembers under "The Plan" tended to be voluntarily self limiting, usually to two short terms of two to four years, before the movement to district elections and heightened partisanship. Compensation of councilmembers was rare under "The Plan," and they often paid their own expenses. Time devoted to council responsibilities was commonly limited to several hours a week; the manager and other employees were expected to perform all full-time work. Except in smaller communities, the earlier practices have changed. Councilmembers in larger cities are now commonly compensated, and most expect expenses to be reimbursed. In larger governments, compensation often approaches levels that encourage some individuals to value it as a desirable, full-time income or as a substantial addition to other resources. Provision of insurance, retirement benefits, and such perquisites as automobiles and telephones is no longer rare.

Continuation in office beyond one or two short terms has increased in cities where partisanship, compensation, and perquisites have expanded. While questions about imposition of charter limits on some maximum number of terms of councilmembers have arisen in recent years, the new model charter of the National Civic League does not provide for such limits, and such limits appear to be unlikely in the future. Terms of mayors are a related issue that is discussed later.

Council Staff and Committees. Council-manager government initially assumed that the entire administrative apparatus would serve, through the manager, as "staff" to the council, and that practice generally continued even in larger cities until the 1970s. The original idea was one variation of the reform movement, election on a short ballot of a visible few who would constitute a government of unity--not one characterized by separation of powers. In the absence of such separation, council staff was not required. However, during the structural orthodoxy period, councils increasingly found themselves fenced off from the administrative apparatus of government, shunted into obscurity by the growing public administration principle of the powerful executive. Also, professional managers sometimes seemed to dominate policy initiatives. When the social activism period followed, council workloads increased, councilmembers often found themselves hard pressed to fulfill constituents' demands, and pressures grew to provide them with staff assistance.

Staffs developed in two directions in the 1970s and 1980s: (1) liaison staff to serve the council as a whole and (2) staff to individual councilmembers. Liaison staff, in turn, commonly took two forms: (1) under the control of the manager and (2) under the control of the mayor and other councilmembers.

Individual council staff also developed in two directions: (1) secretarial and other office staff, commonly nonpartisan careerists, and (2) district and policy staff, often exempt from civil service and commonly partisan. Today, councilmembers in larger jurisdictions often utilize both sorts of staff, and the council as a whole may also rely on some common "legislative affairs" organization.

As councils have expanded in size and as workloads have grown, some have taken on other trappings of legislatures also, most notably committee forms of organization. These committees have sometimes employed staff functioning as budgetary and functional policy analysts.

As a result of the development of specialized council staff--a legislative apparatus--council-manager government in a few cases has almost come to resemble a system of separation of powers. Following the Future Horizons project, some of those on that committee started reemphasizing the value of unity of authority in the council, as in a parliamentary system, with the manager and other top administrators responsible for provision of direct staff assistance to councilmembers. Bill Hansell, the ICMA executive director selected after that period, quickly adopted that parliamentary focus in an effort to highlight merits of unity of authority and responsibility in the council. These alternative ways of approaching council-manager relations--separation of powers versus unity of authority--seem certain to continue at the forefront of future issues over forms of local government.

However, the development of automated information systems and related high-tech capacities in local governments are impacting council-manager government in ways that are reshaping the issue. One contradiction between the old principles of the structural orthodoxy period and the realities of new information technology illustrates this change. The old doctrine was that the manager was the single channel of communication between the council and the administrative apparatus. Today, council offices are sometimes linked by computers to information systems that provide relatively real-time knowledge of tax rolls, budget status, physical planning projects, and varied policy agendas. Such information, and much more, is available at computer work stations to administrative and council staff at most levels. Citizens can sometimes access such information through personal phone lines or at public-access computer stations at municipal or county facilities. This new openness of information facilitates some renewed unity or "community" in council-manager government. It has already altered the environment of council-manager relations dramatically, and that trend will continue.

The Manager--Control of Expertise and Implementation

While technology is eroding the barriers to information flow from the administrative apparatus to the council (and sometimes in the reverse direction), managers still control most administrative expertise as well as the methods of implementation of council policies. Some exceptions to that relationship have been common from the early days of "The Plan," however, and others have emerged as important.

Old Exceptions, New Forms. Civil service and planners are two relatively old exceptions to nearly exclusive managerial control of administration. These were exceptions because of the special value placed on them during the political reform period.

Civil service commissions were commonly created to exercise control of personnel operations in the early decades of the council-manager plan. They sometimes controlled all personnel, including recruitment and examination of key administrators. In other cases, they provided oversight of police and fire personnel functions. That old structure has been significantly altered in many governments since the 1960s. Personnel operations have been transferred to the control of managers, and functions of civil service commissions have eroded, except for continuation of appellate oversight of decisions. Expansion of collective bargaining has been the chief cause of the change; bilateralism requires a "management" party not only at the bargaining table but in the day-to-day implementation of labor-management agreements. While unionization and collective bargaining have declined in the private sector, they remain vigorous in the increasingly political environment of government, and this development appears likely to continue.

While managers have gained enlarged authority over personnel operations vis-a-vis civil service commissions, collective bargaining has resulted in pressures in support of greater council intrusions into labor-management relations. While collective bargaining orthodoxy in local government is against such council involvement, except possibly for ratification of final contract provisions, political realities often bring union leaders into direct relationships with councilmembers. Police and fire fighters are commonly involved in highly visible electoral campaigns, and other employee unions often engage in similar politics. *Quid pro quos* are expected in labor-management relations, and they are often paid. With the escalation of partisanship and the costs of council elections, this new form of the old "civil service exception" to managerial control is likely to continue. Rather than an exception to promote merit employment, however, this new form is closer to the old transactional politics of spoils.

Physical planning and land use constitute the other old exception. It never moved far in the direction of managerial dominance, but it has changed in ways that are likely to continue. The old reform ideal was linked to the garden-city movement and thus to the value of high citizen involvement in planning and beautification; but it was also realistic in efforts to insulate physical planning and zoning from the corrupting influences of land speculators, railroads, and other special interests. Thus, "insulated" citizen planning boards were created and professional planners commonly reported both to them and to the manager in addition to attending many or most council meetings. As land speculators became "homogenized" as developers during the years following World War Two, planning operations came increasingly under their influence. By the 1970s, development and developers again became important sources of political finances, and councils became more directly involved in planning and land use. By the 1980s, such council involvement was common. Professional planners turned increasingly to managerial leadership, during the years of these changes, in efforts to maintain reasonable levels of expertise and integrity in their operations. Thus, new forms of both managerial control and exceptions to it have developed, and these complex council-manager-planner-citizen-developer relationships will continue.

New Exceptions, Varied Forms. Police review boards constitute a new exception to managerial control over administration. Some other citizen-control and involvement mechanisms that developed out of the 1960s and 1970s also remain important and controversial.

Police review boards have been created in many larger cities in response to political action by varied minority groups who have alleged brutality by police. Law enforcement personnel have almost always opposed such boards. In council-manager cities, this controversy has a special twist to it. If, like other administrative units, the police department is under the direction of the manager, should a review board be appointed by and/or report to (or advise) the manager or the police chief--or the council? Often, exceptions to managerial control existed prior to the emergence of the police review board issue in appointments of police and/or fire chiefs. Councils have sometimes made these appointments directly; more often the manager has made them, sometimes subject to council consent. Local situations determine how these decisions are made. Where professionally oriented or employee-controlled public safety services are desired, insulation from citizen oversight is workable; where politically responsive services are preferred, enhanced popular control is workable. In either case, because of the escalating importance of partisan politics and the political power of police and fire unions in local elections, extensive employee control is likely to continue over public safety operations.

Varied forms of citizen-involvement were developed during the "Great Society" years and later as a result of New Public Administration thinking. One feature of these mechanisms distinguishes many of them from citizen-involvement practices of the political reform period, and that difference is vital in contemplation of the future of council-manager government. The old citizen involvement was outside the arena of administration. The "new civism" of the 1960s injected citizens into administrative processes, as in neighborhood advisory councils to comment on implementation of physical plans and zoning policies or as in increased use of volunteers in law enforcement, recreation programs, and public education.[8] The Future Horizons Committee generally favored such citizen involvement and urged professional managers to facilitate these and other mechanisms of self governance--but with disciplined means to reduce chances of their takeover or manipulation by special interests with objectives contrary to those of "the essential community." Despite this injunction of a decade ago, retrenchment pressure and other national political pressures resulted in reduced attention to citizen-involvement mechanisms in the 1980s. Those cutback pressures continue to be powerful and are likely to characterize the future.

Accountability: Changed Technology/Shared Information. The executive budget became a fixed tenet of public administration even before the structural orthodoxy period. An annual external audit, under the control of the Council, became an expected accountability tool. Public financial operations in larger jurisdictions have multiplied in complexity in recent decades, requiring internal controls that facilitate unbroken tracking of all receipts and expenditures. Automated internal financial controls routinely perform these functions today, making it possible to track expenditures from initial authorizations through preaudited approvals of spending, delivery, payments, internal post audits, and periodic external audits.

Typically, the council-manager charter still provides that the council is completely responsible for the external audit function. But with respect to internal financial controls, the comptroller function is essentially an administrative responsibility of the manager. Neither function can be independent of the other, however, and today automated systems facilitate widely shared information among councilmembers and their staffs, managerial officials, line administrators, external auditors, and possibly others, including interested citizens. This may result in new forms of council "intrusions" into administrative processes; the old rule that councilmembers are to deal with the administrative apparatus only through the manager is out of date when computer terminals in council offices can be used to probe for information with no personal contacts with subordinate administrators. Managerial flexibility may be significantly limited. These realities of council-manager government will continue in importance.

The Mayor--Visible Brokerage and Focus

The most obvious challenge to the future of council-manager government has been in the means of selection and the roles of the mayor. These changes have resulted from the growing partisan politicization of local government since the start of the social activism period. Changes that have strengthened the mayors in many council-manager governments are likely to continue in the future because they have facilitated visible brokerage and focus. On the other hand, even more drastic changes--adoption of mayor-council government or mayor/manager-council government--will continue to be proposed. Deficiencies of mayor-dominant systems may continue to help defeat such drastic changes, however, in an era of economic stringency and public-sector complexity.

Changes within the Council-Manager Plan. The authority of mayors has been strengthened in varied ways to provide political leadership in council-manager cities. Three changes have been common and are likely to continue into the future, at least in larger governments; a fourth change, mayoral veto authority, remains uncommon.

Changes in the selection of mayors have taken a variety of forms. "The Plan" provided for selection by councilmembers from among themselves, and the office was usually rotated. Direct popular election of mayors at large is not unusual now and governments which adopt district election of councilmembers and at-large election of the mayor, by that means alone, greatly enlarge the relative authority of the mayor. The mayoral election may or may not be synchronous with council election. Partisan politics escalates with direct election of the mayor, and politicians are more attracted to the office as a stepping stone toward other political offices. Costs of elections increase, with resulting changes in the influence of contributors.

The mayor in council-manager government now typically exercises considerable authority over the council agenda. Traditionally, professional managers formulated council agendas in consultation with the mayor or council, and most still do. Even then, without wholly dominating formulation of the agenda, a mayor typically manages it during meetings. A council which is organized with the trappings of a legislature, however, may have a rules committee to control the agenda, and that can be an instrument of enhanced mayoral power only if the mayor chairs it and controls appointments of council committees. Bureaucratization of councils--with expanded use of council committees and legislative staff offices--was a tendency in large cities following politicization in the 1960s and 1970s, and it was typically designed to strengthen the mayor. Rules and finance committees may both be chaired by the mayor in such arrangements. A central legislative services office may also be controlled by the mayor.

Appointment by the mayor of citizen boards and nonadministrative commissions and officials is a common source of enhanced power. Advice and consent of the council to such appointments remains the rule, however. That relationship will likely continue.

In 13.6 percent of council-manager cities surveyed in 1988 by ICMA, the mayor has a weighted vote or may exercise a qualified veto of council actions in which the mayor is not in the majority.[9] This was the recommendation of the San Diego Charter Review Commission in December 1988. Such developments modify the fundamental character of council-manager government--undivided, community-oriented authority in the council as a whole--and inject elements of separation of powers into the local government.

Mayor-Dominant Forms. Mayor-council government and other mayor-dominant forms have demonstrated weaknesses, as contrasted with council-manager government, and those are likely to continue into the future, generating support for professionally managed government. Three chief contrasts are: (1) mayor-dominant forms are more conflict prone, with increased partisanship and special-interest brokerage; (2) governmental work forces and expenditures are typically larger, proportionately, in mayor-dominant governments; (3) departmental actions tend to be quasi-autonomous, with reduced coordination and collaboration, in strong mayor systems.

Despite its short-ballot origins, council-manager government has generally functioned with some elected or appointed officials who are independent of the manager, especially in county governments. The attorney is commonly independent, and managers often find that troublesome--particularly when an "abominable no man" fills that office. The clerk generally has a community power base and distinctive responsibilities. Police chiefs may be independent of the manager, and sheriffs are almost always elected. Judges are virtually all independent. No trends are discernible with respect to such deviations within council-manager governments. Situational variables will continue to determine them.

Structural Alternatives: 1990s Precursors?

Diversity characterized council-manager governments at the time of the Future Horizons Committee, and variations have continued to increase. Nonetheless, it remains possible to contrast council-manager and mayor-council governments in terms of three sets of ideal characteristics which will continue to be important in the future. All of these were illustrated in the preceding discussion:

1. Council-manager government facilitates more collaborative civic authority, combined with coordinated, institutionalized administration. Mayor-council government encourages separation of powers with the focus on mayoral leadership, but administration is more fragmented and *ad hoc*.
2. Transformational politics is the ideal of the council-manager form, searching for a collaborative, community wide orientation. Transactional politics is the ideal of the mayor-council form, facilitating brokerage among differing interests.
3. Professionally expert administration is the ideal in council-manager government, with neutrally equal access and responsiveness. Politically sensitive administration is the ideal in the mayor-council form, with nonroutinization to facilitate responsiveness.

The positive values associated with mayor-council government have been increasingly incorporated into council-manager forms. Orthodoxy of "The Plan" has eroded, and diversity now prevails. The ideals of council-manager government persist as fundamental. However, changes in the environment of local government will continue to challenge those ideals in the future. Those changes and challenges are the concluding subject here.

Changes and Future Challenge

Corresponding to developments considered by the Future Horizons Committee, at least six categories of environmental changes will affect the future of council-manager government: (1) economic, (2) natural resource, (3) demographic, (4) social, (5) science and technology, and (6) political and governmental.[10] The first five are only briefly sketched here as one set of factors to impact the future, and then relevant political conditions are summarized.

Broad Horizons

Worldwide economic interdependence will continue indefinitely, and the United States's peculiar position as the world's largest debtor nation will persist into the foreseeable future.

Water, air, and energy resources--and possibly weather patterns--will continue to be threatened. Environmental protection costs will rise or resources will be seriously impaired.

The older population, which grew at twice the rate of other age groups during the 1970s-1980s, will continue to increase disproportionately.[11] Females, whose life expectancy averages over seven years longer than that of males, will continue to outlive men, although the gap will narrow slightly. Anglos will constitute less than two-thirds of the population by the year 2000. Hispanic and black females are younger, with the highest projected birthrates.

Only 15 percent of new entrants into the workforce will be Anglo males during the years to the turn of the century. With 62 percent of all working-age women in the workforce in 1988, females will continue to expand their share of jobs. Retirement age may cease to decline or level off and then begin to rise during the next decade, reversing a downward trend in which nearly two-thirds of workers in the mid-1980s retired before age 65, over half by age 62. Changes in Social Security retirement eligibility, mostly due to begin in the next century, will ratchet up the retirement age. This is to account for the already present, coincidental approach to retirement age of the post-World War II baby boomers and the relative shortage of young workers to replace and support them.

Drugs and AIDS will probably continue to be plagues through the next decade.

Poverty and homelessness will also continue. Poverty, once chiefly a problem of the elderly, has changed; 40 percent of the poor in 1988 were children. Homelessness, once a problem of detached, adult males, became a family problem in the 1980s. Low and middle-income housing declined. Those trends may continue.

Science and technology will continue to fuel the communications and information revolutions and facilitate further shifts in health services and behavioral sciences. Fewer jobs will be created for the marginally literate. The gap will widen between the educationally advantaged and the marginally skilled.

Political and Governmental Changes

Two broad, national political trends since the late 1960s were identified earlier: partisan politicization and deinstitutionalization. Nationally this is an era of New Spoils, dominated by the executive, but enthusiastically shared by many legislators, feeding on large government and financing costly, media-dominated elections and related political operations.

A precursor to these developments was a shift that occurred in much of political science during the 1950s and 1960s. That change was driven by the new technologies of opinion polling, elections analysis, and media campaigning. Old philosophical outlooks were largely shunted aside, along with traditional concerns about constitutional values, disciplines, and institutions. Power became the purpose of politics; authority was displaced as a political foundation; legitimacy, determined by politics, became the final test of power. And the new technologies were quickly put to work to manipulate public opinion to win elections and power. Presidential primaries and the general election in 1988 illustrated that this development is growing, not abating.

Executive aggrandizement was noted earlier as a tenet of public administration that was elevated as a high principle during the structural orthodoxy period of council-manager government. That orthodoxy dominated the entire field, far more at the national level than in local government. The doctrine took a crucial turn during the 1970s. Responsibility of employees of the executive branch of the United States national government--public servants--had generally been first to the law and then to authoritative missions before the 1970s. Expectations of loyalty then shifted; first loyalty to the President became the expectation in a system that turned away from traditional practices of shared constitutional authority to a conflict-oriented concept of separation of powers. This outlook also increasingly characterizes state governments and many mayor-council jurisdictions. In short, it is the growing climate of transactional American politics.

Council-manager government is increasingly pressured by these two interrelated political paradigms: *legitimacy of power, without regard for legal authority, and loyalty to the powerful.*

Besides council-manager government, other forces support continued efforts to sustain alternative values of constitutional institutions and popular self governance. Many political leaders at national, state, and local levels support traditional values of nonself-serving civic duty. The National Commission on the Public Service (the Volcker Commission) in 1988-1989 was one of several organized efforts to restore transformational values to government. By 1988, the National Academy of Public Administration, while continuing to support extensive executive power, had turned increasingly toward the shared-powers concept of the Constitution, and NAPA supported first loyalty to the law in its 1988 transition report, *The Executive Presidency: Federal Management for the 1990s.*[12]

Future Challenges

The greatest challenge for council-manager governments in the United States in the 1990s is to help restore to the nation the transformational disciplines of constitutional democracy: civic duty and public service in support of human dignity and the rule of law. This can be done by focusing on "The Essential Community," as urged by ICMA's Future Horizons Committee. Writing in 1979 and 1980, that group expected the challenges to be difficult in the 1980s and to become easier in the 1990s. They did not foresee the creation of a national government debt that, by fiscal year 1990, required nearly 15 percent of the annual budget of the United States to service. They did not anticipate an AIDS plague that is expected to consume extensive resources in the 1990s. They did not expect low-income and moderate-cost housing to dwindle as disastrously as it did in the 1980s.

Because of the national debt and incapacities of the United States government, local governments must now deal with many of these problems in the 1990s without much help. In a new sense, local governments are the hope of essential community not only at the important level of neighborhoods, as projected in the 1970s, but nationally as well.

Council-manager government remains the strongest institutional force of transformational politics in practice in the United States. Its basic tenet of collaborative, community-oriented politics, combined with the qualities of disciplined institutions and professionally responsible expertise, stand in contrast to more visible trends in national politics and government.

Which political forces, transactional or transformational, will prosper in the 1990s remains an open question. Only the seriousness of the answer is clear. That is a high challenge worthy of the transformational idealism of council-manager government. It is a challenge that demonstrates again a lesson of long experience: in constitutional democracy, realism requires the disciplined practice of ideals.

Notes

1. ICMA Committee on Future Horizons, ". . . *New Worlds of Service*" (Washington: International City Management Association, 1979).

2. Laurence Rutter, *The Essential Community: Local Government in the Year 2000* (Washington: ICMA, 1980).

3. ICMA Committee, *supra.*, cover page.

4. Keith F. Mulrooney, symposium editor, "The American City Manager: An Urban Administrator in a Complex and Evolving Situation," *Public Administration Review*, vol. 31 (January/February 1971), pp. 2-46.

5. Aaron Wildavsky, "Ubiquitous Anomie: Public Service in an Era of Ideological Dissensus," *Public Administration Review*, vol. 48 (July/August 1988), pp. 753-755; Robert B. Denhardt and Edward T. Jennings, "Image and Integrity in the Public Service," *Public Administration Review*, vol. 49 (January/February 1989), pp. 74-77; Aaron Wildavsky, "Ubiquitous Anomie: Reflections and Rejoinder," *Public Administration Review*, vol. 49 (January/February 1989), p. 77.

6. ICMA Committee, *supra.*, p. 1.

7. *Thornburgh* v. *Gingles*, 106 S.Ct. 2752 (1986) is the leading case. See: Tari Renner, *Municipal Election Processes: The Impact on Minority Representation*, Baseline Data Report, vol. 19, no. 6 (Washington: International City Management Association, November 1987).

8. H. George Frederickson and Ralph Clark Chandler, eds., "Citizenship and Public Administration," *Public Administration Review*, special issue, vol. 44 (March 1984), pp. 99-209.

9. Tari Renner, *Elected Executives: Authority and Responsibility*, Baseline Data Report, vol. 20, no. 3 (Washington: International City Management Association, May/June 1988).

10. Elizabeth K. Kellar, "Future Horizons: Then and Now," *Public Management*, vol. 70 (April 1988), pp. 14-15.

11. Numerous publications provide insights on future trends. Sources used in this section include these: Special Committee on Aging, United States Senate, *America in Transition: An Aging Society*, Serial No.99-B (Washington: U.S. Government Printing Office, June 1985); William B. Johnston and Arnold E. Packer, *Workforce 2000* (Indianapolis: Hudson Institute, June 1987); John F. W. Rogers *et al.*, *Meeting Public Demands: Federal Services in the Year 2000* (Washington: U.S. Government Printing Office, January 1988).

12. Elmer B. Staats *et al.*, *The Executive Presidency: Federal Management for the 1990s* (Washington: National Academy of Public Administration, September 1988).

Response

Enrique G. Serna
Tucson, Arizona

What does the future hold for the council-manager form of government? Chester Newland contends that there is a certain predictability to this question. In 1978, the Future Horizons Committee studied the prospects for local government. Observations made then still hold true in that they are still valid points of departure upon which to continue the inquiry. In fact, the committee's characterization of "new worlds of service" implicitly suggests redefining or questioning, on an on-going basis, both the environment and public service.

Newland's paper raises expansive and provoking thoughts too numerous and complex to digest or summarize here. As with all people, this city manager has a quest to make a contribution in life. The most significant contribution that this city manager might make to Newland's paper is in selecting but one or two issues that relate to a very specific "world" or "community." As a city manager in a predominately Hispanic and Native-American community, the issues of leadership and single-member district versus at-large elections might have atypical ramifications. These issues will be discussed briefly after springing off another point of departure that complements Newland's formal comments.

San Antonio's Mayor, Henry Cisneros, in his address at the 1988 ICMA conference, addressed the same themes of the environment and public service. He touted the council-manager form of government while suggesting that it is the best form of government for anticipating changing policies and policy implementation in an environment of changing demography. A crystal ball is not needed to predict the increased demands that will be placed on urban areas with dilapidated housing and an already dense, poor, and undereducated (or illiterate) population.

It seems clear, then, that most areas of inquiry related to the council-manager form of government can be indexed under this dual category of environment and public service. This concept is cemented in the philosophical concept of the social contract. That is, Americans are born into an environment with already defined expectations (rights and services) and implicitly agree to play by the rules (obey laws) and regularly review the contractual declaration of services.

The professional manager, as stated by former Dallas City Manager George Schrader, has been thrust into brokering and negotiating among often conflicting interests in the community. Leadership is defined as a "relationship and a set of processes in which unequal authority operates to achieve common purposes." The professional manager often finds that he or she is expected to be instructive and bring political insights to the council's attention.

Said differently, in a minority community wherein the rules, through court mandates, side with the disenfranchised and they become electable, new obstacles towards achieving equal authority are appearing. It is perhaps a conflict between western representative democracy and small "d" democracy. Minorities are finally becoming proportionately represented in elective offices.

272

A recent phenomenon which dilutes decision-making empowerment is the multitude of neighborhood associations. It does seem to be more representative of needs, but it surely does not account for the disguised advantages implicit for those economically and organizationally empowered. This manager's understanding of the Future Horizons Committee's "neighborhood level" service challenge is that it cannot help but be predicated on political demand. Political questions are pervasive in such a dilemma! Sociological commentaries related to voluntary associations and the extended families, for example, greatly affect expected behavior patterns. The dilemma is that minority enclaves are in many ways already more cohesive, but they lack a need or ability to organize formally. Council members are the obvious articulators anytime such issues arise and professional managers, especially in small communities, must sometimes be prospector, assayer, and mediator in such conflicts. Leadership will always be of significant importance in the council-manager form of government as both partners must lead from their respective arenas of authority.

The single member district versus at-large election (and partisan) variables serve only to compound the problem. Single member district class-action lawsuits in the early 1970s raised questions of representation that may or may not still reinforce restrictive obstacles. At-large elections either at the primary or general election level presume a "community at-large" orientation which is a superhuman standard by anyone's expectations. Most communities through their elective officials and often with the requested collaboration of their managers are already redefining the needs. They are, as Mayor Cisneros predicts, anticipating the implications of service need by growing disadvantaged minorities.

As the Future Horizons Committee noted in *The Essential Community* (p. 136), "In the next twenty years the concept of representative democracy will be seriously challenged." Newland's detailed analysis of the major futures issues reminds us all of the many philosophical tenets which must be reconciled as departures are attempted.

It should be of no surprise that the environment and public service are equated with human dignity and rule of law. These standards of inquiry by professional managers and academicians are our assurance that the old perceptions about seat of the pants, line of sight governmental management is a myth. There is, however, a lot to be said about compensating for the prevailing winds through good ol' Kentucky windage.

Response

David F. Watkins
Lenexa, Kansas

Dr. Newland's paper is a reflection on the ICMA sponsored Future Horizons effort launched ten years ago to examine the future of the city management profession in the year 2000. The Horizons study focused briefly on the history of the council-manager plan as instigated by Dr. Childs, its evolution during the post World War II era, the social activist days of the 1960s and 1970s, and the structural changes in the council-manager plan occurring in the 1980s.

Dr. Newland's premise is that the council-manager plan, while undergoing political pressures in the 1980s to become more politicized and responsive to community needs and demands, is still the ideal form of local government to deal with the challenges of the 1990s.

There is no question that the council-manager plan still provides many of the positive attributes that the reformers envisioned. However, just as the Constitution has been amended to respond to the demands of the body politic, so has the council-manager plan been subjected to evolutionary pressures.

The future of council-manager government is at a crossroads. Local papers in Kansas City in 1988-1989 were filled with attempts by citizen groups, local leaders, even a road contractor, to initiate changes in the city's charter to respond to a perception that the city government is weak politically and controlled by City Hall bureaucrats. This trend is commonplace and represents an attempt by citizens to have more say in what happens in the day-to-day operations of local government.

Some of the original precepts of Dr. Childs' plan need review. In many communities, particularly fast growing ones, at-large elections are stifling participation of potential leaders, especially new residents, who lack the name identification necessary to garner communitywide support. In Olathe, Kansas, a commissioner-manager community until 1987, three out of five commissioners lived within one block of each other in a community of over 55,000 people. This political disenfranchisement of a large part of the community led to a change in the form of government in an effort to guarantee ward representation.

Other tenets of the plan, such as a pyramid based organization with no staff contact with elected officials, are impossible in the age of elected officials wanting instant information.

Another basic element of the original plan undergoing transformation is the idea of the neutral administrator. The increasing complexity of intergovernmental relations requires someone who can steer the governing body through the political and bureaucratic labyrinth in order to accomplish objectives. The manager seems the ideal person to help develop consensus by informing the governing body of policy alternatives and helping to lead and to obtain consensus.

The council-manager plan, just like the Constitution, has to be flexible enough to respond to changes going on in the country. The Future Horizons program identified changes that would affect the council-manager plan in the future. ICMA should convene a group to study alternatives to the original council-manager plan that still embraces professionalism in management but are more adaptive to the political changes occurring in local government.

It is hard to argue with the successes occurring in cities like Indianapolis, Baltimore, and Seattle that have highly visible dynamic mayors functioning very well in a strong-mayor system. We all know the history of abuse that occurred in the "boss era" that led to the inception of the council-manager plan. City managers will be guilty of burying their heads in the sand if collectively they do not recognize that time honored principles such as the policy-administration dichotomy, POSDCORB, efficiency and effectiveness, short ballot, at-large elections, etc. are coming under political and in some cases legal attack, and alternatives need to be suggested.

Newland states that council-manager government remains as the strongest institutional force of transformational politics in practice in the United States. This is because the plan mixes the best attributes of representative democracy and professional management. However, the plan has to be flexible to respond to future challenges ranging from a realization of Grodzin's marble cake theory of federalism to national problems that are becoming local, such as the homeless, AIDS, and the drug crisis.

Such "unreformed" city practices as directly elected mayors, ward representatives, partisan elections, higher compensation for elected officials, should be seen as efforts to enhance the policy side of local government as opposed to weakening the administrative side. However, efforts to inject politics into the administrative arena (hiring of council staff members, hiring of department heads by the council, mayoral submission of budgets) are obvious underminings of the basic elements of professional management and should be resisted.

In conclusion, professional managers have to be cognizant of the changes occurring in local government at the political level. Managers should resist changes which undermine administrative responsibilities but should accept structural changes designed to enhance the political effectiveness of the governing body.

Discussion

Branscome: I've been frightened twice this week. The first time was yesterday when what John Nalbandian was saying really sank in that elected officials are no longer effective in the process; therefore, for city managers to be legitimate, they have to reflect the values of the community at large. That is how they gain legitimacy. I'm still not willing to give up the role of the elected officials based on that discussion.

The other thing that really frightened me was today when Dr. Newland said that we are the idealists. This business is based on idealism, process, form, and technology. Managers brought technology to local government many years ago. We're not doing new things here. We are in a society and a phase now where even legitimate liberals will not admit that they are liberals. Is there room in society, a legitimate role and acceptance for the idealist? Is there a place for our underlying values?

Novak: Let me expand on that with a personal anecdote. I mentioned yesterday that one of my personal transformations in city management was several years of marriage counseling. I followed that by divorce. I'm remarried to a clergy woman. People always laugh and say, "That must really be a strange marriage, a city manager and a clergy woman," but it's extraordinarily mutually supportive. What you've done in this phase of idealism of transformational politics is to label this idealism for me. There's a power that flows from this idealism. It's something that we all could use in our daily affairs. I'm not speaking in a religious context necessarily. It's something that we have to keep and magnify.

Keller: I want to make a couple of observations about things that fascinate me. All but one or two participants at the Constitutional Convention were college-educated people in a society where less than one percent of the people had college educations. It always amuses me to think of the founding fathers taking a poll and saying, "This thing will never fly." They didn't do that. Instead, they transformed the society. We tend to accept our culture as given, but culture is not a given. How government is conducted determines a society's culture. By building traditions, you can change that culture over time.

Hale: I want to build on what Terry Novak said, too. The other word that Dr. Newland used besides idealism was realism. City management is an interesting blend of those two aspects. I would hate to see us lose that precious combination.

Watson: There is a place for home rule and differences in all of our cities. We don't want to all be the same; we want to be different, and we want to be able to handle problems in many different ways. Maybe people who are changing these political systems are not really looking for social equity. Maybe they're looking for advantage. A neighborhood organization that organizes for some purpose is not looking for equity; it is looking for advantage. There have been inequities in education. They don't teach Spanish in Mission, Texas, for example because they feel the advantage is to learn English.

Banovetz: Coming back to this notion of idealism and realism, an upward sloping line represents society's expectations regarding public service behavior. Thirty years ago one could hold to a high standard of personal behavior but engage in public corruption and get away with it. Today one can engage in diverse personal behavior but not public. That gap is inherently unstable as it reflects public service. People whose personal behavior is loose can't be expected to hold to a high standard of public behavior. Yet that expectation is coming, and it's going to create a major challenge to this profession. We've got to be able to deal with it.

Let me give you a specific example. Over the last half-dozen years I've used an exercise in my class when we work with ethics. We've got a number of case studies that focus on the question of honesty in dealing with the public. They deal with the question "Should you lie to promote the public interest?" Initially, when I started using these exercises students would say, "No, of course you can't." Now students say, "Yes, you can." In our own staffs this kind of value system is evident. Sooner or later, those who lie for the public interest are going to get hoist with their own petards. This involves a clash of personal and professional ethics. As a profession and particularly as managers who ultimately must take the guff for what their staffs do, you must deal with idealism and ethics. It's going to be more than a staff issue. I think it's also going to have consequences for our society.

This politics of advantage is also inherently unstable in the public realm. We have to move back toward transformational politics or we're going to be in trouble. The leadership for that movement can't come wholly from the city management profession. It's better to light one candle than to curse the darkness. The management profession had better be prepared to start lighting candles in hopes that some others will join us.

Novak: Let me add one comment to this question of ethics. In my part of the world, the Northwest, if you count the managers who have been fired lately and look at the reasons why, seldom is anybody canned for incompetence. It's almost impossible to judge competency. Most often, individuals are fired because of problems relating to their personal affairs, their sexual practices, or their orientation towards alcohol.

Tipton: I want to share an experience that this discussion brought to mind. Perhaps I hadn't identified it until we started talking about idealism. I recently defended the council-manager plan several times in Florida. I debated a local hero who proposed a strong mayor form of government. In each of those cases, we have won. I think it is the idealism of the council-manager plan that wins. It is really a beautiful plan to defend.

Gleason: We're in this business because we're public servants. Nothing chafes me more than to hear people call me a bureaucrat. I'm a public servant and that's a calling. One of the places where we have to do some preaching is with council members. I spend a lot of time praising the council members, both individually and collectively, when they reflect the collective will of the community and when they sincerely concern themselves with public service. It doesn't take very long before they start to reflect that and expect that of each other. We, the managers, are the principal agents in re-reform. One of the principal vehicles for expressing our re-reform is inspiring the council about public service. It's surprising to me how crass people can be one week and then they suddenly catch on. It really ignites. Once they get the drift, they don't seem to drift back.

Ruder: Every time I hear you, Dr. Newland, it's inspirational. It reminds me of why I got in this business. But I still have an uneasy feeling related to the disparity between our ideals and the practical way we manage. A lot of the discussion has revolved around concerns that managers have about the difficulties of good policy leadership. The issue is how do we help create transformational politics at the same time that we promote political leadership in the community. What is my role in trying to live up to that ideal in the future?

King: One thing we can try to do is to better define what we do in terms of the combination of the reality and the ideal. I don't think our words have kept up with our practice.

Newland: In my paper I tried to provide concrete information woven into the thesis of realism and the practice of ideals. I remember when Charldean Newell was thinking about being a city manager and did her internship in Fort Worth. In those days a woman couldn't be a city manager. The world has changed. Charldean's turned out a lot of brilliant managers. Of course, I've thought also about how the national challenges have changed. I cited three instances where ten years ago we didn't foresee what was going to happen: massive indebtedness of the United States, AIDS, and the problem of the homeless. Not one of us in 1978 and 1979 foresaw that we would have a $2.6 billion indebtedness with the certainty of a $3 trillion indebtedness before that is turned around. Fifteen percent of the national budget will be used to pay interest, mostly to people from other countries, as a result of the irresponsibility of these past ten years. That says a lot about the next ten years; the national government can't help us with many of these big problems. In major cities huge resources are being spent to combat the AIDS crisis. We're faced with this problem at a time when the national government is the greatest debtor nation in the world. And we call that transactional politics.

The homeless population is no longer just adult males. Today it's forty percent children and families. This is a massive problem compared to what we expected. Earlier, Gene Denton used the wonderful phrase "the 24-hour courthouse." I too thought of similar examples. When I lived in Fairfax, I could call the county courthouse and I could find out what my neighbor's tax bill was and whether he'd paid it. I could call in 24 hours a day on an automated system and really participate in government. In San Diego in every council member's office, a computer can provide access to information from the time of proposal of any expenditure right down to pre-audit, expenditure, and post-audit. I thought back to the time when I first came onto the city council in Texas as an old school teacher who had been accustomed to wandering all over the city hall. As soon as I was elected, the manager sat down with me and said, "Now in the future you can not secure any information or talk to anyone except me." All information in that system is closed to you because you have been elected to government.

Now technology alone has turned that whole concept around. Ours is a government of self-governance and service to a broad range of humanity. It is not government by the lowest common denominator but government by the highest possible denominator through the leadership of experts. That's what we really mean when we talk about realism in the practice of ideals. The decay of values is widespread; yet, I'm convinced that our hope is in our institutions. The council-manager government is the institutional base that is strongest and shows that we can practice ideals as realism.

Ideal & Practice in Council-Manager Government

Composition
Department of Public Administration
University of Kansas
Lawrence, Kansas

Printing and binding
St. Mary's Press
Hollywood, Maryland

Cover design
Susan Gubisch